Praise for Michael Bess's

CHOICES
UNDER FIRE

"Beautifully written. . . . A volume that belongs on every World War II bookshelf." —*America in World War II*

"Impressive. . . . Bess's appreciation for moral context is as compelling as the book itself. Highly recommended." —*CHOICE*

"[Bess] frequently engages in meticulous and subtle military and moral analysis. . . . Well-informed and deeply impressive. *Choices Under Fire* is a book with great strengths." —*American Heritage*

"Fascinating. . . . Bess unhesitatingly tackles some of the moral dilemmas presented by the war. These, of course, are difficult [issues], and those who prefer pat answers will have little patience with these ruminations. Yet the strength of this book is that it forces us to acknowledge and confront them." —*Booklist*

"Shakes many of the certainties which [the reader] may have entertained before opening it." —*History News Network*

"Bess combines vivid descriptions of the historical events at hand with a careful canvassing of the ethical issues they raise. He is eager in nearly every instance to bring out the complexity of matters and the difficulty of arriving at simple moral conclusions." —*Christian Century*

Michael Bess

CHOICES UNDER FIRE

Michael Bess is Chancellor's Professor of History at Vanderbilt University. His book *The Light-Green Society: Ecology and Technological Modernity in France, 1960–2000* won the 2004 George Perkins Marsh Prize for the best book on environmental history. He lives in Nashville, Tennessee.

Also by Michael Bess

The Light-Green Society:
Ecology and Technological Modernity in France, 1960–2000

Realism, Utopia, and the Mushroom Cloud:
Four Activist Intellectuals and Their Strategies for Peace, 1945–1989

CHOICES UNDER FIRE

MORAL DIMENSIONS OF
WORLD WAR II

Michael Bess

Vintage Books
A Division of Random House, Inc.
New York

FIRST VINTAGE BOOKS EDITION, MARCH 2008

Vintage and colophon are registered trademarks of Random House, Inc.

Due to limitations of space, permissions to reprint previously published
material can be found following the index.

The Library of Congress has cataloged the Knopf edition as follows:
Bess, Michael.
Choices under fire : moral dimensions of World War II / Michael Bess. —1st ed.
p. cm.
Includes bibliographical references and index.
1. World War, 1939–1945—Moral and ethical aspects. I. Title.
D744.4.B45 2006 200645253
172'.42—dc22

Vintage ISBN: 978-0-307-27580-6

Book design by M. Kristen Bearse

www.vintagebooks.com

Printed in the United States of America
10 9

For my children,
Natalie and Sebastian

CONTENTS

How solemn as one by one,
As the ranks returning worn and sweaty, as the men
	file by where I stand,
As the faces the masks appear, as I glance at the faces
	studying the masks,
(As I glance upward out of this page studying you,
	dear friend, whoever you are,)
How solemn the thought of my whispering soul to
	each in the ranks, and to you,
I see behind each mask that wonder a kindred soul,
O the bullet could never kill what you really are,
	dear friend,
Nor the bayonet stab what you really are;
The soul! yourself I see, great as any, good as the best,
Waiting secure and content, which the bullet could
	never kill,
Nor the bayonet stab O friend.

—Walt Whitman, 1865

ACKNOWLEDGMENTS

I owe a tremendous debt to the students and graduate teaching assistants in my annual course on World War II at Vanderbilt University: over the years, they have forced me again and again to rethink my positions on the major moral controversies of the war. In class discussions, in skeptical questions raised during lectures, in quietly intense debates walking back from class, these students have helped to shape this book: their curiosity, moral passion, and incisive critical questioning have enriched my life.

I completed this book during the first few months of a sabbatical leave from Vanderbilt in 2004–2005: my heartfelt thanks to the Vanderbilt University Research Scholar Grants Program, which helped to fund my year away from the classroom; and to the College of Arts and Science at Vanderbilt, for granting me the sabbatical. Without the sustained and generous support of these institutions, this project could never have been completed.

The reflections presented in this book have been in gestation for some twenty-five years, since the time when I wrote my first research paper on Leo Szilard in a graduate seminar with Martin Jay at the University of California, Berkeley. Among the many persons whose influence marks these pages, I would like to single out the following for particularly warm thanks (needless to say, they are not responsible for the conclusions I reach): Bev Asbury, John Barrow, Susanna Barrows, Alain Beltran, Barton Bernstein, Richard Blackett, Claude Bourdet, Tim Boyd, Gene Brucker, Roy Brunkenhoeffer, Bill Caferro, David Carlton, Mark Cioc, Simon Collier, John Compton, Paul Conkin, Beth Conklin, Katie Crawford, Dennis Daniels, Basil Davidson, Charles Delzell, Danilo Dolci, Marshall Eakin, Jean Bethke Elshtain, James Epstein, Sarah Farmer, Peter Felten, Devin Fergus, Gerald Figal, Carole Fink, Mona Frederick, Paul Freedman, Peter Fritzsche, Lawrence Frohman, Johan Galtung, Gordon Gee, Jay Geller,

Joseph Goldstein, G. Allen Greb, Peter Haas, Mark Hampton, Joel Harrington, Helen Hawkins, Gabrielle Hecht, J. León Helguera, Nelly Trocmé Hewett, Nikolaus Hohmann, Lynn Hunt, John Hurst, Yoshikuni Igarashi, Martin Jay, Lionel Jensen, Ingrid Jordt, Mary Kaldor, Amy Kirschke, Steve Kotkin, Cathy Kudlick, Jane Landers, Thomas Laqueur, Thomas Lindsay, Amanda and Billy Livsey, Kaspar Locher, Peter Lorge, Martin Malia, Deanna Matheuszik, Richard McCarty, Walter McDougall, Sam McSeveney, Douglas Mitchell, Michael Nagler, Michael Norman, Bill Partridge, Tom Patten, Bill Peck, Elisabeth Perry, Lewis Perry, Pierre Pflimlin, Allison Pingree, Alain Poher, Matthew Ramsey, David Reeve, Ruth Rogaski, Michael Rose, John Saville, Franz Schurmann, Tom Schwartz, Vanessa Schwartz, Jonathon Scruggs, Ed Segel, Becky and Michael Sharpe, George Sheer, Bob Sherwood, James Skelly, Helmut Smith, Rob Spinney, Dorothy Thompson, E. P. Thompson, Arleen Tuchman, Owen Ulph, Dan Usner, Meredith Veldman, Justin Vitiello, W. Warren Wagar, Kenneth Waltz, Frank Wcislo, Meike Werner, Lawrence Wittner, David Wood, Donald Worster, David Yarian, Herbert York, Reggie Zelnik, and Nick Zeppos.

Working with Ash Green, my editor at Knopf, has been a writer's dream: from the rewording of individual phrases and sentences, to the conceptual integrity of chapters, to the structure of the book as a whole, Ash brought to bear the kind of clear eye and literary flair that make all the difference. I felt as though the spirit of E. B. White, kindly but unsparing, were hovering over me: "It's no cinch to write standard English." Ash's editing made this a much better book than it was. Many thanks also to all the others at Knopf who helped bring this book into existence: Sara Sherbill, Luba Ostashevsky, Kristen Bearse, Maria Massey, and Carol Carson.

I owe a special debt to my colleagues John Compton, Gerald Figal, Yoshi Igarashi, Helmut Smith, Frank Wcislo, and David Wood; and to my wife, Kimberly, for their perceptive and constructively critical comments on earlier drafts of some of the chapters that follow. Many thanks to the librarians at Vanderbilt's Central Library for all their assistance: Peter Brush, David Anderson, LaRentina Gray, Marilyn Pilley, Janet Thomason, and Jim Toplon. And thanks as well to the staff in Vanderbilt's History Department: Brenda Hummel, Vicki Swinehart, Lauren Henderson, Heidi Welch, and Jane Anderson.

My literary agent, Mildred Marmur, has sustained my writing through more than two decades with extraordinary patience and good cheer; her expertise, encouragement, and insight, as well as her insider's knowledge of the publishing world, have been truly invaluable. My gratitude to my graduate school mentors, Susanna Barrows and Martin Jay, only grows deeper as the decades go by. Marshall Eakin has been a source of inspiration to me through the years, as a teacher, as a scholar, as a human being. The teachings of Joseph Goldstein, Jack Kornfield, and Stephen Levine enrich my life every day.

My heartfelt gratitude also to my extended family: the Western Besses, David, Patty, Theresa, and Daniel; the Danielses, Elrods, Hoheners, Tharauds, Warwick-Smiths, and Christensens; and to the Allisons, Beatons, Cavaliers, Coopers, McCrums, Tracys, and Van Buskirks. *E profondo riconoscimento anche a tutti i miei cari in Italia: le famiglie Carrara, Corti, Dolza, Jona, Paglietta, Passera, Pilone, Tomatis, e Viale.*

To my oldest friends I give a silent, happy bear hug: David Baty, Hollis Cline, Jed Diamond, David Hurwith, Walden Kirsch, Doran Larson, Roberto Malinow, Bryan Tracy, and Ruth Weizman.

As for my parents, Rina and Donovan Bess, my wife, Kimberly, and my children, Natalie and Sebastian:

Such fullness in that quarter overflows
And falls into the basin of the mind
That man is stricken deaf and dumb and blind,
For intellect no longer knows
Is from the Ought, or Knower from the Known—
That is to say, ascends to Heaven . . .

EVALUATING THE SECOND WORLD WAR

Celebration, Doubt, and Complexity

When we were fleeing the burning city
And looked back from the first field path,
I said, "Let the grass grow over our footprints,
Let the harsh prophets fall silent in the fire,
Let the dead explain to the dead what happened.
We are fated to beget a new and violent tribe
Free from the evil and the happiness that drowsed there.
Let us go"—and the earth was opened for us by a sword of flames.
—Czeslaw Milosz, Goszyce, Poland (1944)[1]

On the morning of June 4, 1942, three American naval aviators—the torpedo squadron leaders John Waldron, Gene Lindsey, and Lance Massey—led their formations of TBD torpedo bombers across the bright expanse of the Pacific Ocean, two hundred miles to the north of Midway Island. Behind them, over the horizon, steamed the carriers *Hornet, Enterprise,* and *Yorktown,* from which they had taken off two hours before. Somewhere ahead, below the puffs of white cloud that dotted the sky, a huge Japanese carrier task force was advancing toward Midway. Each of the American squadrons was flying on its own, in isolation from the others, maintaining strict radio silence—anxiously looking to make contact with the enemy.

Between 9:35 and 10:15 a.m., at intervals spaced about twenty minutes apart, they found the Japanese ships. Waldron, Lindsey, and Massey knew that the odds were not good: they were coming in with little or no fighter protection, facing swarms of superior Japanese fighter planes. They would have to make their attack runs along a low, straight line, skimming just above the water, in order to release their torpedoes accurately—a long,

Torpedo squadron leaders in the Battle of Midway, June 4, 1942.

(Upper left) John Waldron (Hornet), (upper right) Eugene Lindsey (Enterprise), and (lower left) Lance Massey (Yorktown).

slow approach, entirely unprotected, under conditions of extreme vulnerability. This was a textbook case of how *not* to conduct a torpedo attack; but this, nonetheless, was the situation they now confronted.

One by one, the three squadron commanders plunged down to sea level and led their planes in. One after another, their formations of lumbering TBDs were chopped to pieces by the defending Japanese fighters. All three men, along with most of their squadron members, were killed in the attack. In taking this action, however, they opened the way for one of the greatest upset victories in the history of naval warfare. At 10:25 a.m., just as the last wave of TBDs was being dispatched into the sea by the wheeling Zeros, two squadrons of dive-bombers from the *Enterprise* and *Yorktown* arrived on the scene, high in the sky above. Through a combination of grit, intuition, and blind luck, they happened to have found the Japanese task force at the very moment when all the defending Zeros had come down to sea level to fend off the successive waves of torpedo plane attacks. The American dive-bombers encountered virtually no opposition as they dove down and pelted three Japanese carriers with five-hundred-pound and one-thousand-pound bombs. By nightfall all three giant ships had either sunk or been scuttled. The Japanese disaster at Midway not only turned the tide of the Pacific War, but ultimately allowed the United States to devote the bulk of its vast resources, until the spring of 1945, to the defeat of Nazi Germany.

The decision made by Waldron, Lindsey, and Massey that June morning was not just a military decision: it constituted, in an important sense, a moral choice as well. These men chose to sacrifice their own lives because of a rich and complex set of allegiances they felt toward their fellow fighting men, and more broadly toward the nation they served. Their deed cannot be understood solely in terms of military discipline, rigorous training, or the logic of tactical attack: it only makes sense when we bring into play such concepts as duty, honor, valor, altruism. We rightly cherish the memory of their deed, not just because it resulted in a pivotal victory, but because of what it says, more broadly, about the society that produces such men as these.

Long before Niccolò Machiavelli put pen to paper in writing *The Prince*, the idea had already been firmly established that in times of war the principles of morality tend to take a back seat. In warfare, as Thucydides famously put it, "the strong take what they can, and the weak yield what they must."[2] Warfare is all about *winning*, and what therefore matters most for a nation at war is the calculus of effective force: military assets, economic resources, technological innovation, accurate intelligence, preparation of the fighting men, skills of leadership.

This is all true, of course; but it is only at best a very partial truth. When nations go to war, they do not, as it were, check their morality at the door: they do not construe the decisions and policies of wartime as if they were taking place in an amoral vacuum. Indeed, the exact opposite is the case: nations in wartime tend to paint their own actions and those of their enemies in especially stark colors of righteousness and wickedness.

Machiavelli, being an astute connoisseur of social reality, realized this fact
all too well: he argued that the skillful prince needed to take the moral
dimension of warfare seriously into account, making sure that the *impression* of just conduct would always be upheld. Though the real motivations
of the prince should aim primarily at maximizing and consolidating
power—disregarding all ethical and religious constraints—a cunning
leader should always take care to keep up moral appearances.

In actuality, however (*pace* Machiavelli), it turns out that a great many
political and military leaders, like the citizens and soldiers who follow
them, are incapable of operating at such high levels of cynicism: they
really do care deeply about whether or not their actions in wartime are
morally justifiable. How a nation conducts its wars, and how an individual
citizen or soldier chooses to behave during wartime say a great deal about
who they are. Moral considerations, in other words, are not just a froth
playing on the surface of war's campaigns: they permeate the policy-
making and the conduct of military action in countless ways.[3] In this
book I seek to show how the moral choices made by individual persons—
military and civilian, on both sides of the global conflict, and at all levels of
society—played a pivotal role both in shaping World War II and in determining its long-term impact on the postwar world.

This moral dimension of the war revealed itself in three distinct ways:

- in the political and military policies adopted (or rejected) by the belligerent governments;
- in the sometimes momentous decisions made by individual civilians and
  soldiers;
- in the broader patterns of small, everyday choices—relatively isolated
  choices that were seemingly less consequential in themselves, but that
  became highly significant when cumulatively played out and repeated
  across large numbers of people.

A good example of the first of these factors—the impact of moral considerations on national policy—lies in the story of the American strategic
bombing campaign. When the United States Army Air Force first began
setting up bases in Britain in the spring of 1942, preparing to launch large-
scale bombing attacks against Germany, it faced a fundamental choice:
whether to bomb by day or by night. Officers in RAF Bomber Command
warned that daylight bombing missions would exact an extremely high
price in U.S. planes shot down: they urged the Americans to adopt the
British tactic of hitting enemy targets under cover of darkness. But the

Americans would have none of it. On the one hand, they confidently maintained that their B-17 bombers, bristling with gun turrets and equipped with the superb Norden bombsight, would be able to fend off German fighter planes and deliver a far more accurate and crippling blow through daytime precision bombing of enemy industrial and military targets. On the other hand, they argued (without mincing words) that the British technique of nighttime bombing was of extremely dubious morality. Because nocturnal raids were unavoidably far less accurate than daylight bombing, and therefore required the indiscriminate plastering of German cities with a dense carpeting of bombs, they often resulted in substantial civilian casualties. American citizens back home, the USAAF officers believed, would never abide this kind of warfare being conducted in their name.[4]

As the historian Ronald Schaffer has exhaustively shown in his book *Wings of Judgment*, this moral consideration played a major role in the ongoing debates within the USAAF between 1942 and 1945. Even though, as the war years went by, the United States gradually drifted more and more toward a de facto adoption of British-style area bombing, it nonetheless continued to hold fast to the "precision bombing" doctrine all the way to the war's end; and a significant portion of American bombing missions continued to be governed by this doctrine through the spring of 1945.

The second factor—the influence of moral allegiances on key decisions made by individual civilians and soldiers—has already been illustrated above, in the sketch drawn from the Battle of Midway. Such examples could be repeated many times over. The Hungarian scientist Leo Szilard conceived the principle of the nuclear chain reaction in 1933, but made a carefully reasoned moral decision to keep it secret for as long as possible; he then changed his mind in 1939, revealing his secret to President Franklin Roosevelt and assisting in the launch of the Manhattan Project. A French pastor, André Trocmé, decided in 1940 to lead his village in sheltering Jews from the Gestapo, and ultimately helped save the lives of thousands of men, women, and children. A Japanese medical doctor, Shiro Ishii, made the judgment in 1940 that considerations of national security outweighed those of human rights: he led a team of researchers that conducted deadly biological warfare experiments on thousands of Chinese peasants and political prisoners. The émigré German physicist Klaus Fuchs decided in 1942 that his duty as a communist outweighed his loyalty to England and America, where he had taken shelter from Nazi persecution; he gained entry to the Manhattan Project and passed vital atomic secrets to the Soviets throughout the second half of the war. Pope Pius XII, while personally abhorring German anti-Semitic practices, concluded that a policy of prudence would be best for the Vatican to follow: he refrained throughout the war from issuing any explicit condemnation of the Nazi racial deportations and atrocities, and did nothing to stop the devoutly Catholic governments of France and Slovakia from direct collaboration in the roundup of Jews. All these kinds of stories testify to the pivotal importance that individual moral choices could have in marking the history of this global war.

But even ethical decisions that appeared to carry far less momentous consequences could also end up playing a major role in determining the war's ultimate course and legacy. Here we encounter a third type of moral factor, discernible among patterns of behavior manifesting themselves across entire populations. When we consider the story of the Holocaust, for example, it rapidly becomes apparent that this event could not have occurred, in the way it did, had it not been for a recurrent phenomenon taking place among the majority of the European citizenry: *When they came to take my Jewish neighbors away, I closed my door and kept silent, hoping to avoid trouble for myself and my family.*

Those who opted to take this path undoubtedly found all manner of ways to rationalize it, explaining it to themselves in terms of prudence, the lack of viable alternatives, the sense of powerlessness, or some other such line of reasoning. Nevertheless, this seemingly rather small and isolated moral choice, repeated in literally millions of day-to-day episodes throughout the Continent over the course of six years, added up to a collective phenomenon that ultimately allowed a genocide to proceed unimpeded.

On the more positive side of this story, however, we must also observe that some European populations made decisions that went very differently. A large proportion of Danish citizens quietly threw themselves into the rescue of their Jewish compatriots in 1943, after the Nazis had declared their intent to round them up for deportation. As a result, 98 percent of Denmark's Jews survived the war. Very significant portions of the Italian population also chose to resist or ignore the anti-Jewish measures imposed by their fascist government and by the occupying Germans after 1943: once again, the direct consequence was that 85 percent of Italy's Jews escaped the Holocaust. What these more positive examples underscore, therefore, is precisely how decisive the element of individual moral choice could prove to be, once manifested in cumulative patterns emerging across a broader population.

In all these dimensions—government policy, individual decision, collective patterns of action or inaction—the "moral factor" really mattered: it profoundly affected the way events unfolded, at all levels of society, and on both sides of the conflict. This book tells the story of World War II through the lens of these myriad moral choices, tracing the common threads that run through them and assessing their enduring impact on the world we have all inherited. The argument falls into three chronological parts: it starts with the moral issues surrounding the causes of World War II; works its way through the war's most contested episodes and policies; and concludes by assessing the conflict's long-term moral consequences and implications.

My goal is twofold. At one level I seek to offer the reader a vivid *tour d'horizon* of the war's moral "hot spots"—those areas around which the most intractable and acrimonious controversy has tended to emerge. At a deeper level, by exploring the underlying thematic linkages among seemingly far-removed events and decisions, I hope to shed new light on the forces that shaped this epochal conflict, and to offer fresh conclusions about its far-reaching legacy.

Three main themes recur throughout the discussion that follows: the reader will hopefully recognize them as they emerge (albeit in very different contexts) in successive chapters.

1. *The centrality of race.*

In the context of World War II, the word "racism" is most likely to trigger immediate associations with Nazi anti-Semitism and the death camps. Yet, in fact, racism existed just about everywhere in the world of the 1930s and early 1940s: the entire globe was drenched in it—many different kinds of racism, with equally diverse origins and nuances. Rioting black GIs in Kansas, enraged at second-class treatment; Korean women forced into prostitution for Japanese troops; complacent U.S. military officers at Pearl Harbor, totally underestimating the capabilities of the Japanese navy; murdered Slavs in Warsaw; massacred Filipinos in Manila; gang-raped young girls in Nanking; emaciated white POWs in Thailand; interned American citizens of Japanese descent—all these take their place in the story of the racisms that permeated the Second World War, alongside the unspeakable ashes of Auschwitz.

This is by no means to imply that all these people should be lumped together in the same category. On the contrary, each group, each dyad of perpetrator and victim, deserves its own dismal chronicle. The Holocaust still stands on its own, a unique exemplar of the human capacity for industrial-strength malice. Yet it is striking, when one reflects on it, just how pervasive was the racist mentality in the 1930s and 1940s: race is arguably one of the central concepts of the entire conflagration that we call World War II, both in causing the conflict and in shaping its course.

2. *The barbarization of warfare.*

When the Japanese bombed civilian populations in China during the late 1930s, the United States and Britain voiced great outrage. Franklin Roosevelt, according to his biographers, was genuinely shocked by this atrocity, and developed a far more hostile and uncompromising attitude toward the Japanese as a result. Newspapers in the United States and Britain issued vehement denunciations of Japan, and some politicians called for a full-scale economic embargo against this nation that practiced warfare in such a barbaric manner. Partly this reaction reflected the smug sense of moral superiority that many Americans and Europeans reflexively felt in dealing with the Japanese; and partly it reflected a sincere belief, on the part of many, that the large-scale bombing of civilian populations lay completely beyond the pale of civilized behavior. This was not, in the eyes of most British and Americans, something that you would *ever* find us doing.

Scroll forward a mere seven or eight years, however, and what do we encounter? Hamburg, Dresden, Tokyo—entire cities, tens of thousands of noncombatant civilians at a time, incinerated or blasted to bits under a steady torrent of British and American bombs. The large-scale killing of children, women, and old people had now become routine facets of Allied warfare. Judging by our own moral standards, repeatedly and emphatically articulated as recently as 1937, we had become unequivocally barbarized.

To varying degrees, this kind of phenomenon affected all the major belligerents in World War II: atrocious behavior came to characterize "normal" warfare, not just among the Axis aggressors, but also among those nations fighting a defensive war. The strafing of helpless sailors whose ships had been sunk; the brutal maltreatment of POWs; the taking of gruesome war trophies such as severed enemy body parts; the shooting of prisoners; the wholesale slaughter of civilians during military operations; the invention of fiendishly clever incendiary devices and other technologies of enhanced butchery—all these grim realities form part of the rigorously documented history of wartime conduct on both sides of this all-out conflict.

Once again, we should not conclude from this—as Hermann Göring sought to argue at the Nuremberg trials—that because all sides committed atrocious acts, all hands were equally and indiscriminately stained. No: each nation, each people, has to deal with its own measure of accountability for the moral transgressions it committed. We need to make detailed, exacting distinctions among the barbaric behaviors of wartime, assigning proper responsibility to each perpetrator in due proportion to the gravity of the deeds done and the policies pursued.

3. *The internationalist imperative.*

World War II led to an enduring transformation in global politics: an unprecedented commitment among the majority of the world's peoples to erecting common institutions of humane and lawful planetary governance. Some of the new international institutions were primarily political in nature (United Nations, Council of Europe); some were economic (International Monetary Fund, World Bank, Marshall Plan, European Economic Community); some were military (Western European Union, NATO, Warsaw Pact, SEATO); some were juridical (Nuremberg and Tokyo trials, International Court of Justice, Fourth Geneva Convention, Universal Declaration of Human Rights).

Partly this new commitment grew out of the manifest inadequacy of the League of Nations and the other international agencies of conflict resolution during the 1930s. Partly it grew out of the keen awareness, among formerly isolationist powers like the United States, that in the new environment created by twentieth-century military technologies, national security could only be assured through proactive engagement in truly globe-spanning institutions. Partly it grew out of the sheer suffering directly experienced by so many of the world's peoples during the war itself. Partly, no doubt, it grew out of a chastened humanity's coming face-to-face with the implications of Auschwitz and Hiroshima—the stark realization that the human capacity for cruelty and large-scale violence was seemingly without limits.

For all these reasons, the Second World War brought about a tremendous acceleration in the quest for a global legal order, for a new system of fair and effective conflict resolution among the world's peoples. Even during the worst years of the Cold War, this multifaceted process of international institution-building continued to advance, step by painstaking step—despite frequent crises and setbacks. It has constituted one of the most significant moral and political legacies of the World War II experience.

World War II is widely considered one of the most morally unambiguous military conflicts in all history—the quintessential "Good War," as Studs Terkel famously described it in his Pulitzer Prize–winning book, *The*

"Good War": An Oral History of World War Two.[5] And yet, as the decades have passed since 1945, the myriad complexities and ambiguities of this conflict have also come increasingly to the fore, as both historians and those who directly experienced the war have cast their evaluative gaze on those momentous years. Many of the war's fundamental moral questions still remain vividly relevant in today's world, and thus it is not surprising that the debates over those seemingly distant issues still retain the power both to fascinate and to enrage.

Exploring the moral dimensions of the Second World War thus presents the historical observer with an unusually difficult challenge, because it was really two kinds of conflict at the same time: a morally straightforward war of defense against unprovoked aggression, and a morally complex conflict pervaded by ambiguities, trade-offs, agonizing choices, and unre-solvable dilemmas. Doing justice to this irreducible duality of the war experience—the purely black-and-white dimension and the far messier gray areas—is necessary in order to capture accurately the full range of the war's many contradictory realities.

Consider, for example, the magnificent oral history of the World War II generation that Studs Terkel put together during the early 1980s. As he conducted his interviews, Terkel expected to hear all sorts of moving tales of woe and horror—and he did indeed—but he was also astonished by another dimension that began to emerge, in one testimonial after another. People looked back on the war years with unabashed nostalgia. One of the core experiences of this war, strikingly revealed in Terkel's interviews, was about feeling the thrill of moral clarity—a just cause, in which you could truly give your all. Both the Allied soldiers who fought overseas and their relatives and fellow citizens who toiled on the home front referred again and again to the exhilaration they experienced during those years. What lay at stake in this military contest amounted to nothing less than a dras-tic realignment of world power, with enslavement and genocide looming on the horizon. People knew that they were fighting for the defense of their families, their country's independence, their entire way of life; they threw themselves wholeheartedly into an all-out campaign against a vicious aggressor whose brutality and culpability in starting the war were utterly beyond doubt. Once the moral stakes had become so sharply defined, even the ultimate risk of sacrificing one's life, if necessary, could make sense and prove profoundly meaningful. Perhaps equally important, both civilians and soldiers could simultaneously feel a deep sense of comradeship with their fellow citizens who were likewise giving their all to the same overriding cause. Those of us who only know World War II through the history books cannot help but reflect: it must have been quite a sensation.

But there was also another side to Terkel's interviews. Here, for example, is the testimonial given to Terkel by Nancy Arnot Harjan, a San Francisco woman who was thirteen when the war began and seventeen when it ended. In Harjan's account, we can certainly recognize the strong element of nostalgia, the crusading fervor that permeated so many of Terkel's chronicles; but we also see something else emerging in the questions raised by this precociously perceptive young woman. Side by side with the moral certainties, disturbing intimations arise, and the plot begins to thicken.

We had in our employ a beautiful Japanese woman named Mae. The edict came that all Japanese in California be sent to relocation camps. We didn't speak about it until one morning Mae brought it up herself. It was spring 1942. I was upstairs, overhearing the conversation. I heard their voices rising, my mother's and Mae's. It frightened me. She said, "Mrs. Arnot, it's really a concentration camp I'm going to." My mother was caught in a bind. She did know that it was wrong. "It's for your own good," she said, "for your own protection." Mae was saying, "Ah ha, I thought *you* had to be protected from *us*. Now you're telling me I have to be protected from you." I was so blown away by that as a fourteen-year-old, an idealistic teenager.

Mae started to cry. I remember my mother's voice, rising and crying. She seldom did that and it distressed me. So I stayed upstairs. Mae was bitter. She had been saving her money to go to school. She was beginning to think things were getting better for the Japanese.

When she did leave, everybody put on a brave front. We said goodbye and wished her well. I wanted to get away as soon as possible. I ran upstairs to my room. I don't know what happened to her. We never saw her again.

We had another person in our employ, a gardener. He was an Austrian Jew who had escaped from a Nazi concentration camp. He came to this country in 1941. He [wrote down] his story, twenty, thirty pages of what happened to him and his family. My mom handed Albert's little portfolio to me. She said, "Nan, read this, because there's a lot of Americans who hear but do not believe what is happening in Nazi Germany. This is living proof." Losing his whole family. It almost makes you go crazy if you try to comprehend the human cruelty and barbarism. Especially if you are fourteen and have been treated kindly all your life.

We were a very comfortable, privileged family. White Anglo-Saxon Protestant. My father was a successful physician. He was a kind of groovy conservative Republican. Very magnanimous on a one-to-one level, but very naive politically. Did not like Roosevelt and the New Deal. Hated Roosevelt. . . .

Some of my schoolmates were antisemitic and played down what was happening in Nazi Germany. We were all very patriotic. The girls at this private school and I would knit all kinds of scarves and caps for the boys in the service. We'd go down to the USO and bring sailors home for dinner. *(Laughs.)* I donated blood at the age of seventeen. I was underage but patriotic. I was delighted to give my blood. It didn't hurt and I was so proud of myself. *(Laughs.)*

Before the war was over, I went down to the WACs and tried to enlist. They were very nice, but they wouldn't take me. I really wanted to be a woman in uniform and support this terrible war and overcome evil with good. America represented nothing but good to me. Our boys were good. They weren't trained to be malicious killers. We took *Life* and *Look*. Everything seemed so right and good, I even liked Bob Hope.

We saw many war films that showed our boys fighting the Japanese and pictured the Japanese military as utter brutes. I bought all that. But I couldn't hate Mae. We loved her. Yet I felt this detachment. We knew that people of German descent were not being picked up.

I do remember V-E day. Oh, such a joyous thing! It was in early May. It was my younger brother's birthday and my older brother would most likely be coming home. And San Francisco was chosen for the first session of the UN. I was ecstatic. Stalin, Churchill, and Roosevelt met, and somehow war never again would happen. . . .

My dad, my younger brother and I, and my mother went to the Sierras for a two-week vacation. In the middle of it came August 6, the bombing of Hiroshima. The war was over. This wonderful new bomb had ended it all. I remember my father organizing everybody in camp, he was so happy the war was over. He had everybody dancing the Virginia Reel. He was up there clappin' his hands. I was just so proud of him.

Within a week or two, bit by bit, it sank in. Seventy thousand or a hundred thousand or two hundred thousand civilians? It came as a shock after seeing so many war movies with the Japanese portrayed as militaristic brutes. To see women, children, and old innocent civilians brutally burned. And Nagasaki! Two of them?

As the war came to an end, I was totally blown away by how quickly our former enemies became our friends and how quickly our former friends became our enemies. I couldn't understand that. I began to ask, What was it all about?

Since the end of World War II, I've really had all kinds of questions. I feel let down and disillusioned. I never heard much anti-Soviet talk during the war. My parents may have had some friends who wondered about, ha-ha, these communist allies of ours. But I don't think anyone suggested we were fighting on the wrong side. . . .

When I was that young girl, I saw on the news films the Parisian people, with tears streaming down their faces, welcoming our GIs. They were doing what I wanted them to do. When the Holocaust survivors came out, I felt we were liberating them. When the GIs and Russian soldiers met, they were all knights in shining armor, saving humanity. *(Laughs.)* I believed in that. It's not that simple. It's true, Nazism is evil. But Nazism is not totally gone. We still have the seeds of all these evils here.

World War II was just an innocent time in America. I was innocent. My parents were innocent. The country was innocent. Since World War II, I think I have a more objective view of what this country really is.[6]

Swirling about in the memory of this San Francisco schoolgirl, arising almost randomly before us, we find all manner of morally contradictory realities coming to life: the bitter sense of betrayal felt by a young Japanese-American woman; the horror of a Holocaust survivor's story; the strains of anti-Semitism among some American schoolchildren; the fervent patriotism felt by most Americans, and the sincere idealism that animated so many of them; the clash between a propaganda image of the Japanese and the affection felt for a real Japanese-American acquaintance; the initial elation over Hiroshima and the war's ending, followed by troubled questions about the horrible deaths of so many civilians; perplexities over the strange alliance with the Soviet dictatorship and the rapid disintegration of that alliance after 1945; tremendous pride in belonging to the victor nations that saved the world from Nazi and Japanese barbarism. America's war, in the memory of Nancy Arnot Harjan, is neither black, nor white, nor even a straightforward tint of gray: it is a collage of countless gradations and shades, mottled and striated and irreducibly messy. In these memories we find many elements of the "Good War," of the righteous crusade against fascism, of pride, fervor, and elation; but we also find significant dissonant notes of shame, pain, and doubt. America's war, in this rendering, was a great deal more complicated than it is often made out to be.

Both these contradictory dimensions—the crusade and the ambiguity, the elements of triumph and the elements of doubt and shame—have recurred like leitmotifs in the popular and scholarly literature on World War II that has emerged over the past sixty years. And this should not surprise us: for both these aspects of the war are equally real, and both have an equally valid claim on our attention. As historical observers surveying the moral dimensions of wartime, we find ourselves compelled to wear two very different hats—alternating somewhat awkwardly between them as we move from story to story. One hat represents what might be called the stance of celebration: the imperative one feels to recapture vividly the drama, sacrifice, and extraordinary achievements that culminated in Allied victory. The other hat represents what might be called the stance of critical scrutiny: the imperative one feels to reconstruct the full story of what happened as accurately as possible—which means, among other things, confronting forthrightly those aspects of wartime that are controversial, ambiguous, or in some cases just plain disgraceful.

These two stances do not coexist comfortably together: they tend to elicit very different emotions from us as we seek to refine our comprehension of those tumultuous years. Nevertheless, if we want to avoid presenting a grievously distorted picture of World War II, we have to keep both these dimensions of the conflict clearly in mind. In our ongoing effort of understanding, we somehow have to do justice to both the triumphant crusade and the troubling elements of moral controversy that refuse to go away.

The TV newsman Tom Brokaw, in his book *The Greatest Generation*, gives an eloquent account of his own reaction as he learned more deeply about the nature of this titanic military conflict. In 1984, Brokaw was sent by his network, NBC, to cover the commemoration ceremonies of the fortieth anniversary of D-Day, in Normandy:

> [When I arrived in Normandy,] I was simply looking forward to what I thought would be an interesting assignment in a part of France celebrated for its hospitality, its seafood, and its Calvados, the local brandy made from apples.
>
> Instead, I underwent a life-changing experience. As I walked the beaches with the American veterans who had landed there and now returned for this anniversary, men in their sixties and seventies, and listened to their stories in the cafés and inns, I was deeply moved and profoundly grateful for all

they had done. I realized that they had been all around me as I was growing up and that I had failed to appreciate what they had been through and what they had accomplished.[7]

Brokaw's response is an entirely understandable one. His narrative focuses primarily on the American experience of the war, rather than on the equally impressive British, Russian, and other Allied contributions to the defeat of the Axis; but to anyone who reflects for a moment on the consequences that would have followed if the Allies had not prevailed, his account cannot help but ring true. It is hard not to feel a sense of admiration, bordering on amazement, at the successes achieved—against truly daunting odds—by the Allied soldiers, most of them in their late teens and early twenties when they packed off to join the fight. Only the most callous ingrate could fail to acknowledge the immense debt owed to that generation by the generations that have followed. Remembering and celebrating the sacrifices they made in defending our freedom is surely a civic duty we should take great pleasure in fulfilling.

This is the underlying intention that appears to have inspired Steven Spielberg in crafting his masterly film *Saving Private Ryan*. As the movie plot develops, you come to look on the Tom Hanks character, Captain John Miller, with a kind of awe. He is quiet, understated, modest. He fights with intelligence and great valor. He manages to remain humane and decent, despite the brutality of the conflict in which he has been forced to engage: he even spares the life of a German soldier, although, as we come to see later in the film, that soldier eventually comes back and joins in the attack that kills him.

In one of the film's final scenes, Miller has been mortally wounded. His last words, spoken to Private Ryan almost in a whisper, are simple and totally unexpected. They take hold of you completely. He says: "*Earn this.*"

Half a century later, Ryan comes back to Normandy to stand before the grave of this extraordinary, ordinary man, Captain John Miller. Ryan turns to his wife, his face furrowed with emotion, and softly asks her: "Tell me I've led a good life. Tell me I'm a good man." And she replies: "You are."

It is a singularly powerful moment. You realize that those young men back in 1944 died to give us a chance to live the lives we have today. You realize what a privilege it is, simply to have the chances we have in ordinary life: to be alive, to pursue our careers, to have families, to smell the scent of a spring day in the air. They gave this up, so that we might have it. "*Earn this.*" It is hard not to find yourself thinking, as a member of the audience, "I'll try. I'll do my best." Spielberg puts his audience very vividly into a position in which we see noble behavior as something to be remembered, and honored—and to the extent that this is possible, something to be emulated.[8]

In their distinctive ways, both Brokaw's book and Spielberg's film offer compelling examples of the stance of celebration. These works aim to express the gratitude felt by postwar society for the sacrifices and achievements of the men and women who helped bring about the Allied victory of 1945. Such works, not surprisingly, tend to elide the more ambiguous or morally troubling aspects of wartime, placing their accent instead on the innumerable heroic and altruistic actions, great and small, that characterized the struggle against the Axis powers. This emphasis on the positive side of the war's stories—a portrait painted largely in clear black-and-white—constitutes a kind of war memorial crafted out of words and images rather than stone. It allows today's generations, for whom the Second World War would otherwise remain a distant abstraction, to reach back across the long decades and say, in effect, to those who died and to those dwindling numbers who still survive: "Your deeds will not be forgotten."

It has fallen to another category of works, therefore, to explore the darker sides of the war's stories: those episodes or aspects in which moral certainties break down, and painful questions compel our attention. This body of literature, which is equally as vast (and equally as legitimate and important) as the literature of celebration, has gradually uncovered, over the years, a great many of the war's gray areas—those intractably controversial aspects of the conflict in which a straightforward moral judgment proves difficult or downright impossible to reach. Such elusive and troubling aspects of the World War II experience are perceptible among virtually all the principal belligerents.

Many Germans, for example, still wrangle among themselves over the question of popular complicity in the crimes of Nazism: how widely into German society must the net of moral accountability be cast? Japanese and Chinese citizens continue to exchange acrimonious accusations over the nature and implications of the 1937 Rape of Nanking. Russians today are only beginning to come to grips with the extent to which their triumph in the "Great Patriotic War" was tainted by the grossly inhumane policies of the Stalinist regime—policies of unblinking, feral violence directed both toward enemy populations and toward the Russian soldiers and civilians themselves. Italians erupt periodically into raucous disputes over the legacy of fascism—particularly on such occasions as the elections of 1992, when a Mussolini granddaughter won election to parliament on an unabashedly neo-fascist ticket. On every major anniversary of the great incendiary raids against Hamburg and Dresden, Britons break into bitter arguments over whether the wartime policies of Sir Arthur "Bomber" Harris have irreparably tarnished their nation's "finest hour." In 1992 the French president François Mitterrand publicly refused to apologize, on behalf of the French state, for the deportations of Jews carried out fifty years earlier by the Vichy regime: the resultant national furor raged with an intensity that reminded some observers of the Dreyfus Affair.

The United States, for its part, has experienced plenty of such controversies surrounding some of its actions during the World War II era: the relatively weak measures taken during the late 1930s to offer assistance or asylum to Europe's Jews; the forcible internment of Japanese-American citizens; widespread racist policies within the U.S. military; the large-scale killing of civilians in the strategic bombing campaign; the flawed conduct of justice in the Nuremberg and Tokyo trials. The most recent outburst came in 1994–1995, when the Smithsonian Museum in Washington attempted to exhibit the *Enola Gay*, the B-29 bomber that dropped the atomic bomb on Hiroshima. In the passionate (and sometimes quite nasty) debates that ensued, Americans grappled with exceedingly tough questions about patriotism, historical honesty, and public memory. Was the dropping of the bomb a just and reasonable way to end the war, or was it an atrocity that blackens the history of the United States with an indelible stain? And more broadly: what is the most constructive way for such controversial issues to be confronted within the nation's civic culture? All these ongoing debates offer a poignant testimonial, both to the enduring prominence of World War II in the nation's self-image, and to the deep cleavages that still divide Americans as they look back on the war years.

In this book I try to remain sensitive to both the stance of celebration and the stance of critical scrutiny. World War II was a time of extremes: it gave men like John Waldron, Gene Lindsey, and Lance Massey a chance to show their true mettle; and it afforded individuals like Shiro Ishii or Josef Mengele the resources and the opportunity to make choices of a very different nature. At the same time, for millions of soldiers and civilians in Europe, North America, and Asia, World War II presented moments of decision that were far less clear or trenchant in nature: decisions that took the form of painful dilemmas, uneasy trade-offs, awful but unavoidable compromises. Taken together, these countless choices—these moral bifurcation points great and small—decisively shaped the course and character of a global war, and left their powerful mark on the decades that have followed.

———————

This book benefited enormously from the debates I had with my students and colleagues over the years. Those debates are, of course, still under way: most of the moral controversies arising out of World War II are far from being definitively settled or resolved. In this spirit of ongoing exchange of views, I would like to invite the readers of this book to join in the conversation. I have established a Web site bulletin board where readers can go to post their responses to my arguments, to see the responses left by other readers, and, if they feel so inclined, to engage each other (and me) in open discussion. The Web site address is www.choicesunderfire.com. I look forward to reading your comments.

PART ONE

★

FOMENTING WAR

Chapter One

A WIDE WORLD OF RACISMS

It's a question of whether the white man lives on the Pacific Coast
or the brown man.

—Austin Anson,
California Grower-Shipper
Vegetable Association, 1942[1]

World War II was not a race war, but it was—to an extent that
is often overlooked—a conflict in which race played a central
role, from start to finish and in every theater of combat. To speak of a
"race war," in the conventional sense, is to imply a military struggle for
supremacy between two groups who perceive themselves as being racially
distinct. The Second World War was far too complex to be contained
within such a clear-cut rubric: this conflict was just as much about territorial expansion, economic resources, and global hegemony as it was about
racial purity; it ended up pitting Asians against other Asians, and led Germany into a mortal struggle with Great Britain—a nation categorized by
the Nazis as falling clearly within the Aryan fold.

Nevertheless, if we conduct a careful survey of this global conflict, bearing the concept of race in mind, we may be astonished at the result. It is
hard to find many significant aspects of this war in which racial distinctions did not play an important role. Racial ideas shaped both German and
Japanese war aims, and helped spur these two peoples to take the aggressive actions that precipitated military hostilities. Racial prejudices on the
Allied side led to a gross underestimation of Japanese capabilities in
1941—a misperception for which Britain and the United States paid dearly
in December 1941 and the early months of 1942. Racial distinctions per-

Japanese-American girl in California awaiting transfer to internment camp (April 1942).

meated the American war economy and the American military; they also led to one of the greatest breaches of constitutional governance in the nation's history, the forced internment of a racially demarcated subset of American citizens. Racial hatreds animated soldiers on both sides in the Pacific War, leading to unprecedented levels of brutality in the conduct of combat and the treatment of prisoners. And racism, of course, lay at the heart of the Nazi genocide that has marked World War II as a chapter of unique horror in human history.

This chapter explores some of the manifold ways in which racial thinking shaped the Second World War; it is an exploration that continues in subsequent chapters, as we take up such diverse subjects as the "bystander" phenomenon during the Holocaust; the psychological mechanisms that allowed seemingly ordinary Germans to become mass murderers; the stereotyped imagery surrounding kamikazes; the clash between Germans and Russians on the Eastern Front; the atomic bombing of Hiroshima and Nagasaki; the war crimes trials at Nuremberg and Tokyo; the postwar occupation of Japan; and the enduring transformation that the war brought about for racist ideas and practices around the world, in the decades since 1945.

In order to understand World War II, we need to understand why three disparate and physically far-removed nations—Germany, Italy, and Japan—ended up fighting as part of a single alliance, the Tripartite Pact of 1940. What did they perceive themselves to be fighting for? And how did this bind them together? There are two ways to go about answering these kinds of questions. The first approach lies in the realm of politics, economics, and military power: we trace what these three nations wanted by looking back on their diplomacy, their wars, their economic troubles, the domestic political upheavals they experienced in the period twenty or thirty years before the outbreak of the Second World War.

This is a perfectly valid approach (and we duly take it up in chapters 2 and 3), but by itself it is not enough. If we really want to get at the motivations of the Germans, Japanese, and Italians, then we have to go deeper, into the realm of ideas. Ultimately, it is here that the war really began—in a basic set of attitudes that came to be quite widely held throughout Europe and the United States (and later in Japan) around the last decades of the nineteenth century, a cultural current that historians call Social Darwinism.

Charles Darwin published his *Origin of Species* in 1860. At its heart lay the notion of natural selection—the evolutionary process resulting from the interaction between random genetic mutations in animal populations and the special challenges and opportunities presented by particular habitats. It amounted to a genuine intellectual revolution. But this complex, subtle notion came to be popularized, in the decades after 1860, as "survival of the fittest"—a much simpler, cruder vision of all nature's creatures engaged in a ruthless competition for scarce resources. All life, everywhere, was unavoidably caught in this relentless struggle for survival, for domination of the available ecological niches.

From here, it was a relatively easy intellectual move to take these ideas out of their context in the physical world of zoology and botany and reapply them to the human world of society and history. Hence the term "Social Darwinism"—survival of the fittest, readapted as an interpretive guide to understanding all human interactions, from the behaviors of individuals to the mass movements of entire nations or races. Everywhere the message was the same: If I don't dominate you, you'll dominate me. If I survive, it will have to be at someone else's expense. Resources are scarce, and only the most efficient competitors—the smartest, the strongest, the most ruthless—will live to struggle another day. Whenever you see two groups of people coexisting peacefully, it is merely an illusion, or a temporary truce. Underneath the surface, they cannot help but be secretly preparing a coup against each other. Such are the realities of Human Nature.

Social Darwinist thinkers of the late nineteenth century also added a twist to this logic, an intriguing moral tone. If I have succeeded at dominating everyone else, then this is a sign that I *deserve* to be the leader, the privileged arbiter of everyone else's destinies. By exercising domination over others, by mercilessly weeding out the weak and unfit, I am performing a higher service to the species as a whole. I am keeping the species strong and vigorous, primed for successful competition against other species. This process may appear cruel at times, but the logic of natural selection looks to the species, not to the individual. Weak and unfit individuals place an unacceptable burden on the rest of their group, and though it may appear heartless, they must be periodically selected and cast away, if the collective organism is to remain dynamic and healthy.

Once one had accepted this line of argument, it became easy to apply the logic to entire racial groups. In the millennial struggle, the Social Darwinists argued, some races had clearly emerged as superior competitors. How do you tell which races are better suited to rule and to dominate than others? Simply look and see who's on top of the heap. By definition, they are the fittest, and therefore the ones who are also morally justified in exercising control over all the rest. This is Social Darwinism in a nutshell.

It is worth noting that this ideology was not born in Germany, Italy, or Japan, but rather in England and France.[2] Thinkers like Gustave Le Bon in France or Herbert Spencer in England—or, in the United States, the popular writer William Graham Sumner—were among the key proponents of this ideology during the late nineteenth century. Social Darwinism proved attractive for many reasons. At one level, it was refreshingly simple and straightforward, so that just about anyone could grasp it: "Either dominate or be dominated; it may not be pretty, but that's the way life is." At a more visceral level, it was also flattering to think of oneself (or one's social group) as King of the Hill. Finally, it meshed neatly with the widespread phenomenon of imperialism, conveniently justifying all kinds of excursions into the rest of the world, subjugating other peoples in the name of Progress and the Higher Good of the Species. The fact that Europeans had planted their flags all over Asia, Africa, and the Middle East could be easily explained by this relatively accessible and simple rationale: "We Europeans are superior to all other peoples on earth. It is our right to go and conquer them. In fact, it is our duty to do so, for in conquering them we are bringing them the benefits of our superior civilization: our religion, medicine, technology, customs, literature—everything that makes us so obviously more advanced than they, the primitive ones."

In some cases, moreover, the Social Darwinist thinkers added the piquancy of paranoia to this heady mix of ideas. It is certainly true, they argued, that the non-European races are weaker and less advanced than us white Europeans, but the plain fact is that they reproduce like rabbits. A real possibility exists of their swamping us by their sheer numbers, the way parasites or viruses can eventually overwhelm a healthy animal's body. Hence, we have to move aggressively in preempting them from gaining too much ground, bringing them firmly under our tutelage, so that we can restrain not only their actions, but their reproductive rates as well. We have to master them completely, assuming full control over their lives, before they simply overwhelm us.

Since the nineteenth century, a long succession of critics have passionately argued against the Social Darwinist vision, denouncing it as dangerous and simplistic nonsense. Their key argument has been that the principles of natural selection discovered by Darwin only applied within the realm of animals and plants. Animals obeyed instincts, the inflexible behavior patterns with which they were born; they submitted blindly to the demands and limitations imposed on them by their biology and their surroundings. Animals could certainly adapt, through natural selection, but this was not a matter of conscious, deliberate choice: it was an unconscious process that happened to them collectively over many generations, not something they undertook as individuals acting on their own initiative.

Human beings were fundamentally different, according to the opponents of Social Darwinism, because humans inhabited a culturally mediated social world. Here, one entered the realm of free will, of deliberate reshaping of environments. Humans were not *only* animals: they also had language, ethics, religion, complex social networks of cooperation, elaborate legal systems to regulate their competition. Concepts like justice or morality played at least as important a role in shaping the human world as did the struggle to get ahead: both these forces, competition *and* cooperation, combined to give humans the power they enjoyed over their physical environment. Precisely because the human world was qualitatively different from that of the animals, applying the same set of rules to both realms could not help but yield fundamental errors and contradictions.

Many Europeans, however—especially in the late nineteenth century—

remained unaware of this critique, and found the adaptation of Darwinian ideas to the human world quite compelling. In the half-century following 1860, the Social Darwinist ideology became highly influential throughout Europe and America (and later in Japan as well): ultimately, one of the most important converts to this grim worldview was Adolf Hitler himself.

Hitler was in many ways an extremely complex, devious, enigmatic person; yet in one respect he possessed a character trait that rendered him predictable and transparent: he saw nearly everything in the light of this Social Darwinist vision. For him, human life, at its deepest essence, was about ruthless, unremitting competition. At the level of individuals, it was Me against You; at the level of collectivities, it was Our Group against Your Group.

One anecdote from the last days of Hitler's life is particularly revealing in this regard. It was March 1945, and the Russians were closing in on his bunker in Berlin. The Third Reich lay in ruins all around him, and he had finally given up hope that any of the secret weapons he'd been frantically pursuing might still emerge, like a deus ex machina, to save Germany. Hitler called in Albert Speer, his armaments minister, and issued a scorched-earth order calling for the total destruction of any surviving assets that might prove useful to Germany's enemies—factories, bridges, mines, railroads. Speer was appalled: How would the German people live after the war, he asked his führer, if such a policy were implemented? Hitler replied: "There is no need to consider the basis for even a most primitive existence. On the contrary, it is better to destroy even that, and to destroy it ourselves. The nation has proved itself weak, and the future belongs to the stronger Eastern nation."[3] The great life-or-death struggle between Aryans and Slavs had played itself out: the Aryans had failed in the contest, and now deserved to disappear from the earth. Even in the face of death, Social Darwinism gave Hitler a handle for making sense of the world that was crashing down around him on all sides. It must have been an agonizing choice, but in the end he preferred to cut himself loose from his own sense of Aryan superiority, rather than relinquish the pitiless vision that had imparted fundamental orientation and purpose to his life.

This worldview of unending competition among peoples is not, in itself, enough to explain why World War II occurred, but it amounts to what philosophers call a "necessary condition" for the war. The Japanese, Germans, and Italians, despite all the profound differences in their cultures and histories, shared a fundamental set of ambitions in common: to redress perceived injustices and raw deals of the past; to stop being treated as second-class citizens; and ultimately, to climb to their rightful place at the top of the world heap.

Japan, after centuries of isolation, wanted to be a great power and colonial empire like France and Great Britain. The Japanese people perceived themselves as being isolated on relatively small island territories, confined in living space, and intolerably vulnerable to military and economic strangulation. Japanese elites felt rage at the condescending and racist treatment they had received at the hands of Europeans and Americans, who openly regarded Japan as a second-class nation.

Germany in the 1930s was still seething with bitterness and humiliation at the loss of the First World War and the harsh peace treaty of Versailles. Hitler promised, most significantly, not only to rescue the German economy from the woes of the Great Depression, but to lift the nation back to its rightful place at the very front rank of international power.

Italy, after centuries of foreign occupation and internal strife, had only achieved national unity as recently as 1870. Amid deep disappointment with the peace settlement of 1919, and incipient social and economic chaos in the early 1920s, Benito Mussolini swept to power, promising the Italians that he would regain for them the glory of the old Roman Empire.

In all three cases we find a similar constellation of grievances and ambitions, all built around the imagery of millennial struggles among peoples, the never-ending quest for domination. To be sure, significant numbers of Japanese, Germans, and Italians ignored this kind of imagery, or rejected it outright. Among those who did find it compelling, there were innumerable variations and subcurrents, each emphasizing one aspect or another of the core ideology. But the nationalist leaders who formed the Tripartite Pact—Fumimaro Konoe, Hideki Tojo, and Yosuke Matsuoka for Japan, Hitler and Mussolini for Germany and Italy—would never have succeeded in mobilizing their peoples for war if significant portions of those populations had not accepted, at some basic level, the intuitive appeal of Social Darwinism. History had not been kind to them, their leaders claimed, and they had taken more than their share of knocks and humiliations. Now their time had come, and they would seize their rightful place as leaders of humankind.

Hitler never explicitly laid out a cogent long-term plan for his Thousand Year Reich, but historians have gone over his speeches and writings, from *Mein Kampf* in the 1920s to the conversations with his inner circle in the

early 1940s, and pieced together a sense of his overall vision.[4] His foreign
policy goals comprised three basic phases:

1. *Consolidation of domestic power base; rearmament.*

In order to project German power effectively on a global scale, the
nation first had to overcome the internal divisions of the democratic but
chaotic Weimar era of the 1920s. This process came to be known in Nazi
terminology as *Gleichschaltung*—getting all parts of German society
firmly behind the national leadership, with the entire *Volk* marching in
lockstep toward a common set of goals. At the same time, the Nazi government would cast off the restrictions of the Versailles treaty and pursue a
vigorous program of rearmament.

2. *War with France; coordination with Britain and Italy.*

Hitler regarded England with a measure of respect, as a country whose
people were rather close to the Teutonic Aryans in many ways. Perhaps, he
hoped, the British might be induced to recognize the inevitability of German dominance over the European continent, and a historic deal might be
struck: Germany would leave Britain her far-flung empire over the seas,
and Britain would accept the emergence of a German empire over the
lands of Europe.

The primary obstacle here was France. Hitler assumed that, once the
British had been persuaded to remain neutral, German armies would
defeat the French in a swift and decisive war—leaving Northern Europe
under German hegemony and Southern Europe under the dominance of
Germany's Italian allies.

3. *Expansion to the east.*

The path would then lie open for the great onslaught against the Soviet
Union—a war for increased living space for the German people, a war to
liberate Europe from the communist threat. Hitler believed that despite
the size and resources of Russia, this war would prove relatively easy for
Germany because of the inherent superiority of the Aryan race over the
Slavic and Jewish Bolsheviks. From this expanded Eurasian power base
Germany could then play its historic role as a leading world power. The
Americans might seek to intervene at some point, but Hitler dismissed
them as a mongrel people whom the Germans and their allies would
inevitably come to dominate.

Central to this expansionist plan—indeed, inseparably interwoven with
it—was the Nazi racial doctrine. Here, too, the führer never formulated a
single clear vision, but the rough outlines of his understanding may

nonetheless be gleaned from the many references he made to it over the years. The Nazi racial policy divided humankind into four levels:

- the master race on top, calling the shots;
- Aryan but non-German peoples like the Swedes, British, or Dutch (and to a certain extent the Italians and French) in the second tier, who would be allowed a relative autonomy as long as they played by rules that suited Germany;
- a third level comprising Slavs, like the Russians and Poles, to provide slave labor;
- and finally, at the bottom, Jews, Gypsies, homosexuals, and anybody infected by left-wing ideology, who would be systematically eliminated.

Precise policies and methods for the implementation of this racial hierarchy—including the extermination of the bottom tier—were not clearly established in advance; they were improvised as the Nazis went along. The killing began in the late 1930s with a euthanasia program in Germany, aimed at strengthening the Aryan race by weeding out the feebleminded or the severely disabled—*Lebensunwertes Leben*, or "life unworthy of life," in the Nazi parlance. It expanded rapidly between 1939 and 1941, with death commandos fanning out through the occupied territories in Central Europe, and the first, rather primitive death camps taking form. It reached its apotheosis starting in 1942, with the industrial-scale murder of hundreds of thousands of people per month in a network of advanced "processing facilities" such as Treblinka, Auschwitz, and Chelmno.

Where the Japanese would fit into this global hierarchy is an interesting question—one that clearly posed serious practical problems for the German-Japanese alliance during the war. Asians, according to the German racial vision, could not possibly stand as equals of white Europeans: the very notion struck Nazi theorists as self-evidently preposterous. But there *was* a way to finesse the issue: for within Asia as a whole, the Japanese were clearly the local master race. Therefore, in the multitiered pyramid of the world's peoples, the Japanese could still be seen as occupying a fairly elevated position—as subordinate but still respectable allies, administering an important subregion of a Nazi-led world. (The satirical magazine *The Onion* neatly captures the retrospective ironies of this situation in an imaginary newspaper headline for September 27, 1940, after the signing of the Tripartite Pact: "Japan Forms Alliance with White Supremacists in Well-Thought-Out Scheme.")[5]

The Japanese leadership, for their part, had their own vision of the middle- and long-term future; and it, too, entailed a vast sphere of geopolitical power, structured by an explicit racial hierarchy. They invented a delightfully Orwellian euphemism for it: the Greater East Asia Co-Prosperity Sphere.

Like Hitler and his entourage in Germany, the Japanese leaders hungered after space for their rapidly growing population. Japan lacked natural resources, and those resources were plentiful in the lands of China and Southeast Asia. Colonization seemed the perfect solution: it would offer an outlet to surplus population at home, and simultaneously consolidate Japanese power around the western Pacific. Asia was weak and internally divided; it seemed natural to the Japanese that a vigorous and dynamic people like themselves should take over the region and run it properly. Besides, they said, if we don't do it, the Europeans and Americans will do it for us. And this was certainly true.

The historian John Dower has painted a vivid portrait of the racial ideology that animated Japan's vision of overseas empire.[6] The Japanese, he explains, saw themselves as the Yamato race, an ancient people of exceptionally pure blood and high culture, destined to lead all the other Asians into a glorious future. Genocide did not form part of this vision, as it did with the bottom tier of the Nazi racial hierarchy; rather, the Japanese self-image bore a greater similarity to traditional European colonial ideologies like the White Man's Burden. Asia, under the vigorous and enlightened leadership of the Japanese, would at last throw off the exploitive shackles of European colonialism; the multifarious Asian peoples, finally moving beyond their millennial rivalries and working together under Japan's firm guidance, would create a powerful and prosperous bloc in world politics. Each Asian national or ethnic group would have its own proper place in the new order, and that order would be strictly hierarchical, with the Japanese unambiguously at the top. The central fact about the Yamato vision and the Co-Prosperity Sphere, Dower maintains, lay in the fundamental Japanese certainty that the other peoples of Asia were racially inferior—each in their own distinctive ways—and that the Japanese were the only ones who deserved the position of master. The "sphere" was actually a pyramid.

By August 1942, the Japanese had gone remarkably far toward the creation of this pan-Asian empire. They had taken over nearly all the former European colonies or American protectorates: Burma, Malaya, Singapore, the East Indies, the Philippines, and Indochina. They had conquered extensive portions of China. They were advancing on Australia, and were poised to move into the Indian Ocean and threaten British India. Initially, many Asians actually believed the egalitarian Japanese rhetoric about "co-prosperity." As they watched the Japanese in 1942 routing the Europeans and Americans, many of them reacted with enthusiasm. The Japanese were finally kicking out the arrogant whites: "Asia for the Asians!" became the battle cry that animated many Indonesians, Vietnamese, Burmese, Cambodians, and Indians.

But they were quickly disabused. In concrete practice, the Japanese racial vision resulted in callous, condescending, and often brutal treatment of the native peoples in their newly "liberated" territories. The official language of the Co-Prosperity Sphere was of course Japanese: both schoolchildren and adults were forced to start learning it. A broad policy of cultural Japanization held sway: local teachers had to present their pupils with a highly celebratory version of Japanese history; the idiosyncratic Japanese calendar replaced local measures of time; Japanese holidays supplanted indigenous holidays. Every encounter between indigenous people and a Japanese soldier or official became an occasion for symbolic subordination: the non-Japanese were required to bow before any Japanese person they met, and also to bow in the direction of Tokyo at the start of any public gathering. Resistance or even sullenness were routinely met by the Japanese with swift and unflinching punishment: a slap in the face, a beating, or worse.

And these were only the relatively milder aspects of the Japanese policies. Tens of thousands of Korean women—referred to as "comfort women"—were forced into prostitution for Japanese soldiers. Throughout the Co-Prosperity Sphere, Japanese officials compelled farmers to grow new crops, such as cotton, to meet the needs of Japan's war economy; worse still, they often ordered the wholesale confiscation of farmers' crops and food stocks, remorselessly disregarding the obvious fact that this would bring starvation on entire regions. In 1944, for example, the Japanese occupation army in Indochina seized nearly all of the annual rice crop to feed its troops: the direct result was a famine that killed approximately one million Vietnamese.[7] All indigenous Asian males became fair game for forcible impressment into hard labor, the official doctrine being to wring as much work as possible out of the native labor force, while discouraging the creation of local industries that might undermine Japanese economic dominance. Hundreds of thousands of such laborers—Indonesian, Korean, Chinese—died under the extremely harsh conditions in which their Japanese masters forced them to toil.[8]

The racist Yamato vision undoubtedly lay at the heart of the countless atrocities, great and small, that have blackened the name of wartime Japan throughout Asia ever since the 1930s and 1940s. Racism often shades all too easily into full-scale dehumanization of the "other." The helpless person quivering beneath the heel of the master race may initially be seen as a subordinate or inferior breed of human; but it does not take much for that person to lose the quality of humanity altogether, becoming a pawn, a parasite, a valueless specimen to be abused or killed without the slightest regard or remorse.

Throughout their conquered territories, Japanese soldiers in World War II indulged in an orgy of sadistic violence that leaves the historical observer dumbstruck: in China they routinely raped civilian women, sometimes killing them afterward; in Singapore they massacred five thousand Chinese by beheading them, shooting them, or taking them far into the ocean in boats and pushing them overboard to drown; in Hong Kong they bayoneted the doctors, nurses, and patients in hospitals; at Tjepu, in Java, they killed all the captured Dutch men and boys, in many cases chopping off their arms and legs, then gang-raped the women and girls; in the POW camps they freely bayoneted or tortured Australian and British soldiers, a common practice being to tear out their fingernails; in Malaya they tortured English prisoners to death, then cut off their genitals and stuffed them into their mouths, displaying the mutilated corpses on trees; at Manokwari, in New Guinea, they engaged repeatedly in acts of cannibalism, killing Asian POWs and eating their flesh; in Manchuria they performed biological experiments on Chinese men and women, exposing several thousand of them to deadly diseases, and subsequently dissecting many of them while they were still alive.[9] The mortality rate among Anglo-American POWs held by Germany and Italy was 4 percent; the mortality rate for Anglo-American POWs held by Japan was 27 percent. Close to 100,000 civilians were massacred in Manila by retreating Japanese soldiers in February and March 1945. Recalled Carlos Romulo, a Filipino who entered Manila with the forces of General Douglas A. MacArthur:

> These were my neighbors and my friends whose tortured bodies I saw pushed into heaps on the Manila streets, their hands tied behind their backs, and bayonet stabs running through and through. This girl who looked up at me wordlessly, her young breasts crisscrossed with bayonet strokes, had been in school with my son. I saw the bodies of priests, women, children, and

babies that had been bayoneted for sport, survivors told us, by a soldiery
gone mad with blood lust in defeat.[10]

No doubt it is true that any war produces its share of needless slaughter.
But the atrocious track record of the Japanese, in their treatment of occupied peoples and captured enemies, is simply too pervasive, too repetitive,
to be explained away as the "excesses" of a few sadists run amok. It follows
a pattern that can only be explained by something more systematic: the
powerful dehumanizing effect of a widespread racist ideology—an ideology that had already been building up in Japan since the early twentieth
century (one thinks of the bloody rampage against Koreans in Japan after
the Kanto earthquake of 1923), and that now revealed itself in all its fath-
omless cruelty. This was not a proud period in the history of Japan.

The racism that marked the United States during these years was of a different order of magnitude from that of the Germans and Japanese. It was
(apart from extreme cases) much less violent; it was less systematic; and
for the most part it went against the laws and stated policies of the federal
government. Yet it was there in all its ugliness—an important part of our
history, which we must face and acknowledge. It hurt our fellow citizens in
many ways, taking away their dignity, their opportunity and hope, and in
some cases their very lives.

America's participation in World War II was supposed to be about fighting fascism and aggression, and about defending the values of equality
and freedom that the Western democracies had written into their constitutions and their way of life. But in the case of Japanese-Americans and
African-Americans, we find a profound contradiction between these ideals
in theory and their actual enactment in practice. Both these groups faced
pervasive forms of injustice and discrimination. Both groups resisted discrimination, to varying degrees and in various ways. And both of them
ended up contributing, to the best extent they were allowed, to the American war effort.[11]

At the time of the Pearl Harbor attack, some 270,000 Japanese-
Americans lived in the United States, for the most part in Hawaii and California. About 64 percent were American citizens, and about 50 percent
had been born on United States soil.[12] They constituted a large minority
(about 40 percent of the population) in the territory of Hawaii, and a much
smaller minority (about 1 percent) in California—yet it was in California

that their presence had aroused the most significant racist backlash. Ever since the turn of the century, the rhetoric of the "Yellow Peril" had constituted an important undercurrent along the West Coast: according to this vision, eagerly propounded by the sensationalist Hearst newspapers, these new Asian-Americans threatened to swamp the white European populations of the western United States. Hearst's scurrilous attacks against Asian immigrants had not only sold papers, but had brought harsh legislative action as well. In California, new state laws passed after World War I prohibited Japanese citizens from owning land. Then in 1924 the new federal Immigration Act banned all further Asian immigration to the United States: this legislation was openly racist, since it placed much milder restrictions on immigration from other (presumably more "suitable") regions such as Northern Europe.

Somewhat surprisingly, given this tradition of racial fears, most Americans kept their cool in the first few weeks after Pearl Harbor: only a few openly racist organizations called for special measures to be taken against Japanese-Americans. But the mood swiftly changed in the early months of 1942, as news came in from the western Pacific of Japan's navy and army rampaging from victory to victory: many Americans suddenly began feeling genuine fear of an attack against the West Coast. Rumors spread of imminent invasion, of Japanese-American spies communicating by radio with offshore submarines, of sabotage, of Japanese-American farmers planting their crops in cryptic formations that would direct incoming aircraft to vulnerable military installations.

The American people—to put it simply—went into a panic. "A Jap's a Jap," the saying went: no matter how long their families had lived in the United States, no matter how perfect their American accent or how completely they had assimilated into American culture, they were regarded as unavoidably and automatically taking the side of Japan in the war. Every one of them was instantly regarded as a potential traitor. Soon even so august a commentator as the journalist Walter Lippmann was calling for stringent measures of surveillance against all Japanese-Americans—the Constitution be damned. "Nobody's constitutional rights," he declared, "include the right to reside and do business on a battlefield."[13]

The public clamor for action rapidly became so strong that the federal government felt compelled to respond. After nervous consultations in the War Department and the Department of Justice, President Roosevelt signed Executive Order 9066 in February 1942. The decree, claiming "military necessity" as its justification, authorized U.S. officials to designate areas of the nation in which they could round up anyone they chose (it did not specifically mention Japanese-Americans) and deport them to detention facilities as they saw fit.

The authorities acted swiftly. Within three months, more than 110,000 Japanese-Americans from California, Oregon, and Washington had been ordered to pack a few suitcases, close down their homes and businesses, settle their personal affairs on very short notice, and board trains and buses to the new camps deep in the interior of the country. One sees them in photographs in the National Archives: quietly lined up to get on the trains, flanked by long rows of stern-looking U.S. Army soldiers, rifles at the ready.[14]

The camps were spartan but survivable. One internee, the Stanford University professor Yamato Ichihashi, stoically reported in his letters to friends that the sanitary facilities were adequate and the food was good.[15] From inside the camp, an internee could peer out through two layers of barbed-wire fences at the world he or she had left behind. From the observation towers, uniformed guards looked down, wielding machine guns. At night, powerful searchlights swept to and fro.

Some brave Japanese-Americans fought the internment policy in the courts, but they got nowhere, because the U.S. Supreme Court repeatedly upheld the relocation order. In one landmark case, *Korematsu v. United States* (December 1944), the majority of judges voted (6–3) to sustain the internment policy, directly addressing the issue of racism:

> Korematsu was not excluded from the Military Area [California] because of hostility to him or his race. He was excluded because we are at war with the Japanese Empire, because the properly constituted military authorities feared an invasion of our West Coast and felt constrained to take proper security measures, because they decided that the military urgency of the situation demanded that all citizens of Japanese ancestry be segregated from the West Coast temporarily. . . . There was evidence of disloyalty on the part of some, the military authorities considered that the need for action was great, and time was short.

Justice Frank Murphy was one of the three judges dissenting:

> No one denies, of course, that there were some disloyal persons of Japanese descent on the Pacific Coast who did all in their power to aid their ancestral land. Similar disloyal activities have been engaged in by many persons of German, Italian and even more pioneer stock in our country. But to infer that examples of individual disloyalty prove group disloyalty and justify

discriminatory action against the entire group is to deny that under our system of law individual guilt is the sole basis for deprivation of rights. . . . [It] is to adopt one of the cruelest of the rationales used by our enemies to destroy the dignity of the individual and to encourage and open the door to discriminatory actions against other minority groups in the passions of tomorrow. . . . I dissent, therefore, from this legalization of racism.[16]

By this late point in the war, however, several facts had become evident to most Americans: the United States was going to win the war; the Japanese were not about to disembark at Santa Monica or Coos Bay tomorrow night; not a single verified case of Japanese-American subversion had ever come to light; and above all, several battalions of Japanese-American volunteers had gone and distinguished themselves so bravely in the fighting in Europe that they finally made a dent in public opinion.

So on December 17, 1944, the policy was ended and the internees released—ironically, one day before the *Korematsu* ruling came through. "We were given $25 in transportation fare," recalled one of the freed internees, Estelle Ishigo (a white woman who had refused to be separated from her Japanese-American husband and had chosen to accompany him in internment). "We were poorly clad, dirty. We marched like prisoners into the waiting buses and trains. I felt like I was part of a defeated Indian tribe."[17]

No such large-scale internment was ever put into practice for Italian-Americans or German-Americans.

African-Americans entered the war under rather different circumstances than the Japanese, for American society had been even more profoundly and pervasively discriminatory against blacks well before the war began. The tradition continued in wartime, both in the area of civilian work and in military service. African-Americans joined the flood of other working-class citizens who poured into the new jobs that the war industries provided: by 1945, some 1.2 million blacks had left the South, heading for employment opportunities in the North and out West. Even though they occupied the lowest rung of the social ladder, the sheer demand for labor in the war economy had reached such a level that they found unprecedented new chances to receive education and to make money. This unintended demographic shift was to have a profound impact on the black population and its experiences during the postwar decades.

The historian David Kennedy offers the story of one black woman as a typical example of the war's transformative impact:

> When defense production began to gear up, [Sybil] Lewis left her position as a $3.50-per-week housemaid in Sapulpa, Oklahoma, and headed for Los Angeles, where she found employment as a $48-per-week riveter at Lockheed Aircraft. "When I got my first paycheck, I'd never seen that much money before," she remembered, "not even in the bank, because I'd never been in a bank too much." On the Lockheed assembly floor she was teamed with a "big strong white girl from a cotton farm in Arkansas." Like many of the white women in the plant, for her workmate "to say 'nigger' was just a way of life. Many of them had never been near, let alone touched a Negro." But shared work meant that "both of us [had] to relate to each other in ways that we never experienced before. Although we had our differences we both learned to work together and talk together." Repeated in thousands upon thousands of wartime workplaces, mundane encounters like Sybil Lewis's with her Arkansas co-worker began to sand away the stereotypes that had ossified under segregation. "We learned that despite our hostilities and resentments we could open up to each other and get along. . . . She learned that Negroes were people, too, and I saw her as a person also, and we both gained from it."[18]

Unfortunately, not all whites could quite bring themselves to see that "Negroes were people, too." In small towns and large cities throughout America the influx of black workers was deeply resented—and sometimes violently resisted—by whites. The whole city of Detroit erupted in race riots in June 1943 after white workers in the defense factories protested the promotion of several blacks; twenty-five blacks and nine whites had been killed by the time federal troops arrived to quell the violence. In another episode, black soldiers at a base in Salina, Kansas, rioted when they were barred from eating at a local restaurant: the restaurant owner showed no compunction about regularly serving white German prisoners of war who were interned nearby, but adamantly refused entry to the uniformed American blacks. Seventeen blacks were lynched in the United States between 1940 and 1943.

Some blacks began to organize to protest the inequalities of their condition. They started referring to the "Double V" of America's war, meaning V for Victory over fascism abroad, but also V for Victory over racism at home. One African-American labor leader, A. Philip Randolph, formed a powerful political organization among American blacks, the March on Washington Movement (MOWM), which helped to focus the discontent of blacks into cogent political action in Washington, and was instrumental in prodding the federal government to enact laws protecting blacks' rights. It was direct pressure from Randolph—the threat of a huge protest demonstration in the capital—that caused President Roosevelt to finally assume the political risk in June 1941 of issuing a landmark decree, Executive Order 8802, which banned all forms of racial discrimination in the war industries. Though the law was unevenly enforced, this pivotal action by the MOWM helped lay the basis for the postwar civil rights agitation that ultimately abolished the Jim Crow system and desegregated the South.

In the U.S. military, meanwhile, systematic injustice prevailed. Even though racial discrimination in the armed services was technically illegal, 95 percent of African-Americans serving in the navy were restricted to mess hall duties or menial jobs. The secretary of war, Henry Stimson, stoutly upheld these policies, claiming that blacks were "less capable of handling modern weapons."[19] In the army, black GIs slept in segregated barracks, ate in Jim Crow mess halls, and were forced to spend their leisure time in "colored only" recreational buildings. When they were sent overseas to the combat theaters, they were mostly restricted to support and logistical assignments, and deliberately kept away from the main battles. Late in the war a few segregated black combat units were finally created, but almost always with the unstated but ironclad rule that they would be led by white officers. One black GI, the writer Bill Horton, summed up the situation in a 1944 poem:

> I'm just a Negro soldier
> Fighting for "Democracy,"
> A thing I've often heard of
> But very seldom see . . .
>
> Yet I must be patriotic
> Must not grumble or complain
> But must fight for some "four freedoms"
> On which I'll have no claim.[20]

In June 1944, as Allied armies approached Rome and prepared to liberate the city, Pope Pius XII quietly contacted the staff of General Mark Clark with a polite but firm demand: could the American officers see to it that black soldiers not be included among the Allied units stationed in

Rome? The pontiff did not elaborate on why he wanted this, and General Clark—to his credit—ignored the Vatican's request.[21] Despite these indignities (and thousands more), the African-American soldiers in their segregated combat units did their best to fight hard for their country overseas.[22] The 99th Fighter Squadron, also known as the Tuskegee Airmen, distinguished itself in the air battle over Italy: between 1943 and 1945 these black pilots downed more than a thousand German aircraft and received 150 Distinguished Flying Crosses. Farther north, as the Allies advanced into Germany, the 761st Tank Battalion helped to turn the tide against advancing German units in the Battle of the Bulge; one black soldier in the battalion, Staff Sergeant Ruben Rivers, was later awarded the Congressional Medal of Honor:

Citation: For extraordinary heroism in action during 15–19 November 1944, toward Guebling, France. Though severely wounded in the leg, Sergeant Rivers refused medical treatment and evacuation, took command of another tank, and advanced with his company in Guebling the next day. Repeatedly refusing evacuation, Sergeant Rivers continued to direct his tank's fire at enemy positions through the morning of 19 November 1944. At dawn, Company A's tanks began to advance towards Bougaktroff, but were stopped by enemy fire. Sergeant Rivers, joined by another tank, opened fire on the enemy tanks, covering Company A as they withdrew. While doing so, Sergeant Rivers' tank was hit, killing him and wounding the crew. Staff Sergeant Rivers' fighting spirit and daring leadership were an inspiration to his unit and exemplify the highest traditions of military service.[23]

By 1945, 883,000 black soldiers were serving in the U.S. armed forces. Here is one story that captures what it was like for them. It comes from an interview by Studs Terkel with an African-American veteran named Alfred Duckett.

In France, we were at Camp Lucky Strike. It was huge, a town. Its function was to hold German prisoners who had been captured at the front. They were brought to us to be guarded and worked.

There was an almost psychotic terror on the part of white commanders that there would be a great deal of association with the white women. We had a chaplain who made it his business to visit in advance every place we were going to. He'd warn the people in those communities that in America white people did not associate with us and—I'm not kidding—that we had tails. That we quite often, without provocation, cut people up. A man of God. There was an edict issued by the commanding officer of the camp that no black troops were to associate with French civilians. They meant women, of course.

One night in a Red Cross tent, a member of our regiment, Allen Left-ridge, was talking to a French woman who was serving doughnuts and cof-fee. When a white MP ordered him not to stand there talking to this woman, Allen turned his back on him. He was shot in the back and killed. Another black, Frank Glenn, was also killed during this incident.

Word spread like wildfire among all the black regiments at Camp Lucky Strike. Since we were not combat troops, they used to lock our arms up every day. We would only get arms when we'd drill. When the killings hap-pened, the fellows in my outfit broke into the supply room and got their guns. They started to march. They were determined to avenge the deaths even if they got wiped out. Luckily there were a couple of white officers who everybody respected: "You can't win. The odds are against you." The next day, our outfit was moved out.

I was sending stories back to the black papers, as letters. They were get-ting through. I sent the one about how Leftridge and Glenn were killed. Allen had about two weeks to go before going home on rotation and for the first time would see his little daughter.

After the war, I ran into one of the fellas from the outfit: "You remember Allen Leftridge?" How could I forget him? He said, "Remember how when Allen died, he called out his wife's name? Well, I ran into her. Would you believe the army refused to give her a pension because they said he was killed due to his misconduct? She has been trying to find out what caused his death, and they give her a lot of doubletalk. She read the article you wrote and she'd like to meet you, 'cause maybe she could get more informa-tion." It wasn't written under my name, but a lot of people knew it was me.

I went to see her, and she had this adorable little girl running around, bein' bad. We talked real late. I noticed that when they started playin' "The Star-Spangled Banner" on the radio she got up and turned it off.[24]

Making distinctions among the various racisms of World War II is important; but it is equally important to recognize the underlying com-monalities among them. The black GI thrown out of a segregated mess hall did not face the same dangers as a Jewish father cradling his child at the ravine of Babi Yar, but for all their differences, they were victims of a fun-damentally similar gesture, rooted in hatred and dehumanization. It is essential to recognize the distinctions between the lynch mobs of the

American South, the rampaging Japanese in Manila, and the coldly methodical Nazis in the Ukraine; but it is also too easy to classify these phenomena as totally separate, totally removed from one another. They were not. They were part of the same deep disease, erupting simultaneously all over the planet. We, as Americans, are falsely comforting ourselves if we fail to see the common lines that connect all these things beneath the surface—linking our clean, bright, familiar hometowns to the ghastly hellholes on the other side of the world.

Chapter Two

CAUSES OF THE PACIFIC WAR

A Longer View on Pearl Harbor

Ever since the ships
from foreign countries
came for the jeweled
silkworm cocoons
To the land of the gods and the emperor . . .

—Matsuo Taseko, 1860s[1]

When you see Hollywood films about the outbreak of World War II in the Pacific, the impression you often get is that it all started with a Japanese sneak attack at Pearl Harbor. You see pictures of the battleships burning, the dive-bombers wheeling and plunging. You see newsreel footage of Roosevelt standing in Congress, solemnly proclaiming, "December 7, 1941, a date which will live in infamy." And that's pretty much it. We Americans were minding our own business in Hawaii, and the Japs actually had the effrontery to come across the ocean and launch a totally unexpected attack against us without declaring war—killing 2,400 Americans.

This view of the war's origins could be called the "Out of the Blue" narrative. They attacked us, out of the blue. We recovered and fought back and won.

Sometimes, though, the explanation for the war goes into a bit more depth. At the National D-Day Museum in New Orleans, for example, the visitor watches a documentary film and goes through an elaborate exhibit: both the film and the exhibit lay out the origins of the war in a more detailed manner, starting in 1931. This second approach to explaining the war's origins could be called the "Ten Years of Aggression" narrative.

It goes roughly like this: in 1931, the Japanese began a policy of aggres-

Commodore Matthew Perry arrives in Kurihama, Japan (July 18, 1853).
Painting by Gessan Ogata.

sive imperial expansionism that was to last for more than ten years, and eventually led to World War II.

- *1931:* Japan illegally annexes the Chinese province of Manchuria.
- *1937:* Japan launches another major wave of attacks in China.
- *1940:* Japan joins an alliance with the other expansionist fascist powers, Germany and Italy.

- *July 1941:* Japan seizes French Indochina. The United States responds by joining the British and Dutch in imposing a severe embargo on shipments of food and oil to Japan.
- *December 1941:* Japan attacks the United States.

This is certainly a more sophisticated account than the "Out of the Blue" narrative, but ultimately it leads to the same rather straightforward conclusion: the Japanese had embarked on a path of brutal aggression, and the United States tried to stop them all through the 1930s, at first through diplomacy and then through economic pressures. They responded by attacking the United States militarily. World War II is about the Americans fighting back.

These two renditions of the story, while accurate in a limited way, fail to give us a satisfactory understanding of why the Pacific War took place. The full story is more complicated, and ultimately a lot more interesting, than either of these two narratives can convey.

Our narrative must go back much further than 1931—all the way to 1853. In that year, an American naval officer, Commodore Matthew Perry, arrived with a flotilla of warships in Edo Bay, off what is today the city of Tokyo. The Americans did not mince words: they told the Japanese that if they did not start trading with American merchants, U.S. military forces, with their superior technology, would attack Japan. This came to be known as the Opening of Japan.[2]

For the preceding 250 years, Japan had been a feudal society under the Tokugawa shogunate, fairly stable and isolated on its islands, and utterly closed off from the rest of the world. But the international situation was swiftly changing. Ever since the early 1800s, the British, French, and Dutch had been moving more and more aggressively into Asia, establishing colonial settlements, seeking markets and raw materials. British merchants had begun reaping a significant profit dealing in opium along the China coast, and when the Chinese government tried to stop this, the British navy simply crushed them by force. Free trade, it was called: the inalienable right of British merchants to come and sell addictive drugs, for high profits, to the citizens of any Asian nation they saw fit. The crumbling Chinese monarchy was simply too weak to do anything about it.

The Japanese watched all this with growing anxiety. They knew that the French, British, Dutch, Russians, and Americans were all eager to expand their trade in Asia, carving out handsome markets there. They realized, to their profound shock, that they were basically naked before the superior military technology of the Westerners.

In 1858 the Japanese government was compelled to sign a treaty with the United States, followed quickly by a series of similar treaties with the other Western powers. These came to be known as the Unequal Treaties, because they clearly reflected the lopsided power relations between Japan and the white foreigners from Europe and the United States. The treaties set tariff levels for imports and exports, stipulating that the Japanese government could not alter these tariffs. If a foreigner committed a crime on Japanese territory, the laws and courts of Japan would hold no jurisdiction over the case: all such trials would be conducted by foreign judges, applying the laws of the accused person's home nation. This was known as the legal principle of extraterritoriality. In these and other ways, the treaties brazenly infringed Japan's sovereignty, imposing obviously unfair terms to which the Japanese had no choice but to submit.

These treaties were not substantially altered for forty years, until 1899. According to the historian Andrew Gordon, the experience of forced submission to the Unequal Treaties exerted a decisive impact on Japanese mentalities, and thus played a pivotal role in the formation of modern Japanese national feeling:

> These "unequal treaties" were humiliating in theory and in practice. [They] imposed a semicolonial status on Japan. Politically and economically, Japan became legally subordinate to foreign governments. Over the next few decades, petty insults were heaped one upon the other. Numerous nasty crimes went lightly punished [by the foreign judges], if they were punished at all. In the 1870s and 1880s, these injustices—a rape unpunished or an assault excused—came to be front page material in the new national press. They were experienced each time as a renewed blow to pride, yet another violation of Japanese sovereignty.
>
> Yet it would be misleading to conclude simply that these treaties trampled a *preexisting* national pride and sovereignty. Rather . . . the very process of dealing with the pushy [foreigners] *created* modern Japanese nationalism. [A] new conception took hold of "Japan" as a single nation, to be defended and governed as such.[3]

Japanese nationalism, in other words, was born in the second half of the 1800s as a reaction against foreign aggression and maltreatment. It was the Japanese who had been "minding their own business" in the mid-

1800s, and it was the Americans who came across the ocean, unbidden and unwelcome, with guns at the ready. The histories of Japan and the United States had already become entwined in important ways, almost a century before the Second World War.

This straightforward fact gets lost, somehow, in many histories of World War II. Yet the humiliation of those four decades between the 1850s and 1890s—the raw realization of standing helpless before the over-whelming power of domineering foreigners—constitutes one of the pivotal factors in modern Japanese history. We cannot understand the lam-entable trajectory of Japanese society in the first half of the twentieth cen-tury unless we look to its direct roots in the closing decades of the nineteenth. Out of that brush with colonial subjugation was born a deter-mination among the Japanese people that they would never allow this kind of inferior status to be imposed on them again: they would do whatever it took to become strong, to take their future back into their own hands, to gain and defend their national independence.

Unfortunately, these kinds of sentiments are hard to extinguish, once they are kindled. The tragedy of Japanese history between 1900 and 1945 can be seen, from one perspective, as the story of these nationalistic senti-ments running gradually out of control, strengthening the enemies of democracy in Japan, and ultimately delivering the nation's polity into the hands of brutal militarist leaders hell-bent on foreign conquest.

After the 1860s, Japan underwent a major social revolution. The Tokugawa system was dismantled in 1868 and replaced with a new government that drew its authority directly from the Meiji emperor. What followed was an absolutely breathtaking crusade for economic and social modernization— arguably the most rapid and successful industrialization of any economy in the world's history, rivaled only by Soviet industrialization under Stalin in the 1930s. Over less than four decades, Japan transformed itself from a largely agricultural, feudal society into an industrial powerhouse, far and away the most modern and dynamic economy in Asia by the year 1900. The Japanese became famous for their skill in emulating the Europeans and Americans, mastering their technology and adopting many aspects of the Western social and political systems.

But this was not the only way the Japanese patterned themselves after the West: they also imitated the European enterprise of imperial conquest. Starting in the 1880s, Japanese elites began systematically putting into place a policy of imperial expansion, carried out by a rapidly built-up army and navy. Japanese businessmen eagerly extended their connections and trade relationships all over Asia, particularly in Korea and China. In 1895 Japan fought a brief war against China and won decisively: it immediately annexed the island of Taiwan, severing it from the decrepit Chinese empire. By 1899 Japan's position had become sufficiently strong that it renegotiated the Unequal Treaties, replacing them with much more equitable agreements that restored national sovereignty.

Then, in 1904, the Japanese clashed with the Russians over who would dominate the northern Chinese province of Manchuria, a territory rich in natural resources. This imperialist rivalry culminated in a short war in 1904–1905; a war in which all bets were on the much larger Russian empire. To the astonishment of the entire world, the Japanese not only held their own, but trounced the czar's navy and army in a series of brilliant battles. Since neither side felt it could afford a protracted war, they entered peace negotiations, which resulted in Japan adding the southern half of the Sakhalin Peninsula to its imperial holdings. This victory also paved the way for rising Japanese dominance in Korea, which was formally annexed as a Japanese colony in 1910.

The Japanese rationale in piecing together this overseas empire went roughly as follows: We are merely doing the same thing that the European great powers have been doing for centuries. The only difference is that we are an Asian nation, and hence have a superior moral right to establish an Asian empire. The Europeans have no such right and should leave Asia to us. We are the natural leaders of Asia, and it is our destiny to liberate Asia from Western domination and lead it to prosperity and justice under our flag.

This rationale—it must be emphasized—bore a striking similarity to those being offered by the major European powers for their own empires: the French ideology of the *mission civilisatrice*, the "White Man's Burden" of the British. The principal difference, of course, was that France and Britain had never themselves been the objects of semi-colonial status, as the Japanese had been for forty years under the Unequal Treaties. The Japanese, having narrowly escaped being colonized themselves, argued that the creation of their empire constituted nothing less than an act of self-defense. In this dog-eat-dog world of imperialism, only the strong would remain independent—and to be strong in today's world meant having a large imperial territory of your own. This line of thinking became widely popular among the Japanese population, among both elites and common people, and across the political spectrum. During the 1920s, to be sure, some liberal or left-wing intellectuals and politicians did question the policy of imperialism, but they remained a relatively small minority.[4] The majority of Japanese strongly supported the idea of building up an empire, just as the European great powers had done.

During the First World War, Japan sided with the Allies, which meant that at war's end Japan was awarded some of Germany's small colonial possessions in China. In 1922, the British, Japanese, and Americans held a conference in Washington, D.C., in the postwar spirit of peacemaking and avoiding arms races and future wars. Together these three dominant Pacific naval powers negotiated a treaty that established a basic ratio in the total tonnage of their warships: 5:5:3, respectively, for the United States, Britain, and Japan. The American and British navies would remain equal, while the Japanese navy would weigh in at 60 percent of the other two. The British and Americans justified this ratio by the argument that their far-flung geopolitical interests required a two-ocean navy, whereas Japan's interests lay solely in the Pacific region. Not surprisingly, this rationale failed to carry much weight with the Japanese, but they accepted the unequal terms in exchange for a British and American pledge not to estab-lish new naval bases in the Asian-Pacific region.[5] Nevertheless, some Japanese leaders regarded the Washington Naval Treaty as nothing short of insulting—a return to the old system of unfair treatment at the hands of the arrogant Western powers.

Until the late 1920s, Japanese society had been roughly balanced between two diffuse attitudes toward foreign policy.[6] On one side were those who wanted to go slowly and cautiously in building the empire, respecting international agreements as much as possible, and avoiding making ene-mies among other great powers. On the other side were those who said, in effect, "To hell with international agreements and international opinion: we have our national interest at stake here, our very long-term survival, and we should build up our empire quickly and aggressively before it's too late." This hard-line attitude became particularly influential among the top echelons of the army and navy, but it had strong civilian backers as well.

The sad story of the 1930s is one in which this latter group, the mili-tarist hard-liners, not only got the upper hand, but ultimately succeeded in hijacking Japanese national policy altogether. They used assassination and other forms of illegal intimidation to silence their opponents, and by the late 1930s no one remained who could effectively oppose them. The militarists of the 1930s, unhindered by any countervailing domestic political force, created an increasingly authoritarian government, and single-mindedly pushed Japan toward a foreign policy of war and conquest.

The first target of this stepped-up policy of aggression was Manchuria, the large province of China conveniently located right across the Sea of Japan. Ever since the Chinese revolution of 1911, China had been a republic, nominally under the leadership of Chiang Kai-shek and his nationalist Guomindang Party. But in reality, China was in semi-anarchy, as feuding warlords in various provinces struggled to gain power at one another's expense. As far as the Japanese militarists were concerned, the vastness of China beckoned as a trove of precious land and resources, ripe for the picking.

In 1931, secret agents of the Japanese army created a minor "incident" along one of the railway lines in Manchuria—a bomb blowing up a section of track. In the ensuing days Japanese army units poured in and occupied large portions of Manchuria, claiming that this was a humanitarian mission to "restore order." What is particularly fascinating about this incident is that the Japanese army acted entirely on its own initiative in seizing Manchuria—without getting any orders from the political leadership in Tokyo. The army was basically dictating policy to the central government, presenting it with a fait accompli that no civilian politician felt strong enough to repudiate.

Not surprisingly, the Chinese government appealed to the League of Nations. This constituted as clear-cut a case of unjustified aggression as one could find, the Chinese argued: one League member state had simply invaded and annexed a large province of another League member state. Indeed, by 1932, the Japanese had already installed a pliant puppet government in Manchuria, renaming the province with the Japanese name Manchukuo. The League of Nations dispatched a commission to investigate, and in 1933 issued its verdict: it deplored the Japanese act of annexation and asked the Japanese army to withdraw from Manchuria. But the League's action had no teeth: it imposed no sanctions against Japan, and wielded no credible threat of military action in the event of Japanese defiance. The reality was that no nation—neither the United States, nor Britain, nor anyone else inside or outside the League—really cared enough about China to risk war in the name of undoing this brazen violation of international law. Japan angrily withdrew from the League of Nations in 1933; Manchukuo remained under Japanese control. The Japanese army's expansionist move had succeeded.

Within Japanese society, however, there were still many who looked with horror on the policy of aggressive expansionism and international isolation that the militarist leaders were pressuring the government to adopt. On February 26, 1936, a group of rabidly nationalist young army officers launched a rebellion against the moderates in the government. They seized control of Tokyo and assassinated many of the political figures who had spoken out in recent years against increased military spending, or against the Manchurian invasion. Anyone who had been looking for peaceful ways to advance Japan's national interests was seen by the fanatical nationalists as a traitor, and became a target of the murderous rampage.

Eventually, after four days of violence, the rebellion died out. The principal leaders were arrested, and a number of them were subsequently court-martialed and executed. But many among the broader Japanese population, and especially among the military, openly regarded these rebels as heroes whose self-sacrifice should be revered and emulated. From 1936 until the outbreak of the Second World War, any Japanese politician or military leader who voiced counsels of caution, or of peaceful compromise, ran the serious risk of being labeled a traitor and assassinated. The hardliners were increasingly setting the tone for their country's strategic decisions—by intimidation and the threat of deadly force.

The success of the Manchukuo adventure had greatly emboldened the army leadership. They were itching to accelerate Japan's expansion into Chinese territory, and were eagerly looking for a pretext. That pretext came on July 7, 1937, when a group of Chinese soldiers skirmished with a Japanese patrol on the Marco Polo Bridge near Beijing. Skirmishes of this sort were not all that uncommon, given the fact that Japanese troops were patrolling on many parts of Chinese territory. This time, however, the Japanese army chose to hit hard, launching a major attack that rapidly escalated to all-out war between China and Japan. Starting in August, the Japanese began full-scale aerial bombardment of defenseless Chinese cities, killing thousands of civilians in Beijing, Tientsin, and Shanghai. The poorly equipped Chinese army retreated pell-mell.

This retreat left exposed the city of Nanking, just inland from Shanghai—a city of considerable symbolic importance because it had formerly constituted the official seat of government for the Chinese leader Chiang Kai-shek. On December 13, 1937, Japanese forces occupied Nanking. Evidently, the Japanese army leaders decided that they stood a good chance of terrifying the Chinese into surrender if they made an example of the occupied city. So their troops went after the civilian population. At least twenty thousand Chinese noncombatant men were rounded up, taken outside the city, and massacred. They were used as living targets for bayonet practice by Japanese soldiers; they were machine-gunned; they were buried alive; they were doused with gasoline and burned to death; they were tied to trees and kicked to death. The same was also done to untold thousands of Chinese soldiers who had surrendered or been captured.[7]

Meanwhile, inside the city, Japanese troops were gang-raping every Chinese woman they could get their hands on. Over and over, at least twenty thousand women, day after day: pregnant mothers, old women, young girls. First rape, then mutilation and murder. The orgy of sadistic violence went on for six weeks. Japan's military leadership and the government in Tokyo did nothing to stop it.

This incident has gone down in history as the Rape of Nanking.[8] Historians still debate over the total number of Chinese men, women, and children killed in the rampage. The range of plausible estimates lies between 50,000 and 300,000 dead; one prominent expert, John Dower, believes the figure of 200,000 is the most convincing.[9] Not surprisingly, the massacre instantly became a source of outrage in nations all over the world. In the United States, FDR responded in 1938 by calling for a voluntary boycott among American arms manufacturers of any further sales to the Japanese.

From this point onward, the United States and Japan were increasingly on a collision course. As the Japanese saw it, the United States and the Europeans had no business meddling in the affairs of East Asia and the South Pacific, half a world away from their own shores. As the Americans viewed it, Japan's expansionist ambitions had become too dangerous to ignore any longer; the entire balance of power in Asia lay at risk. Moreover, many Americans felt that the barbarous way the Japanese had behaved in China placed them beyond the pale of civilized nations.

In October 1939, Roosevelt ordered the U.S. Pacific Fleet to shift its home base from San Diego, California, to Hawaii, in the mid-Pacific. This aggressive body language would show the Japanese that the United States meant business when it expressed its disapproval over Japan's ongoing war of conquest in China. But all that this move accomplished was to alarm and infuriate the Japanese.

Meanwhile, the war in Europe had just begun. The Japanese looked on with admiration and amazement as Hitler carved up Poland, Norway, Denmark, Belgium, Holland, and France, pushing the British ignomin-

iously back onto their island. On September 27, 1940—while the RAF and
Luftwaffe fought it out over the skies of Britain—Japan signed the Tripartite Pact with Germany and Italy: a firm military alliance. If any of the
three signatories was attacked by an outside party, the other two would
leap to the defense.

On the Japanese side, two men were primarily responsible for this
move. The first was General Hideki Tojo, a fanatically nationalist army
officer who had helped lead the Japanese campaign in China in the late
1930s. Tojo became minister of war in July 1940, and from this post he was
able to exert enormous pressure on the more moderate-minded members
of government, arguing that a major war was inevitable in the coming
year or two, unless the Japanese were willing to accept a permanently inferior status. The second was Yosuke Matsuoka—a civilian, but a devoted
ally of the most extreme faction of nationalists in the Japanese army.
He became Japan's foreign minister in July 1940 (at the same time as
Tojo became war minister): together these two appointments substantially
increased the probability that Japan would go to war.

Early in 1941, unbeknownst to the Japanese, U.S. intelligence broke the
Japanese diplomatic cipher, which meant that the innermost diplomatic
discussions of the Tokyo government during the entire year of 1941 were
secretly being read by U.S. leaders. It was clear that the Japanese were
preparing for war. The breaking point came in July 1941, when their troops
took over the French colony of Indochina, despite repeated American
warnings that such an act would constitute a serious breach of the precarious status quo, and would bring strong American sanctions. The Japanese
government thought the Americans were bluffing; only a few days later,
they discovered their mistake.

Roosevelt and his secretary of state, Cordell Hull, felt the time had
come to send a very tough message to the Japanese: on July 25, 1941, acting in concert with the British and Dutch governments, the United States
imposed a full-scale embargo on trade with Japan, thereby cutting Japan's
foreign trade by 75 percent, and oil imports by 90 percent. Initially, FDR's
intention had been to impose this embargo through a series of incremental steps, giving the Japanese a chance to rethink their aggressive actions
under steadily mounting pressure; but in actual practice the economic
impact of the trade ban hit Japan immediately with full force. Under this
draconian embargo, Japan's oil reserves would last for between nine to
eighteen months; then its whole economy would grind to a halt.

The Japanese saw this measure—quite reasonably—as nothing less
than a declaration of economic warfare. The Americans, they said to them-

selves, have now presented us with a clear and peremptory ultimatum: we must withdraw from Indochina and China altogether, or face economic collapse. So we Japanese have a choice: We can retreat from our newly acquired territories the way the Americans are demanding. Or we can fight.

This did not seem like a hard decision. The Japanese leaders ordered their military to start finalizing plans for war with the United States. Negotiations between the two governments continued through the fall, with the Japanese hoping that Washington might back away from its stance of confrontation, and the Americans wishing that Tokyo would finally recognize the unacceptably high cost of its imperialist aggression. Unfortunately, the situation had developed to a point in which neither side felt there was much room for compromise.

What did the Japanese leaders expect to gain from this war, in concrete terms, and how did they intend to achieve it? Briefly put, they aimed to command the entire western Pacific Ocean—a huge sphere that included coastal China, most of Southeast Asia, all the western Pacific islands, and Australia. They realized full well that they were embarking on a historic gamble, for they admitted that a relatively small island nation like Japan could never prevail in a war of attrition against a great continental power like the United States, whose resources were twenty times larger.

Instead, they reasoned as follows: We won't try to beat the Americans in an all-out military confrontation. What we must do is grab as much territory as we can in the Asia-Pacific region, quickly, ruthlessly—and rapidly fortify it, building up a very impressive defensive perimeter. We'll take the Europeans and Americans by surprise.

And then the Americans will be faced with a difficult choice: They can come and fight us to liberate those territories, or they can accept the fact that the map of Asia has been redrawn, and that they must henceforth learn to deal with a Japanese-led Asian bloc. If we make it clear that kicking us Japanese out of our new Asian empire is going to require a long, bloody fight, then there is a good chance that the Americans will regard the battle as simply not being worth the high cost in lives. Controlling the southwestern Pacific is not a vital interest of the United States. The American people will say: Why should the United States fight a protracted war, merely to give back to the British and Dutch and French their Asian colonies? Why should we send our citizens to fight and die, merely to regain possession of a worthless protectorate in the Philippines? Antiwar movements will spread, and in the end, the American government will simply have to accept Japan's fait accompli. They may not like it, but they won't have the popular support to do much about it. Japan's best ally, in other words, will be the deep-rooted American tendency toward isolationism. As long as no vital American interests are in play, the Yankees can be counted on to stay put.

This was actually a fairly shrewd calculation. A few decades later, in the Vietnam War era, something came to pass that rather closely resembled the scenario that the Japanese envisioned. Faced with the mounting tally of body bags coming home from Vietnam, the American people began to question the need for fighting a war on the other side of the earth. Eventually, a great antiwar movement rose up in the United States, arguing that this was an evil and unnecessary war because American national security was not deeply threatened: regardless of who controlled this far-off Asian nation, it would not decisively affect America's vitality and independence back home.

Even in the 1960s and 1970s, in other words—when Americans had abandoned isolationism and accepted a much more active role on the world stage—the American people were still unwilling to shed a great deal of blood in a war they perceived as entailing no direct threat to national security. How much more plausible, then—in the early 1940s—for the Japanese to expect that an ardently isolationist United States would balk at full-scale war in Asia, as long as Japan's expansionist actions fell short of directly attacking American security or vital interests. It was a big gamble, to be sure: no one can really know what would have happened if the Japanese had held to this original plan. But it arguably had a certain cogent logic to it.

Of course, the Japanese didn't stick to their plan. Instead, they adopted Admiral Isoroku Yamamoto's much more aggressive idea of striking a crippling blow against the U.S. Pacific Fleet at Pearl Harbor. Yamamoto thought he understood the Americans well, having lived in the United States and studied at Harvard from 1919 to 1921. He believed that destroying the Pacific Fleet would achieve two goals: at the immediate military level, it would shield the Japanese from American counterattacks throughout the first half of 1942. But still more important, at the psychological level, Yamamoto argued, experiencing such a devastating military debacle at the war's outset would break the Americans' fighting spirit, rendering them even less likely to oppose Japanese imperial expansion over the long haul.

One wonders what Yamamoto learned while at Harvard, for he certainly failed to grasp the effect that such a move would have on the American public. Without a doubt, the Pearl Harbor attack constituted one of the worst strategic blunders of the entire war. After December 7, the American people *did* regard Japan as posing a clear and present danger to their country—and worse still, they now vowed to avenge this despicable attack no matter what the cost.[10] In this sense, the Pearl Harbor operation presented a classic case of tactics versus strategy. This brilliant tactical victory completely contradicted the one long-term strategy that might have allowed the Japanese—perhaps—to get away with their aggression in Asia, and still keep a large part of the spoils.

The narratives we most commonly encounter of how the Pacific War began are tendentious and inadequate: they make it look as though the Japanese acts of conquest in the 1930s were a unique thing in world affairs, a sudden aberration from the conduct of international relations in Asia. The story we have told, by contrast, paints a more complicated picture.

The Japanese came close to being colonized in the mid-1800s. They reacted with understandable outrage at the unfair treatment they received at the hands of Europeans and Americans. Out of this nineteenth-century crucible, modern Japanese nationalism was born. The Japanese resolved to beat the Europeans and Americans at their own game: they would become imperialists along with the best of them. Eventually, they hoped, Japan would become the dominant imperial power in Asia, supplanting the hegemony of Europeans and Americans with a new hegemony of its own.

The tragedy of twentieth-century Japanese history is that this imperialist policy strengthened the hand of those factions in Japanese society who were enemies of democratic politics, and who were not afraid to use violence to realize their goals. The result was the collapse of Japanese democracy during the 1930s, and the rise of a vicious and militarist leadership, untrammeled by domestic opposition and bent on dominating all Asia. The result was atrocities like the Rape of Nanking, a blight on Japan's history that should never be forgotten—particularly since some right-wing Japanese today are actively trying to sweep it under the carpet. The result, finally, was a catastrophic war with the most powerful nation in the world, a war that ended with Japan prostrate, nuked, and under foreign occupation in 1945.

To cast the story in this way—situating its origins within the broader context of European imperialism and American penetration of Asia—is by no means to condone the savage Japanese policies of the 1930s and 1940s. The war against China after 1931 was both unjustifiable and bestially conducted; the attack on Pearl Harbor was both dastardly and strategically stupid. Nothing can ever justify these actions.

But telling the story in this way does help us to avoid the disingenuously self-serving picture that often emerges in the American and European framing of the Pacific War. Japan's actions in the lead-up to World War II were not, unfortunately, a historical aberration: they were rooted in a pattern of imperialist domination in Asia that went back to the late nineteenth century—a pattern in which Europeans and Americans had figured very prominently as aggressors. Japan's imperialist expansion was far from unique: it was merely the latest brutal round in a very long catalogue of brutal subjugation of the Asian peoples.

Admittedly, this is a dangerous thing to say. An apologist for Japan could presumably use this logic to make a cynical argument: "At Pearl Harbor, the Japanese were merely paying back the United States for the aggression of Commodore Perry ninety years before." We need to reject this preposterous argument just as firmly as we reject the self-righteous image of the Europeans and Americans as paragons of international virtue. The fact of European and American aggression against Asians in the 1800s does not justify in any way the Japanese aggression of the 1900s—but it does help us to understand how it came to pass. We need to be able to state both truths at the same time:

- The Japanese were engaged in a monstrous enterprise in the 1930s and 1940s, and the United States was absolutely right to oppose them; and
- Japanese imperialism did not come out of nowhere: it was rooted several decades earlier, in the searing experience of helplessness before European and American domination.

Was war between the United States and Japan avoidable?

In the end, it may not have made much difference if the United States had adopted a more conciliatory policy between 1939 and 1941. By that point, Japan was being led by men who would have interpreted any such act of conciliation as weakness, as a sign that they could further step up their imperialist aggression. Sooner or later, the United States would have had to draw the line—or else acquiesce in the emergence of a vast Asian military bloc, dominated from Tokyo by a brutal and expansionist leadership. It is not reasonable to expect the United States to have stood by indefinitely, allowing such a clearly threatening development to continue unopposed.

For war to be avoided, one would have to turn back the clock all the way to the late 1920s, and find a way, somehow, to alter the outcome in Japan's domestic politics that allowed the militarist hard-liners to gain the upper hand. If there had been a solid balance between hard-liners and more moderate leaders in Tokyo during the 1930s, and a democratic government whose policies reflected that balance, then it is unlikely that the world would have witnessed the kind of outrageous Japanese aggression that marked those years. Japan's foreign policy would have been more cautious, more subtle—more intelligent, ultimately, in achieving its long-term aims without isolating the nation in world affairs.

It is worth recalling, in this context, that between 1895 and 1910 Japan had acquired control over Taiwan, southern Sakhalin, and Korea, all while retaining the approval of world opinion. This kind of cautious, piecemeal approach might well have continued to yield modest imperial dividends during the 1930s and 1940s as well. But modest gains were not acceptable to the men who actually did gain power in Japan during the 1930s. They wanted it all, they wanted it now. And they brought ruin on themselves, their country, and much of Asia.

Chapter Three

CAUSES OF THE WAR IN EUROPE
The Paradoxical Legacy of Munich

> Hitler asked whether he was to understand that the British, French and
> Czechoslovak governments had in effect agreed to the transfer of the
> Sudeten territory from Czechoslovakia to Germany.
>
> The Prime Minister replied: "Yes."
>
> There was a slight pause, a silence in which Hitler appeared for a
> moment to be making up his mind. He then said decisively: "*Es tut mir
> fürchbar leid, aber das geht nicht mehr.*" ("I am terribly sorry, but that
> won't do anymore.")
>
> —Sir Nevile Henderson, September 1938[1]

After the First World War, historians began heatedly debating what
had caused this cataclysm of violence—and the debates still go on
today. In the 1920s some European historians claimed that World War I
had been caused by poor leadership and a rigid system of alliances; others
thought that arms manufacturers (in all nations) had diabolically prodded
the hapless peoples to slaughter one another; still others blamed the capitalist system itself, or the bitter rivalries spawned by colonial empires.
Then, in the 1960s, a book by the German historian Fritz Fischer rekindled
the debates anew: Fischer offered abundant documentary evidence to
reveal a systematic pattern of aggressive expansionist goals among the
German leadership both before and during World War I—a pattern that
made it look as though it was the Germans who truly held the smoking
gun of primary responsibility for the war.[2] But other writers soon weighed
in, arguing that Fischer's book did not absolve the other belligerent powers
from their share of responsibility for the bloodshed. The war, they maintained, did not spring from any one cause. It was the tragic result of multiple causal strands coming together—a highly complex convergence of

Benito Mussolini and Adolf Hitler in Munich (June 1940).

forces in which virtually all levels of historical process had played their part: popular attitudes, economic pressures, statecraft, political constraints, military exigencies, technological developments. The origins of World War I, in short, were inherently and profoundly complicated: no particular nation or individual, no sole factor, could be singled out to bear the blame.

World War II in Europe is completely different: it was, and no doubt always will be, Adolf Hitler's war.[3] Apart from a small and utterly marginal rabble of pro-Nazi apologists, only one serious scholar—the puckish British historian A. J. P. Taylor—has ever offered a sustained argument that this disastrous conflict was anything but Germany's fault. And even Taylor was stretching his point considerably. He did not deny that Germany was the aggressor, but only insisted that France and Britain also bore serious blame: they had capitulated to Hitler so consistently during the 1930s that the German tyrant was misled into believing he could get away with his conquest of Poland in 1939.[4]

This question of the appeasement of Hitler during the 1930s has arguably provided one of the most powerful and enduring "lessons" of World War II for the generations that followed. The lesson has been:

never give in to an opponent who is making peremptory demands at gunpoint; *always* move in swiftly and resolutely to nip aggression in the bud.
In this picture Britain's prime minister, Neville Chamberlain, and France's
premier, Edouard Daladier, invariably appear as craven, shortsighted
statesmen who caved in unnecessarily to Hitler's bullying tactics. This
chapter's argument is that the complex story of "appeasement" actually
demands a finer set of distinctions on our part; and that in the end, paradoxically, Chamberlain and Daladier bequeathed to the Allies—however
unwittingly—one very significant advantage in their conduct of the war.

Three main factors led Germany into the Second World War: the bitterly
aggrieved nationalism spawned by the loss of World War I and the harsh
peace terms that followed it; the Great Depression; and the leadership of
Adolf Hitler.

From a military point of view, Germany's achievements in the First
World War were nothing short of breathtaking. Fighting alongside a weak
ally, Austria-Hungary, German armies succeeded in holding down the
combined forces of Britain and France through four grueling years of
trench warfare; at the same time, German forces in the east systematically
smashed the czar's armies to pieces, bringing down the government and
forcing the Russians out of the war. Only the intervention in 1917 of the
United States, with its immense reserves of weapons and manpower,
finally tipped the scales decisively against Germany.

The victorious Allies imposed a notoriously punitive peace treaty on
Germany in 1919: the German monarchy was replaced by a republic; Germany lost significant lands in both the east and west; portions of German
territory along the Rhine were occupied by French and British soldiers; the
German army was cut down to 100,000 troops; Germany was compelled to
pay astronomical war reparations to France and Britain; and finally—
adding insult to injury—the German government was forced to declare
publicly that Germany had started this war, that the guilt for all the bloodshed lay solely on German shoulders. The majority of Germans seethed in
outrage at all this. They perceived the Treaty of Versailles as a grossly
unfair diktat—a Carthaginian peace forced on them at gunpoint. Adolf
Hitler deeply and sincerely shared this sentiment, and his openly avowed
obsession with overturning Versailles became one of his strongest selling
points with the German electorate.

Then came the Great Depression. After a terribly rocky period in the early 1920s, including hyperinflation and a humiliating occupation of the German Ruhr by French troops, the German economy finally began to pick up nicely in the second half of the decade. Hopes were rising, and extremist parties like the communists and Nazis could not muster more than a dozen deputies or so in the 500-member German parliament. The economic blizzard of 1929 brought this to a swift end. Within a year, major banks and industries had collapsed in bankruptcy; roughly half the German workforce was unemployed; bread lines snaked their way down city blocks. Many Germans blamed the harshness of their economic woes directly on the iniquities of Versailles, arguing that the reparations payments had fatally destabilized the German economy; they began harking ever more eagerly to the extremists of both left and right who inveighed against parliamentary democracy and liberal capitalism. Within two years, by 1932, the communists had grown to 100 deputies in the Reichstag; the Nazis had vaulted to 230 seats, becoming the second-largest party in German politics. Weimar democracy was lurching from one grave crisis to another, slowly tearing itself apart under the pressure of a dire economic hardship that its squabbling political leaders seemed powerless to end.

Hitler accordingly came to power in January 1933, not through a coup d'état, but through the regular and legal workings of a German democratic process that had finally reached the end of its rope. Many conservative politicians and influential industrialists outside the Nazi Party gave Hitler their backing at this crucial juncture, thinking they could easily control this upstart demagogue: they regarded him as a useful pawn who would help Germany get through the crisis and fend off a communist revolution. Later, they assumed, when things calmed down, they would quietly push aside this gesticulating fanatic, and put their own men back in the driver's seat.

But Hitler astounded them all. Within a year, by 1934, he had imposed an iron dictatorship on Germany, one of the most ruthless, all-encompassing tyrannies the world had ever seen. By 1936, Hitler's economic programs of massive rearmament and public works had ended the Depression: Germany was actually having to import laborers from other countries to man the bustling factories. The German people looked around themselves, and it seemed as though they were living in a different world from that of a mere three years before. The political freedoms and liberal rights of Weimar democracy had seemingly gone hand in hand with economic chaos and feckless leadership; the hard-edged system of dictatorship apparently offered prosperity, order, national self-confidence. To many Germans, this amounted to a perfectly acceptable trade-off: they flocked to the Nazi banner, raising their arms in enthusiastic salute.

Back in 1919 U.S. president Woodrow Wilson had insistently pushed on the French and British his idea for an international agency, a club of nations, that could help avert another disastrous war like the one they had just survived. The key to Wilson's vision lay in creating an international forum where two countries that were having a dispute could seek to work out their differences peacefully. The League of Nations—as he proposed to call it—would provide arbitration through an international tribunal. It would set up a system of international laws. And when some nation refused arbitration, and persisted in breaking the agreed-upon international norms, the League would offer a flexible but potent mechanism for collective security: economic sanctions for mild infractions; military force for serious violations.

Somewhat skeptically, the French and British went along: on January 10, 1920, the League duly set up its offices in Geneva, Switzerland. Unfortunately, the idea proved to be ahead of its time. To Wilson's great chagrin, his own country refused to join the organization: isolationist sentiment ran high in the United States after World War I, and the president simply could not persuade a sufficient number of his fellow Americans that this would be a valuable instrument for the long haul. Many nations did join the League—some seventy in all—but they refused to surrender any sovereignty or military forces to this international body. This left the League basically impotent: it could make all the resounding proclamations it wanted, but possessed no real clout to back up its decisions.

Italy had been a founding member of the League in 1920, and Germany was allowed to join in 1926; but by the 1930s both these nations had become what political scientists call "revisionist powers"—a rather polite way of saying that they were deeply unhappy with the international status quo, and were looking for ways to improve their geopolitical situation by any means available (through diplomacy if possible, through war and conquest if necessary). The Italians and Germans had much in common: they had both forged their national unity a mere six decades before, in 1870; they both felt they had missed out on the great imperialist spree of the late nineteenth century; they both harbored deep bitterness at the outcome of World War I (the Italians had hoped to gain territory at the 1919 peace conference, but came away disappointed). The story of the 1930s, from this perspective, is one of Hitler and Mussolini doggedly pursuing a "revision" of the map of Europe; it is a story of the League of Nations, weakly led by the French and the British, trying and failing again and again to restrain them.

Here was the argument one heard in Rome and Berlin during these years: "France and Britain already have their colonial empires. The United States and Soviet Union possess immense territories rich in natural resources. Those nations are the 'haves,' and we Italians and Germans are the 'have-nots.' But when we ask for a reasonable share of the world's lands, proportional to our importance as nations, the haves sternly tell us that we should not challenge the delicate balance of the status quo. They tell us we are being aggressive expansionists. But that's easy for *them* to say: They've already got their vast lands! They are seeking to hold us down in a permanently inferior position." Out of this mixture of aggrievement and expansionism came the sad litany of aggression that marked the 1930s.

Japan opened the decade with its invasion and annexation of Manchuria, which (as we saw in chapter 2) the League proved powerless to reverse. In October 1933 Hitler withdrew Germany from the League, citing the unfairness of his country's disarmament under the Treaty of Versailles. At first covertly, and then much more openly, Germany began ramping up its arms industries, flagrantly violating the Versailles strictures. Neither the League nor any national government did anything to stop this.

In October 1935 Mussolini's Italy abruptly invaded Ethiopia, the last surviving black African kingdom that had not been colonized by Europeans. While the Ethiopians rallied and fought back, their leader, Haile Selassie, appealed to the League of Nations. This time the League responded more vigorously than it had in the case of Manchuria: in November 1935 it imposed economic sanctions against Italy and demanded the withdrawal of all Italian forces. But in reality the sanctions were only a slap on the wrist: neither the French nor the British wanted to alienate the Italians too harshly, and they saw to it that the League embargo would only cover such nonessential items as Italian exports of olive oil and typewriters. Italy had very low petroleum reserves, and a full ban on petroleum imports would have stopped the Italian armed forces in their tracks; but the League proved unable to muster the will for so serious a measure. Mussolini's armies stepped up their attacks, ultimately using poison gas against the massed Ethiopian troops, and clinched their conquest in May 1936.

Almost simultaneously, in March 1936, Hitler took another foreign policy gamble, defiantly sending 22,000 troops into the demilitarized German Rhineland territory—a clear violation not only of the Versailles treaty but of a second pact signed with France and Britain in 1925. His timing was perfect: the British were caught up in a political crisis over the abdication of their king, Edward VIII; the French were in the midst of a hotly contested national election. Neither France nor Britain took any serious steps to oppose the provocative German action.

All these bold moves had met with considerable approval among the people of Italy and Germany: they were seen as forceful statesmanship, proudly and defiantly asserting national prerogatives in the face of the hegemonic French and British. Hitler's next gambit proved more popular still: in March 1938 he sent troops into neighboring Austria, formally annexing his native country to Germany. Pro-Nazi agitators had been fomenting unrest in Austria for more than a year in preparation for this maneuver: large segments of the population had been clamoring for annexation to the Third Reich. Again, France and Britain did nothing to oppose this development. Germany's total population now stood at 80 million.

Almost immediately after his successful *Anschluss* with Austria, Hitler turned his attention to neighboring Czechoslovakia. Here the situation was of course completely different, for the majority of Czechs were profoundly committed to the national independence they had only recently won at the Peace of Paris in 1919. Hitler's point of leverage lay in the western region of Czechoslovakia, a province known as the Sudetenland that nestled against the German border. Some portions of the Sudetenland were populated by a sizable minority of ethnic Germans—some 3 million German-speaking Czech citizens (out of a total Czechoslovakian population of 16 million) who thought of themselves as being of German ancestry and cultural background. Up until 1933, these German-speaking Czechs had been fairly satisfied with their situation, but as soon as Hitler came to power he sent Nazi agents into the Sudetenland to stir up discontent. This proved relatively easy to do, amid the ongoing economic hardship of the Depression.

Now, in September 1938, Hitler made his move: he demanded the immediate cession of the Sudetenland to Germany. All Germans everywhere, he insisted, must have the right to form part of the Fatherland. The Czech government promptly issued an adamant refusal to even consider Hitler's demands, and proclaimed martial law. Hitler responded by massing German troops along the Czech border. A major war scare flashed throughout Europe: in Britain and France, some cities began evacuating children to the countryside in case of air raids.

The British prime minister, Neville Chamberlain, decided to try to handle this crisis in a face-to-face encounter with Hitler. On September 15 he boarded an airplane for the first time in his life and flew to the führer's alpine retreat at Berchtesgaden. Here he told Hitler that Britain was prepared to accept the "detachment"—in a series of incremental phases—of the Sudeten areas from Czechoslovakia. Hitler, quite amazed at the British offer, replied that he would wait to see how the Czechs reacted.

Chamberlain then flew on to meet with President Eduard Beneš, telling the thunderstruck Czech leader that he had to accept the partial dismemberment of his country: Britain and France would not go to war over the defense of the Sudetenland. Beneš realized he had no choice but to bow to the inevitable. Germany was a hundred times stronger than tiny Czechoslovakia, and the Czechs had always relied on their diplomatic ties with France and Britain to secure their independence. Now they were being sold down the river.

Chamberlain got back on his plane and flew to Germany to tell Hitler the good news. Hitler was secretly furious, because he didn't want a compromise settlement—he wanted to smash the Czechs completely and subjugate the entire country. So he told Chamberlain, *"Das geht nicht mehr."* ("That won't do anymore.") He now added two new demands: the cession of the Sudetenland to Germany would have to take place in three days' time; in addition, several Polish and Hungarian territorial claims against Czechoslovakia would have to be settled at this time as well. Taken together, Hitler knew, these fresh demands would constitute an insurmountable deal-breaker.

Chamberlain flew back to London, angry and frustrated. He had put himself at considerable risk, politically, in order to broker this extremely favorable offer to Hitler; and he now despaired that any peaceful solution could be found. On September 27 he ordered the mobilization of the British fleet and began preparing his government for war.

Suddenly Mussolini stepped forward with a last-minute offer to negotiate a compromise. The Italian dictator proposed that a four-power conference should convene in Munich within two days, in hopes of salvaging the peace. Hitler, knowing the conciliatory mood in Paris and London, and astutely wagering that he had nothing to lose from such a meeting, issued invitations for an emergency summit conference in Munich. The führer's message arrived in London at 8:30 p.m. on September 28, in most dramatic fashion (described here by the historian William Manchester):

Chamberlain, addressing the House of Commons in its first session since the August adjournment, was describing the tangled diplomatic skein when a messenger arrived. Normally so important a dispatch would have been taken straight to the front bench. This one was delivered to Halifax, seated in the Peers' Gallery. He passed it down to Simon, who read it and pushed it in front of the prime minister. The House watched all this with mounting interest. In a voice that could be heard throughout the hall, Chamberlain asked: "Shall I tell them now?" and, when Simon smiled and nodded, announced: "Herr Hitler has just agreed to postpone his mobilisation for twenty-four hours and to meet me in conference with Signor Mussolini and [Monsieur] Daladier at Munich." . . . "For a second, the House was hushed in absolute silence. And then the whole House burst into a roar of cheering, since they knew that this might mean peace."[5]

The next morning, Chamberlain got back on his plane for the fifth time in two weeks and flew to Munich. (Soviet leader Joseph Stalin formally requested that a representative of his government be included at the conference, but he was quietly rebuffed.)

What basically happened at Munich on September 29 was that Hitler got everything he wanted, with a few face-saving trivialities thrown in to cover up the fact that France and Britain were abandoning Czechoslovakia. All parts of the Sudetenland would be transferred to German control at once. Plebiscites would be held in any additional area with 20 percent or more ethnic Germans. Hitler pledged in writing to respect the autonomy of the remainder of Czechoslovakia.

Chamberlain and French premier Edouard Daladier returned home from Munich, hailed as heroes for bringing "peace in our time." The newsreel footage of Chamberlain emerging from his plane in London, waving the document with Hitler's signature, has become part of the mythic iconography of the lead-up to World War II. Here, in the judgment of posterity, lay one of the last steps taken along the road to war: the dictator had been (temporarily) appeased.

Sure enough, six months later—on March 15, 1939—German troops moved out of the Sudeten areas, and took over the entire Czech portion of Czechoslovakia (roughly half the country). The remaining Slovak areas were allowed to establish a separate national government, closely aligned with Nazi Germany. This clear violation of the Munich accords finally awakened Chamberlain, and the rest of Europe, to the fact that Hitler could not be appeased, could not be satiated. Hitler had now incorporated, for the first time, territories that were not populated by German-speaking peoples. His expansionist designs finally became clear to everyone.

Poland was next. The Polish nation had disappeared completely from the map of Europe for more than a century: it had been swallowed up by its neighbors in the 1700s, and was duly resuscitated by the diplomats of 1919, out of deference to the Wilsonian principle of national self-determination. But the mapmakers in Paris had created a nation with very strange features: to the west of Poland lay the main body of Germany, and nestled along Poland's northeastern border lay the large German region of East Prussia. In between these two areas of sovereign German territory lay a strip of land, known as the Polish Corridor, which connected Poland to the Baltic coast, giving the Poles access to the sea. Unfortunately, the Polish Corridor ran through an area populated since ancient times by ethnic Germans; and smack in its middle lay the German-speaking city of Danzig.

In the spring of 1939 Hitler began demanding that these ethnic Germans under Polish rule be returned to the Fatherland: the Polish Corridor would need to be "revised." The Poles, not surprisingly, defiantly rejected any such idea; Hitler made increasingly threatening noises; and the drums of war began to beat again. This Polish crisis, however, proved different from the Czech crisis of 1938, because by this point the French and British governments had witnessed the dismemberment of Czechoslovakia in March 1939: their willingness to trust Hitler had evaporated. They issued a formal warning to Germany that any attack against Poland would mean general war.

Hitler thought they were bluffing. He reasoned that Poland was far more remote and less easily defensible than Czechoslovakia had been: if the French and the British had been serious about stopping him, they would have done so in the fall of 1938. He fully expected them to acquiesce in his latest conquest, just as they had done throughout the preceding decade.

The German leader, moreover, had one more powerful card to play. In August 1939 he astounded the rest of the world by announcing that his government had just signed a nonaggression treaty with Stalin. On the surface of it, the Nazi-Soviet Pact seemed to fly in the face of all logic. Hitler had long proclaimed that one of his main goals in politics was to defend against the evils of communism. Stalin had been saying for a decade that Nazism was Public Enemy Number One. How could these two archenemies cut a deal?

The answer lay in pure and cynical self-interest. Stalin feared the total isolation of the USSR in the war that he saw looming on the horizon; he believed that the capitalist nations were secretly encouraging Hitler to expand eastward at Russia's expense; he also was concerned about the possibility of a war with Japan, especially after large-scale clashes between Soviet and Japanese troops took place along the Chinese border during the summer of 1939.

Hitler, too, had the old German nightmare of a two-front war to worry about: he knew that his plans for Western Europe required war with France, and that his longer-term plans for Eastern Europe would eventually mean war with Russia. A pact with Stalin at the war's outset would allow Germany to deal with these goals one at a time, rather than having to face both military challenges simultaneously. Early in August 1939, therefore, Hitler sent his foreign minister, Joachim von Ribbentrop, to see if he could work out a deal with Stalin.

The result came on August 23: the Nazi-Soviet Pact. Ostensibly a mere nonaggression treaty, the secret clauses of the agreement stipulated how Central Europe would be divided between the two tyrants in the coming war. Hitler would get western Poland and all of Lithuania. Stalin would get eastern Poland, Finland, Estonia, Latvia, and parts of Romania.

All that now remained was the fabrication of a pretext for military action. On the night of August 31, Hitler ordered a secret unit of SS troops, commanded by Sturmbannführer Alfred Naujocks, to stage a mock Polish attack against a German radio station at Gleiwitz on the German-Polish border. Naujocks and his SS men took a dozen prisoners from a Nazi concentration camp, dressed them in German and Polish army uniforms, and shot them, leaving their bodies strewn about as if a fierce gunfight between German and Polish forces had occurred. The next morning German newspapers stridently proclaimed that an unprovoked Polish incursion into German territory at Gleiwitz had resulted in the deaths of several German soldiers.

At dawn on September 1, 1939, Hitler unleashed his blitzkrieg: sixty-three divisions marched across the Polish border, six of them deadly panzer units, fully motorized and equipped with the stunningly effective combination of tanks and Stuka dive-bombers. From the other side the Polish military charged to meet them: one sees them in archival photos, advancing on horseback, brandishing long lances like knights from another era.

World War II had begun.

The appeasement of the 1930s was clearly a disastrous policy. It not only failed to avert the war its proponents dreaded, but may actually have contributed to the war's outbreak, by emboldening the expansionists in Germany and Italy and repeatedly rewarding their tactics of threat and deceit. Why, one might ask, did the French and the British not do more to oppose the string of bullying moves by Hitler and Mussolini? They certainly possessed the military resources to do so. Germany was still in the process of rearmament throughout much of the 1930s, and as late as 1938 the French and British armies outnumbered and outgunned those of Germany and Italy. Why did they not stop the aggressors in their tracks?

We face a double challenge in addressing this question. On the one hand, we need to avoid a facile approach that heaps scorn on the French and British policymakers of the 1930s from the all too comfortable perspective of hindsight. It is tempting to dismiss Chamberlain, Daladier, and their colleagues as timorous statesmen, blinded by wishful thinking, foolish enough to believe that they could buy peace at any price. Such a judgment comes easily, given the tragic outcome that we know all too well, but it fails to capture the complex reality of the 1930s. On the other hand, we must explain how the leaders of the democracies actually reached the profoundly flawed decisions they did: what their motivations and reasoning were, how they came to apply the wrong policy to the wrong man. What factors led them to misread Adolf Hitler so egregiously?

According to the historian Robert O. Paxton, three tacit assumptions undergirded Chamberlain's foreign policy, and more broadly the enterprise of appeasement:[6]

1. Another all-out war in Europe would result in catastrophe for everyone involved. Such a war would not only devastate the continent and kill millions, but would also severely weaken Europe as a center of world power.

2. Nazism was a temporary extremist aberration caused by the lingering iniquities of Versailles. Remove those iniquities—addressing them point by point in good faith—and the Germans would quiet down.

3. A new war would result in the triumph of communism in Europe. Given the widespread socialist revolutions or revolts brought about by World War I—in the USSR, Hungary, Italy, Germany—one could expect even worse to come after another war.

Were these assumptions misguided or unrealistic? Not at all. The first assumption turned out to be quite accurate. The war did devastate the con-

tinent, and it did result in the long-term eclipse of Europe as a center of
world power—an eclipse from which the region was only just beginning
to emerge seven decades later.

The second assumption turned out to be partially right and partially
wrong. Hitler and his ilk had indeed come to power partly as a result of
German resentment over the harsh terms imposed at Versailles. Chamberlain failed to realize, however, that once the Nazis were in control, their
Social Darwinist ideology would impel them to embark on a program of
aggression that went far beyond a mere rectification of Versailles. He was
dealing with a regime whose aims entailed not merely a readjustment of
the post-1919 status quo, but a veritable revolution in world politics, culminating in the violent creation of a global racial empire.

The third assumption also turned out to be partially accurate: World
War II did result in the Bolshevization of half of Europe, "from Stettin in
the Baltic to Trieste on the Adriatic," to use Churchill's phrase. Communist dictatorship was one of the war's great beneficiaries.

Above all, Chamberlain's efforts to avoid war stemmed from a keen
awareness of the passionate pacifism that animated the majority of people
in Britain and France. The nightmare of World War I remained fresh in
their memories: an entire generation of young men had been decimated,
and they rightly feared that a new war would result in still worse suffering. Pacifism is sometimes portrayed as a naïve belief in the potential
goodness of human nature, as a blindly idealistic hope that reason and justice can prevail. For the most part, however, the pacifism of the 1930s did
not take this form: its roots lay in pessimism, not optimism. It resulted
from the direct experience of shattered lives, on a vast societal scale, and in
this sense sprang from a profoundly realistic source: what terrified these
people was the prospect of once again unleashing the mindless slaughter of
modern warfare. Between 1914 and 1918 this generation had been horri-
bly, disfiguringly burned: they now understandably shied away from fire.

Hitler saw this and ruthlessly capitalized on it. The German people, too,
had suffered in the First World War—but he knew that their fear of war
could be outweighed by the sense of rank injustice that still seethed among
them. One measure of this man's utter cynicism lies in the way he played
on the pacifist sentiments of the other peoples of Europe, exploiting them
for his own purposes.

And it worked. If one reads the editorials in British and French newspapers from these years, one finds again and again the evidence of thoughtful people trying earnestly to deal with the looming threat of war.[7] It
makes for poignant reading. Much of their thinking was not at all utopian

or far-fetched, but revealed rather a clearheaded effort to put themselves in the shoes of the Germans and to empathize with their grievances. Was it not possible, they asked, to despise Nazism and all that it stood for, while nonetheless acknowledging that some of the German claims were legitimate? Germany wanted to rearm: wasn't this only fair, given that all other nations refused to disarm? The German government wished to place troops within a part of sovereign German territory, the Rhineland: how would the British feel if they were forbidden to place troops in Herefordshire or Kent? Germany hoped to unite with Austria: wasn't this just the sort of national consolidation that Wilson's Fourteen Points had advocated in 1917?

Unfortunately, as we know from hindsight, all this was wrong. It was intelligent, noble, and proactive diplomacy—applied to a man who scornfully regarded it as weakness, who saw nothing in it but an opportunity for Germany's unilateral gain. Should the statesmen of the 1930s have recognized this fact at the time? Certainly they can be faulted for having clung so long to their hopes that Hitler could be satiated, when the evidence was steadily accumulating in the opposite direction. If Winston Churchill could sense where the Nazis were aiming, then surely other statesmen in Britain and France could have made the connections as well.

But in another sense this judgment is unfair. It is almost always possible to look back in history and find someone who appears to have predicted a war, a natural disaster, an economic downturn, before it actually happened. Churchill was the Cassandra for Britain in the 1930s; Charles de Gaulle played that role in France. Is it reasonable, though, to expect the majority of European citizens and statesmen to have accurately read Adolf Hitler before he broke his Munich promise in March 1939?

The key to addressing this question lies in acknowledging the difference between the perspective of hindsight and the perspective of the 1930s. Today, looking back, we know all too well who Hitler was: a racist maniac, totally without moral scruples, nihilistically bent on world conquest. We know where the story begins and ends—with the ravings of *Mein Kampf* in 1923, and with Auschwitz and a continent in ruins in 1945. But the Europeans of the 1930s did not have this story line inscribed in their minds, like a road map with which to read the events of the day as they unfolded. They had to make sense of contemporary developments one headline at a time, amid the clamor and confusion of misleading or inadequate information, amid the welter of hopes and fears with which humans inevitably tinge their perceptions of breaking news.

It is therefore unreasonable to judge too harshly the European citizenry and leaders of the 1930s for having failed to discern in *Mein Kampf* a clear signal of Hitler's long-term intentions: there was no way they could have known, at the time, how many of the elements in that turgid screed would eventually become a reality. Nor can we really fault those Europeans for their soft responses to the major foreign policy initiatives undertaken by Germany between 1933 and 1937—the withdrawal from the League of Nations, rearmament, the remilitarization of the Rhineland, and the *Anschluss* with Austria. All these moves could be plausibly construed as legitimate expressions of a traditional nationalist foreign policy on the part of the German government.

It is at Munich, however, that we must draw the line. Here, the British and French leaders went well beyond their conciliatory policy of offering redress for reasonable German grievances. At Munich, Hitler's demands were no longer reasonable: they were deliberately crafted to provoke a crisis. The cession of the Sudetenland to Germany, under the draconian conditions accepted at Munich, could not be justified by even the most cynical casuistry: it seriously violated Czech sovereignty, and fatally compromised Czechoslovakia's western defense network along its border with Germany. In agreeing to Hitler's peremptory demands, Britain and France were openly reneging on a commitment they had made to the Czechs as early as 1919—a security guarantee they had repeatedly reaffirmed through the diplomacy of the intervening years. By going to their knees at Munich, Britain and France were sending the worst of all possible signals to Hitler and Mussolini: in the name of peace, they would be willing to yield to the most blatantly unjustifiable demands—even if this required betraying their long-standing allies. Faced with such an Anglo-French capitulation at Munich—a move that was in equal measure immoral, cowardly, and strategically counterproductive—it is not surprising that Hitler should have concluded he would have an even easier time with Poland. At Munich in 1938, the policy of appeasement underwent a qualitative change: from an intelligent and morally defensible policy of addressing reasonable German grievances, to a dishonorable and self-defeating policy of caving in to the grossly unfair demands of a bully.

"It is misleading," writes the historian Anthony Adamthwaite, "to describe international affairs after 1918 as one long slide to inevitable catastrophe. Different policies might have averted disaster at several turning points."[8] What were these turning points?

It is difficult to envision any realistic scenario for avoiding World War II at any point after Hitler's accession to power in 1933. One might argue, for example, that France and Britain could have invaded the Rhineland with massive force in March 1936, resolutely kicking out the relatively small contingent of troops that the German dictator was illegally placing there. But even if this stark showdown had occurred in 1936, would it ultimately have stopped Hitler? Some historians have argued that the shock of such a foreign policy defeat might have caused an insurrection against the Nazi regime among the German people. But it seems far more likely that such a situation—yet another invasion by the detested French and British— would only have exacerbated the nationalist ire of the German population, further consolidating their support for Hitler's expansionist agenda. He would have grimly proceeded with rearmament, and would ultimately have launched his war of conquest just the same.

One faces the same element of unreality in discussions of diplomatic alternatives. What if the Russians, for example, had been more effectively integrated into a common European security system with the French and the British? The problem with this scenario, as with so many others, lies in the way it presupposes the very conditions that were lacking in Europe in the 1930s: the French and British governments feared Bolshevism and distrusted the Soviet leadership (with good reason). A strong capitalist-communist alliance to surround Hitler proved elusive in peacetime: it took the desperate conditions of wartime to cement that bond (a bond that promptly dissolved at war's end). Hitler's alliance with Stalin in 1939 was profoundly different: far from being a defensive pact, it amounted to a coldly calculated arrangement for dividing the spoils in the coming war.

The more plausible chances for averting World War II all lie in the pre-1933 period—and even here we have to engage in some large counterfactual what-ifs. If the United States had joined the League of Nations, and made good on Wilson's promise of a guarantee for the German-French border, this might have led the French to adopt a less truculent policy toward Germany in the early 1920s, thereby cooling the fires of German revanchism somewhat. If the French and the British had cooperated more actively with each other, instead of jockeying distrustfully for position, then their strong alliance might have given greater pause to German expansionists. If all nations had avoided economic policies of "every man for himself" after 1929, this might have mitigated the Depression crisis in Germany, thereby undermining the appeal of extremists like Hitler and the communists. If the League of Nations had been endowed with credible military forces of its own, then this body might have proved far more effective in nipping aggression in the bud.

In all these alternative cases, what we are really presupposing is wiser leadership: the United States forsaking isolationism and engaging constructively in world affairs; Great Britain partnering with France in assuming a leading role on the Continent; France avoiding provocative moves like the Ruhr occupation of 1923; Russia resisting the temptation to spread communism everywhere, and focusing instead on forging diplomatic ties with the capitalist West; France and Britain setting aside their distrust of Stalin, in the name of establishing a resolute anti-fascist front; Germany seeking redress for Versailles through legal and peaceful means.

Such counterfactual reasoning is always a rather dicey matter: one is reminded of the old dictum "If we had ham, we could have ham and eggs—if we had eggs." Nevertheless, what we have assumed in these alternative scenarios is far from impossible: it merely postulates that both the citizens and the statesmen of the great powers in the interwar years might have rejected the politics of intransigent nationalism, and opted instead for collective security, moderation, and compromise. The problem, of course, lies in getting a sufficient number of players in the game of international politics to accept these more constructive rules at the same time. The temptation, unfortunately, is always to go for the short-term gain that beckons from a narrowly self-interested national policy.

The appeasement of the 1930s, for all its tragic nature, did bring with it one highly significant advantage. Once war began, everyone knew whose fault it was. The image of Neville Chamberlain bending over backward to satisfy Hitler at Munich, the steady string of concessions made to Germany and Italy in the 1930s, the blatant violation of the Munich accords by Hitler in March 1939—all this meant that even the most scrupulously evenhanded person knew instantly in September 1939 who the real aggressor was. There was no ambiguity here, no wiggle room for German apologists.

The historian Richard Overy considers this "moral edge" a crucial factor in determining the war's eventual outcome, because it sustained the fighting spirit of the Allies through the dark years of 1939–1942, and contributed mightily to the crumbling of Axis morale after the war started to turn against fascism in 1942:

> The belief that their cause was on the side of progress in world history gave
> a genuine moral certainty to the Allies, which the Axis populations largely
> lacked. Popular commitment to war in the aggressor states was half-hearted
> and morally ambiguous. In the Allied communities, on the other hand, there

was a powerful crusading rejection of the forces of fascist darkness. This helped to mask the deep doctrinal and political differences between the three major Allies, and encouraged the greatest of efforts, particularly from the Soviet people, in destroying their enemies. The moral forces at work on the Allied side kept people fighting in a common cause; but as the war went on Axis populations suffered a growing demoralisation, a collapse of consensus, and increasingly brutal regimentation of the home front.[9]

Unlike the First World War, this war could appear to those who were fighting it on the Allied side as truly a struggle against an unmitigated evil. Rarely in history has a war seemed so just to so many; and it would be a serious error to underestimate the importance of this psychological factor in contributing to the ultimate Allied victory. Part of the reason why World War II ultimately became the "Good War" is precisely because Hitler's neighbors had gone to such abjectly extreme lengths in the late 1930s to appease him—and he had revealed himself to be insatiable. The paradoxical legacy of Munich is that it rendered the defensive character of the war that followed so starkly clear.

PART TWO

★

MAKING WAR

Chapter Four

BYSTANDERS

How Much Is Not Enough?

What hurts the victim most is not the cruelty of the oppressor but the silence of the bystander.

—Elie Wiesel[1]

Two nations stand out, among the Axis-controlled territories of wartime Europe, as the safest places to live if you happened to be a Jew: Denmark and Italy. Perhaps Denmark is not so surprising: Danish Jews had been well assimilated before the war, and the Danish people reacted with both courage and (perhaps still more important) a high degree of unanimity in rushing to the defense of their Jewish fellow citizens. When the Germans commenced in October 1943 to round up Denmark's 7,500 Jews for deportation, the Danish police refused to cooperate. A large number of Danes swiftly organized a massive rescue operation, moving the Jews first into hiding, then ferrying them on fishing boats across the Baltic Sea to neutral Sweden. When some five hundred Danish Jews were captured by the Germans and deported to the Nazi concentration camp at Theresienstadt, the Danish government strongly and persistently pressured the Germans not to allow their transfer to the death camps: remarkably, the Germans complied. Partly because the Jewish population of Denmark was relatively small, partly because Germany relied on Danish agricultural imports, and partly because Nazi ideologues regarded the Danes as fellow Aryans, the Hitler regime accorded special treatment to the Danish Jews at Theresienstadt, allowing most of them to survive the war. By 1945, the Holocaust had claimed the lives of some one hundred Danish Jews—about 1.3 percent of the prewar population, by far the lowest of any Axis-occupied nation.[2]

Cardinal Eugenio Pacelli, the future Pope Pius XII, signs the Vatican's Concordat with Hitler's government (July 20, 1933).

Fascist Italy is more unexpected. This was, after all, Germany's closest ally—a nation whose government had promulgated severe anti-Jewish laws in 1938, slavishly modeled after the German Nuremberg Laws of 1936. Nevertheless, the fact remains: approximately 85 percent of Italy's fifty thousand Jews survived the Holocaust.[3] Why?

One reason was that the Italian fascist regime was itself halfhearted in its anti-Semitism. Although some rabid Jew-baiters did hold high office in the party, the duce himself had never founded his quest for consensus on racial hatred, as Hitler had: his rhetoric revolved instead around the promise of restoring the glories of ancient Rome. Mussolini knew full well that the majority of Italians regarded German racial policies with either indifference or outright revulsion. Italian Jews made up about one-tenth of 1 percent of the nation's population: their families had lived in Italy for centuries, and most Italians simply saw them as being no different from themselves.

One should not conclude from this that the situation for Italian Jews after 1938 was ever benign or safe. Jews in Italy faced a broad range of humiliations, injustices, and violence against both their property and their person, and the fascist regime established detention camps in which it forcibly interned several thousand Jews between 1940 and 1943. But these were not death camps, and the government steadfastly resisted pressure from German officials to hand over the camp inmates for deportation.

Overall, the relative level of the anti-Semitic persecution in Italy remained far lower and less pervasive than in other areas of Axis Europe. Though Jews were purged from positions in government, education, and public life, the fascist police and administration showed extreme reluctance (and inefficiency) in pursuing the full enforcement of the 1938 anti-Jewish laws. For example, when Mussolini issued the order in 1939 for all Jews to be dismissed from the Italian army, one general immediately wrote him back, saying that he refused to obey this order because it violated his honor as an officer. Though the duce was not usually one to take lightly such a blatant act of insubordination, in this case no disciplinary action against the dissenting officer ever materialized: the general simply ignored the duce's order, and the duce simply ignored the general's disobedience.

Many Italians adopted a similar approach: they pretended the anti-Semitic laws didn't exist. Some went one step further, actively aiding and sheltering their Jewish neighbors when they became objects of official persecution. Such acts of protection usually entailed fairly low risks as long as Italy remained a sovereign nation, with the relatively lax Italian police in charge of enforcing anti-Jewish laws. But all this changed dramatically after July 1943, when the Allies invaded southern Italy, the duce's government fell, and the Germans imposed direct rule over the central and northern portions of the peninsula. At this point the deportations began in earnest, under the supervision of the Gestapo, and any Italians who gave aid to Jews were truly risking their necks.

Nevertheless, they did it anyway, in surprisingly large numbers. Some hid Jews in the countryside or in cellars, but the most effective route was to smuggle them southward, through the battle zones in southern Italy, into the safety of Allied-controlled territory. One such brave rescuer, for example, was Giovanni Palatucci, the chief of police in the northern city of Fiume, who saved hundreds of Jews by providing them with false identity papers and organizing safe passage for them to southern Italy or to Switzerland. Palatucci was arrested by the Gestapo in 1944 and sent to Dachau, where he died at the age of thirty-six—just weeks before the camp was liberated in April 1945.[4]

In April 1998, the Vatican published a fourteen-page report on the role played by the Catholic Church vis-à-vis the European Jews during World

War II. It was written by an American cardinal, Edward Cassidy, and had the full authority of the pope behind it. Here is an excerpt from it:

> At first the leaders of the Third Reich sought to expel the Jews. Unfortunately, the governments of some Western countries of Christian tradition, including some in North and South America, were more than hesitant to open their borders to the persecuted Jews. Although they could not foresee how far the Nazi hierarchs would go in their criminal intentions, the leaders of those nations were aware of the hardships and dangers to which Jews living in the territories of the Third Reich were exposed. The closing of borders to Jewish emigration in those circumstances, whether due to any anti-Jewish hostility or suspicion, political cowardice or shortsightedness, or national selfishness, lays a heavy burden of conscience on the authorities in question.
>
> In the lands where the Nazis undertook mass deportations, the brutality which surrounded these forced movements of helpless people should have led to suspect the worst. Did Christians give every possible assistance to those being persecuted, and in particular to the persecuted Jews?
>
> Many did, but others did not. Those who did help to save Jewish lives as much as was in their power, even to the point of placing their own lives in danger, must not be forgotten. During and after the war, Jewish communities and Jewish leaders expressed their thanks for all that had been done for them, including what Pope Pius XII did personally or through his representatives to save hundreds of thousands of Jewish lives. Many Catholic bishops, priests, religious and laity have been honored for this reason by the State of Israel.
>
> Nevertheless, as Pope John Paul II has recognized, alongside such courageous men and women, the spiritual resistance and concrete action of other Christians was not that which might have been expected from Christ's followers. We cannot know how many Christians in countries occupied or ruled by the Nazi powers or their allies were horrified at the disappearance of their Jewish neighbors and yet were not strong enough to raise their voices in protest. For Christians, this heavy burden of conscience of their brothers and sisters during the Second World War must be a call to penitence.
>
> We deeply regret the errors and failures of those sons and daughters of the Church.[5]

This is, by any standard, a rather extraordinary document: the world's largest Christian church basically admitting that it didn't do nearly enough. What role did the Catholics of Germany play, both before and after the Nazi seizure of power? Hitler had become chancellor of Germany in 1933 partly through the support of the Catholic political party in Germany, which was one of the largest in the Reichstag. In March 1933 the Catholic party joined the Nazis and right-wing Nationalists in passing the Enabling Act, which handed Hitler virtually dictatorial powers. When Hermann Göring met with Pope Pius XI in Rome on April 10, 1933, the pontiff "remarked how pleased he was that the German government now had at its head a man uncompromisingly opposed to communism and Russian nihilism in all its forms."[6] The Nazis and the Vatican signed an official Concordat in July 1933, laying out the terms for their peaceful coexistence under the Third Reich: this diplomatic coup gave Hitler crucial political support at a time when he was still consolidating his grip on power.

Later on, after his position had become unchallengeable and he no longer needed the Catholics, Hitler went back on his word. He abolished the Catholic youth organization, disbanded the Catholic political party, and severely curtailed the public activities of the Catholic Church. The Vatican protested, but did nothing else.

Throughout the rest of the 1930s, the Vatican never spoke out explicitly against the persecution of Jews in Germany. A 1937 papal encyclical, *Mit Brennender Sorge,* condemned the Nazis for their neopaganism and "idolatric doctrine of the race," but made no specific mention of the anti-Jewish violence taking place in Germany.[7] Although individual Catholic clergy outside Germany did condemn the anti-Semitic policies of the Nazi regime, the Vatican remained conspicuously silent in this regard. Meanwhile, inside Germany, some Catholic churches were handing over their parish records so that the Gestapo could identify people of Jewish origin.

As for Germany's Protestant churches, the story is not much different.[8] Hitler wanted to subordinate them to the authority of the Nazi Party, and tried to impose a Nazi political appointee, or imperial bishop, as supreme leader of the church hierarchy. This maneuver was vehemently resisted by the Protestant rank and file, and ended up becoming one of the few cases in the history of the Third Reich in which Hitler was forced to back down. The Protestants of Germany—nearly two-thirds of the population—made it clear that they would never accept a Nazi as their ultimate spiritual authority.

But what did they do about the persecution of the Jews? A small minority of clergy did speak out very bravely, condemning the treatment of Jews. These men, the most famous of whom were Dietrich Bonhoeffer and Martin Niemoller, were arrested by the Gestapo and put in concentration camps. The rest of the church leadership remained silent; the vast majority of German Protestants did not lift a finger against the mounting anti-Jewish violence.

Once the war began, the Vatican, under the newly elected Pope Pius XII, adopted a position of official neutrality—enjoining both sides in the conflict to seek a way toward peace. Much strident controversy has surrounded the wartime role of Pius XII vis-à-vis Europe's Jews: the literature tends to divide starkly down the middle, with ardent papal supporters claiming that the pontiff was a saintly paragon of philosemitic activism, and fervent papal detractors claiming he was an anti-Semite, a coward, even a tacit collaborator in genocide.[9] Between those striving to "get" Pius XII, and those struggling to beatify him, little middle ground exists.

Nevertheless, a tentative assessment of the evidence leads to the following conclusions. At a personal level, Pius XII appears to have been appalled by what was happening to European Jews: in private conversations, he strongly condemned the Nazis' racial policies. Between 1939 and 1945 he used his own family's funds to help a small number of Jews to be hidden from the Nazis; he allowed a few to stay in his summer residence at Castelgandolfo; he actively supported the rescue of sizable groups of Jews throughout Europe on several occasions. For all these deeds, he has been formally recognized since 1945 by some Jewish organizations.

However, at a public level, as leader of the Catholic Church, Pius XII followed a much more cautious path. He evidently made the calculation that speaking out against the Holocaust would be counterproductive, and might result in many Catholics being deported and killed along with the Jews. So the pope kept quiet, and avoided any act that could be interpreted by the Germans as openly confrontational. He confined his public statements to vague sentiments of empathy for the victims of injustice throughout the world, and appealed to the belligerent nations to conduct the war in a more humane fashion. That was all. The result is that, at an institutional level, the Catholic Church gives the historical observer a marked impression of silence, detachment, and inaction as it confronted one of the greatest crimes that humankind has ever witnessed.

Some Catholics did go out of their way to save Jews—but they did so on their own, and not because their church had openly enjoined them to do so. Other Catholics, faced with the silence of the Vatican, evidently interpreted this as a license to cooperate with the Nazis. French Catholics, for example, faced no condemnation from their church as their government, led by the devoutly Catholic figures of the Vichy regime, handed over 75,000 Jews to the Gestapo. In Slovakia, a Catholic priest, Monsignor Josef Tiso, became head of state during the war: his government cooperated closely with the Germans, actively participating in the Nazi roundups and deportations of tens of thousands of Jews. The Vatican did nothing to put a stop to this.

Today, defenders of Pope Pius XII argue that he was acting with reasonable prudence and caution when he avoided an open confrontation with Hitler, choosing instead to oppose the Nazis more furtively, operating behind the scenes. But this argument seems unconvincing. What if the pope had stood up one day in St. Peter's and issued a formal proclamation to all Catholics along these lines: "The policy of the Nazi regime toward the Jews is utterly wrong. We cannot tolerate it; we will do our utmost to oppose it. All good Catholics are hereby enjoined to resist this Evil that is being done, in any way they can. Any Catholic who participates in this Evil, even indirectly, will be excommunicated."

This would have been the risky path—the one taken by the Danish citizenry, and by individuals like the devout Catholic Giovanni Palatucci. It would have amounted to a "declaration of war" by the Vatican against the Nazi regime and its policies. What would have resulted? We can be relatively sure that such a policy would have led to death and suffering for many European Catholics. But how would the Nazi regime have fared, in an open and frontal confrontation with the world's largest Christian church? Germany's population was about 30 percent Catholic: would they all have just stood by and let themselves be slaughtered by the Nazis? On the contrary: it is probable that Germany's Catholics would have rallied very strongly to the moral leadership of their church, if they had seen the Vatican pitted in a profound and dangerous conflict with the dictatorial regime of their nation.

German Catholics would have been faced with a choice: am I a Christian first, or a supporter of Nazism first? Some might have opted for the latter, but it seems likely that, if push came to shove, a significant number of German Catholics would have risen up with great passion to save their church and their religious community. Hitler would have ignored this at his great peril. Under these conditions, the Nazis might well have been the ones who would have had to back down, or risk an insurrection by a huge segment of the German population.

This logic applies even more strongly to the Catholics of the rest of Europe—in Hungary, Slovakia, Italy, Austria—all those countries with large Catholic populations, whose regimes were actively supporting Hitler.

What would a dramatic confrontation between pope and führer have brought about in those countries? How would Hitler, for all his fury, have been able to face this down?

But push never came to shove, because the Nazis pushed, but the Vatican did not shove back. The defenders of Pius XII argue today that he was merely trying to avoid having even more people killed than were already being killed. He was doing the best he could, under the awful circumstances. He was adopting a responsible policy of caution and prudence.

This argument is unpersuasive. Today, we remember the citizenry of Denmark and the isolated rescuers like Giovanni Palatucci, and their story warms our hearts still. But the "prudence" of most European Christians—their relative inaction and timidity in this time of trial—fills us with anguish and a sense of tarnish, of moral weakness.

And what about the Americans, on the other side of the Atlantic? Lest one might think that the Yanks were morally separate from this story about bystanders, it is worthwhile to narrate one episode from the year 1939.

The persecution of Jews in Germany had reached widespread and deadly proportions by that year. The whole world knew this. Those Jews who could still escape Nazi Germany counted themselves very lucky indeed. One such group was the passengers of the German cruise ship *St. Louis*—936 Jewish men, women, and children. They managed to embark from Hamburg on May 13, headed for Cuba. From Cuba, most of them hoped to apply for visas for immigration to the United States.[10]

But while they were crossing the Atlantic, the Cuban government abruptly changed its immigration policy, demanding that Jewish refugees post a $500 bond per head. Without this bond—a large sum of money in 1939—they would not be allowed to disembark in Havana. Most of the ship's passengers simply did not have such a sum.

They arrived in Havana on May 27, but were forbidden to land. They pleaded with the Cuban government; Jewish organizations pleaded on their behalf. To no avail. Finally, in desperation, the *St. Louis* sailed from Havana, headed for Miami. Frantic negotiations ensued with the U.S. government to let these people in. The State Department's response was that if it made an exception for the *St. Louis,* the nation would soon face similar demands from thousands of other desperate Jews.

The United States had imposed severe restrictions on immigration in 1924. The same legislation that completely blocked Japanese from settling in the United States also imposed firm quotas on refugees coming from

Europe (especially Southern and Eastern Europe). Great Britain had similarly limited the number of Jews it allowed to emigrate from Europe to Palestine, which was under British control in the 1930s. Earlier in 1939, two U.S. congressmen had submitted a bill in Congress to allow a onetime special permission for twenty thousand Jewish children to enter the United States from Europe. The bill languished in the committee process, and was ultimately abandoned for lack of support. Nor was this congressional reluctance particularly surprising: an opinion poll conducted in 1939 by *Fortune* magazine found that "83 percent of Americans opposed relaxing restrictions on immigration."[11]

As the *St. Louis* waited four miles offshore, Washington remained adamant. American Jewish organizations repeatedly begged U.S. officials at all levels to make an exception, reminding them of the fate that awaited these people if they were compelled to return to Europe. By way of reply, the Coast Guard was ordered to shadow the ship as it sailed off the Florida coast, making sure none of the desperate passengers tried to swim ashore.

The German government, which had been monitoring these developments with great interest, quickly saw the propaganda value of the episode. America's treatment of the *St. Louis*, its officials proclaimed, clearly showed that the Jews were distrusted and rejected by everyone, and that the Germans were not alone in despising them.

Faced with the Americans' refusal to budge, the governments of Britain, France, Belgium, and Holland finally relented, and agreed to accept the 936 Jews of the *St. Louis*. The ship sailed back to Europe and disembarked its passengers in those four countries. Three of these nations, of course, were overrun by the Nazis the following spring. By the end of 1940, more than six hundred of the passengers from the *St. Louis* had wound up again in German hands. Though they had gotten close enough to U.S. shores to see the lights of Miami at night, most of them did not survive the war.[12]

Chapter Five

BOMBING CIVILIAN POPULATIONS

A Case of Moral Slippage

For everybody knows or else should know
That if nothing drastic is done
Aeroplane and Zeppelin will come out,
Pitch like King Billy bomb-balls in
Until the town lie beaten flat.
—W. B. Yeats, "Lapis Lazuli" (1938)[1]

The Second World War so drastically expanded the scope of war's violence that it scarcely resembled what had always been meant by the word "war" in the centuries and millennia that had gone before.[2] Even apart from the advent of the atomic bomb, this conflict utterly transformed the very nature of war, and in this sense, it amounted to a genuine revolution in the history of human society.

The nerve gas and mustard gas of the First World War had already opened a new dimension in weaponry: suddenly you didn't have to shoot people anymore, individually aiming a rifle or a cannon at them. Now you could simply let loose an immense floating cloud of death, and everyone in its path would be wiped out. Like a child spraying poison on an anthill, you could feel your power as you watched your enemies writhe in their terminal spasms. But there was still something very clumsy about poison gas weapons. They depended on prevailing wind direction, and wind was a notoriously fickle phenomenon: people on your own side might wind up floundering about in the deadly cloud. By a kind of tacit agreement, therefore, all parties began avoiding these kinds of weapons; after the war, the great powers signed a treaty that banned their use, the Geneva Gas Protocol of 1925.

London children outside the wreckage of their home (September 1940).

During these same years, however, a new dimension in mass destruction also came into play: the aerial bombing of civilian populations in cities.[3] The first to do this had been the Italians, even before the First World War, in the fall of 1911. They used biplanes to drop bombs on the city of Tripoli, Tunisia, as part of an attempt to conquer and annex this strip of uncolonized African territory. The attack was fairly small-scale and ineffectual, but reports about the bombing elicited considerable bad press throughout the rest of Europe. "This was not war: it was butchery," exclaimed a writer for the London *Daily Chronicle*.[4]

Almost as soon as hostilities began in World War I, both sides started experimenting with the techniques and technologies of aerial bombardment. Germany sent in a few zeppelins and small aircraft to drop bombs on Belgian and French cities in August 1914; the British and French soon responded with small-scale attacks of their own. Both sides aimed their bombs at military targets within urban areas, but the rudimentary nature of the aircraft and the limited experience of the pilots resulted in a high level of inaccuracy, with civilian casualties an inevitable side effect of the raids. At this stage in the war, both the military efficacy of the bombardments and the harm to civilians remained relatively low.

This steadily changed, however, as the war went on. By 1917, both sides had developed large new aircraft capable of delivering far deadlier payloads: the German Gotha bomber and the British Handley Page could carry well over a thousand pounds of ordnance. Both sides gradually abandoned the restraint shown earlier in the war, and now regularly plastered the industrial areas of each other's cities with bombs. And on both sides, air force officers began voicing hopes that aerial bombardment might sap the morale of the enemy population, eroding their will to continue the war. Approximately 1,400 British citizens, most of them civilians, perished in German air raids during the war; in 1918 alone, some 1,200 Germans were killed by English and French bombs.[5] The trajectory of airborne slaughter was moving ominously upward; only the U.S. intervention and the subsequent German surrender interrupted it.

But the bombing did not stop: indeed, it became a regular instrument of European colonial policy in the interwar years. British planes battered rebel sections of Baghdad in 1923; Spanish aircraft assaulted Moroccan villages in 1924; not to be outdone, the French repeatedly bombed Druze populations in Syria in 1925. In all these cases civilian casualties formed a large proportion of the dead on the ground, but the aerial actions were justified, in the eyes of European opinion, because they formed part of the imperialist policing function that the Europeans had taken on themselves, "pacifying" rebels and keeping order in their colonial territories and mandates.

During the Spanish Civil War, General Francisco Franco's Nazi allies began dropping bombs on Spanish towns in the north of the country: the blasted village of Guernica, captured in the harrowing imagery of Pablo Picasso's famous painting, now became a fixture in the iconography of modernity. The next major step was taken by the Japanese in 1937, when they systematically bombed the coastal cities of China, killing thousands. The Japanese took the scale of aerial bombardment to a new level: both the number of bombs dropped, and the number of dead on the ground, set grim records. From around the world, the chorus of outraged condemnation of the Japanese reached unprecedentedly high levels. Such condemnation was, to be sure, highly disingenuous on the part of peoples like the British and the French, who had already bombed civilians (albeit on a smaller scale) within their own colonial empires—but it was also understandable, given the overall ferocity of the Japanese attack against China.

By the late 1930s, meanwhile, a substantial science fiction literature had built up in Europe and the United States, depicting the horrors of future wars—wars, it was believed, in which civilian populations would be swiftly wiped out in massed air bombardments. One of the most celebrated of such literary works was *The World Set Free*, by H. G. Wells, which had been published on the eve of World War I. Wells, with astonishing prescience, envisioned the harnessing of nuclear energy and the development of atomic bombs: he foresaw the widespread devastation of modern civilization, and the emergence of a new era of international peace out of the radioactive ashes. But other writers did not see a need to venture so far into the technological future: existing explosives would suffice quite nicely, they predicted, to bring an end to civilization as it was currently known. Future wars would be quickly decided from the air; entire populations would be held hostage; any outbreak of all-out war, in such a context, would bring suffering on an unimaginable scale, and a swift descent into barbarism.

Nevertheless, most European and American citizens of the late 1930s did not read this frightening science fiction literature. While they had a vague sense that advancing military technologies would render the next war even bloodier than the last, they were unprepared, on the whole, for the vertiginous acceleration that airborne bombardment would undergo in the six years that followed 1939. Once war began, the dynamics of this acceleration arguably went through four main phases.

1940–1941

During the summer of 1940, while the Royal Air Force was desperately engaged in fighting the Battle of Britain, the German Luftwaffe initially concentrated its attacks primarily on British airfields, aircraft factories, and similar military targets. Some historians have argued that, had the Germans persisted with this strategy throughout the fall, they might well have succeeded in bringing the RAF to its knees.[6] But Hermann Göring, the Luftwaffe chief, had promised his führer that he could rapidly achieve air superiority over the English Channel, as a prelude to the amphibious invasion of Britain that the German army and navy were busily preparing. When Göring saw that the air battle was proving far more difficult and drawn-out than he had expected, he grew increasingly impatient. The tipping point came in late August, through a series of events that started with a simple navigational error on the part of a flight of German bombers: on the night of August 24 they lost their way and accidentally released bombs over the heart of London. Though the damage was slight, Churchill felt he could not allow this attack to go unchallenged. The very next day he sent a flight of eighty British planes to attack Berlin. The British inflicted modest and widely scattered damage on a few neighborhoods of the German capital, and killed ten German civilians on the ground. Hitler responded with unbridled fury: "The British will know that we are now giving our answer night after night. Since they attack our cities, we shall extirpate theirs."[7]

On September 7, Göring ordered his bombers to stop focusing on airfields and aircraft factories, and to commence targeting military assets inside London itself.

It was a fateful decision. Not only did this change in German tactics give the RAF a crucial breathing space in which to recover its fighting strength, it also altered the nature of the air war. Given the inaccuracy of the aerial bombardment technologies of the time, attacks on such targets as the London docks, in heavily inhabited areas, inevitably killed large numbers of civilians on the ground. Hitler and Göring thought that this new tactic might bring home to Churchill and the British people the folly of continuing the war. It had the opposite effect. The British rearranged their lives around the Blitz—as they came to call the nightly pummeling from the skies—and fought harder than ever. On September 17 (unbeknownst to the British) Hitler was forced to admit that Göring's Luftwaffe had failed in its bid for air superiority: he postponed the amphibious invasion of Britain until further notice. But the aerial bombardment continued; a ten-hour attack on Coventry during the night of November 15, for example, resulted in major devastation and the deaths of some five hundred civilians. All told, the German airborne attacks on British cities claimed some forty thousand civilian lives during the war.

Throughout the rest of 1940 and 1941, British bombers continued to launch attacks against a wide variety of targets in southern and western Germany. Two facts soon became clear to the leaders of Bomber Command. First, daylight runs over Germany resulted in unacceptably high numbers of planes succumbing to the increasingly effective German anti-aircraft defenses. Second, the bombardments themselves were proving terribly inaccurate: it was impossible, given the technology of the time, to hit precise targets with any degree of reliability. As a result, Bomber Command shifted its strategy. Henceforth, British planes would only fly missions under cover of darkness; and since this would further increase the inaccuracy of their bombardments, the planes would adopt a new technique. Instead of aiming at specific points on the ground, they would seek instead to cover a wider area surrounding the target point with a dense rain of ordnance—a technique that therefore came to be called area bombing.

To those who objected that this new tactic would inevitably result in far higher numbers of noncombatant casualties on the ground, the leaders of Bomber Command replied that they had no choice: area bombing at night was the only effective way to carry the war to the German territory, while limiting aircraft loss rates to a level that could be sustained over the long haul. The leadership, in other words, continued to speak in terms of waging the air war primarily against military targets in Germany; but they frankly admitted that these kinds of operations would also take a considerable toll among enemy noncombatants.

1942

When units of the U.S. Army Air Force started arriving in Britain during the spring of 1942, they decided that the British practice of nighttime area bombing was technologically outdated. They felt confident that American B-17 bombers, equipped with their superb Norden bombsights and bristling with gun turrets, would be able to launch far more successful missions by daylight than the British could ever hope to achieve at night. In addition—although they did not admit this publicly—some American air force officers believed that the British bombing practices would never prove acceptable to public opinion in the United States. If word got out that American planes were hitting German military targets by plastering entire swaths of cities indiscriminately with bombs—killing large numbers of civilians in the process—they feared that a dangerous domestic backlash against the USAAF might ensue.[8] As a result, the British and Yanks adopted a straightforward division of labor between themselves: American planes would hit the Germans by day, seeking to take out key military targets through precision bombing; British planes would strike the Germans by night, relying primarily on their established method of area bombing.

As the months went by in 1942, however, the Americans were forced to admit—through cruel experience—that the British had a point. The B-17s, it turned out, could not defend themselves effectively against the fast and well-piloted German fighter planes that swarmed up to meet them: they got shot down in droves, especially when their missions forced them to fly beyond the range of escorting Allied fighter planes. In addition, follow-up reconnaissance photos of bombarded targets revealed that, in too many cases, the damage resulting from American daylight raids remained far too low to justify their cost in lost planes and men. On many days, moreover, the dense cloud cover over Germany rendered the Norden bombsights useless, and American planes had to either turn around and return to Britain, or (after 1943) attempt to aim their bombs with airborne radar—a method that offered little hope of a direct hit on the intended target.

Gradually, therefore, the American strategic bombers developed what amounted in practice to a dual policy. In good weather, they would continue to try for precision bombing, even though they acknowledged that a significant percentage of their bombs were hitting far wide of the mark. And in cloudy weather, they would continue to fly combat missions, but would rely on the relatively crude method of radar-guided targeting. Both methods, they admitted, were proving far more indiscriminate than they had initially expected: the whole idea of "precision bombing," given the technology available in 1942, was turning out to be something of a pipe dream. In public, however, American military leaders never deviated from their original stated policy: they were aiming solely at military targets over Germany, and were doing the best they could to minimize civilian casualties.[9]

1943–1944

Starting in 1943, and even more clearly in 1944, the air war over Europe began—gradually, but unmistakably—to undergo a qualitative shift. The sheer number of both British and American aircraft continued to rise; their quality kept improving, as new models were introduced; the number of fighter escorts slowly but steadily grew; important modifications to the Norden bombsight rendered it considerably more effective; Allied scientists developed several ingenious techniques for defeating German radar; new types of bombs, both incendiary and high-explosive, were brought on line; and in 1944 the P-51 Mustang entered service—a fast and highly maneuverable plane that could not only outmatch the best German fighters, but whose fuel drop tanks allowed it to escort bombers all the way to Berlin and back. Under these gradually changing circumstances, a new level of airborne destruction became both technologically and operationally feasible.

The first clear sign of this transformed reality came during the night of July 27, 1943, when 787 British bombers passed in a steady stream over the northern German city of Hamburg, dropping a carefully calibrated mix of incendiary bombs and high explosives. On the ground, the fires that broke out quickly began spreading, joining up with other fires started by other bombs, until the whole city center was engulfed. The colossal flames sucked in air from the surrounding countryside, creating wind effects like those of a hurricane, capable of lifting people off the ground and whisking them away; not surprisingly, this wind further fanned the fires, pushing them to levels of heat that melted metal, exploded bricks, turned asphalt roads into searing rivers. A firestorm, it came to be called. On that night and the day that followed, 45,000 German civilians died in Hamburg. The heat was so intense that rescue efforts could not begin until two days later; when rescuers opened the city's bomb shelters, they often found piles of bodies melted down by the heat into a shapeless mass.

As word got out among the British public that Bomber Command was conducting these kinds of raids, some Britons began voicing strong objections, arguing that this form of warfare was unconscionable, and should be discontinued immediately.[10] But Arthur Harris, the head of Bomber Command, stoutly defended the area bombing strategy. Cruel as it might be in the short run, he insisted, this strategy was proving highly effective in degrading the military capabilities of the enemy, and therefore offered the best chance of winning the war as quickly as possible. By shortening the war, the bombing campaign would end up saving far more lives than it cost. This rationale—an intriguing fusion of military and moral arguments—eventually came to permeate both the British and the American campaigns. In all cases the Allies directly linked the killing of civilians to the moral goal of concluding the war swiftly and thereby saving lives. Thus, for example, the "Most Secret Operation Order No. 173," issued by the RAF's Bomber Command before the attack on Hamburg, ran as follows: "The total destruction of this city . . . would play a very important part in shortening and in winning the war."[11]

A second line of reasoning also began emerging at about this point in the war: the logic of "collateral damage." As it became increasingly clear that Allied bombers could not expect to hit military targets without simultaneously having a significant percentage of their ordnance fall on nearby inhabited areas, they developed this new term to describe what was happening. "Collateral damage" was a euphemism that allowed the Allies to render psychologically tolerable the large-scale killing of civilians. When a British or American flier looked down from his Lancaster or B-17 and saw the spattering of explosions spread across a densely populated German city, he could say to himself, in effect: "I am not trying to slaughter helpless noncombatants. We are doing our best to hit the production centers, but that goal inevitably entails unintended hits on surrounding civilian areas. It is regrettable, but it cannot be helped. This is merely the unavoidable side effect of our morally legitimate campaign to stop the German economy in its tracks."

For those Allied leaders (and airmen) who could not help but step back from what they were doing, reflecting on the nature of what was happening on the ground, the Orwellian terminology of "collateral damage" cloaked the actual realities of strategic bombing within the broader moral purpose of bringing the war swiftly to a merciful end. Few were the Allied officers like Sir Arthur Harris in Britain and Curtis LeMay in the United States (two of the main architects of strategic bombing) who could forthrightly look at themselves in the mirror and say, as LeMay publicly did: "I'll tell you what war is about. You've got to kill people, and when you've killed enough they stop fighting."[12]

At about this point in the war, moreover, some officers of Bomber Command and the USAAF also began openly articulating yet another rationale for strategic bombing: if the Allies could do to a large number of German cities what they had done to Hamburg, this catastrophic level of destruction might well result in a German surrender *without* the need for a bloody invasion of Europe on the ground. "Morale bombing," it came to be called: the deliberate obliteration of one enemy city after another, with the goal of shattering the fighting spirit of the general population. This idea had first emerged in World War I, and had already been articulated in detail as early as the 1920s by the Italian military theorist Giulio Douhet; but now it was no longer a mere theory. By the summer of 1943, the actual wherewithal to carry out this kind of cataclysmic attack was clearly taking shape in Allied hands. Through the use of airpower alone, it might prove possible to shorten the war, saving the lives of vast numbers of Allied soldiers.

But would it work? The debates within Bomber Command and the USAAF throughout the second half of the war never reached a clear point of consensus.[13] Some argued that the strategy would be worth a try. Others claimed that it wouldn't work, and would divert precious resources from the real goal, which was the destruction of the enemy's military capabilities. Still others maintained that even if it did work, it would amount to such a barbaric form of warfare as to taint the victory beyond redemption.[14]

In the end, neither the British nor the Americans ever explicitly embraced the concept of "morale bombing" in its more clear-cut form. What happened, instead, was something rather blurrier. Both the British and the Americans continued to insist in their public pronouncements, all the way through 1945, that their goal was the destruction of the enemy's ability to fight, through the systematic degradation of his military and economic assets; no Allied bombers would ever target civilian populations for their own sake. In concrete practice, however, it became increasingly hard to tell the difference. Some bombing missions, like the raids on Schweinfurt and Ploesti in 1943, could legitimately be characterized as precision bombing efforts aimed at destroying specific military targets. But a growing number of missions fell into a much hazier category, in which the targeted military assets were so closely intertwined with surrounding civilian populations that it became impossible to distinguish meaningfully between the two. In the case of Hamburg, for example, the British could legitimately claim that the city constituted a major center of production for the German war machine; but there can be no denying that this raid indiscriminately destroyed both the city's military assets and a large percentage of its inhabitants in a single sweep.

1945

Both sides in the war applied considerable energy and ingenuity to the challenge of torching the cities of the enemy. British incendiaries used thermite, a blend of iron oxide and powdered aluminum, which burned very hot over a small area, setting off fires in just about any combustible material. German incendiary bombs outperformed the British ones, however, by employing thermite as the igniting material and metallic magnesium as the primary fuel, resulting in fires that could not be extinguished with water. Japanese incendiaries also contained thermite, but were designed most ingeniously to explode at an altitude of two hundred feet, thereby spreading pods of unquenchable fire over a five-hundred-foot radius. The Americans developed a large incendiary bomb, the M-47, which weighed seventy pounds and contained a newly invented substance known as napalm—a gelatinized form of gasoline developed in 1942 by scientists at Harvard. Napalm proved devastatingly effective because the flaming gel stuck to just about anything, burned very hot, and resisted all efforts at extinguishment; but the relatively large size of the M-47 bomb was a handicap because it concentrated the bomb's effect too narrowly on a single point on the ground.[15]

Early in 1945, therefore, the Yanks brought together the aerial cluster design and the napalm fuel, an innovation that resulted in the M-69 bomb—arguably the single most effective nonnuclear killing device of the war. According to the historian Daniel Green, the M-69 "was a simple weapon, shaped like a long tin can and weighing just 6.2 lbs."

> Since dropping quantities of individual bombs from high altitude would be wildly inaccurate, [the M-69] was designed to be incorporated into an "aimable cluster," a type of cluster bomb that contained 38 of the [6.2-lb.] firebombs. Aimable clusters would be released over the target and break apart at about 2,000 ft. altitude, scattering their M-69s. Each M-69 would then eject a long strip of cloth to orient itself and crash nose-first into the buildings below. On impact the payload of napalm would ignite and shoot out of the tail of the bomb in a burning jet. Under ideal conditions, this jet could extend 100 ft.[16]

A single B-29 bomber could carry 1,520 M-69s. Usually they were delivered along with some conventional high-explosive bombs so as to prevent firefighters from approaching the target area until after the planes had left.[17] The Anglo-Americans dropped about 30 million thermite bombs on Germany during the war; the United States released about 10 million thermite or napalm bombs on Japan.[18]

By the beginning of 1945, the Allied air forces had achieved mastery of the air over most of Europe; and in the Pacific Theater the Americans had finally managed to seize a series of island bases from which they could launch large fleets of bombers against the Japanese homeland. In this climactic phase of the air war, the British and Americans were sustaining considerably lower loss rates on bombing missions than earlier in the war. Both the Germans and the Japanese stood increasingly helpless before their colossal daily onslaughts.

But neither the Germans nor the Japanese gave any sign of surrendering. Indeed, the Germans ramped up the firing of their V-2 rockets against British cities, killing thousands of civilians in late 1944 and early 1945; the Japanese dug in for the bloody battle of Okinawa, where their military would sustain losses of 95 percent before being overrun by American forces in June 1945. The war was still very much on, in other words, and the Allies were determined to use their overwhelming advantage in airpower as a means to crush enemy resistance and compel a surrender.

On February 3, 1945, the U.S. Eighth Air Force sent 937 bombers and 613 escorting fighters over Berlin: they leveled large parts of the city and killed some 25,000 persons. On February 14 and 15, 800 British and 400 American bombers flew in over Dresden, igniting a firestorm that burned for a week and killed at least 60,000 noncombatants. In the Pacific, American B-29 bombers systematically pounded the major cities of Japan, using the M-69 incendiaries that worked so devastatingly well on Japanese urban habitats, where most houses were made of wood. Sixty-six Japanese cities experienced large-scale destruction during the first seven months of 1945; approximately 200,000 civilians died in the bombardments and fires. The single deadliest air attack of the entire war (excluding atomic bombs) took place on the night of March 9, 1945, when 334 B-29 bombers went in over Tokyo, laying down incendiaries in a dense grid pattern that rapidly turned the city center into a superheated furnace. Between 90,000 and 100,000 died on the ground, the majority of them noncombatants. They were, to use the memorable words of General Curtis LeMay, "scorched and boiled and baked to death."[19]

At several junctures in the early years of the war, Allied leaders seriously considered calling off the bombing of Germany—or at least scaling it back drastically—not because of moral qualms, but because the campaign seemed to be wasting precious resources of men and matériel on a fairly ineffectual project. As the reconnaissance flights returned from their missions over Germany in 1941 and 1942, reporting the results on the ground, even the most ardent believers in airpower were forced to face a sobering reality: the German war economy seemed to be doing just fine, despite the steady escalation of the Allied bombing offensive. Many Allied leaders began questioning the idea itself of strategic air attack, and by mid-1942 the bombing campaign lay in serious jeopardy.[20]

But here a political factor intervened: Stalin's urgent demand for a second front in the west. The Soviet leader, whose armies were reeling under the massive blows of the Wehrmacht, wanted his Anglo-American allies to mount a direct and immediate attack on Germany, forcing Hitler to divert large numbers of soldiers and weapons from the Eastern Front. This would give the Russians a desperately needed respite in which to recover their balance and strengthen their defenses.

Churchill and Roosevelt struggled to convince Stalin that they were doing their utmost to open such a major new theater on Hitler's western flank. But the submarine threat in the Atlantic stubbornly persisted: despite frantic efforts, the Anglo-Americans proved unable to subdue the German submarine wolfpacks until well into 1943. As a result, the second front had to wait: all that they were able to do was to launch Operation Torch, in northern Africa (1942), and a peripheral attack on the south of the Italian peninsula (1943). Stalin was not impressed, and kept demanding a full-fledged frontal assault on northwestern Europe. He shrugged off Churchill's and Roosevelt's protestations that such an attack would be suicidally risky in 1943.

Seen in this context, the strategic bombing campaign against Germany provided the Anglo-American leaders with a crucial diplomatic alibi. They could tell the Soviet dictator, throughout 1943, that even though the second front would have to wait until the following year, they were already hitting Germany hard from the air, sapping German military production and forcing Hitler to divert significant resources from the Eastern Front. From this point on, therefore, any notion of abandoning the bombing campaign became untenable: it would continue for vitally important diplomatic reasons, regardless of its military cost-effectiveness.

The historian Richard Overy has persuasively argued that strategic bombing ultimately came to constitute a key factor in why the Allies won the war.[21] "By 1944," he writes,

> one-third of all German artillery production consisted of anti-aircraft guns; the anti-aircraft effort absorbed 20 per cent of all ammunition produced, one-third of the output of the optical industry, and between half and two-thirds of the production of radar and signals equipment. . . . An estimated two million Germans were engaged in anti-aircraft defence, in repairing shattered factories and in generally cleaning up the destruction.[22]

German war production began to sag noticeably in 1944, both because of direct damage to factories and rail lines, and because of the severe disruption that the bombing caused to the economy in general. Civilian morale also started to decline at this juncture, and absenteeism among the workforce became a growing problem. Allied mastery of the air, secured at last in the spring of 1944, constituted an essential precondition for the successful launch of Operation Overlord, the amphibious invasion of Normandy. Finally, of course, strategic bombing played a clearly decisive role in the defeat of Japan, speeding surrender on that front as well.

The foregoing discussion, therefore, leaves us with two facts to deal with:

- strategic bombing (excluding atomic bombs) killed between 500,000 and 900,000 civilians in Germany and Japan;[23] and

- strategic bombing constituted an important contributing factor in the ultimate defeat of Germany and Japan.

If killing hundreds of thousands of noncombatants played a key role in securing Allied victory, did this taint the victory with an indelible stain of innocent blood? Defenders of the wartime bombing effort argue, in hindsight, that three powerful factors had rendered it unavoidable:

- the Allies were engaged in a desperate war, in which their very survival was at stake;
- the enemy was using barbaric forms of warfare, and if the Allies had not adopted the enemy's methods then they might not have prevailed;
- the technology was there, growing and developing with a swift and pitiless momentum of its own—and in all-out warfare, if a weapon exists that will save lives on your own side, and hasten the demise of the enemy, you will most likely use it.

These are sensible and compelling arguments, grounded in the harsh reality of the mid-twentieth century. After all, if Churchill and FDR had refused to allow large-scale strategic bombing, how many more Allied soldiers would have had to die in order to secure the final victory? Isn't it all too easy to sit in moral judgment on the Allied policies, half a century later, coming from the comfortable and secure position of a society that has benefited in so many ways from the fruits of Allied victory?

These are all valid considerations. But they do not absolve us from the duty to look back over the strategic bombing campaign and reach a conclusion about the morality of what the Anglo-Americans did. The following three questions cut to the heart of the matter: What kinds of bombing are clearly morally legitimate? How much collateral damage is morally justifiable? What would have been the consequences, for the Allies, of conducting an air war that stopped short of area bombing and firebombing enemy cities?

1. *What kinds of bombing are clearly morally legitimate?*

According to the centuries-long tradition of Western thought regarding the just conduct of warfare, at least two principles must underpin any wartime military action, in order for that action to be considered morally legitimate:

- *Proportionality of means.* The destructive devices and practices used in warfare must be proportionate to the overall aims of the warring parties;

- *Sparing noncombatants.* Innocent civilians and noncombatants should
  never become the direct targets of warfare; only military personnel and
  installations can be legitimately attacked.[24]

Taking these principles as our guideline, one can see that the strafing
and aerial bombing of enemy positions in battle clearly lies within the
bounds of morally defensible military practice. Similarly, attacking enemy
airfields and bases, transportation lines, rail hubs, or munitions depots all
qualify as unambiguously legitimate military actions—even though in
some cases an airborne attack on such targets might inadvertently kill
some noncombatant bystanders. Certain types of factories clearly qualify
as well: those that produce weapons, aircraft, military vehicles, munitions,
gasoline, or any essential instruments of warfare. Under these criteria, for
example, the attacks on the German ball-bearing plants at Schweinfurt in
August and October 1943 would count as legitimate, because ball bearings
constituted an essential component of Germany's highly mechanized military services. (The factories also happened to be located on the outskirts of
Schweinfurt rather than in the main inhabited area of the town.)

2. *How much collateral damage is morally justifiable?*

Within the enemy population, we can distinguish four types of people
and things that are destroyed by aerial bombardment:

- Military installations, assets, and personnel;
- Industrial assets and personnel that directly support the war effort;
- Industrial assets and personnel that support both civilian life and the war
  effort (for example, factories that produce clothing and food);
- Persons within the enemy population who have little or nothing to do
  with the war effort: babies and toddlers, old men and women, the severely
  handicapped; individuals employed in literary, humanistic, or artistic professions that have no direct impact on the war effort; persons who teach
  elementary school, doctors and nurses who tend primarily to the needs of
  civilians, scientists engaged in basic research that is irrelevant to the war
  effort.

Those who are killed in this fourth category are being killed simply
because they are enemy nationals. The majority of them have most likely
done very little to harm or threaten the Allies directly: most are simply
living out their civilian lives as best they can under the hard conditions of
wartime. To kill even one such person is to incur a heavy moral burden: it
is, from one perspective, tantamount to murder. According to the Western

tradition of "just war" thought, soldiers engaged in combat are morally bound to make every reasonable effort to avoid harming such persons.

As we have seen, the Allied justification for killing such people lay in the concept of collateral damage: We were definitely *not* trying to kill them, only those in the first two categories. But where to draw the line? From one perspective, attacking a large food-processing facility might be considered a valuable contribution to the war effort, since soldiers need food in order to keep fighting. From another perspective, of course, such an attack is clearly illegitimate, for several reasons: destroying a single food production facility would not seriously undermine the enemy's war machine; the bombardment itself would no doubt kill many noncombatant workers and bystanders; and in the long run it would probably inflict greater food deprivation on local civilians than it would on the enemy's armies. The moral judgment needs to be worked out on a case-by-case basis, weighing the benefits of degrading the enemy's military capabilities against the costs of inflicting direct harm on a civilian population. Unless the proportion of harm done is clearly weighted toward the military side, and unless the target is crucial to the enemy war effort, the attack should not take place.

In general, the higher the number of noncombatants likely to be killed, the higher must be the threshold set by air force officers in deciding whether or not a site constitutes a morally acceptable target: how important is the target as a component of the enemy's war effort, and how does this compare with the human cost of conducting the mission? Thus, for example, even though the American attacks on Schweinfurt killed about six hundred civilians, this consideration was legitimately outweighed by the fact that the ball bearings produced there constituted absolutely essential elements in Germany's continued prosecution of the war.[25] The Americans, moreover, did not obliterate Schweinfurt. They did not indiscriminately wipe out the town's entire population of forty thousand, but rather concentrated their attacks as closely as they could on the immediate vicinity of the four main factories that produced the precious ball bearings.

But what about the other great raids of the war, in which area bombing and firebombing devastated large swaths of entire cities such as Hamburg, Dresden, or Tokyo? Here for example is a description of how American B-29s went about bombarding Tokyo on the night of March 9–10, 1945:

> At the head of each squadron moving toward the target area, one wing of bombers carried M-47 incendiaries, each containing enough napalm to generate 600,000 BTUs and produce a blaze that could tie up an entire fire

engine company. The M-47s were to mark out patterns of equal size, enabling the planes that followed to distribute their bombs evenly, covering all sectors with more than sixty tons per square mile. Air force analysts had calculated that this density would produce an uncontrollable conflagration.

A few minutes after midnight, Tokyo time, the lead Superfortresses began to drop their marking bombs, using precision bombsights. Planes following behind them circled and crisscrossed the target zone individually. Flying at altitudes of 4900 to 9200 feet, they unloaded clusters of M-69s which created giant rings of fire. The remaining bombers filled the rings with showers of incendiaries.[26]

What we see happening here is instructive. By 1945, the technology of bombardment had become sufficiently sophisticated that relatively high levels of accuracy could be attained: on a B-29 (as on the most recent generation of B-17s in Europe) the Norden bombsight was directly linked to an autopilot that took over the plane's controls in the final moments before "bombs away." This innovation yielded a level of accuracy that, according to USAAF claims at the time, could under ideal circumstances allow a dropped bomb to hit a 100-foot circle on the ground from an altitude of 21,000 feet. On that night of March 9, therefore, the leading B-29s dropped their large M-47 incendiaries as markers to lay out a precise gridwork over downtown Tokyo, as if they were plotting out squares on a piece of graph paper. Once those marker fires were burning, the rest of the bomber force could then proceed to methodically fly back and forth over the city, filling in the grids with incendiaries, according to a carefully thought-out pattern. In this manner, far fewer bombs were wasted on redundant hits, and the bombers could be certain of achieving a homogeneously dense coverage of the entire target area.

This method of bombing virtually ensured that, in a sixteen-square-mile trapezoidal area of central Tokyo, practically nothing could survive unscathed: the raid of March 9–10 was, by definition, an act of indiscriminate destruction, visited knowingly on a major population center. Scattered throughout that zone was a mixture of military installations, industrial assets, and civilian residences—in some cases within one and the same building. Many civilian homes in Tokyo had been equipped with lathes and heavy machinery, so that the inhabitants could work around the clock to produce war matériel: the decentralized nature of this mode of production had been specifically devised to thwart American attacks against large factories. Tokyo, in other words, like many other Japanese and German cities, constituted a classic case of a "mixed target"—a site in which important military assets existed side by side with purely civilian workplaces and residences. The raid of March 9–10 devastated all the military assets within the firestorm area, and simultaneously killed tens of thousands of noncombatants who bore no direct connection whatever to the Japanese war effort. "We knew we were going to kill a lot of women and kids," General LeMay later observed. "Had to be done."[27]

But did it really? Can such an attack be morally justified? It is hard to see how it possibly could be. The military assets scattered throughout downtown Tokyo were certainly important components of the nation's war machine, but they were not essential components of that war machine; they were definitely not the kinds of assets whose destruction would cripple Japan's war-making ability. As the historian Ronald Schaffer explains it:

> The most flammable zones did not contain the most important war plants. Some of the workshops and factories that were destroyed could not have contributed to the Japanese military effort in any case, since American attacks on transportation had shut off their supplies and made it impossible to ship what they produced. While area raids set back production for a while, they could not interfere quickly and decisively with Japan's ability to fight—which meant that despite all the damage the fire raids had done, Allied troops could anticipate severe casualties if they landed on the Japanese main islands.[28]

It is impossible to avoid the conclusion that the military value of Tokyo, as a target, came nowhere near the horrific loss of life that resulted from its destruction. From a moral standpoint, it was one thing to kill six hundred civilians in a raid against Schweinfurt, one of the most important nodal points in Nazi Germany's military production line. It was quite another to wipe out tens of thousands of noncombatants in order to neutralize military assets of middling importance that were widely dispersed throughout downtown Tokyo. The devastation of this city did not appreciably dampen the Japanese government's determination to continue the war; nor did it significantly degrade its capability for doing so.

There comes a point, along the escalating gradient of bombardment, where the damage inflicted on the enemy's military capabilities, and that borne by the enemy's noncombatant population, are about equal. Beyond that point, the balance of harm lies on the side of the noncombatants: more innocents are being killed than those who are legitimate targets of attack. At precisely that point, therefore, the concept of collateral damage breaks down, because the collateral effect is greater than the main intended effect of the raid. Beyond that point, the lives of civilians are being squandered by attackers who have lost all sense of proportion in their conduct of warfare: they are willing to kill any number of helpless noncombatants indiscriminately, in the single-minded pursuit of their military goals.

3. *What would have been the consequences, for the Allies, of conducting an air war that stopped short of area bombing and firebombing enemy cities?*

All these moral considerations would be rendered moot, of course, if the Allies had possessed no other viable option for seriously degrading the enemy's war-making capability. But they did possess such an option: they could have resolutely refused to engage in area bombing and firebombing, and focused their airpower exclusively on the destruction of military assets and the most essential sectors of the military economy.

Considerable debate has surrounded the question of what would have resulted from such a decision. Essentially, two schools of thought have emerged, with one group of military historians arguing that such a policy might well have shortened the war, and another group maintaining that it would probably have prolonged the war.[29] Those in the former school base their argument on the premise that area bombing and firebombing—while destructive and disruptive—nonetheless wasted tremendous resources on the neutralization of many nonessential targets. If instead the rain of destruction had been concentrated primarily on absolutely vital enemy assets, the resultant strangulation of the enemy's economy might plausibly have compelled a surrender at an even earlier date than actually resulted. In particular, these historians maintain that the Allies would have achieved far more by focusing on three categories of target: oil, transportation, and the enemy air force. To inflict crippling damage on any one of these three would have severely diminished the enemy's ability to fight effectively; to cripple all three would be to bring the enemy to surrender.

Those who believe that such a policy would have lengthened the war, by contrast, argue that—wasteful as it was—the policy of firebombing and area bombing still produced a cumulative effect that ultimately proved decisive by the spring of 1945. The indiscriminate devastation of cities forced the enemy to divert tremendous resources into air defenses, assisting the homeless and wounded, and repairing the damage. It grievously disrupted the economy, particularly after 1943. Over time, it also began to exert a significant impact on morale, on the will of the population to carry on the fight. Last but not least, it also possessed an important legacy for the postwar era: it impressed the sheer horror of warfare very force-fully on the enemy population, and rendered both the German and the Japanese peoples extremely reluctant to engage in any military adventures after 1945.

Let us assume, for the sake of argument, that a decision to avoid fire-bombing and area bombing would have extended the war. It is still reason-able to conclude that such a policy would probably not have prolonged the war by much. Even without firebombing and area bombing of cities, the rain of airborne destruction over Germany and Japan would have been colossal: it merely would have concentrated on a narrower set of targets. Hitler would still have had to divert vast resources from the east to defend against it. The Allies would still have achieved mastery of the air over Europe and Japan at about the same point in the war. Starting in mid-1944, the Allies could increasingly go in at will over enemy territory with air superiority, under the shield of highly effective fighter protection. They could often defeat enemy radar. Their planes were getting both qualita-tively better and far more numerous, and they faced steadily dwindling enemy resistance. Their capabilities for accurate targeting were steadily improving, both because of refinements in the technology itself, and because the acquisition of air superiority meant that they could take their time and bombard targets repeatedly—without incurring the devastating losses in planes and men that had plagued them between 1940 and 1943.

Richard Overy, in describing the wide variety of military targets hit by the Allies during the culminating phase of the air war over Germany, gives us a good depiction of what this kind of warfare might have looked like—without the need for indiscriminate area bombing and firebombing of entire cities:

> Over the last year of war the bombing of Germany was relentless. . . . Oil supplies for Germany's war effort were critically reduced. Chemical produc-tion was emasculated, reducing the output of explosives by half by the end of [1944]. From the autumn, attacks were concentrated against transport targets, which could now be hit accurately by fighters and fighter-bombers flying unmolested in German air space. The railway system was fatally debilitated. By December 1944 the number of freight-car journeys was half those of the previous year, and only half the quantity of coal needed by Ger-man industry could be moved by rail. Bombing gradually dismembered the economic body. By the winter of 1944–5 Germany was carved up into iso-lated economic regions, living off accumulated stocks, while frantic efforts

were made to divert essential military production into caves and salt-mines and vast, artificial, concrete caverns built, like the pyramids, by an army of wretched slaves.[30]

The key point to note here is that by 1944 all these kinds of vitally important targets—oil, chemicals, rail, and so on—could be seriously damaged or destroyed, without resorting to large-scale area bombing or firebombing of cities. The combination of air superiority and improved bombing accuracy meant that by this point in the war the Allies could severely weaken the enemy's war machine, while stopping well short of indiscriminately plastering enemy cities with firebombs.[31]

Such a relatively restrained air campaign would still have inflicted thousands upon thousands of civilian casualties on Germany and Japan. Hitting all those essential factories and key transportation lines would inevitably have caused a great many deaths among noncombatants. But in such a case the term "collateral damage" would truly have been legitimate, because the guiding principle of the Allied bombing campaign would have been to minimize as rigorously as possible such civilian deaths.

Unfortunately, the exact opposite turned out to be the case: as the months went by, and the Anglo-American air forces grew steadily bigger and more technologically sophisticated, they embarked instead on ever-escalating indiscriminate attacks against enemy population centers. Instead of using their technological prowess in a serious effort to limit the destruction they inflicted on noncombatants, they ever more blatantly ignored the distinction between military and civilian targets. It was not in the first half of the war, when the Anglo-American air forces were still flying desperate missions against long odds, that they pursued the policy of incinerating vast numbers of enemy civilians. Rather, they did so primarily in the second half, at a time when they were steadily moving toward total domination of the skies. The airborne slaughter of noncombatants climaxed in the spring and early summer of 1945, precisely when the Anglo-American air forces had reached the apogee of their numerical strength and technological sophistication.

We come, therefore, to our moral bottom line. Strategic bombing, we have seen, constituted a crucial element in securing Allied victory. Many of the Anglo-American bombardment practices can be justified, in retrospect, either because they did not cause large numbers of noncombatant deaths, or because the moral burden of such deaths (as in the case of Schweinfurt or Ploesti) was offset by the vital importance of the targets being destroyed. To argue, as some have done, that all forms of strategic bombardment were morally wrong is to lose sight of the realities of an all-out war in progress. If we try to imagine what World War II would have been like without the strategic bombing campaign, the resultant questions reveal just how crucial a part this campaign played in the overall shaping of the war. How much more powerfully would the German and Japanese war machines have worked if they had not been compelled to deal with Allied bombardment? If not for the great Allied resources that went into the conduct and support of strategic bombing, would the Allies have ever gained mastery of the air in Europe? How much longer would the Pacific War have lasted, if the aerial bombardment of Japan had not come into play? How many civilians would have been killed in the series of climactic military campaigns fought primarily on the ground?

We are left, ultimately, with no choice but to draw a line somewhere in the gray areas, along the slippery slope of Allied bombing practices. At some rather blurry point along that gradient, as the slaughter of noncombatants kept steadily setting new records, we encounter a transitional zone where the military benefit of a bombing operation begins to be clearly outweighed by the human cost. At first, the distinctions might seem hard to make: we agonize over the relative assessment of all the factors. How much less important would ball bearings have to be, for example, before we would be forced to balk at the six hundred noncombatant deaths of the citizens of Schweinfurt? This is, quite clearly, an exceedingly difficult judgment to make, in which all manner of probabilities and intangibles have to be set off against one another.

But there does come a point, along the escalating gradient of aerial bombardment practices, where we emerge from the gray areas once again, and the moral judgment gels more easily. Few could really argue, with any conviction, that the destruction of Hamburg, Dresden, or Tokyo yielded military advantages sufficient to counterbalance the deaths of 45,000, 60,000, or 80,000 noncombatants. No amount of casuistry about "collateral damage" can obscure the fact that the area bombing and firebombing of such cities amounted to little more than indiscriminate butchery—a form of warfare in which the military benefit of the operation was overwhelmingly outweighed by the colossal human cost. Such, indeed, was the conclusion reached in May 1945 by the American secretary of war, Henry Stimson. The nuclear physicist Robert Oppenheimer later recalled Stimson's words, as the elderly statesman presided over a top-level meeting of Manhattan Project scientists and government leaders:

[Stimson emphasized] the appalling lack of conscience and compassion that the war had brought about . . . the complacency, the indifference, and the silence with which we greeted the mass bombings in Europe and, above all, Japan. He was not exultant about the bombings of Hamburg, of Dresden, of Tokyo. . . . Colonel Stimson felt that, as far as degradation went, we had had it.[32]

There can be no excuse, in the end, for the practices of large-scale area bombing and firebombing of cities: these were atrocities, pure and simple. They were atrocities because the Anglo-Americans could definitely have won the war without resorting to them. They were atrocities because, starting in 1944, the Anglo-Americans increasingly possessed both the technology and the know-how to conduct a very different kind of aerial warfare: far more precise, measured, and controlled. But they chose instead to "scorch and boil and bake" tens of thousands of noncombatants at a time, month after month, on an ever-escalating scale. Here—in this sorry fact—lay the single greatest moral failure of the Anglo-American war effort.

Chapter Six

DEEP EVIL AND DEEP GOOD

The Concept of Human Nature Confronts the Holocaust

I made the effort, and it was possible for me, to shoot only children.
—Friedrich M.,
German Reserve Police,
at his trial in the 1960s[1]

I t would offer some comfort, as one reads the stories of the Holocaust, to be able to believe that this event was an anomaly, a freak of history. It was the Germans: they were uniquely cruel. It was the nature of the times: those years were uniquely barbarous.

But this would be false comfort: the past six decades of scholarship and reflection on the Nazi campaign against Europe's Jews have led in the opposite direction. The Holocaust was unique in some respects, and yet in others it was also not unique. Though it remains impossible for us to "understand" the Holocaust, in the sense of encompassing in one's mind the full monstrous reality of what transpired, we have nonetheless made substantial progress in charting the dimensions of this event: what kinds of causal factors led to it, what actually happened, and who did what. The more deeply we probe, the more the conclusion seems to emerge: what the Germans did to the Jews was in one sense historically unique, because it ultimately took on a scope and a character that had never before been witnessed in human affairs. But there was another side to it as well: this event also reflected broader patterns of human cruelty, visible at other times and in other societies. As we learn more about the motivations of the perpetrators, about the machinery of death that they put into place, we begin to discern social and psychological factors at work that extend beyond Nazi

*Magda and André Trocmé (left) and Mildred and Edouard Theis in
Le Chambon-sur-Lignon, circa September 1944.*

Germany and twentieth-century Europe. We recognize the distinctive signature of certain pathologies of human culture that already existed in various forms long before the 1940s, and that have continued to plague
society long after 1945.

The Holocaust is a singular crime, unparalleled in its combination of
malice, industrial efficiency, and sheer scale of consistent ruthlessness; but
it also holds up a mirror to all humans, forcing each of us to ask, Could
something like this happen again, in my own country, and during my own
lifetime? If I were to find myself caught up in such a situation, how would
I respond? These questions might seem rather naïve, like the awestruck
response of a schoolchild upon first reading the diary of Anne Frank. But
they are not, in fact, naïve. They follow as a consequence of understanding one fundamental fact about the Holocaust: many of the forces that
brought about this event are still at work, all around us, in our "normal"
everyday lives. They manifest in forms that sometimes speak subtly in
understated tones, sometimes shriek into our faces with terrible intensity.
But they are there.

The story of the Holocaust, in other words, remains starkly and
painfully relevant: it resonates directly with many of the most intractable
hatreds and cruelties that we continue to face in today's world. This chap-

ter focuses on two stories from the Holocaust, two episodes in which Europeans responded to the moral demands of their times in strikingly different ways. The contrast between these episodes sheds light on both the potentials, and the limits, of our ability to shape a moral universe out of the world that surrounds us.

Between June 1942 and May 1943, a group of some five hundred German men—middle-aged, working-class men, many of them married, with families waiting for them back home—worked their way through occupied Poland, killing Jews.[2] During those eleven months they killed approximately 38,000 men, women, and children—face-to-face, one by one, shooting them in their homes, in the streets of their villages, in the forests nearby. This was not the machinelike, impersonal murder of the gas chambers in the death camps: it was close-up, messy, and laborious. These men got the brains of their victims spattered on their uniforms; in the shooting pits, where the bodies piled up as they did their work, they had to literally wade knee-deep through the blood of entire villages.

The story of these men has been pieced together and recounted by the historian Christopher Browning, in his book *Ordinary Men: Reserve Police Battalion 101 and the Final Solution in Poland*.[3] It leaves the reader dumbstruck. What we discover is that these men were not, as is commonly believed, *forced* to become killers: they were not following adamant orders, the refusal of which might have resulted in severe punishment. On the contrary, Browning shows that they were given plenty of opportunities to choose not to participate in massacring civilians: their commanding officer openly invited any of his men who felt they were not "up to the task" to request reassignment to other duties. Some did so, in full view of the others: those men underwent no special punishment or ostracism. Yet most of the five hundred members of the battalion—80 percent of them—stayed in the ranks and voluntarily went ahead with the killing.

At first, during the initial massacres in June 1942, the majority of these individuals were horrified and disgusted by the duty to which they had been assigned. These were not, after all, hardened SS members, rigorously trained and ideologically steeled for the task of liquidating large civilian populations. They were reservists in the Order Police, a low-level, semimilitary organization whose purpose was to serve as a home guard in Germany and to administer the areas conquered by advancing German armies in the east. Some of them were career policemen, some were too old to serve in the army, some had joined the Order Police so as to avoid conscription into the Wehrmacht. Their job—so they thought—would be to patrol the streets of occupied cities, to guard captured enemy soldiers, to enforce the laws in the harsh Pax Germanica that had descended on Eastern Europe. They came from humble social origins, mostly from Hamburg and its environs: dockworkers, construction workers, salesclerks, waiters. Only the officers of the battalion were SS men, and only 25 percent were members of the Nazi Party. Neither officers nor men had the slightest idea of the job that awaited them when they were transferred from Hamburg to central Poland in 1942.

But most of them got used to it, after a while. Some continued to hate their task to the end, and had to struggle to get through it. Some became utterly deadened to their job, calloused enough to make crude jokes about it at the end of the day. Some gradually acquired a taste for it, ultimately turning into enthusiastic and sadistic torturers as well as killers. When desperate Jews fled into the nearby forests, there were always volunteers for the exciting "Jew hunts" that ensued.

They drank a lot: plenty of vodka was always on hand to numb their emotions and ease their work. One junior officer took considerable pride in the efficiency of his job performance: he even managed to arrange for his new bride to come visit and personally witness one of the roundup operations as the Jews were hounded from their homes. Another man developed severe stomach cramps every time a mass killing was announced for the following day: he did his best to conceal his infirmity, so as not to be thought weak by his comrades. A thirty-five-year-old metalworker from Bremerhaven even found a way to construe "mercy" in what he was doing:

> I made the effort, and it was possible for me, to shoot only children. It so happened that the mothers led the children by the hand. My neighbor then shot the mother and I shot the child that belonged to her, because I reasoned with myself that after all without its mother the child could not live any longer. It was supposed to be, so to speak, soothing to my conscience to release children unable to live without their mothers.[4]

During these same months, on the other side of Europe, in a remote area of south-central France, something very different was happening to Jewish children. One at a time, passing through a thousand dangers, families of desperate Jewish refugees made their way to the mountain hamlets of a region known as the Plateau Vivarais-Lignon. They came from all over

Europe, as the net of the Gestapo and SS tightened over the Continent. The villagers of the plateau took them in, hid them on outlying farms, fed them and clothed them, gave them forged identity papers, and, whenever possible, arranged for their escape to safe areas such as neutral Switzerland. Under the very nose of the Gestapo and the dreaded Milice, the Vichy secret police, the people of the Vivarais-Lignon saved the lives of more than 5,000 refugees, including 3,500 Jews, between 1940 and 1944.

The story of wartime rescue on the Plateau Vivarais-Lignon has only gradually come to be known. It has long been associated primarily with a single village, Le Chambon-sur-Lignon, which has formed the subject of two widely noted works, the philosopher Philip Hallie's book *Lest Innocent Blood Be Shed;* and the filmmaker Pierre Sauvage's documentary, *Weapons of the Spirit.* Nevertheless, recent work by French historians has shown that a dozen other communities in the region also engaged in significant rescue efforts of their own. While the account that follows focuses on the better-known activities in Le Chambon, it is worth underscoring that what happened in this village was not unique, but exemplified the extraordinary initiatives undertaken simultaneously throughout much of the surrounding countryside.[5]

At the nucleus of the story of Le Chambon-sur-Lignon stands one remarkable man, the Protestant pastor André Trocmé, who, with his assistant, Edouard Theis, served as a spiritual catalyst for the village's enterprise of sheltering refugees; but even more remarkable is the way several thousand villagers gradually came to form a loose but potent network of rescue, acting with quiet determination under conditions of great peril.

Trocmé was, by all accounts, a formidable character: passionate, deeply charismatic, quick to rage, fiercely independent-minded. Born in 1901 in northern France, he had become a Protestant minister in the late 1920s, and openly defied his superiors in the church by announcing that he was a believer in uncompromising nonviolence, and would preach nonviolence and conscientious objection among his flock. He and his wife, Magda, with their four children, moved to Le Chambon to take up the vacant pastorship there in 1934. Edouard Theis joined him as assistant pastor in 1938.

Most of the villagers of Le Chambon, like the other inhabitants of the Plateau Vivarais-Lignon, were French Protestants whose ancestors had fled to the remote mountains of the Massif Central at the time of the wars of religion in the sixteenth century. The Chambonnais of the 1940s still felt a deep kinship with their persecuted ancestors—their hymns and cultural traditions derived in direct lineage from the religious conflict experienced centuries before—and it was perhaps this that helped them to empathize more strongly than other French citizens with the plight of the fleeing Jews. Since they were themselves a religious minority in over-whelmingly Catholic France, they knew what it was like to be outsiders.

After the defeat of France in June 1940, the Germans divided the country into two parts: a northern region directly occupied and governed from Paris by Nazi authorities, and a southern region left in the hands of a French puppet dictator, the eighty-five-year-old hero from World War I, Marshal Philippe Pétain. The capital for this semi-autonomous southern zone was set up for the duration of the war at the health spa of Vichy; the Plateau Vivarais-Lignon lay in the heart of this zone, under the jurisdiction of Pétain's Vichy government.

Pétain was an arch-right-winger, authoritarian and anti-Semitic, who saw the Vichy regime as his chance to set up a traditional society in France, under the conservative values of work, family, and patriotism—in close cooperation with the Catholic Church. He therefore decided to collaborate actively with the Nazis. Part of this policy meant that all the Jews in France, whether citizens or not, were kept under careful surveillance by the French police, with some of them gradually rounded up in detention camps. After 1942, when the Germans dramatically heightened the pace of the Final Solution, Pétain's police helped to round up Jews for the deportation trains to Auschwitz and the other death camps. Most French citizens did nothing to stop this.

Even in remote Le Chambon, the pressure to conform to the new racial laws and quasi-fascist rhetoric of the Vichy government soon made itself felt. And from the start, Pastors Trocmé and Theis took a clear stand of resistance. Already in the fall of 1940, they were preaching to their parishioners about noncooperation with the racist laws of Vichy. They organized a way for local schoolchildren to avoid having to salute the Vichy flag. Even in these relatively small symbolic acts, they believed, it was important to show that one could stand firm and say no. "We will resist," they told their parishioners, "whenever our adversaries will demand of us obedience contrary to the orders of the Gospel. We will do so without fear, but also without pride and without hate."[6]

The first refugee Jews started arriving that fall, seeking shelter and hiding places in the backwoods of the Massif Central. Several village households, including the Trocmé and Theis families, opened their doors to them. Gradually, as the number of refugees grew, the two pastors had a flash of understanding: this was more than just a matter of extending a hand to help a few despairing individuals who presented themselves at one's door. This was a test of Christian faith. Nonviolence and charity, for

Trocmé and Theis, meant more than just being kind to one's neighbor: they were dynamic forces that reached out to transform the world. In dark times like these, true Christian faith required taking the initiative to go out and oppose the evil that was being perpetrated throughout Europe. The moment had come to go into full-fledged opposition against Nazism— wielding not weapons but the more potent, enduring force of active non-violence.

Trocmé and Theis did not explicitly ask their parishioners to harbor Jewish refugees; instead, in their weekly sermons, they made clear the connection between the present wartime plight of the refugees and the teachings of the Gospel: they urged their flock to look into their own conscience and take whatever steps they deemed appropriate. The result was the gradual emergence, among the townsfolk and farmers from the surrounding countryside, of an improvised, secret, and highly decentralized network of rescue—a kind of "underground railroad" for Jewish refugees. Most of the Chambonnais were well aware that their neighbors were also harboring Jews and aiding their escape; but in the interest of secrecy, they avoided discussing with one another the details of who was doing what. The enterprise of rescue in Le Chambon, like the broader one taking place across the Plateau Vivarais-Lignon, never developed a central organization or coordinating body: such a body would have rendered it vulnerable to infiltration by informers from the Gestapo. Instead, each participating household quietly made its own arrangements for taking care of its own refugees, working on a need-to-know basis with other households, with the specialized individuals who forged documents, with the underground guides who led Jews to safety.

The danger was great. Both the Gestapo and the Milice had agents and informers operating throughout the area. As news gradually filtered out by word of mouth among France's refugees that a safe haven had been created in the mountains of the Massif Central, it did not take long for Vichy and German authorities to conclude that something untoward was happening on the Plateau Vivarais-Lignon. One German official referred to the region as "that nest of Jews in Protestant country."[7] Nevertheless, despite the authorities' repeated investigations and interrogations, the secret held; each time Vichy police descended on the remote villages in search of refugees, the Jews had already been alerted and spirited off to their hiding places. Only one of the Gestapo's raids, conducted in Le Chambon in June 1943, succeeded in ferreting out hidden Jews: on that occasion nineteen teenage refugees, most of them Jewish, were arrested and deported. Included among them was André Trocmé's cousin, the schoolteacher Daniel Trocmé, who had been looking after the youths, and who insisted on accompanying them after their arrest. Many of the deported youths are known to have perished in the Nazi death camps; Daniel Trocmé was gassed on April 2, 1944, in the Polish camp of Majdanek.

André Trocmé and Edouard Theis themselves faced deadly peril. In February 1943 they were arrested by Vichy police, along with one of their closest associates, Roger Darcissac. The three men were held for a month in an internment camp near Limoges, and were only released after Protestant church officials and other acquaintances with good political connections interceded with the Vichy government on their behalf. Then, shortly after the Gestapo raid on Le Chambon in June, Trocmé was tipped off by a friend in the Resistance that he was on a target list for agents of the Gestapo: his life was in danger. He and Theis both went into hiding for the remainder of the war: Theis assisted in the underground railroad efforts between the Massif Central and Switzerland; Trocmé lived in another part of the mountains, under a pseudonym, until the liberation of France that began in June 1944.

But through it all—even with Trocmé and Theis gone—the villagers of Le Chambon continued to save Jews. The loose but efficient network they had put into place, the tough solidarity of these unlikely conspirators, their quiet faith in what they were doing: these never faltered. One sees them, captured on camera many years later in the film by Sauvage, asked by the interviewer to reflect on how they managed to do this remarkable thing: an old farmer and his wife, standing in front of the weathered stone façade of their ancient farmhouse. They shrug their shoulders. They look down. They give a soft little smile. The interviewer persists: Where did you find such courage? Again the shrug, the smile. "Oh, you know. After a while we got used to it."

On one side, the men of Reserve Battalion 101; on the other, the inhabitants of the Plateau Vivarais-Lignon. How do we make sense of the chasm that separates them?

Perhaps the most disturbing fact about these two groups is that, if you had encountered any of these individuals in the year 1939—say, as a tourist visiting Hamburg and Le Chambon—you would have had no inkling of the difference that their behavior would be manifesting a mere three years later. A waiter in a Hamburg restaurant, a waiter in the café at Le Chambon; a dockworker in Hamburg, a plumber plying his trade in the villages of the Plateau Vivarais-Lignon: these men would all have struck you as perfectly "normal" Europeans peaceably going about their daily business. Even if you had gotten to know them better, as individuals, it would still have been hard to tell. In Hamburg just as in Le Chambon, they were law-abiding citizens; they had families; many of them had children. They had friends, relationships, pets, hobbies. They were kind to some people at times, nasty to others at other times: they were, in short, human beings like anybody else. And yet, three years later . . .

Were the profound differences between them already present in 1939, lurking beneath the surface? Such a question cannot help but shake one's faith in all human beings. As we look around at the "ordinary" people in our community, we cannot prevent ourselves from wondering, What extremes of cruelty or of compassion lie latent beneath the seemingly unremarkable gestures and habits of that man or woman? If dark times should come again, on which side of the chasm will each of them turn out to live? And most disturbing of all: On which side will my neighbors find *me*?

Not surprisingly, these issues have attracted a great deal of attention from scholars in many disciplines over the past few decades.[8] Part of what it means to come to terms with the Holocaust is precisely this: to seek an understanding of how seemingly ordinary people could wind up as mass murderers or as heroes—or, in most cases, as passive bystanders, seemingly indifferent to the atrocities that went on under the very windows of their homes. Three broad schools of thought have emerged: those who argue that a person's character—upbringing, values, philosophy of life— proved decisive in determining behavior during the Holocaust; those who argue that situational factors—conformism, peer pressure, group power dynamics, subordination to authority—were the key to shaping behavior, regardless of the character of particular individuals; and those who argue that only a combination of both elements—personal character as well as situational factors—can take us in the direction of a deeper understanding.

In *Ordinary Men*, Christopher Browning provides an exhaustive analysis of the possible causes for the behavior of his police reservists. Wartime brutalization, he argues, cannot account for these men's atrocities, because they had not been subjected beforehand to the feral cruelties of combat (as had, for example, the soldiers at Stalingrad): they had just been transferred from the civilian environment of Hamburg when they commenced their killing. Any brutalization that occurred took place after they had begun their killing, and could not therefore be adduced as a precipitating cause of it. Nor can we attribute the behavior of these men to the kind of machinelike and desensitizing conditions that prevailed in the death camps: the "depersonalizing aspects of bureaucratized killing" did not apply to them, since they killed in a way that remained relentlessly "up close and personal." While their action did eventually settle into a sort of routine, it was a routine of direct and ever-fresh brutality, not one that might have afforded them the comfort of psychological distancing—as, for example, with the attack carried out by an aircraft bombardier from an altitude of twenty thousand feet.

Was the composition of Battalion 101, Browning asks, the result of some sort of explicit or even tacit selection process? Were these men, at some level, chosen for this task because they showed attributes that boded well for a career as callous murderers of helpless civilians? Not at all: their selection was, if anything, highly unpropitious for the duty to which they were assigned. They were not thugs or ultra-zealous Nazis, but working-class men, some of them from socialist backgrounds, many of them too old to have participated in the Hitler Youth or other such organizations. Far from being specially selected, they constituted "the 'dregs' of the man-power pool available at that stage of the war . . . the only kind of unit available for such behind-the-lines duties."[9]

Were they ideologically indoctrinated, then—systematically brain-washed into becoming killers? Once again, Browning answers in the negative. Many of these men were old enough to have been raised long before the years of Nazi racial indoctrination. Although the whole battalion did receive a certain amount of regular propaganda, it was vague and ineffectual fare—hardly the kind of material that would be expected to whip normal men into a frenzy of racial bloodlust. No, Browning concludes: these men had certainly imbibed the general atmosphere of anti-Semitic hatred that prevailed in Nazi Germany, and some of them were undoubtedly ferocious racists; but such ideological motives simply cannot suffice to explain the extreme violence in which the majority of them engaged. They may have regarded their victims with hatred or disgust, but nothing in their ideological education had explicitly prepared them for the task of shooting large numbers of unarmed civilians.

Where does this leave us, then? Browning concludes that "situational factors"—peer pressure within the battalion, a generalized submission to authority, and the psychological reactions of individuals wielding absolute power over others—all played key roles. He cites two famous studies conducted since World War II by psychologists in American universities—studies that suggest the surprisingly potent influence exerted by such factors in determining an individual's behavior. Though these kinds of elements cannot by themselves fully explain the behavior of Reserve Battalion 101, Browning argues persuasively that they do go a long way toward helping us understand what took place in the minds of these men.

The first study was conducted by the psychologist Stanley Milgram at Yale University over a three-year period in the early 1960s.[10] Milgram wanted to see how far people would be willing to go in blind obedience to authority—even to the point of overriding their inner moral scruples and inflicting harm on helpless victims. He devised a singularly ingenious experiment to test this, and applied it (with variations) to more than a thousand male volunteers from the surrounding community in New Haven, Connecticut.[11]

The test subject was told that he was participating in an experiment on learning and memory, in order to determine if people learned more rapidly under the threat of physical punishment. In the lab, Milgram set up an apparatus that looked like a machine for administering electric shocks: these, he told the subject, would provide the "punishment." Under the supervision of a man in a white lab coat—the "Scientist" in charge—each test subject was paired up with another person, and the two drew straws to see who would be the "Teacher" and who would be the "Learner." In reality, however, the selection was rigged so that the test subject would always function as the Teacher, while the Learner would always be (unbeknownst to the test subject) a member of Milgram's staff, playing a carefully scripted role.

Then the experiment began. The Teacher would follow the Scientist and Learner to a separate room and watch the Learner being strapped into a chair, so that he could not move. Then the Teacher and Scientist would return to the main lab, and the Teacher would take his place at the shock console. Teacher and Learner would communicate through a microphone and speakers, and commence working together with memorizing pairs of words: every time the Learner made a mistake, the Teacher was instructed to administer an electric shock. With each mistake, the shock level grew by a 15-volt increment.

It was all a charade: the machine never produced any shocks, and the Learner (a Milgram staff member) only pretended to cry out as if he had been shocked. But the test subject did not know this: he earnestly believed he was testing the ability to learn, and administering real electric shocks to another volunteer just like himself, along a steadily escalating scale of voltage. The shock generator had a series of labels, culminating in words like "danger," "severe shock," and finally (after 450 volts) just "XXX."

As the shocks got stronger and stronger, the Learner began to complain (as per the experiment's script), "Hey, this really hurts!"[12] The Teacher, in most cases, turned to the man in the white lab coat, looking for instructions. "Continue," the Scientist would say. On with the word games: more mistakes, more shocks, steadily growing in intensity. Finally the Learner would shout, following the script, "Experimenter! That's all. Get me out of here. I told you I had heart trouble. My heart's starting to bother me now. Get me out of here, please. My heart's starting to bother me. I refuse to go on. Let me out."

Once again the Teacher would look to the Scientist for directions, and the Scientist would calmly say, "Continue, please." At this point most Teachers rebelled: "But he says he has a heart condition. He says he wants to stop." To which the Scientist stonily replied, "The experiment requires that you go on. Please continue, Teacher."

The Teacher then faced a choice: he could refuse to go on, or he could submit to the authority of the man of Science. To the utter astonishment of Milgram and his associates, 65 percent of his test subjects continued to administer shocks to a Learner who was howling with protestations of pain in the adjoining room. The test subjects did not do so happily: they complained, they argued with the Scientist, they sweated, they twitched with severe anxiety. But on they went, prodded by the stolid man in the white lab coat, even after the cries of pain suddenly—and ominously—ceased altogether in the adjoining room, making it seem as though the Learner had finally collapsed from duress. They proceeded to administer shocks at the 450-volt level, fully aware that by this point they might be shocking a man in cardiac arrest—or a corpse. The transcript of these experiments makes for chilling reading:

(Experiment continues with Learner refusing to answer, and, finally, failing even to grunt or groan. At 375 volts, the subject stands up.)

SUBJECT: I think something's happened to that fellow in there. I don't get no answer. He was hollering at less voltage. Can't you check in and see that he's all right, please?

EXPERIMENTER (*with same detached calm*): Not once we've started. Please continue, Teacher.

SUBJECT (*sits down, sighs deeply*): "Cool—day, shade, water, plant. Answer please. Are you all right in there? Are you all right?

EXPERIMENTER: Please continue, Teacher. Continue please. (*Subject pushes lever.*)

SUBJECT (*swiveling around in his chair*): Something's happened to that man in there. (*Swiveling back.*) Next one. Low——dollar, necklace, moon, paint. (*Turning around again.*) Something's happened to that man in there. You better check in on him, sir. He won't answer or nothing.

EXPERIMENTER: Continue. Go on, please.

SUBJECT: You accept all responsibility?

EXPERIMENTER: The responsibility is mine. Correct. Please go on.

(*Subject returns to his list, starts running through words as rapidly as he can read them, works through to 450 volts.*)

SUBJECT: That's that.

EXPERIMENTER: Continue using the 450-volt switch for each wrong answer. Continue please.

SUBJECT: But I don't get no anything!

EXPERIMENTER: Please continue. The next word is "white."

SUBJECT: Don't you think you should look in on him, please?

EXPERIMENTER: Not once we've started the experiment.

SUBJECT: But what if something has happened to that man?

EXPERIMENTER: The experiment requires that you continue. Go on, please.

SUBJECT: Don't the man's health mean anything?

EXPERIMENTER: Whether the Learner likes it or not . . .

SUBJECT: What if he's dead in there? (*Gestures toward the room with the electric chair.*) I mean, he told me he can't stand the shock, sir. I don't mean to be rude, but I think you should look in on him. All you have to do is look in on him. All you have to do is look in the door. I don't get no answer, no noise. Something might have happened to the gentleman in there, sir.

EXPERIMENTER: We must continue. Go on, please.

SUBJECT: You mean keep giving him what? Four-hundred-fifty volts, what he's got now?

EXPERIMENTER: That's correct. Continue. The next word is "white."

SUBJECT (*now at furious pace*): "White—cloud, horse, rock, house." Answer, please. The answer is "horse." Four-hundred-fifty volts. (*Administers shock.*)[13]

Milgram ran this test many times, using as test subjects both men and women, people from all walks of life, individuals of low and high levels of education. The result remained disturbingly constant: about 65 percent of the subjects proved obedient, going all the way to 450 volts as instructed. Then Milgram created dozens of variations on this basic situation: he placed the Teacher and Learner in the same room (the obedience level dropped somewhat); he removed the Scientist from the lab (the obedience level plummeted); he required the Teacher to make physical contact with the Learner while administering the shock (obedience dropped considerably); he moved the lab from Yale to a nondescript office building in Bridgeport, Connecticut (no appreciable difference in results); he allowed the Teacher to choose which level of shock to administer (almost none went beyond 135 volts, labeled "strong shock").

One set of experiments also aimed to test the effects of peer pressure on obedience. When Milgram embedded the subject within a group of other Teachers (all members of Milgram's staff following a script), the results were striking: if the other Teachers refused at some point to go on with shocking the Learner, the test subjects' average obedience level dropped to a mere 10 percent; but if the other Teachers went all the way to 450 volts, fully 92 percent of test subjects did so as well. Peer pressure, in other words, strongly reinforced the already powerful pull of authority. "Ordinary people," Milgram concluded,

simply doing their jobs, without any particular hostility on their part, can become agents in a terrible destructive process. Moreover, even when the destructive effects of their work become patently clear, and they are asked to carry out actions incompatible with fundamental standards of morality, relatively few people have the resources needed to resist authority.[14]

For Christopher Browning, the Milgram experiments cast important retrospective light on the behavior of Reserve Battalion 101. The differences between the two situations were profound, of course. But if citizens of Connecticut—in the civilian context of peacetime—could so easily be made to inflict pain and perhaps even death on helpless victims in a laboratory setting, the implications for the far more extreme circumstances of Nazi-occupied Poland were grim indeed. The men of Reserve Battalion 101 were operating during wartime in a semimilitary unit, in a foreign land in which their power over local citizens was absolute; they were obeying the commands of a state-sanctioned power hierarchy that carried tremendous authority; they were ordered to kill victims who had been systematically portrayed, over many years, as subhumans, as the archenemies of their nation.

Browning places particular emphasis on the element of peer pressure in assessing the behavior of his police reservists. Many military historians and psychologists have noted the importance of group cohesion in determining the effectiveness of a fighting unit: when the men have a chance to bond with one another they are often moved to do extraordinary things to help one another in battle.[15] In the case of Reserve Battalion 101, the bonding did not take the form of bravely facing combat together; rather, it consisted in steeling oneself to do one's part in carrying out the awful duty that they all shared. In the postwar testimony of these men, this was a salient and recurring factor: it became vitally important to them not to let one another down, not to be perceived by the others as being too "weak" to carry out the battalion's horrific assignment. In this context, paradoxically, the act of refusing on moral grounds to massacre civilians became a "betrayal" of the unit as a whole: it violated the ethic of comradeship in wartime. Peer pressure, under such circumstances, was not just a matter of imitating one's fellows, of going along with the crowd: it also became a matter of loyalty, and a test of manhood.

Here another key situational factor came into play as well: the psychological reaction of a person wielding absolute power over other human beings. Browning cites the work of another psychologist, Philip Zimbardo, whose 1971 Stanford Prison Experiment has become just as renowned as the Milgram experiments (perhaps even more so, in the wake of the 2004 Abu Ghraib prison scandal in U.S.-occupied Iraq). Zimbardo wanted to study "the psychological effects of prison life," assessing (among other things) the extent to which ordinary individuals would prove capable of inhumane behavior if they were placed in an institutional setting that gave them complete power over other people. After he had placed an ad for volunteers in a local newspaper, Zimbardo received applications from seventy college students who were willing to participate, earning $15 per day over a two-week period. He submitted this group to a battery of standard psychological and sociological tests, weeding out all those whose personality profiles deviated from that of "normal, well-adjusted" persons. This left him with a test group of twenty-four "healthy, intelligent, middle-class males."[16]

He randomly divided the young men into two groups: prisoners and guards. In a mock jailhouse constructed in the basement of a Stanford University building, the young men quickly began settling into their roles. The prisoners were subjected to treatment that aimed to reproduce the psychological effect of a real arrest: strip-search, delousing, prison garb, an ID number, an ankle chain, small cells with bars. The guards wore uniforms and dark glasses ("like Cool Hand Luke," as one of them remarked): they were not allowed to harm the prisoners physically, but beyond that restriction, Zimbardo deliberately left them considerable leeway in performing their roles. They were told to improvise.

At first, neither the prisoners nor the guards took their roles too seriously: it seemed an interesting and even amusing game. But this soon changed. On their own initiative, the guards began imposing harsh discipline on the prisoners, waking them at 2:00 a.m. for roll calls and searches, and forcing them to do push-ups. On the second day the prisoners staged a rebellion, barricading themselves in their cells and refusing to obey the guards. The guards responded by clamping down hard: "[They] broke into each cell, stripped the prisoners naked, took the beds out, forced the ringleaders of the prisoner rebellion into solitary confinement, and generally began to harass and intimidate the prisoners."[17]

Over the days that followed, an astonishing transformation took place. The prisoners got so caught up in their roles that they felt genuine anguish and terror: some became defiant and uncooperative, others totally submissive and compliant. The guards, for their part, steadily turned more abusive and arbitrary in exercising control over their wards. Within thirty-six hours, Zimbardo had his first real crisis: one of the young prisoners suffered an emotional breakdown, and had to be let out.

With each passing day, the tension and conflict increased. A rumor of an impending jailbreak brought down a further escalation in the guards' aggression: they punished the prisoners by forcing them to clean toilets with their bare hands, and by making them do push-ups and jumping jacks for hours on end. One of the men, referred to simply as #819, got singled out by the other prisoners as a weakling and a "bad prisoner": the taunts and torment inflicted by the guards were now complemented by the ostracism of his fellows. This proved too much for him to bear, and he too suffered a breakdown. Zimbardo was forced once again to intervene.

At that point I said, "Listen, you are not #819. You are [his name], and my name is Dr. Zimbardo. I am a psychologist, not a prison superintendent, and this is not a real prison. This is just an experiment, and those are students, not prisoners, just like you. Let's go." He stopped crying suddenly, looked up at me like a small child awakened from a nightmare, and replied, "Okay, let's go."[18]

On the sixth day, Zimbardo decided he had no choice but to call the experiment to a premature halt:

We had learned through videotapes that the guards were escalating their abuse of prisoners in the middle of the night when they thought no researchers were watching and the experiment was "off." Their boredom had driven them to ever more pornographic and degrading abuse of the prisoners.[19]

In a mere six days, a group of twenty-four college students had evolved into sadists and victims—while under the continual supervision of psychologists, and under clearly simulated conditions. Once again, the parallels with the behavior of Reserve Battalion 101 are too striking to ignore: seemingly normal individuals, placed in a position of absolute power over other human beings, rapidly degenerating into an astonishing array of inhumane behaviors. If the Milgram experiments had revealed that humans could be induced all too easily to override their moral sentiments, the Zimbardo experiments suggested that human cruelty always lies, like an untapped reservoir, not far beneath the surface of everyday life.

Should we conclude that, given the right conditions, just about anyone can be maneuvered into carrying out such cruel and immoral behaviors? Certainly not. In all three cases—Reserve Battalion 101, Milgram, Zimbardo—we find a minority of individuals who steadfastly refused to go along with the inhumane acts that surrounded them. A couple of Zimbardo's guards (16 percent of the twelve) went out of their way to treat prisoners kindly; about 20 percent of Milgram's test subjects indignantly broke off their participation early in the experiment, when the Learner began protesting. A handful of Browning's reserve policemen adamantly refused to kill civilians from the start, while about 20 percent subsequently took measures to be excluded from the massacres.

We may take comfort in the fact that this minority existed. But the very fact that it remained a minority—hovering around 20 percent—cannot but lead to sobering conclusions. The ability to resist even the most blatant evil, it turns out, is not nearly so robust as we might be inclined to believe. One of the most dismal lessons suggested by the Holocaust, and subsequently reinforced by psychological research, is that given the right conditions, an astonishingly large proportion of a human population can willingly participate in monstrous acts.

But what about that 20 percent? From where did they draw their power to resist? What kinds of factors led them down the path of dissent, rebellion, and even active self-sacrifice? Here we can look to the villagers of Le Chambon for illumination.

Three elements seem central to explaining the behavior of the Chambonnais during World War II: the power of their Christian faith; the relative homogeneity and social compactness of the village population; and the spiritual leadership of their ministers. As we saw in chapter 4, the mere fact of being devoutly religious was not—alas—sufficient to guarantee boldly altruistic action during wartime. On the contrary, most European Christians responded to the Holocaust in ways that paralleled the behavior patterns of the general population: a minority of perpetrators, an even smaller minority of rescuers, a majority of passive bystanders. In study after study of rescuers during the Holocaust, the factor of religious conviction has been repeatedly found to constitute a poor predictor of bravery or self-sacrifice on behalf of saving Jews.[20]

Religion clearly played a pivotal role in Le Chambon—but what made all the difference was the radical interpretation of Christianity espoused by pastors Trocmé and Theis. One scholar, René Girard, has aptly referred to it as "disruptive empathy": a combination of ardent solidarity with persecuted people, coupled with a willingness to shatter conventional behavior patterns in the act of reaching out to them.[21] Trocmé and Theis read the words "love thy neighbor" as requiring more than just sending out sweet thoughts from the window of one's house: it meant going out the door, into the turmoil of the world, to perform deeds that blocked the advance of injustice and hatred, actively replacing them with the transformative power of charity. It meant, in short, laying it on the line.

The Chambonnais responded to this vision, partly because they found their pastors' personal example inspiring, and partly because it resonated with their own simple but piercing understanding of Scripture. It is important to realize, however, that they did not all serve the rescue operation in the same way. Some became regular and devoted contributors to the cause;

others took part on a more occasional basis; still others opted not to participate at all, while still sharing in the commitment to maintain secrecy.
Indeed, one of the more striking aspects of the village's story lies precisely
in the fact that nobody ratted; nobody seized a single one of the countless
opportunities for personal gain that betrayal would have offered. The open
secret lived among them over four years of shifting fortunes: their solidarity with one another proved as true as their solidarity with the people they
saved.

This tension between the communal and the personal appears to have
lain at the heart of the villagers' motivation. At one level, a powerful form
of bonding must have taken place in Le Chambon during the war years—
a "unit cohesion" perhaps not dissimilar to that experienced by groups of
fighting men under combat. For the Chambonnais were in combat, too:
they lived at great risk, and their very lives depended on one another, day
after day. When they attended church services on Sundays, listened to the
sermons preached by their ministers, and looked around at the congrega-
tion, they cannot but have felt very keenly the unity of purpose and commitment that bound them together.

At the same time, however, the ultimate roots of their motivation
remained deeply personal in nature. Trocmé and Theis did not impose
their views by force of will, but primarily by their own example. Each villager's choice to join the rescue effort, or to remain more on the sidelines,
was left entirely up to that individual's temperament and conscience—just
as the pastors' own positions reflected decisions taken in private and for
themselves alone. According to Philip Hallie,

> [Trocmé] believed that if you choose to resist evil, and you choose this
> firmly, then ways of carrying out that resistance will open up around you.
> His kind of originality *generated originality* in others. It did not stifle that
> originality, the way a dictator using fear and hypnotic charisma stifles the
> originality of his followers.[22]

In the end, the impulse that motivated the Chambonnais appears to
have reflected a delicate equilibrium between group and individual. It was
an impulse that came from within one's own conscience, as one observed
the example of others around oneself, acting in ways that elicited respect.
It was the impulse of living up to values in which each of them had long
believed, and in this sense it grew out of the fullness of each villager's
personal history. It was the impulse of making real one's own innermost

convictions, and of doing so alongside one's neighbors who were simultaneously doing the same thing. Looking back on it, the historical observer cannot help but reflect: it must have been quite a feeling.

One of Stanley Milgram's subjects who became "disobedient" was a thirty-two-year-old Dutch engineer—a man who had grown up in Europe and had lived through the Second World War as a teenager under Nazi rule. When he got to 255 volts, he pushed his chair back from the shock console and refused to go on.

> MR. RENSALEER: Oh, I can't continue this way; it's a voluntary program, if the man doesn't want to go on with it.
>
> EXPERIMENTER: Please continue.
>
> *(A long pause.)*
>
> MR. RENSALEER: No, I can't continue. I'm sorry.
>
> EXPERIMENTER: The experiment requires that you go on.
>
> MR. RENSALEER: The man, he seems to be getting hurt.
>
> EXPERIMENTER: There is no permanent tissue damage.
>
> MR. RENSALEER: Yes, but I know what shocks do to you. I'm an electrical engineer, and I have had shocks . . . and you do get real shook up by them—especially if you know the next one is coming. I'm sorry.
>
> EXPERIMENTER: It is absolutely essential that you continue.
>
> MR. RENSALEER: Well, I won't—not with the man screaming to get out.
>
> EXPERIMENTER: You have no other choice.
>
> MR. RENSALEER: I *do* have a choice. (*Incredulous and indignant.*) Why don't I have a choice? I came here on my own free will. I thought I could help in a research project. But if I have to hurt somebody to do that, or if I was in his place, too, I wouldn't stay there. I can't continue. I'm very sorry. I think I've gone too far already, probably.[23]

Here was a classic case of "disruptive empathy" at work. Rensaleer's reliance on critical reason to assess the situation and reject the Scientist's assurances; his ability to put himself in the other man's shoes ("I know what shocks do to you"); his appeal to higher moral principles ("If I have to hurt somebody to do that . . ."); his unshakable confidence in his own free will; his willingness to submit his own behavior to stern moral scrutiny ("I think I've gone too far already"); his forceful rupture of the situation's momentum, breaking the façade of normality by crying foul after a certain line had been crossed—all these elements paint a portrait of a highly evolved moral agent, the kind of person we would all presumably hope to be, when a time of testing faced us.

How does one become a person like Rensaleer? And how, conversely, does one degenerate to the monstrous level of Browning's "ordinary men"? Perhaps the most striking conclusion to be drawn from these Holocaust stories lies precisely in this: the citizens of the Plateau Vivarais-Lignon and the men of Reserve Battalion 101 may have appeared indistinguishable to a casual passerby observing them in their civilian lives in the year 1939, but in fact this surface similarity concealed a powerful difference operating at a deeper level. The paths of these two groups of people had already begun to diverge—fundamentally—well before the war began.

The villagers of Le Chambon had been quietly but very deliberately preparing themselves, over years and years, for precisely the kind of moral challenge that the war ultimately presented. Partly through their own initiative, and partly through the leadership of their pastors, they had gradually shaped themselves as moral actors: cultivating the critical skills with which to question external authority; honing their sense of right and wrong through reflection; practicing the translation of abstract ideals into concrete action; experiencing their own power to make choices and to see those choices bear fruit; building the tools of moral judgment, and applying those tools time and again to the scrutiny of their own behavior. They carried out this process through the pursuit of their religion, but it was a highly distinctive religious practice that they undertook: the apparent simplicity of their adherence to the Gospel should not mislead us. Like athletes training for a race to be run at some indeterminate point in the future, they incorporated into the course of their daily lives a systematic effort of ethical and spiritual self-fashioning: unobtrusively, without fuss or fanfare, they built up an exceptionally strong constitution of independent thinking and moral fiber.

Perhaps equally important, they did so not merely as individuals, but acting together, in twos and threes, in Bible study groups, in running the local school and the affairs of the town. Over time, the community that emerged proved as tough and resilient as the single filaments of each villager's character—perhaps even more so, since the example that they posed for one another, and the encouragement they gave one another, undoubtedly strengthened their resolve still further. The rescue operation that took place in Le Chambon between 1940 and 1944 did not "just happen" by accident: it grew rather out of a decades-long process of patient work and preparation.

The men of Reserve Battalion 101 were not without moral resources and background of their own, of course. Some of them (a minority) had regularly attended church in Hamburg and considered themselves Christians; we can be confident that virtually all of them had grown up with the basic moral socialization that children acquire in every human society. Though they obviously did so in a manner that differed drastically from that of the Chambonnais, these men, too, felt compelled to make sense of their world through moral language—to infuse the events around them with a set of cardinal directions that assigned positive or negative value to the deeds that made up their lives. They experienced the values of group loyalty and comradeship in a deep way, for example, and those who broke with the group by refusing to participate in the battalion's atrocities often experienced harsh guilt rather than relief: noncooperation, in their twisted moral world, had become a form of wretched betrayal.

The feeling of connectedness lies at the heart of all moral action. It possesses two dimensions: the element of empathy, through which one says, "That person's experience is a part of my own, and I feel something of what he or she feels"; and the element of accountability, through which one says, "That person's situation, for better or worse, is a part of my own situation. We can change each other's lives, and are therefore responsible to each other." The men of Reserve Battalion 101 certainly felt connected to one another in both these ways; but the task to which they had been assigned required them to sever completely any human bond with the Jewish civilians they encountered on a daily basis. It is fascinating to observe how hard these men had to struggle to achieve such a state of disconnection—and how often they manifestly failed to maintain it. Most of them proved unable to wipe out, to will out of existence, the many-layered process of moral socialization and the elemental moral feelings that they had acquired over the course of their lives. "To harm a helpless child is wrong." This simple notion resonates through virtually every human society, and even Nazi Germany was certainly no exception. Thus, the men of Reserve Battalion 101 could deaden their revulsion through alcohol; they could try to rationalize their inner conflict through elaborate justifications; they could appeal to other ideals ("subhuman race," "patriotic duty") that might somehow redeem what they were doing—but all along one senses the resistance, the inner struggle of these men, as they sought to go ahead with actions that incessantly cried out "wrong, wrong, wrong." Though most of them succeeded in hardening themselves to the task, and eventually became relatively inured to it through sheer routine and repetition, one suspects that, in order to do what they did, they had to continually violate a deep part of themselves.

This is what people usually mean by the term "moral integrity." The shooter who specialized in killing children, for example, explained this fact in moral terms: it salved his conscience somewhat to believe that he was "releasing" those helpless young ones from the suffering of an orphaned life. In his own way he was trying to negotiate a way to live with himself, despite the fact that he was inhabiting two incompatible moral universes at the same time: one in which murdering helpless children was monstrous, and one in which such murder constituted his official duty and the daily practice of his comrades. In this sense, he was a man profoundly divided against himself: he lived in a state of the most extreme moral schizophrenia. One wonders, among other things, what his dreams must have been like.

The villagers of Le Chambon, by contrast, achieved a degree of moral wholeness rarely witnessed in human affairs. What their consciences and long-standing belief system dictated became, to an extraordinary degree, what their deeds bespoke, day after day. Above all, what strikes one in the contrast between these two stories is the sense of rootlessness and confusion—of lost moral moorings—that characterizes the Nazi killers, as compared with the clear sense of orientation that pervaded the Chambonnais. The moral background of the police reservists had sufficed quite well to prepare them for roles as upstanding citizens in peacetime; but when faced with the extreme trial of the Holocaust, most of them simply lacked the internal resources—the habits of mind and heart—with which to assert a dissenting voice. Because their "character" remained shallow and immature, the majority of them succumbed to the powerful pull of "situational factors."

The example of the Chambonnais, and the counterexample of the German police reservists, still reach out to us today, across all the years that have passed: the contrast between them suggests that each of us, in the

end, faces three wholly distinct levels of moral choice. At the most immediate level, we are responsible for the actions we undertake, and for the
consequences they bring into the lives of those around us. But these two
stories reveal a deeper dimension as well: we are responsible for shaping
ourselves over decades of time, as ever more effective moral agents. We
have a choice, not only in how to act at any given moment, but also a
broader choice about the long-term orientation of our life's purpose: do
we, or do we not, undertake the kind of patient, systematic effort at moral
deepening that the Chambonnais had been quietly pursuing well before
World War II began? Do we, or do we not, take responsibility for the sustained struggle that is needed to become a different person from who we
are today: more fully sovereign over our fears, more incisively self-aware,
more sharply attuned to the needs of strangers? Whether or not we ourselves will ever face a trial commensurate with the one confronted by the
Chambonnais, their deeds still present us with this question: do we choose
for ourselves their clarity of purpose?

And finally, the third dimension: in what ways might we undertake to
build around ourselves the kind of moral community that the Chambonnais constructed? Most of us do not live in a tiny mountain hamlet of like-
minded rural folk, and thus the challenge facing us is undoubtedly a quite
different one. But the possibility beckons to us nonetheless, in whatever
our circumstances may be, of creating among our neighbors and friends a
certain kind of Le Chambon within the interstices of the complex society
through which we make our daily way.

The historian Inga Clendinnen, in her book *Reading the Holocaust*, speaks
of the "Gorgon effect" that this event tends to exert upon us all—the sense
that we cannot help but be struck dumb by the stories of what happened,
finding ourselves "turned to stone" before the horror and suffering. And
yet, she argues persuasively, we must struggle to overcome this Gorgon
effect.[24] We owe it to those who were lost to retrace their experiences as
best we can, bearing witness to their loss, and undoing (insofar as this is
possible) the erasure of their identity that the Nazis tried so hard to carry
out. And we owe it to ourselves, Clendinnen argues, to know what happened, to struggle with the "hows" and "whys" of this knowledge, and to
integrate it into who we are. The world around us today—our own global
society—still resonates powerfully with extreme forms of hatred and
dehumanization not at all dissimilar to those that brought the Holocaust
into being: we simply cannot afford not to know.

Living with the knowledge of the Holocaust comes down to two contra-dictory imperatives.[25] On the one hand, there is the irresistible need to wrest something positive from this catastrophe, a sense that all that suffer-ing was not for nothing, a hope that subsequent generations like our own can derive from this event the impetus for personal and societal transfor-mation. "Never again!" we say: we feel impelled to do something in our own lives that acts as a small but real counterweight to what happened.

On the other hand, there is no redeeming the Holocaust. It is not right, at another level, to seek resolution, or meaning, or "lessons," in this crime. It is a hole in history, a place of irreducible and senseless loss, and we do violence to it if we try to overlay it with even the most well-intentioned affirmations. No: we must respect its enduring emptiness.

There is really no way out of this contradiction. We come away from these stories with the image of André Trocmé, Edouard Theis, and the peo-ple of the Plateau Vivarais-Lignon, lingering in our minds. At the same time, we have to accept the fundamental uncertainty about ourselves that these stories will always compel.

Chapter Seven

DECISIONS AT MIDWAY, 1942

Moral Character As a Factor in Battle

> The Japanese Combined Fleet, placing its faith in "quality rather than quantity," had long trained and prepared to defeat a numerically superior enemy. Yet at Midway a stronger Japanese force went down to defeat before a weaker enemy.
>
> —Mitsuo Fuchida,
> leader of Pearl Harbor
> air strike force[1]

> I had a feeling, an intuition perhaps, that we had pushed our luck as far to the westward as was good for us. Accordingly, we turned back to the eastward.
>
> —Admiral Raymond Spruance,
> commander of the U.S. fleet at Midway[2]

The Americans were the underdogs in the Battle of Midway—a position they rarely experienced to such an extreme extent during the combat of World War II. It is true that one can find plenty of other instances in which great bravery and self-sacrifice marked the American waging of war: for example, the embattled and underequipped marines' struggle for Guadalcanal in 1942; the army rangers clawing up the Pointe-du-Hoc on the first day of Overlord; the successful attack against overwhelming odds by Admiral Clifton Sprague's destroyers in the Battle of Leyte Gulf; the defiance of the encircled garrison at Bastogne during the Battle of the Bulge. But in most of these cases (with the exception of Guadalcanal) the American fighting men were not going in as underdogs: when one pans out from the particulars of the tactical situation, one finds massive American superiority in weapons, matériel, and manpower. The valor of the men who

Admiral Raymond A. Spruance (April 1944).

fought those battles was extraordinary; but the historical observer knows that, if those soldiers and sailors had failed in their specific tactical mission, and that particular phase of the combat had been lost, the ultimate outcome of the war would most probably have remained the same.

This cannot be said about Midway. The Americans fought this battle not by choice but because the Japanese forced them to do so, through a deliberately contrived attack that directly threatened Pearl Harbor. The Japanese wanted to flush out the U.S. fleet while they still enjoyed massive naval superiority: their aim was to crush the Americans once and for all, driving them back to the shores of the West Coast. Admiral Chester Nimitz, the commander of Pacific naval forces, knew what a miserable gamble he was taking when he sent out his last remaining carriers to meet the oncoming Japanese fleet, but he also realized that he had precious few choices left open. The Japanese were coming; his own forces were no match for them; retreat was not an option, since the loss of Midway would have severely endangered Hawaii itself; and thus the best he could do was to use what he had in a manner that at least gave his men a chance.

The result was one of the most astounding engagements in the history of warfare—a hair-raising combination of bravery, split-second decisions, extraordinary miscalculations, self-sacrifice, and blind luck. Every major belligerent nation during World War II had its moment in the sun: for the British, fending off the Luftwaffe during September and October 1940; for the Russians, the great surprise encirclement of their enemies at Stalingrad; for the Germans, the brilliant string of victories won by Erwin Rommel in North Africa's desert warfare; for the Japanese, the capture of Singapore by a force half the size of the defending garrison. Midway, for the United States, was such a moment.

This chapter seeks to show that the element of moral character played a pivotal part in determining the battle's outcome. Precisely because the Americans went into this engagement outgunned and outnumbered, facing a seasoned enemy who wielded highly advanced technologies, such purely military factors as weaponry, training, and tactics can only go so far in explaining the ultimate American victory: for on the morning of June 4 it was the Japanese who seemed to be holding most of the cards in these domains. Rather, it is only by taking into account the intangibles of duty, honor, and moral fiber—tracing the roles these elements played at key moments in the fighting—that the Midway story can be adequately understood.[3]

In looking back at World War II, it is easy to forget that the war's outcome remained, well into 1943, a thoroughly dicey and unpredictable affair. Today we think of the United States with its nuclear weapons, of the lopsided military and economic preponderance of the two superpowers in the Cold War era, and we wonder how three relatively small nations, pitted against an alliance of such colossal powers, could seriously threaten to take over large portions of the whole planet. Yet in the middle of 1942, it looked as though Germany and Japan might actually succeed in their plans of conquest.

One observer who was well placed to make a judgment of the situation was General George C. Marshall, the U.S. Army chief of staff. Marshall was one of the truly brilliant military men of the century, and FDR had kept him in Washington so that he could, in effect, oversee the whole global strategy of the American war: he was too precious to send overseas to fight in particular theaters of combat. In the late spring of 1945 Marshall put together a retrospective assessment of the war's long course. Precisely because this rather dour, no-nonsense man was well known for measuring his words carefully in both writing and speech, his choice of language to describe "the black days of 1942" remains striking: "In those hours Germany and Japan came so close to complete domination of the world that we do not yet realize how thin the thread of Allied survival had been stretched."[4]

Was Marshall exaggerating? The very thread of Allied survival, stretched to the breaking point? Let us engage in a brief *tour d'horizon* of the military situation in June 1942, as the Japanese fleet bore down on Midway Island.[5]

In the Atlantic, German submarines were sinking Allied ships by the score, right up to the coast of the United States. Horrified onlookers along the eastern seaboard could clearly see the flames at night of sinking merchant ships. A very real danger loomed that the German submariners' stranglehold might effectively cut off the British Isles from resupply, forcing Churchill's government into capitulation. Churchill later wrote in his memoirs, "The only thing that ever really frightened me during the war was the U-boat peril."[6]

The Mediterranean remained unsafe for Allied ships, since the Axis powers held northern Africa, Greece, Italy, and France. Spain, while nominally neutral, tilted heavily toward the side of the Axis.

Meanwhile, the Nazis had advanced deep into Russian territory, and south into the Caucasus. Their forces had conquered the Balkans and driven the British out of Greece. In northern Africa, Rommel had the British army squeezed with its back against the Suez Canal. Three vast German movements were taking shape on the map: southeastward from the occupied Russian heartland in Belarus and Ukraine; eastward out of the Balkans toward the Volga; and northeastward into the Middle East out of Egypt. If those three arrows should link up, the British would be cut off completely, the Middle East would fall to Germany, and the defeat of Russia would become inevitable.

At the same time, the Japanese were consolidating the gains won during their triumphant run since Pearl Harbor. In January 1942 they had gone overland from Malaya, capturing Singapore, the "Gibraltar of the East." One by one, during the first six months of 1942, they had taken over Europe's and America's East Asian protectorates or colonies: Burma, Malaya, the Dutch East Indies, the Philippines, and French Indochina. They had conquered huge swaths of China as well. Now they were threatening Australia, and they roamed unopposed across the Indian Ocean, poised to move against British India.

By June 1942, in other words, the arrows that General Marshall drew on his world map showed the Germans advancing relentlessly eastward across Russia and the Middle East, and the Japanese advancing westward across China and Southeast Asia toward India: all these enemy forces were moving toward a fateful convergence, connecting with one another. In six months' time, if their successes continued, the Axis powers might well have consolidated their hold over the entire Eurasian landmass, one-sixth of the earth's land surface. The human and material resources they would have controlled, at that point, would have exceeded those of the United States by a significant margin.

In Western Europe, the British stood alone against this tide of aggression: their American allies remained cut off on the other side of the Atlantic, struggling to convert their behemoth economy to war production. The Russians were reeling under the blows of a renewed German onslaught, fighting on three battle fronts to hold a defensive line.

In the Pacific, what stood between the Japanese and their triumph? There was Pearl Harbor, with its minuscule outpost at the island of Midway. And the U.S. Pacific Fleet: four carriers, and what warships had been hurriedly repaired or transferred from other theaters since the December attack. That was it.

Poised to move against them was the Japanese fleet, now far and away the largest and most powerful on earth. The Japanese had battleships like the 71,000-ton *Yamato* and *Musashi*, the biggest and most advanced on the seas; these ships carried eighteen-inch guns that fired shells six feet long, weighing one and a half tons, over a range so long that its gunners had to take into account the curvature of the earth when they aimed them.

They had twenty cruisers while the Americans had only eight; they had sixty destroyers, the Americans fourteen; a total of eleven battleships, while the Americans had none. But most important, the Japanese had six heavy carriers and four light carriers, comprising a naval air force of 650 planes: the largest in the world. Their pilots were highly trained and experienced in combat. Their aircraft were manifestly superior to those of the Americans: more maneuverable, more powerful. No wonder even the most cautious of the Japanese felt flush with victory. They truly seemed unstoppable.

In the Battle of Midway, as in the Battle of the Coral Sea a month earlier, the Japanese and American surface ships never even sighted each other. All the fighting was done by aircraft at a distance of a hundred miles or more—partly by land-based planes flying from Midway, but most decisively by carrier-based dive-bombers, torpedo bombers, and fighters. The historian John Keegan paints a vivid picture of what it was like in 1942 to fly a plane off a carrier. The technology was not quite the same as it is today.

Carrier flying excluded all but the best. The technique of launching and "landing on" was extremely rigorous: at take-off, without catapult, aircraft dipped beneath the bows of the ship and frequently crashed into the sea; at landing pilots were obliged to drive at full power into the arrester wires lest the hook missed contact and they were forced into involuntary take-off, the alternatives being a crash on the flight deck or a probably fatal ditching. Flight away from the ship was quite as perilous as launching and landing. In 1942 there was no airborne radar. The gunner of a "multi-seat" torpedo- or dive-bomber could keep a rough check of bearings headed and distance flown, and so guide his pilot back to the sea area in which they might hope to find the mother ship by eyesight—from high altitude in clear weather. A fighter pilot alone in his aircraft, once out of sight of the mother ship, was lost in infinity and found his way home by guess or good luck. Extreme visual range in the Pacific, from 10,000 feet on a cloudless day, was a hundred miles; but strike missions might carry aircraft 200 miles from the carrier, to the limit of their endurance—and perhaps beyond. If the carrier reversed course, or a pilot was tempted by a target to press on beyond his point of no return, a homing aircraft could exhaust its fuel on the homeward leg and have to ditch into the sea, where its crew in their dinghy would become a dot in an ocean 25 million miles square.[7]

It was under these conditions that the Japanese decided it was time to lure the United States into one final, decisive naval engagement. After extensive debate, their admirals concluded that the U.S. base at Midway Island would do the trick. Midway was just a tiny pair of atolls, lost in the middle of the Pacific, about 1,100 miles to the northwest of Hawaii. Nothing but empty ocean surrounded it for a thousand miles on all sides. But the Americans had built a fortified base there, and they would not want to lose it, because a Japanese takeover of Midway would give their navy a valuable forward base for supporting attacks against Pearl Harbor.

So the Japanese put together their plan. We'll launch a diversionary assault on the Aleutians in the northern Pacific: this will distract and confuse the Americans. Simultaneously we'll send an attack fleet against Midway, followed by a landing force to invade the island. The Americans will rush to defend their base against this surprise attack. Our submarines will lie in wait off Hawaii, taking a heavy toll on the American ships as they move to the defense of their embattled outpost. Once the surviving American ships arrive at Midway, our carriers will be waiting to the northwest, ready to devastate them with their superior force and skills. And beyond the carriers, farther to the west, will lie Admiral Yamamoto's main force itself, with its battleships, ready to mop up what's left after the carriers have done their damage. The American Pacific Fleet will be flushed out from Pearl Harbor and systematically annihilated.

The United States will then be compelled to look very differently on the prospect of a negotiated settlement. They'll have nothing left. The Pacific will be ours.

The only problem with the Japanese plan was that, unbeknownst to them, the Americans had been reading over their shoulders from the start. In great secrecy, code-breakers in Washington and Hawaii had succeeded in penetrating the primary Japanese communications codes: here lay the sole advantage possessed by the United States in the early summer of 1942.[8] While the Japanese thought they would be surprising the Americans with their Midway operation, it was they who would be falling into a carefully prepared trap.

The Japanese had three main codes: MAGIC, which covered diplomatic messages; PURPLE, for cloaking army communications; and finally the dedicated code used by the Japanese navy, known as JN-25. American code-breakers, headed by a man named Joseph Rochefort at Pearl Harbor, had been working night and day to crack the secrets of JN-25, and by May 1942 they had begun to read small fragments of Japanese naval messages with a fairly high degree of reliability.

Rochefort was the quintessential nerd-genius *avant la lettre*—a "tall, thin, pale, and driven man"[9] who padded around the Pearl Harbor naval intelligence center in slippers and a red smoking jacket, who spent weeks at a time holed up in his basement offices poring over arcane problems of linguistics and mathematics. "If you desire to be a really great cryptanalyst," he once observed, "being a little bit nuts helps."[10] He and his team spoke Japanese well; they had rows of the latest IBM machines noisily processing tall stacks of data cards around the clock (3 million cards a month); they ran their own radio interception station to ensure the speediest turnaround time in the deciphering effort; they routinely put in twenty-two-hour days, popping caffeine pills and napping on cots in a corner of the cavernous room known as the Dungeon. A casual observer would see only chaos in the Dungeon, with piles of intercepts, IBM cards, and scribbled papers stacked on sawhorse tables or heaped against walls; but underneath the chaos and the frenzied pace lay the grim concentration of a group of ardent patriots—men who felt personally responsible for the December 7 disaster, and who were determined to get the better of the Japanese the next time around. "An intelligence officer has one job, one task, one mission," Rochefort affirmed: "to tell his commander . . . today what the Japanese are going to do tomorrow."[11]

Starting in late April and early May 1942, Rochefort and his team reached the conclusion that the Japanese were preparing a major attack.

The volume of messages between their ships and bases grew enormously; what fragments the Americans were able to decode suggested the kind of widespread logistical preparation that presaged a large-scale military move. But where and when?

Among the decoded message fragments, the letters "AF" kept recurring. Rochefort and his team knew that this type of two-letter combination usually designated a Pacific base or island: AH, they knew from experience, meant Pearl Harbor, while AG referred to a small atoll in the North Pacific named French Frigate Shoals. AF, Rochefort decided as he pored over the intercepts, most probably meant Midway Island; and gradually putting all the pieces together, he reached his conclusion. Midway would be the target of the impending attack.

But he could not simply go to Admiral Nimitz and say, "I have a strong hunch they're going after Midway." He needed positive confirmation, somehow, that this was indeed what AF meant. On May 19 Rochefort had an idea. Using the secure underwater telephone cable that linked Hawaii with Midway, he instructed the Midway command to transmit, on an open radio channel, a rather peculiar message. The message should state that Midway's water purification equipment had broken down, and could Hawaii urgently send out spare parts and a tanker with drinking water? The Midway officers, whose desalination plant was working just fine, were no doubt perplexed; but they obeyed.

Then Rochefort and his men waited, anxiously monitoring Japanese communications. Two days went by. On May 21, a coded Japanese message came through, reporting back to Tokyo that AF was having trouble with its water equipment.

A sleepless night of further analysis placed the probable date of the Japanese attack as June 3 or 4. Rochefort went to tell Nimitz. Acting on Rochefort's information, Nimitz urgently summoned his carriers back from the South Pacific to Pearl Harbor. The *Hornet* and the *Enterprise* arrived on May 26. The next day the carrier *Yorktown*, which had been badly damaged at the Battle of the Coral Sea, steamed into Honolulu, trailing a long oil slick. Its captain had scheduled a ninety-day period of wide-ranging repairs. Nimitz told him, "You've got seventy-two hours."

On May 27 the admiral assembled his top staff for a final decision on the Midway threat.[12] Some of his officers argued that the risks were simply too great: what if the enemy's Midway move was a feint, and the real target turned out to be Hawaii itself? Though Pearl Harbor possessed sizable defenses of its own, sending all three carrier groups to Midway would leave Hawaii vulnerable. In the end, Nimitz decided that the picture Rochefort painted made sense. He knew he had to concentrate his forces if he wanted to achieve an effective attack. He chose to go for broke.

During the last ten days of May, preparations proceeded on Midway: fighter planes and B-17 bombers flying in, stockpiles of food, fuel, and ordnance off-loaded, soldiers digging in for the attack. On May 26 the main Japanese carrier force sailed from Tokyo Bay, headed to its ambush point northwest of Midway. In command of the carriers was one of the nation's most respected naval officers, Admiral Chuichi Nagumo, the man who had presided over the attack on Pearl Harbor. Overall command of the Midway operation lay in the hands of Fleet Admiral Isoroku Yamamoto, following a couple hundred miles behind in an armada of battleships, cruisers, and destroyers arrayed around his flagship, the *Yamato*.

Two days later, on May 28, Nimitz sent his carriers off to spring his countertrap on the Japanese. The American plan was straightforward: While the Japanese carriers are using their aircraft to attack Midway, we'll swoop in with our own aircraft and surprise them.

The man originally slated to lead the attack was Admiral William "Bull" Halsey, an officer well known as an aggressive, daring warrior, and very popular not just among navy men, but among the broader American population. He had become famous for his cigar-chomping interviews, peppered by ribaldly racist remarks such as "The Japs are losing their grip, even with their tails."[13] But in late May Halsey suddenly developed a serious skin ailment all over his body—a condition so debilitating that he required hospitalization. To his great disappointment, it became clear that there was no way he could participate in this battle. He recommended to Nimitz that one of his close friends and subordinates, Rear Admiral Raymond Spruance, assume command of the carrier *Enterprise* in his place.

Unlike Halsey, Spruance was a virtually unknown figure.[14] The officers with whom he had served—those who knew him well—deeply respected him: they described him as cool, introspective, rigorously fair-minded, intellectual. But Halsey's staff, who would now be serving on the *Enterprise* under Spruance, made no secret of their anxiety. Spruance, they now discovered, had captained many ships throughout his career, but had never before commanded a carrier. Worse still, for Halsey's men, was the question of character: would this man have the guts to lead effectively in battle? Spruance had a reputation for caution, for conservative tactics. Would he have the gumption to do what was necessary? As it turned out, this change of personnel probably saved the Americans in the battle that was to come.

On May 30, the hastily repaired *Yorktown* sailed from Pearl Harbor to join the *Hornet* and *Enterprise*. On the bridge of the *Yorktown* was Admiral Jack Fletcher, the man who would have overall command of the American ships in the coming battle. Spruance remained, at this point, his subordinate.

On June 2 the three American carriers joined up at a predetermined position in the open ocean 325 miles northeast of Midway. Someone on Nimitz's staff, out of superstitiousness or perhaps a grim sense of humor, had named the rendezvous spot Point Luck. Hovering about that point the three ships sent out their reconnaissance patrols and anxiously awaited word of the Japanese carriers.

On June 3 the Japanese diversionary force far to the north began its attack on the Aleutians. Early the same day, U.S. planes based out of Midway finally sighted a large Japanese naval force about seven hundred miles to the northwest. High-altitude B-17 bombers from Midway pelted the Japanese fleet with bombs; not a single ship was hit. Catalina flying boats dropped torpedoes on the advancing Japanese ships: all they did was damage one tanker.

So far the officers on both sides felt as though everything was going according to plan. Nagumo knew that Midway would immediately report the approach of this Japanese fleet; Hawaii would respond by sending out the carrier groups to the defense. As of June 2, a cordon of Japanese submarines had taken position just north of Hawaii, ready to pounce on the American ships as they sortied. What Nagumo and the submarine captains did not know was that the U.S. fleet had already slipped past their position three days before.

During the night of June 3–4, Nagumo's carriers closed in on Midway from the northwest. The U.S. carriers also moved in from the northeast, to a point two hundred miles from Midway. The two forces were converging, as if down the lines of a vast oceanic V anchored by a small atoll at its base.

Just before dawn on June 4, the Japanese First Carrier Striking Force went through its final preparations: four carriers in formation, each surrounded by a flotilla of destroyers and support vessels, the whole fleet making ready to turn into the wind for the launching of planes. The weather looked promising: scattered puffs of cloud, good visibility. On each of the great carriers—*Akagi, Hiryu, Soryu,* and *Kaga*—the pilots went through their final routines: a small glass of cold sake, for good luck in battle; the blare of Klaxons and the call, "All hands to launching stations!"; the final check of instruments.[15] Nagumo had decided he would send off half his planes in the first wave, a total of 108 fighters and bombers. Below, under the flight decks, he would hold in reserve another 108 planes armed with torpedoes: they would be ready to launch if any American ships should show up.

On his flagship, *Akagi*, Nagumo issued the order. The formation of ships turned into the wind, adding that precious margin of airspeed to loft the heavily laden planes as they roared down the decks and out over the waves. One by one, the planes lifted off the heaving ships and climbed up to join their squadrons in the sky above. In half an hour's time they were ready: they turned as one and sped off toward the speck in the ocean two hundred miles away.

They were spotted at 5:34 a.m. by Lieutenant Howard Ady, piloting his Catalina flying boat—a giant, lumbering slug of a plane, but perfect for reconnaissance because of its extremely long range. Ady had left Midway about an hour before, and he now radioed back his visual contact with a large formation of enemy planes on a bearing directly toward Midway. Back on the island, the American pilots scrambled their aircraft and rushed to meet them.

What the Americans unfortunately discovered, at this point, was how pathetically outclassed their land-based aircraft were by the Japanese. Once again, the B-17 bombers flew out and found the Japanese carrier strike force, raining down bombs on the four enemy carriers. Once again, not a single bomb scored a hit. The tactic of high-altitude bombing of ships was turning out to be an abject failure.

But the obsolete American fighters defending Midway fared even worse. They were piloted by brave men, but they proved no match for the Mitsubishi Zeros escorting the Japanese dive-bombers: the Brewster Buffalos and Grumman Wildcats attacked as best they could, but the Zeros cut them to pieces, outmaneuvering them with seemingly effortless ease. Within minutes, twenty-three out of twenty-five American fighter planes had been shot down or severely damaged.

The Japanese planes flew over Midway at will, bombing and strafing; the island's three thousand defenders fought back with anti-aircraft guns. After the Japanese had used up their bombs, they wheeled and headed back to their carriers. On Midway, the defenders surveyed the flames and the wreckage. Twenty-four men had been killed; the fuel dump had been destroyed, along with various hangars and buildings. Adding an ironic touch that no one recognized at the time, the water-processing plant lay in ruins.

The historian Walter Lord gives a grim account of the raid's aftermath:

> The all-clear sounded at 7:15, and Midway began to pick up the pieces. On the Eastern island Colonel Kimes radioed his VMF-221 [squadron] pilots: "Fighters land, refuel by divisions, 5th Division first."
>
> There was no answer. Kimes tried again. Still no answer. After trying several more times he began to understand, and new orders were sent: "All fighters land and reservice."
>
> One by one they straggled in—six altogether. . . . VMF-221 was virtually wiped out. . . .
>
> "It is my belief," Captain Philip White observed in his action report, "that any commander who orders pilots out for combat in [these kinds of planes] should consider the pilot as lost before leaving the ground."[16]

But there was worse to come, for the Japanese flight leader, Joichi Tomonaga, had observed, as he was leaving the scene, that Midway's runways remained serviceable and that its antiaircraft batteries were still very much alive. He concluded that the island was not yet sufficiently softened up for the invasion to proceed. Those B-17 bombers would still pose a threat to any approaching troopships. He radioed Nagumo that a second strike against the island would be required to finish the job.

Back on the *Akagi*, Nagumo pondered the situation. So far things were going perfectly. His fleet had withstood attacks by several waves of Midway's planes, and had not sustained any serious damage. The first strike against the island had wreaked havoc there, while incurring the loss of only about a dozen of his planes. But he agreed with Tomonaga's assessment: those runways, and any remaining American planes, would have to be neutralized before the invasion could proceed.

Nagumo decided that, while his first wave was returning from Midway, he would use the 108 planes still on his carriers to launch a second wave against the island. But these planes were armed with torpedoes. Nagumo ordered the torpedoes to be removed, and bombs to be loaded on them for a renewed strike on Midway. If his deck crews hurried, rearming from torpedoes to bombs would take a little less than an hour. It was now 7:00 a.m.

At 5:34 a.m., Fletcher's and Spruance's radiomen had overheard Lieutenant Ady's report, from his flying boat, of sighting a large formation of Japanese carrier-based planes closing toward Midway. Fletcher gave the order to prepare for attack. All three American carriers would move toward the enemy at full speed, closing the gap to 150 miles. At that distance the American dive-bombers and torpedo bombers would be within range to launch their attack and still have enough fuel to return to their mother ships.

Fletcher's ship, the *Yorktown*, still had its dawn reconnaissance patrol out. Frustratingly, he had no choice but to stay where he was, waiting for the recon planes to return so that they could be landed. He ordered Spruance to start off without him, steaming toward the southwest, and he would catch up as soon as he could. Soon the *Hornet* and *Enterprise* (under Spruance) had left the *Yorktown* behind, over the horizon. Now Spruance and Fletcher could not communicate with each other, because they were maintaining strict radio silence, and could no longer use visual signals.

About an hour later, at 7:02 a.m., spotters on the *Enterprise* reported that a Japanese reconnaissance plane had just passed within visual range. Now Spruance had to make a decision. There was a good chance the Japanese pilot had seen his ships and reported his position. He was about to lose the only advantage he had: the element of surprise.

But the *Enterprise* and *Hornet* were still at extreme range: 170 miles out from the presumed location of the Japanese ships. The pilots would barely be able to make it there and back. Should he launch his planes now? If so, how many? What about the coordinated attack they'd been planning? Should he wait a couple more hours, until he was closer? Should he wait for Fletcher to catch up so he could ask what to do?

In the space of a minute, Spruance made his decision. He gave the order to turn the two carriers eastward into the wind and launch every plane they had: sixty-seven dive-bombers, twenty-nine torpedo planes, twenty fighters. Without the element of surprise, he had concluded, the battle was hopeless.

The planes commenced launching off of *Enterprise* and *Hornet*. Slowly. It felt as though they were taking forever. One by one, they roared off the two carriers' decks and assembled above in the sky, forming up by squadrons. Spruance looked on, acutely aware that his ships going at full speed into the wind were headed in the opposite direction from the Japanese. But he had no choice: it was the only way the overloaded planes could take off at all.

The dive-bombers went first. From their holding patterns above, the pilots looked on anxiously as the takeoffs proceeded down below. They circled, burning gas. 7:30. 7:45. Planes continued to rise slowly off the carriers. If this went on much longer, at this range, the first planes up wouldn't even have enough gas left to sustain their attack.

Spruance, down on the bridge of the *Enterprise,* kept glancing from the deck to the sky above. Finally he made his second major decision of the day. *If we wait for everyone to be airborne, we risk losing half our planes because of insufficient fuel.* He gave the order, which was flashed up to the circling planes by visual signal: "Proceed on mission assigned."[17]

The pilots up above were aghast, in disbelief. Proceed with only half the planes? Break up the coordinated attack? In a carrier-based assault of this sort, the three types of planes were designed to work together, complementing one another. The dive-bombers would distract an enemy's fighters, so that the slow torpedo bombers could make their long, vulnerable attack runs. The fighter planes would defend both the dive-bombers and torpedo bombers. To go in like this, without the advantage of coordinated attack, meant terribly bad odds.

The squadron leader for the *Enterprise* dive-bombers was a man named Wade McClusky: forty years old, a veteran flier, one of the navy's best and most experienced. He knew the situation was not good. They were going in totally disorganized, in separate little groups. He formed up his squadron, then wheeled off across the empty ocean, the expanse below luminous under the morning sun.

Meanwhile, back on the carrier *Akagi,* Admiral Nagumo was having to make some quick decisions of his own. At 7:28 a.m. a reconnaissance plane from one of his cruisers, the *Tone,* reported sighting a large force of enemy ships 170 miles to the east, moving toward the Japanese fleet. Nagumo's first reaction was excitement: *so the Americans were coming after all!*

But he needed to know what kind of ships: the recon pilot, most frustratingly, neglected to specify. Half an hour later, at 8:09, the same reconnaissance plane radioed in a second report: five cruisers, five destroyers. *Excellent,* thought Nagumo. *My planes are almost finished being rearmed with bombs: I'll launch them on a second Midway strike soon. Then I'll retrieve the first wave of Midway attack planes, refuel and rearm them with torpedoes, and go after the oncoming American naval force.*

Ten minutes later, at 8:20, the *Tone* reconnaissance plane reported in once more: "The enemy is accompanied by what appears to be a carrier in a position to the rear of the others."[18]

Nagumo was thunderstruck. If those ships included a carrier, it was already in striking range. He was vulnerable at that very moment to attack by carrier-based planes.

Panicking, Nagumo delivered a new set of orders: his deck crews were to begin changing the armament on all his planes a second time, from bombs back to torpedoes. He was going to use these planes, immediately available here on deck, to attack the oncoming American ships.

So the deck crews on all four of Nagumo's carriers suddenly were scrambling to unload the bombs and replace them once again with torpedoes, laboring and sweating under the wings of the planes, amid a tangle of fuel lines, bombs, ammunition belts, and torpedo racks.

While this was happening, the first Japanese planes started coming back from the attack on Midway. All were low on fuel, and many were damaged from the defenders' fire. Nagumo had no choice but to turn into the wind and commence the laborious process of landing these aircraft.

Admiral Fletcher, meanwhile, had landed his reconnaissance flights on the *Yorktown*, and had hurried to the southwest to catch up with Spruance, launching his own squadrons against the enemy as soon as he got within range.

Here they were, then, all the American planes from all three carriers, flying in their squadrons over the open ocean. But they no longer formed part of a coordinated strike force. They flew in small groups and clusters, fighters, dive-bombers, torpedo bombers, each launched separately, each looking for the enemy on its own.

Some of the squadrons reached their designated target point. They found nothing there, because Nagumo had shifted direction several times, either to maneuver against the land-based attacks from Midway, or to head into the wind to launch or land his planes. So the various squadrons of American aircraft found themselves over empty ocean, with half a tank of fuel, and no target in sight. Some headed for Midway, hoping to be able to land there and refuel and resume the search. Some headed back to their carriers, not wanting to have to ditch in the ocean. Some decided to keep hunting for the Japanese. Each squadron commander made these choices on his own, without knowledge of what the others were doing, without knowledge of where the Japanese were and what *they* were doing. In short: the American force was close to total disorganization.

And it was at this point that American bravery showed itself. Three groups of torpedo bombers, one each from the *Enterprise*, *Hornet*, and

Yorktown, had been separately combing the ocean and looking for Nagumo. They found him, in three successive waves, between 9:30 and 10:15 a.m.

The first in was Torpedo 8, off the *Hornet*, commanded by John Waldron; fifteen slow, outmoded torpedo planes without fighter cover. They had to go in low over the water, very slow and straight, to make their drop run, or the torpedo would not be aimed properly. When they did this, the Zeros would be all over them. They knew this quite well.

All fifteen planes were torn to pieces. Only a few even got a chance to release their torpedoes: all torpedoes missed. Only one man from Torpedo 8 survived.

A little later came a second wave, Torpedo 6 from the *Enterprise*, with fourteen planes. The commander, Gene Lindsey, had heard the Torpedo 8 pilots over their radios as they got chopped to pieces. He led his men in anyway. Ten of the fourteen planes were shot down. Four managed to drop their torpedoes and escape, but all their torpedoes missed as well. Only ten men survived.

The last to arrive was Torpedo 3, from the *Yorktown*, commanded by Lance Massey. This group did have a little air cover from six Wildcat fighters. But outgunned and outnumbered, they, too, were massacred by the swarming Zeros. Ten planes were shot down, only two escaped. Five torpedoes launched: all missed. Three men survived.

Of more than 160 planes launched from the three U.S. carriers, only fifty-four now remained.[19] The others had either been shot down, or had gotten lost, or had ditched in the ocean for lack of fuel, or were returning to the carriers, frustrated and empty-handed.

The last of the surviving American torpedo bombers were flying away, closely pursued by Zeros. From the bridge of the *Akagi*, Admiral Chuichi Nagumo looked on.

He had every reason to feel pleased: his forces had withstood everything the Americans had been able to throw at him. His ships were basically unscathed. His rearmed planes were finally ready to get moving. Now he was going to send off a full, coordinated response to devastate the American carriers: 108 planes of all sorts, working together in carefully orchestrated order. It was 10:25 a.m.

"Launch the attack!" Nagumo ordered. The first planes began lifting off his carriers' decks. At this moment, one of the lookouts behind Admiral Nagumo shouted, "Helldivers!" As the Japanese officers wheeled about and scanned the sky, they saw a small line of planes making their way across, skimming below the clouds, headed obliquely toward them.

It was Wade McClusky, leading the dive-bombers from the *Enterprise*.

Half an hour earlier, McClusky had been flying back and forth across the ocean, desperately trying to guess where the Japanese fleet had gone. One can imagine his thoughts. Fuel running lower and lower. The sickening sense of futility. The chances of making it back to the carriers steadily dwindling. No sign of the enemy.

At one point during those long minutes, an officer on the *Enterprise*, Captain Miles Browning, became unable to contain his frustration as he sensed the American chances fading away. He seized a radio microphone and shouted a command at his meandering squadrons: "Attack! I say again, attack!"

McClusky broke radio silence with a laconic reply: "Wilco, as soon as I find the bastards."[20]

Here is the way McClusky himself later remembered those moments:

Arriving at the estimated point of contact the sea was empty. Not a Jap vessel was in sight. A hurried review of my navigation convinced me that I had not erred. What was wrong?

With the clear visibility it was certain that we hadn't passed them unsighted. Allowing for their maximum advance of 25 knots, I was positive they couldn't be in my left semi-circle, that is, between my position and the island of Midway.

Then they must be in the right semi-circle. Maybe they had changed course easterly or westerly, or, most likely reversed course. To allow for a possible westerly change of course, I decided to fly west for 35 miles, then to turn north-west in the precise reverse of the original Japanese course.

After making this decision, my next concern was just how far could we go. We had climbed, heavily loaded, to a high altitude. I knew the planes following were probably using more gas than I was. So, with another quick calculation, I decided to stay on course 315 degrees until 1000, then turn north-eastwardly before making a final decision to terminate the hunt and return to the ENTERPRISE.

Call it fate, luck or what you may, because at 0955 I spied a lone Jap cruiser scurrying under full power to the north-east. Concluding that she possibly was a liaison ship between the occupation forces and the striking force, I altered my Group's course to that of the cruiser. At 1005 that decision paid dividends.

Peering through my binoculars which were practically glued to my eyes, I saw dead ahead about 35 miles distant the welcome sight of the Jap carrier striking force. They were in what appeared to be a circular disposition with four carriers in the center, well spaced, and an outer screen of six to eight destroyers and inner support ships composed of two battleships and either four or six cruisers.

I then broke radio silence and reported the contact to the ENTERPRISE. Immediately thereafter I gave attack instructions to my group.[21]

What McClusky saw was Japanese ships, all across his field of vision, spread out over the water's surface. And no air cover. No Zeros zooming down through the clouds to intercept his attack. Scarcely daring to believe his good fortune, McClusky formed up his squadron for the bombing run. He divided his planes into two groups, one for the closest carrier, one for the next carrier over.

Down below, Nagumo and his officers looked on, helpless, transfixed. Every one of their Zeros had flown down to near sea level to fend off the successive waves of American torpedo bombers. Now it was too late for those fighters to do anything to stop the diving American planes.

One by one, the highly trained American dive-bomber pilots made their runs. Here is the way one dive-bomber's experience was reimagined by the writer Herman Wouk in his novel *War and Remembrance*. Wouk conducted extensive research on the battle, including many interviews with World War II pilots, so as to present the most accurate description he could.

The fictional pilot's name is Warren Henry. His radioman and gunner in the SBD Dauntless dive-bomber is a man named Cornett.

Yet again, *where was the combat air patrol?* That had been his worry right along, unescorted as they were. This thing so far was an unbelievable cinch. He kept glancing over his shoulders for Zeroes pouncing out of the clouds. There wasn't a sign of them. McClusky and the first few bombers, already on their steep way down far below, one staggered behind the other, weren't even catching any AA. Warren had often pictured and dreamed of attacks on carriers, but never of a walkover like this.

He said into the intercom in high spirits, "Well here we go, I guess, Cornett. All set?"

"Yes, Mr. Henry." Matter-of-fact drawl. "Say, where the heck are the Zeroes, Mr. Henry?"

"Search me. Are you complaining?"

"No sir, Mr. Henry! Just you drop that egg in there, sir."

"Going to try. We'll have the sun on our starboard side. That's where they're likely to show up."

"Okay, Mr. Henry. I've got my eye peeled. Good luck."

Warren pulled the lever of his diving flaps. The perforated metal V opened all along his wings. The airplane mushily slowed. The flattop went out of sight beside the fuselage, under the wing. The nose came up, the plane gave its almost living warning shudder; Warren pushed over, dizzily dropped the nose straight toward the water far, far below, and straightened out in a roller coaster plunge.

And there, by God, was the carrier in his telescopic sight, right over the little wobbling ball. Now if the telescope only wouldn't fog up as they plunged into the warmer air! Visibility through the oily film of the canopy wouldn't be very good.

It was an excellent dive. The danger was always overshooting and standing on your head, when the dive was almost impossible to control, but he was dropping toward the flattop at a beautiful angle, maybe sixty-five, seventy degrees, from almost dead astern, a little to port, perfect. He wasn't sitting on his seat now, but hanging facedown in his straps, the pure dive sensation. He always thought it was like jumping off a high dive board. There was the same headfirst feeling, the same queaziness in gut and balls that you never got over. It was a long way down, almost a whole minute, and he had excellent controls to straighten out slips or wobbles, but this dive was going fine. With a pedal jammed in hard to neutralize the SBD's usual yaw, they were skimming down sweetly, the throttled-back engine purring, the air whiffling noisily on the brakes—and that flight deck was sitting right there in his little lens, not fogging over at all, growing bigger and plainer, with the hardwood decking bright yellow in the sunlight, the big red ball conspicuous in the white oblong forward of the island, the planes crowded aft in a jumble, and minuscule Japs running around them like insects. As his altimeter reeled backwards his ears popped and the plane warmed.

All at once he saw the great white splash of a near miss jump alongside the island; and then a huge fiery explosion ripped the white paint all around the meatball, with a blast of smoke. So there was one hit! He could see two bombers zooming away. His ears ached like hell. He swallowed, and they popped again. Right now that carrier was in trouble; one more good hit could really cream it. Warren was at five thousand feet. Doctrine called for the bomb to drop at about three thousand feet, but he meant to bore down at least to twenty-five hundred. Joyously in control, watching his dials, watching the rapidly expanding deck almost straight below him, he was nerving himself for a split-second decision. He intended to slam the bomb in among those aircraft sitting there in his scope. But if this carrier took yet another hit first, then instead of plastering it again with a precious half-ton bomb, he might still veer over and try to hit the third carrier, far ahead.

But what a target, that mess of airplanes rushing up at him now in the telescope sight, so clear that he could see white numbers on the fuselages, and the little Japs running and gesticulating as he plunged toward them! No other hits yet; *he'd go*. Now his heart was racing, his mouth was parched, and his ears seemed about to burst. He yanked the bomb release, felt the jolt of lightness as the missile flew clear, remembered to keep going to make sure he didn't throw the bomb, and he pulled up.

His body sagged to the seat, his head swam, his stomach seemed to plop against his backbone, the gray mist came and went; he kicked the plane's tail and glanced backward . . . Oh, *CHRIST!*

A sheet of white fire was climbing out of those airplanes, billowing black smoke; and even as he looked, the fire spread and exploded along the deck and arched into the air in beautiful colors, red, yellow, purple, pink, with varicolored smoke towering up into the sky. What a terrific change in a second or two! Debris was flying in every direction, pieces of airplanes, pieces of the deck; whole human bodies tumbling upward like tossed rag dolls; what a horrible unbelievable magnificent sight! The whole wild holocaust of fire and smoke went roaring skyward and streaming astern, for the stricken carrier was still rushing at full speed into the wind.

"Mr. Henry, there's a Zero at eight o'clock angels about one thousand." Cornett on the intercom. "He's making a run for us."

"Roger."[22]

What McClusky and his fellow pilots didn't realize, as they dived, was that they were not the only ones who had hit the jackpot. By a complete coincidence, the dive-bomber squadron from the *Yorktown* had also come upon the scene at exactly the same minute as McClusky's. Their leader, Max Leslie, had approached from a different angle, but he had spotted columns of smoke from a distance of thirty-five miles—the smoke from the burning torpedo bombers and wildly maneuvering Japanese ships. Those columns had led him straight in.

Leslie didn't know that McClusky was approaching simultaneously from a more southerly angle. He just headed for the closest carrier he could find and carried out his attack. Like McClusky, he met with virtually no resistance from any Zeros: the Japanese fighters were all down at sea level, busily mopping up what was left of the American torpedo bombers. Max Leslie and his *Yorktown* dive-bombers had a clear, easy run on the northernmost Japanese carrier; they plastered it with half-ton bombs.

Herman Wouk does the best job of summing up what happened between 10:25 and 10:30 a.m. on June 4, out in the ocean to the northwest of Midway: "It was a perfectly coordinated attack. It was timed almost to the second. It was a freak accident."[23]

Nagumo had made several fatal mistakes. He had overconfidently assumed that a single round of reconnaissance flights would suffice to cover his advance toward Midway; if he had stepped up his patrols on the early morning of June 4, he might have received earlier warning of the American carriers' presence, and could have sent off a powerful attack force against them.[24] Then, as the fragmentary reconnaissance information dribbled in, he had flip-flopped in his decision about arming his planes, using up precious time to change from torpedoes to bombs, then back again to torpedoes. This gave the American aircraft just enough time to find his fleet. Then Nagumo allowed all of his Zeros to come down to sea level during the successive waves of torpedo plane attacks, leaving no one up above to guard the skies over his ships. Finally, he permitted his carrier decks to become a veritable tangle of explosive substances, all wildly spread about in disarray: bombs and torpedoes left aside from the shifting of armaments, fuel hoses running to and fro in all directions, piles of ammunition ready for loading on planes, and the planes themselves, all fueled up and armed. It was not just the dive-bombers' bombs that sank Nagumo's giant carriers. It was also the explosives and flammable materials so conveniently strewn about, in the heat of battle, by the Japanese crews. All that the American dive-bombers had to do was light the fuse on this Japanese powderkeg, and watch the result from a distance.

In five minutes' time, between 10:25 and 10:30 a.m., the whole battle turned for the Americans from a dismal fiasco to one of the greatest victories in the history of naval warfare. The carriers *Akagi*, *Soryu*, and *Kaga* were damaged beyond repair: they all sank or were scuttled in the ensuing hours. Nagumo escaped his sinking ship and reestablished command aboard a cruiser.

But the battle was not yet over.

The fourth Japanese carrier, the *Hiryu*, had been steaming farthest away, and hence escaped the dive-bomber onslaught. At 10:40 she launched an attack squadron of dive-bombers and torpedo bombers, which headed out over the ocean along the same bearing as the returning American planes. They found the carrier *Yorktown* an hour later, and fought through vigorous antiaircraft defenses to deliver several violent hits with bombs and torpedoes. Things looked bad for the *Yorktown*, as fires began spreading.

At 1:00 p.m. Admiral Fletcher was forced to leave the *Yorktown* and go aboard the cruiser *Astoria*. This meant he would no longer be able to control the air battle from a firsthand position aboard an active carrier. Fletcher did the most reasonable thing he could under the circumstances: he transferred command of the fleet to Spruance. From this point on the battle lay in Raymond Spruance's hands.

Aboard the *Enterprise*, Spruance immediately began reassembling planes and crews for a renewed attack. He had McClusky's dive-bombers that had returned safely from their spectacular success; he had other *Enterprise* planes that had made their way back after failing to find the Japanese fleet; and he had many of *Yorktown*'s aircraft, which had lost their landing platform as the fires spread on their mother ship, and had landed on the nearby *Enterprise* instead.

All these planes were now patched together by Spruance into a second-wave strike force: he dispatched them at 3:30 p.m., their target the *Hiryu*. At 5:03 p.m. they found her, and in twenty minutes of coordinated attack succeeded in putting four heavy bombs through her bright yellow flight deck. Huge fires broke out, which the Japanese fought desperately for eight hours. At 2:30 a.m. on June 5 the crew of the *Hiryu* were forced to abandon ship.

Admiral Tamon Yamaguchi, who had commanded the *Hiryu* and *Soryu*, together with the *Hiryu*'s captain, opted to go down with their ship. Their sailors solemnly went through the last rites: raising a toast, ferrying the portrait of the emperor to a nearby destroyer, lowering the Rising Sun flag while buglers played "Kimigayo," the national anthem. An officer asked Captain Tomeo Kaku what to do with the money in the ship's safe. "Leave the money as it is," the captain replied. "We'll need it to cross the River Styx." Yamaguchi overheard the exchange, and smiled. "That's right," he said. "We'll need money for a square meal in hell." A few moments later all the sailors had boarded the last cutter to leave the burning ship.

Yamaguchi's final radio message was directed to the nearby destroyer *Kazagumo:* "Scuttle the *Hiryu* with your torpedoes."[25]

As the first hours after sunset went by on June 4, Admiral Yamamoto, three hundred miles away on the battleship *Yamato,* had been following over the radio the emerging picture of his carrier fleet's destruction. Now the final news was coming in, of fires on the *Hiryu* burning out of control. A fourth carrier lost. His subordinate, Nagumo, had let him down.

But Yamamoto was not one to give up easily. He asked himself, Can we still find a way to retrieve some semblance of a victory from this disaster? He tried to get into the mind of his opponent, figuring out what the Americans' next move would be. Two assumptions guided his reflections: first, the man in charge of the American fleet must be William Halsey; and second, the Americans can have no idea that I am hovering nearby with this fleet of battleships and cruisers.

The first of these assumptions, though of course erroneous, was reasonable: Halsey's illness had been kept a closely guarded secret at Pearl Harbor, and such an experienced and bold commander would have been the natural pick to lead this daring raid against superior Japanese forces. Yamamoto's second assumption was correct: Rochefort's intelligence had only provided Nimitz with a picture of *three* Japanese fleets: the diversion fleet in the Aleutians, the Midway landing force, and the Midway carrier group. No one on the American side had any idea about the existence of a major battle fleet just three hundred miles to the west.

Out of these two assumptions, Yamamoto put together a desperate plan.[26] Halsey was famous among the Japanese for his impetuous aggressiveness in battle tactics. And American naval doctrine always called for a fleet to pursue and destroy its enemy after a successful engagement. This meant that, in all likelihood, those American carriers were even now heading westward through the night, seeking to overtake the fleeing Japanese, positioning themselves to send out their planes the following morning and sink what remained of the enemy fleet.

Yamamoto said to himself: This is where we have a chance of annihilating the Americans. If we engage them at night, in the hours to come, they won't be able to use their carrier-based planes against us. With our battleships and cruisers, we'll advance immediately to meet them, trying to find them while the darkness gives our gunners a decisive advantage. We'll close to within visual range of the American carrier groups, then hit them with our guns and our long lance torpedoes and wipe them out. If we can pull this off, the Battle of Midway will become a net victory for Japan: for despite our terrible losses we will still come out of this with the most powerful navy in the Pacific, while the U.S. fleet will have been reduced to a single carrier. And we will still be able to proceed with the occupation of Midway.

Yamamoto ordered all the ships he could muster among his own fleet and the invasion fleet led by Admiral Nobutake Kondo—a total of nine battleships, eleven cruisers, and thirty-three destroyers—to move eastward at full speed, toward the Americans, to find them in the darkness of the coming night. Kondo's ships, which started from a position closer to the U.S. carriers than Yamamoto's, deliberately spaced themselves along a line seventy-five miles wide as they advanced, so as to cover the broadest possible swath of ocean in the hope of maximizing their chances of a contact.[27]

At about that moment, as night deepened on June 4, Spruance was pondering his next move. He had successfully retrieved aboard the *Enterprise* the planes that had attacked the *Hiryu*. Now he made his third major decision of that long day. Just that morning he had shown himself willing to take a tremendous gamble, hurling all his planes against the Japanese carriers, from the outer limits of viable range, in a bid to maintain the element of surprise. But as darkness enveloped his ships, he decided he was going to take exactly the opposite kind of action. At 7:09 p.m. he ordered the American fleet to stop its pursuit of the Japanese, turn around, and head east. Away from the enemy.

His staff officers were astounded. Spruance was turning away from an easy chance to mop up a wounded foe! Halsey would never have done this, they were thinking.[28]

They begged Spruance to reconsider. He listened to their arguments, but in the end remained unconvinced. He reminded them that they had done considerable damage to the enemy that day, and lacked solid information about what kinds of forces were still out there to the west. He pointed out that their ships would soon be approaching the seven-hundred-mile circle within which they would be vulnerable to air attack by Japanese planes based on Wake Island. Above all, as he later wrote in his battle report to Admiral Nimitz, "I did not feel justified in risking a night encounter with possibly superior enemy forces."[29]

And that was it. Spruance wouldn't be budged. His officers could scarcely conceal their frustration: this man, they believed, was missing a historic chance at total victory.

So the *Enterprise* and *Hornet* battle groups turned around and moved eastward at a comfortable fifteen knots until midnight. Away from the Japanese. Then, toward morning, Spruance ordered them to turn around again and take a holding position off Midway. From here, he reasoned, he could simultaneously defend the island base against any possible renewed attack, while giving his carrier force extra air cover.

Spruance did not know, of course, that Yamamoto was searching for him, waiting to engage him in a night fight with his battleships. But Spruance's caution proved almost clairvoyant. He had sensed that this was a gamble he didn't need to take, so he ignored the pressure from his staff, and ordered a retreat to a strong defensive position.[30]

With this decision, Spruance effectively sealed the victory of June 4 and deprived Yamamoto of his chance for revenge. At 2:55 a.m. on June 5, Yamamoto was forced to admit he'd been outfoxed again. The Americans had not done what he'd hoped and expected, and were nowhere to be found. Reluctantly, he issued the fleet order: "The Midway occupation is canceled." Fearing the possibility of renewed American air attacks after daybreak, he turned his armada of ships around and headed back to the west.

The last sputterings of this far-flung battle went on for a few more days. On June 5, Spruance's planes found some remnants of the Japanese fleet, sinking one cruiser and damaging another. But the bulk of the Japanese force had withdrawn to the west, beyond the reach of carrier-based attack. Then, on the evening of June 5, Yamamoto gave his bold night-attack strategy one last try: he assembled his ships and advanced rapidly eastward across a broad stretch of ocean, hoping to catch the Americans probing westward with their guard down. But Spruance had once again given the order for a nighttime withdrawal to the east. Yamamoto, recognizing the futility of his efforts, finally gave up early on the morning of June 6 and ordered his ships to turn around and head for Japan.

On June 7, a Japanese submarine caught up with the badly damaged *Yorktown*, whose crew, in an extraordinary feat of firefighting, had somehow managed to extinguish the conflagration that engulfed her on June 4. The listing but still seaworthy carrier was being towed back toward Hawaii, escorted by a destroyer, when the sub let loose a salvo of torpedoes, sinking both ships.

Farther north, meanwhile, the Japanese diversionary force invaded several islands in the Aleutians: this was to have almost no consequence for the broader war. (In fact, it ended up harming the Japanese, because in the course of the fight a Japanese Zero crash-landed on a remote island and was seized by American forces; close scrutiny of the captured plane by aircraft experts ultimately resulted in the Grumman Hellcat, specifically designed to outperform the Zero in speed, armament, and maneuverability.)[31]

When the *Enterprise* and *Hornet* returned to Hawaii on June 13, their crews were intrigued to find that the press was trumpeting a major victory at Midway—a victory supposedly won by the *land-based planes* stationed on the island. The army was terribly proud of the job those B-17s had done sinking the Japanese ships by precision bombing from an altitude of twenty thousand feet.

The true nature of the engagement was not known to the public until after the war. Spruance rarely discussed his role in the battle. Once, when complimented on the victory, he simply said: "There were a hundred Raymond Spruances in the Navy. They just happened to pick me to do the job."[32]

Overall, the battle toll went like this:

- *Japanese losses:* four carriers, one cruiser, 322 planes, 3,500 dead, including more than 100 highly trained pilots.
- *American losses:* one carrier, one destroyer, 150 planes, 307 killed.

But the real legacy lay deeper. The Japanese never again regained the initiative in the Pacific War: from this point on they fought a long, bloody, defensive engagement, covering a slow but inexorable retreat. They would never be able to launch this kind of aggressive attack again. They had lost their only remotely plausible chance of forcing the Americans to come to terms.

As we have seen, this battle was a near thing. The final outcome was lopsided, but at several key junctures, in the moment-by-moment unfolding of events, the Japanese narrowly missed achieving a crushing victory. What would have been the consequences had they prevailed?

The conquest of Midway Island in June 1942 would have provided Japan with a major forward base for operations in the eastern Pacific: Hawaii itself might have become isolated and ultimately untenable. The Pacific Fleet might have had to switch its home port back to California. If this had happened, what sort of political pressure would FDR have faced, with his insistence on the "Europe-first" policy? Cities like San Diego, Los Angeles, San Francisco, and Seattle would have been under a clear and present danger. Arguably, the president would have had to reconsider the basic strategy of the United States in the war, rethinking the global allocation of resources.

Indeed, one of the crowning ironies of the Midway victory lay precisely in this: it meant that the Pacific Theater could now afford to remain a secondary priority for the Americans. Instead of having to defend against a direct threat to the continental United States from the Japanese, the bulk of the nation's energies could continue to go toward aiding Britain and Russia against the Nazis. What would have been the consequences, for Britain, for Germany, for the USSR, if the United States had been forced to divert significant resources toward the protection of its own West Coast? No one knows. But the fact is that at Midway, the whole shape of the war lay in the balance.

What does this battle tell us about the nature of warfare's unfolding? In answering this question, five kinds of factors come into play.

1. *Intentions and planning.*

The Battle of Midway represented the culmination of long years of preparation by the men on both sides: arduous training for the pilots, sailors, and officers; the gradual buildup of forces; the devising of strategies and counterstrategies. At one level, for example, the fate of the battle hung on the ability painstakingly acquired by Lieutenant Commander Joseph Rochefort to read the intentions of the other side, giving Nimitz that slim margin of tactical surprise that ultimately made all the difference.

2. *The "fog of war."*

A crucial element often elided in historical accounts of combat is the one singled out by Leo Tolstoy in his novel *War and Peace:* the central role played by bad information—fragmentary, contradictory, misleading, or altogether missing information. Sheer cluelessness pervaded the action at Midway—on both sides. The achievements of both the Japanese and American officers become all the more remarkable when one realizes to what an extent they had to make their decisions in a shadowy, rapidly shifting world of guesses, partial glimpses, inaccurate sightings, rumors, and false alarms.

The Americans miscalculated the location of Nagumo's fleet on the morning of June 4, sending their planes to the wrong coordinates. The Japanese were convinced they had sunk two carriers after their attack on the *Yorktown.* One Midway-based B-17 crew reported hitting a Japanese cruiser with so many bombs that it sank in less than a minute: the reality, as it turned out, was that they had bombed an American sub, which had crash-dived to save itself. Again and again, in the eyes of the edgy reconnaissance pilots, destroyers became battleships, cruisers multiplied as if by magic, entire fleets appeared and disappeared here and there on the vastness of the ocean.

Admiral Yamamoto, on board the *Yamato*, still remained so thoroughly out of touch—as late as 7:15 p.m. on June 4—that he issued the following order: "The enemy fleet has been practically destroyed and is retiring eastward. Combined Fleet units in the vicinity are preparing to pursue the remnants of the enemy force and, at the same time, to occupy Midway."[33] Meanwhile, the Americans had no idea about the presence of Yamamoto's Main Fleet: they only discovered this many months later, as intelligence analysts pieced together a retrospective picture of the battle's unfolding. One can only imagine the frisson they must have felt, as the realization dawned that a large Japanese battle fleet had been cruising just over the horizon the whole time.

3. *Avoidable errors and miscalculations.*

The mistakes made by the Americans almost cost them the battle: on the morning of June 4, Fletcher and Spruance should not have found themselves in the position of launching their air strikes in total disarray, sending their planes against the Japanese in a desperate, uncoordinated gamble. But the mistakes made by Nagumo and his staff proved more costly still: neglecting the crucial element of reconnaissance, shifting indecisively between bombs and torpedoes, and leaving themselves unforgivably open to attack from the sky.

4. *Luck: the factor of pure chance.*

It was blind luck that the three waves of American torpedo bombers, coming independently from three different carriers, found Nagumo's ships in the evenly spaced sequence that they did. The result was that they gradually brought all the defending Zeros to sea level, keeping them busy down there for almost an hour, from 9:30 to 10:25 a.m. This had the unintended effect of clearing the skies for the American dive-bomber squadrons. It was supposed to go the other way around: standard practice called for the dive-bombers to provide the diversion, so that the more powerful explosives of the torpedoes could do their job. But it went this way instead.

It was blind luck that Wade McClusky spotted that solitary Japanese warship heading northeast at 9:55 a.m., pointing him conveniently in the exact direction of Nagumo's carriers. It was blind luck that brought McClusky's *Enterprise* dive-bombers into position at precisely 10:25 a.m., the very moment when the Japanese carriers were totally vulnerable, and just minutes before those carriers could launch their own attack wave.

It was blind luck that brought Max Leslie's *Yorktown* dive-bombers into position at exactly the same time as McClusky's, even though Leslie was not in contact with McClusky, was coming from a different direction, and had been following a completely different search pattern.

It was blind luck that Halsey got sick in late May and had to be replaced by Spruance. It was blind luck that the *Yorktown* got hit when it did, causing Fletcher to shift command of the fleet to Spruance when he did.

5. *Moral character.*

At three pivotal moments in the battle, the outcome depended less on purely military factors than it did on the moral fiber of the fighting men. As we seek to understand why the Americans ultimately prevailed in this engagement, we can discern three distinct aspects of greatness in the way they went about pursuing their goal.

The first might be described as steadfastness: the commitment to continue pursuing a worthy course of action, even when prudence—the rational calculus of probabilities—clearly dictated otherwise. Many of the American fliers concluded, between 9:00 and 10:00 a.m., that it was time to turn back: this was a perfectly honorable decision, given the realities of dwindling fuel and the elusiveness of the Japanese fleet. They headed for Midway or their mother ships, eager to refuel and resume the search. But some squadron leaders decided to stretch the probabilities beyond the breaking point. It was not luck that made McClusky choose to keep flying his search pattern that morning, knowing full well that he and his men might have to ditch in the ocean, or that made Max Leslie hang in there when others were giving up; both these men kept cool, logical, level-headed, assessing the possibilities with precision, under the most extreme pressure.

A second crucial element consisted in the willingness for self-sacrifice. It was not luck that made the fliers of Torpedo 8, Torpedo 6, and Torpedo 3 swing their planes into position and head into a hail of attacking Zeros and antiaircraft fire, knowing that this was most probably death, the moment of their death, into which they were throwing themselves. Their duty was to deliver torpedoes against the enemy's ships, and though they could see the terrible odds, they no doubt told themselves, Some of us may yet make it through. It was a task that could only be accomplished by the squadron acting in concert: the success of one or two planes would suffice to fulfill the mission for all. These were odds that the men could accept: they willingly gave over their individual fates for the sake of reaching the collective goal. The final poignant irony, of course, is that their deed succeeded beyond anything they might have dared to hope. Not just a few torpedo hits but a veritable catastrophe for the enemy resulted from their squadrons' sacrifice.

And third, the moral element of leadership. If William Halsey had been in charge of the *Enterprise* on the night of June 4, what would he have done? It is quite possible that the doctrine of hot pursuit—the tantalizing prospect of an even more glorious victory—would have run the *Enterprise* and *Hornet* straight into the overwhelming firepower of the advancing Japanese surface fleets.

It was not luck that made Rear Admiral Raymond Spruance refuse to take this course—made him stand his ground that night, look into the eyes of his staff officers, and say, "We have done just about all the damage we are going to do. Let's get out of here."[34] That took a very rare kind of courage. To know that you are being compared by everyone around you with another, more popular leader, and still retain the ability to think for yourself. To choose caution when you are keenly aware that this would not be the other fellow's choice. To know that, in the eyes of many, you will appear as a lesser man, but nevertheless to go ahead and do what you have concluded is the sensible thing.

Today, Spruance is widely described quite simply as "the most brilliant fleet commander of World War II."[35] The retrospective judgment of history, at some level, is easy. We know that Spruance was right. But that night of June 4, 1942, facing down his staff on the bridge of the *Enterprise*, Spruance did not know what we know.

He was alone.

Chapter Eight

TYRANNY TRIUMPHANT
The Moral Awkwardness of the Alliance with Stalin

> If we see that Germany is winning, we should help the Russians, and if
> Russia is winning, we should help the Germans, and that way let them
> kill as many as possible—although I don't want to see Hitler victorious
> in any circumstances.
>
> —Senator Harry Truman, June 1941[1]

Six months after Senator Truman made this remarkably candid (and cold-blooded) statement, the Russians had of course become America's allies. No doubt this off-the-cuff remark—reported in the *New York Times* on June 24, 1941—ultimately came to prove embarrassing, particularly in 1945 when Truman became vice president and then president. But Truman did have a point: the fact remained that Great Britain and the United States only succeeded in beating down the evils of Nazism through an alliance, shoulder to shoulder, with a regime that was in many ways equally as vicious as Hitler's. This simple fact often gets lost, somehow, amid the celebration of the great triumph over the Germans and Japanese. Here, for example, is the way the historian Stephen Ambrose closes his best-selling book *Citizen Soldiers: The U.S. Army from the Normandy Beaches to the Bulge to the Surrender of Germany:*

> At the core, the American citizen soldiers knew the difference between right
> and wrong, and they didn't want to live in a world in which wrong prevailed.
> So they fought, and won, and we all of us, living and yet to be born, must be
> forever profoundly grateful.[2]

*The signing of the Nazi-Soviet Pact, Moscow (August 23, 1939). Soviet foreign
minister Vyacheslav Molotov is seated at center. Behind him stand the
German foreign minister, Joachim von Ribbentrop, and Joseph Stalin.
A photo of Lenin adorns the wall above.*

The impression one gets here is that *because* the citizen soldiers (good
guys) beat the bad guys (Nazis), then wrong (general badness) did *not* prevail. This is misleading in two ways. First, the overwhelming bulk of the
killing of Nazis was not done by the citizen soldiers at all, but rather by the
soldiers of the Red Army: the ratio is about four German soldiers killed
by the Russians for every one killed by the British and Americans. And
second, the triumphant powers at the end of World War II included one of

the most ruthless, pathologically murderous regimes in the history of humankind: our Soviet allies. Badness was actually having a very good day on May 8, 1945.

My uncle, Demaree Bess, was a correspondent for the *Saturday Evening Post*, covering the inaugural meeting of the United Nations in San Francisco in July 1945. On July 7 he wrote a piece that more soberly reflected the realities facing the postwar world:

> The war in Europe was not fought against totalitarianism, because totalitarian states were engaged on both sides. . . . Totalitarianism, far from being wiped out by our victory, has emerged stronger than ever. We can be grateful that this was not a war between totalitarian states and western democracies, because if it had been such a war, then the outcome might have been quite different.
>
> What Americans should understand now, if we really want peace to follow this war, is that the central problem of the whole postwar world is to figure out how totalitarianism and parliamentary democracy can get along peaceably together in the same world.[3]

Here lay prefigured the long struggle of the Cold War—a conflict that some historians consider inevitable precisely because of the unmitigated ruthlessness of Stalin and his regime. That complicated tangle of a story is not our topic here: but my uncle was squarely confronting one of the more uncomfortable facts about World War II. The Russian people had shown a heroism and self-sacrifice in this war that boggled the mind; but they were led by a government whose catalogue of crimes was extraordinarily heinous, even by the standards of the twentieth century. We won World War II partly through our own courage and self-sacrifice, and partly through the hammerblows struck by our extremely powerful, and extremely nasty, ally.

It was in the east that Hitler committed the preponderance of his forces. From June 1941 until the war's denouement in 1945, at least 55 percent (and usually more) of the Wehrmacht's total resources were continuously engaged on the Eastern Front.[4] It was also in the east that Germany got bled to death. Seventy-nine percent of its military casualties during the war were incurred on the Eastern Front, in the fight against the Soviet Union.[5]

The scale of the conflict was colossal—to the point that we have a hard time grasping it. The battle front stretched over 1,900 miles, longer than the diagonal distance from Fargo, North Dakota, to Miami. German troops penetrated a thousand miles into Soviet territory, which is equivalent to the distance from California to Kansas.[6] German and Russian supply lines feeding these fronts extended across four time zones.

In the battles themselves, human lives in the hundreds of thousands were tossed around like dust motes in a gale: 300,000 surrendering here, 200,000 killed there, half a million brought in on the right flank, 700,000 thrown into the fray on the central front. In the Battle of Kursk (July 1943), a total of 3.1 million German and Russian men, 43,000 artillery guns, and 6,600 tanks slammed into each other on the Russian plains.[7] The German-Soviet conflict was like an Okinawa played out on a continental scale—over four *years* rather than four months. On and on it raged, this cataclysm of violence between two titans of twentieth-century military force: violence of bullets, bombs, rockets, and high-explosive shells, violence of hand-to-hand combat, personal and brutal.

To lose sight of all this is to lose sight of one of the defining features of the Second World War. And yet, the conflict on the Eastern Front remains strangely muted in the awareness of most Americans and Western Europeans—like the distant rumble of an unseen thunderstorm over the horizon. The majority of popular histories and mass-audience movies about World War II continue to focus overwhelmingly on the battles in Western Europe, Asia, or Africa, while the tectonic clash on the Eastern Front gets relatively short shrift. There is something perversely lopsided about this—as if a crowd of onlookers were to gather anxiously around an automobile collision, while paying no attention, just behind them, to the flaming head-on wreck of two eighteen-wheel tractor-trailers.

Part of the reason, of course, lies in the natural tendency of the English-speaking peoples to focus on "our" war—the one in which our own boys gave their lives. The defeat of Japan was an overwhelmingly American affair; the war in Europe remains, from an Anglo-American perspective, primarily about northern Africa, Italy, France, and the breaching of Hitler's West Wall. It is also hard to root for the Russians, to identify with their struggle, because they themselves have shrouded their war experience under a veil of official secrecy. During the conflict itself, they maintained an attitude of hostile suspicion toward their allies, refusing to share even the most basic and tactically vital military information; after 1945, they quickly became the new enemy during the long years of the Cold War, and it was not fashionable among Westerners to admit what a pivotal role they had played in the defeat of fascism. Soviet archives remained hermetically sealed until the 1990s, while the regime perpetuated a blandly heroic, cartoonlike mythology about the "Great Patriotic War," deliberately playing down the human dimensions of the conflict.

Nevertheless, despite these distortions of perspective, the incontrovertible fact remains: it was the Russians who broke the back of the German army. They first absorbed and then stopped the German onslaught into their country. They rebuilt their factories and war production. They produced excellent tanks and artillery faster than any other nation, including the United States. Their men died by the millions; yet their comrades kept on fighting. The number of Russian soldiers who died in the Battle of Stalingrad exceeded the number of U.S. soldiers killed in the entire war. Many Germans remarked on this in their diaries: the amazing willingness of these Russians to fight to the death. Russian soldiers and civilians, men and women, fought with the desperation and savagery of cornered animals—but they fought also with increasing skill as the months ground by, taking advantage of German mistakes, biding their time, marshaling their strength, then hammering the Germans hard, repeatedly, implacably.

Just as the Americans turned the tide of war in the Pacific with the Battle of Midway, it was the Russians who turned the tide of war in Europe, in the Battle of Stalingrad. After the German surrender at Stalingrad in February 1943, the names of the epic battles pile up: Minsk, Kursk, Bryansk, Kharkov, Leningrad. The Russians had built up the greatest war machine on land in the world. They had superb tanks, rocket launchers, and artillery pieces, thousands and tens of thousands of them: in July and August 1943—two months' time—they pounded the Germans with 42 million artillery rounds.[8] The Red Army by this time had huge reserves of well-trained and well-equipped men, grim and efficient fighters. Their leaders had developed excellent battlefield tactics, overseen by a whole new group of ruthless and innovative generals: men like Georgi Zhukov, the most famous of Soviet military men, but also others like Rokossovsky, Konev, Vatutin, Vasilevsky, Timoshenko, and Chuikov. "By 1944," conclude the military historians David Glantz and Jonathan House,

> the typical Soviet offensive was preceded by careful planning and deception measures, designed to concentrate forces at the designated breakthrough point. The attack began with a wave of reconnaissance battalions that infiltrated the German defenses and seized key positions, thereby rendering the rest of the German positions untenable. This infiltration was accompanied or followed by massive, carefully orchestrated air and artillery offensives.

When the whirlwinds of artillery fire shifted from the front lines toward the German rear areas, infantry, heavy armor, and engineers conducted the conventional assault to eliminate the remaining centers of German resistance. As quickly as possible, senior Soviet commanders committed their mobile forces through the resulting gaps. . . . These highly mobile, combined-arms groups of 800 to 2,000 soldiers avoided pitched battle whenever possible, bypassing German defenders in order to establish large encirclements and seize the bridgeheads for the next offensive.[9]

Starting in 1943, and even more during 1944, the Russians were doing to the Germans precisely what the Germans had become famous for achieving in 1940 and 1941: bringing to bear a confident, methodical, and shrewd application of military force, in a tactically flexible sequence of dismembering attack—and all on a gigantic scale, backed up by overwhelming reserves. The Red Army had become a master of land warfare.

By June 1944, the time of D-Day in the west, the Germans in Russia had been in retreat for over a year. It was a slow, bitterly fought retreat—a disciplined withdrawal, punctuated by fierce counterattacks. But as we look back on it now, the overall pattern is clear: through 1943, 1944, 1945, what we see on the Eastern Front can only be viewed as a gradual disintegration of German power. They were slowly being ground to bits by an increasingly stronger foe.

To say this—to acknowledge that the Second World War's strategic fulcrum lay squarely on the Eastern Front—is by no means to detract from the indispensable role played by the United States and Britain (and the other Allies) in the defeat of Nazi Germany. The strategic bombing campaign against the German heartland, the antisubmarine war in the Atlantic, the combat in North Africa, Italy, and northwestern Europe: these were all crucial to the ultimate Allied success. They absorbed large quantities of German resources and manpower, keeping them spread much thinner than they would have wanted. In the final campaign, during the winter of 1944–1945, Hitler threw major forces into the defense of his Western Front, compelling the Allies to fight and win the terrible Battle of the Bulge. All this played a key part in shaping the war.

Nor must we underestimate the role played by American and British aid to the Soviets, particularly early on, in 1942, when the Russians were on the brink of collapse: the Anglo-Americans diverted precious resources to the Soviet Union in a bid to keep the Russians alive, to give them a chance to recover and regroup. None of this should be forgotten, in our assessment of the big picture.

Nevertheless, if we want a good sense of where things stood in the overall balance of forces bearing down on Nazi Germany, we need only consider for a moment *why* the Anglo-Americans launched the D-Day invasion of Normandy in June 1944. They did it because they felt they had no choice. It was beginning to look as though the Russians might crush the Germans on their own, if the Americans and British didn't jump in from the west. In June 1944, the Red Army, advancing from the east, stood within five hundred miles of Berlin.

This is a point worth dwelling on for a moment. An amphibious assault like Operation Overlord is an inherently risky endeavor, in which the odds heavily favor the defenders. This was precisely why Hitler in 1940 had finally shied away from Operation Sealion, the cross-Channel invasion of Britain. He knew his troops and ships would get chopped to pieces by the RAF. Why, then, did the Allies insist on attacking in exactly this precarious way, across the Channel into northern France, in June 1944? The reason was quite simple. To fight their way all the way up the Italian peninsula, into Austria and France from the south, would have taken well into 1945. The Alps and other mountain ranges provided the Germans with countless natural features to use to their own defensive advantage.

Churchill and FDR had been looking on with increasing nervousness as Stalin's Red Army blasted its way westward during the twelve months following Stalingrad, advancing like an armored steamroller, mile after mile, day after day. By the time the Anglo-American forces would have finally made their way up to Germany from the southern approach, struggling laboriously through the mountains of Italy, Austria, and southern France, the Russians might already have arrived not just at Berlin, but maybe at Amsterdam and Paris. All of northwestern Europe would be under the occupation of the Red Army.

This was clearly unacceptable to FDR and Churchill. To have the Russians liberate all of northwestern Europe would mean the communists would exert huge postwar influence there—a politically disastrous outcome. So the British and Americans went for the attack across the Channel, directly into the heart of Hitler's Festung Europa. It was, in a very real sense, a race—an undeclared race, because the two competitors were ostensibly allies, fighting on the same side. But beneath the surface, no one had any illusions: this was a high-stakes contest to defeat the Germans and liberate as much European territory with one's own armies as possible.

Five main factors contributed to the Soviet Union's survival and ultimate victory:

1. *Industrial reconstruction.*

Forty percent of the Soviet population and three-quarters of Soviet productive capacity had lain in the western regions taken over by the Germans in 1941. The Soviets retreated, scorching the earth as they went, packing onto trains anything that could be dismantled, unbolted, pried loose. They moved everything into new industrial centers east of the Urals and rebuilt their factories beyond the reach of the enemy—some 1,300 new factories, a wave of makeshift industrialization conducted at breakneck speed under desperate conditions, with survival itself at stake.

2. *Patriotism.*

Stalin deemphasized communist ideology during the war, stressing instead the defense of the Russian Motherland. World War II became the "Great Patriotic War"—with Soviet propaganda harking back unabashedly to the defeat of Napoleon 150 years before. Here the Germans helped out, by systematically massacring and starving the Russian people in the territory they occupied. Many Russians in 1941 hated Stalin and communism, and might well have switched to the German side if the advancing Teutons had been shrewd enough to assume the mantle of anti-communist liberators, promising freedom and prosperity in a postwar *Pax Germanica.* But the cruelty of the Nazi occupation turned such people into devoted patriots. Most Russians genuinely believed they were fighting for their lives— and in this belief they were almost certainly right.

3. *New talent.*

After the decimation of the Red Army leadership in the purges of the 1930s, the future of the Soviet military looked grim indeed. But Stalin quickly changed his tune when war broke out in the west: his fear of being ousted by an internal military coup gave way to the more pressing (and realistic) fear of foreign invasion, and he began systematically cultivating a new generation of military leaders. Georgi Zhukov rose from colonel to marshal in three years.

4. *Lend-Lease.*

Half of American Lend-Lease supplies during the war went to Great Britain; about one-quarter went to the Russians—$9.5 billion worth out of a total of $43 billion. The Americans sent shoes, food, aircraft, weapons, ammunition—and 200,000 excellent Studebaker trucks. Most of these materials came through three long and precarious supply routes: over the

Arctic Circle, and then south through the port of Murmansk; up through Iran in the south; or across the North Pacific, into Siberia.

All totaled, approximately 7 percent of Soviet fighting matériel during the war came from outside aid provided by the United States and Britain.[10] The rest was produced in Soviet factories working without respite from 1941 on. Seven percent might not sound like much, but it was the timing of the aid that made the difference: during the winter of 1941–1942, and the summer battles of 1942—when the Soviets were still struggling to get their newly transplanted factories up and running—the American supplies and weaponry provided an important lifeline to the Russians.

5. German errors.

Hitler judged that the Soviet government would quickly collapse under attack. He was wrong. After the war, his generals held that the führer made his biggest mistake when he diverted forces southward from the Moscow front in July 1941, and again in 1942, in an effort to seize the oil and grain areas of southern Russia. This realignment allowed Zhukov to organize the defense of Moscow during the grim autumn of 1941, holding off the Germans until winter, when the Red Army had the advantage.[11] Needless to say, the führer's adamant refusal late in 1942 to allow a tactical withdrawal from Stalingrad, as the German Sixth Army there faced impending encirclement, does not rank high in the annals of military astuteness either.

Leon Trotsky, the creator of the Red Army during the civil war of 1917–1921, was forced into exile by Stalin in 1929; he never tired of repeating his passionately held belief that Stalin had betrayed the revolution, hijacking the Soviet state and systematically destroying the social edifice that Lenin had so painstakingly built. Stalin's USSR, for Trotsky, represented a pathological degeneration of communism's ideals—a monstrous inversion of the humane values that had animated the communist movement since its inception in the mid-nineteenth century. Stalin, annoyed by Trotsky's rants, dispatched an agent to Mexico City in 1940 to find the old Bolshevik and bash his head to bits with an ice pick.

Historians still debate intensely over the causes of the Stalinist phenomenon.[12] Were the essential features of this brutal regime already lying latent in the heart of communist ideology, because that ideology sanctioned deception and ruthless force in the name of "building socialism"? Or was socialism's promise truly richer and more humane, as Trotsky had believed, and the Stalinist tyranny merely the result of a historical accident—the wrecking of a noble social experiment by the machinations of a single horrible man? Whichever side one inclines toward in this debate—and both possess significant elements of validity—the fact remains that the USSR under Stalin became a truly nightmarish state, both for its own citizens and for its hapless neighbors. On a scale of historical nastiness, it easily holds its own with Nazi Germany and with any number of the other abominations that humans have produced over the past few millennia.

In the early 1930s, Stalin decided to push through the collectivization of Soviet agriculture, and unleashed a two-year killing spree in which millions of Russians perished, either through state-ordered murder, imprisonment in the Gulag, or starvation in the devastated countryside. He marked the second half of the decade by launching several waves of terror purges through Soviet society, ordering the show trial and summary execution of his old Bolshevik comrades, large portions of the Communist Party leadership, and much of the officer corps of the Red Army. Soviet citizens lived in a perpetual agony of fear of the NKVD (secret police) and the all too familiar process of arrest, interrogation, and disappearance. Thousands upon thousands of devoted communists suffered this fate—arrested and liquidated for reasons neither they nor their families ever discovered.

As war approached, Stalin made a marriage of convenience with his archenemy, Adolf Hitler. Any Soviet citizen foolish enough to mention to a neighbor that this perfidious alliance contradicted every tenet of communist ideals was in danger of disappearance. Sometime during the spring of 1940, after Soviet forces had taken over the eastern half of Poland, Stalin quietly ordered the murder of some four thousand captured Polish military officers: they were dispatched one by one by NKVD troops, with a bullet to the back of the head, their bodies stacked in shallow graves under the trees of the Katyn Forest, near Smolensk. An even larger number of prominent Polish civilians—somewhere on the order of ten thousand—were also killed in this manner, their bodies dumped at various sites in the Russian countryside. The reason? Stalin planned to impose Soviet-style rule in Poland, and he wanted no trouble from these well-educated Polish patriots, many of whom would have ardently resisted the subjugation of their country by the Russians.[13]

Four years later, in August 1944, the Red Army had beaten the Germans back as far westward as the Vistula River—on the very edge of Warsaw, where the Germans had established their occupation government over Poland. Inside the city, on August 1, Polish resistance fighters launched an insurrection against the German garrison, aiming to take part in the liberation of their city. Stalin regarded the Polish uprising uneasily: did these Poles, many of whom openly admitted their alignment with the

West rather than the USSR, really think he would allow them to run their own country? He ordered the Red Army to stop at the Vistula, just short of Warsaw, claiming that logistical problems temporarily prevented any further advance. For sixty-six days the Red Army camped by the Vistula, silently standing by while the Germans rushed in reinforcements and methodically went about massacring 55,000 insurgent Poles inside Warsaw. Stalin was letting the Germans do his dirty work of killing large numbers of Polish patriots. When every last remnant of Polish resistance had been wiped out, the Red Army's logistical problems mysteriously cleared up, and Soviet forces advanced once again, driving the Germans out of Warsaw.

Recent scholarship by military historians has clarified much of the controversy that long surrounded this awful episode. On the one hand, it is now widely acknowledged that Soviet forces had reached Warsaw after a long, aggressive drive, and truly needed time to consolidate their position, bring in reinforcements, and make badly needed repairs to their equipment. Thus, the Polish Home Army's choice of August 1 for launching its insurrection against the Germans was undoubtedly premature: had the Poles waited another five weeks, the Russians would have been much better positioned to come to their assistance. On the other hand, the preponderance of evidence suggests that—regardless of the timing—the Russians would still not have done so. When Soviet forces had fully recovered a state of preparedness for advance and attack, they did so by moving across the Bug and Narew rivers, instead of coming to the aid of the struggling freedom fighters in Warsaw. "The intent," according to the historians David Glantz and Jonathan House, "was to gain starting points to facilitate future operations rather than to help the Polish insurgents in the short run."[14] Still more telling was Stalin's adamant refusal to allow American planes access to nearby Soviet airfields—which the Americans wanted to use as bases for dropping desperately needed supplies to the Warsaw insurgents. Stalin delayed granting this permission until mid-September, when it was clear that the Poles no longer held a sufficiently large section of the city for the dropping of supplies from the air. "It was politically convenient [for Stalin]," conclude Glantz and House, "to have the Germans and Poles kill each other off."[15]

As the Red Army advanced into Germany, its soldiers exacted a fearsome revenge for the myriad cruelties that the German invaders had visited on the Russian people. Hundreds of thousands of fleeing German women and children were massacred, or allowed to starve to death, as the tide of fighting moved westward. Russian soldiers looted freely, killed civilians with impunity, and raped or gang-raped more than 2 million German women aged between ten and eighty.[16] They also raped—it should be underscored—thousands of Russian women and girls whom they found as they liberated German POW camps. "By the time the Russians reached Berlin," observes the historian Antony Beevor, "soldiers were regarding women almost as carnal booty; they felt because they were liberating Europe they could behave as they pleased."[17]

But there is another dimension of Soviet wartime behavior that proves even harder to fathom: the systematic and seemingly limitless cruelty shown by Stalin's government toward its own people—even as those citizens defended their country. The Red Army continually terrorized its own soldiers, demanding total obedience and self-sacrifice from them at all times. Anyone who fell short was quite simply branded a traitor and shot—either by his own military superiors, or, most often, by special corps of the NKVD who shadowed Soviet soldiers' every movement.

Historical accounts of the experiences of Russian soldiers and civilians during the war, such as Alan Clark's *Barbarossa* or Antony Beevor's *Stalingrad*, all describe this recurrent element of ruthlessness—the utter disregard that seems to have prevailed among many in the Soviet military and political leadership for the lives of their own people.[18] When Russian infantry charged into battle shouting their war cry—Urrah! Urrah!— behind them would silently advance a detachment of NKVD troops, ready to machine-gun anyone who lagged behind. The stories accumulate: Russian children shot by the NKVD for begging bread from the Germans. Russian women shot for sleeping with German soldiers in exchange for scraps of food. Injured Russian soldiers, regularly accused of self-inflicted wounds, and executed on the spot. Russians who escaped from German prisoner-of-war camps, returning to their own lines to rejoin the fight— met by grim-faced NKVD officers, interrogated, branded as spies, and shot. Russian soldiers hauled before a field tribunal and executed because they had failed to shoot down comrades who were trying to desert. Again and again, throughout the country, tens of thousands of such cases: a total of 13,500 summary and judicial executions in the Battle of Stalingrad alone.[19]

This was not "wartime discipline." It was the senseless, unthinking violence of a regime that regarded human beings as nothing more than disposable instruments. The systematic ferocity used without hesitation by Soviet leaders against their own fighting men, and against their own civilian population, is enough to leave the historical observer speechless. It arguably stands as one of the most damning statements about the underlying mentality at the heart of Soviet communism.

Winston Churchill was asked by a radio interviewer in June 1941 whether he had any misgivings concerning the alliance with Stalin. He replied: "Any man or state who fights against Nazidom will have our aid. Any man or state who marches with Hitler is our foe."[20] He famously remarked to his secretary John Colville, "If Hitler invaded hell, I would make at least a favorable reference to the Devil in the House of Commons."[21] Neither Great Britain nor the United States was in any position to be choosy about its allies during the dark days of 1941 and 1942. It would have been the height of folly for the Anglo-Americans to do anything but embrace the embattled Soviet Union as best they could, and provide it with all the assistance they could muster.

But we should at least be clear about the nature of what followed. The great victory on the Eastern Front presents an awe-inspiring, and simultaneously horrifying, spectacle: a complex picture rather far from the straightforward ticker-tape jubilation that we usually associate with V-E Day. Soviet bravery, Soviet resourcefulness, Soviet ruthlessness, Soviet mass murder; the suffering of the Russian people, a suffering unlike anything else in this war except perhaps that of the Chinese and the Jews; a will to survive, a will to revenge; a war machine that absorbed the frightful impact of German power and then struck back, smashing its enemy; a nightmare state, led by a cunning and remorseless man, looming over world politics in 1945, casting shadow where there might have been hope.

Chapter Nine

KAMIKAZE

Wartime Suicide Attacks in Anthropological Perspective

> The Japanese are prone to make light of their lives and to be too ready to die. . . . On the other hand, Occidentals place high value on the life of the individual. They do not die so readily, and, therefore, they cannot comprehend the psychology of kamikaze pilots.
>
> —Masanori Oshima, *Reflections upon Our National Character* (1947)[1]

When U.S. sailors and soldiers first saw the Japanese suicide bombers in action, off Leyte in the fall of 1944, they couldn't believe their eyes. Those people were actually crashing their planes deliberately into American warships. Time after time. They were turning themselves into human bombs.

It was profoundly disconcerting—not least because these suicide attacks proved hard to repel, and were highly effective in damaging American ships. American carriers still had wooden flight decks in World War II, and were therefore extremely vulnerable to a plane coming in at a nearly vertical angle: that particular contingency had simply not occurred to the ship designers. In the battle off Okinawa during April 1945, Japanese suicide attacks succeeded in sinking or crippling more than *four hundred* American ships.

It was terrifying, and awe-inspiring, watching those planes circle in. Eyewitnesses report having felt almost mesmerized by it. Here is Admiral Bull Halsey, recalling his experience at the Battle of Leyte Gulf, October 29, 1944:

Kamikaze plane diving into the light cruiser Columbia *off Lingayen Gulf, the Philippines (January 6, 1945).*

Intelligence had warned us that the "Divine Wind Special Attack Corps" had been organized, but . . . I think that most of us took it as a sort of token terror, a tissue-paper dragon. The psychology of it was too alien to ours; Americans, who fight to live, find it hard to realize that another people will fight to die. We could not believe that even the Japanese, for all their *hara-kiri* traditions, could muster enough recruits to make such a corps really effective.

We were violently disillusioned the very next day. They missed the *Enterprise*, in Davison's group, but they hit two of his other carriers, the *Franklin* and *Belleau Wood*, killing a total of 158 men, destroying forty-five planes, and requiring the withdrawal of both ships for repairs. Our CVs [carriers] were obvious targets: their huge tanks of aviation gasoline were as vulnerable as they were inflammable, their firepower was light, their armor was thin, and damage to their flight decks meant the neutralization of around a hundred planes.[2]

Halsey's reaction was typical. There was something alien and repugnant to an American in this act of deliberate self-immolation. Already U.S. forces had become painfully familiar with Japanese soldiers' readiness to die rather than surrender—their banzai charges, their holding out in caves and foxholes to the last man, their suicides when capture appeared imminent. Now the Americans had to take stock of this new phenomenon, and, as the historian John Dower notes, the image of the kamikaze only served to bolster the picture that most Americans had of the Japanese as "a people with a compulsive death wish."[3]

Dower has exhaustively documented, in his book *War Without Mercy,* the myriad ways in which both sides in the Pacific War produced racial stereotypes of the enemy. In the eyes of many Japanese, the Americans were a mongrel people, soft and pampered, undisciplined, shallowly materialistic, selfishly individualistic—a bunch of arrogant and hypocritical bullies. In the eyes of many Americans, by contrast, the Japanese were virtual subhumans: irrational, cruel, aggressive, treacherous.

One particularly common trope in the Western portrayal of the Japanese was perfectly embodied by the kamikaze: the Japanese did not value human life as highly as Westerners—not only the lives of captured prisoners and of the "lesser races" of Asia, but their own as well, which they threw away in patently hopeless attacks. They seemed to embrace death almost eagerly; they committed suicide in droves; their leaders heedlessly squandered both troops and civilians. It all added up to a simple conclusion: these Japanese people might appear to possess the fundamental attributes common to virtually all human populations, but this was an illusion. In reality, they lacked the most basic human quality of all: the instinct of self-preservation. They were so strange as to lie beyond the pale of normal humanity. "By his atrocities," writes Dower,

> the enemy had become identified as a savage. By these banzai charges and mass deaths, he became known as a madman. And from these battlefield hell scenes emerged the picture of an entire race whose growth was stunted in every way: in cultural evolution and in mental and emotional development, both as individuals and as a group.[4]

Reflecting on the kamikaze phenomenon offers a way to explore not only the morality of extreme forms of warfare, but also broader questions about how to interpret what these behaviors say about the culture that engages in them.[5] How did the Japanese themselves view the kamikaze program? What does the imagery surrounding the kamikazes reveal about the processes of cultural stereotyping through which one nation sometimes perceives another? How do we account for the undeniable pattern of life-denying or brutal behaviors exhibited by many Japanese during World War II—without perpetuating simplistic and dehumanizing national or racial stereotypes? These kinds of questions possess an especially grim relevance today because, as we know all too well, the phenomenon of the suicide bomber did not fade away after 1945: it spread like a metastasizing cancer into the postwar era, and has become a regular feature of contemporary world politics. The conceptual tools we bring to bear in gaining a better understanding of the kamikaze can perhaps help us to confront more constructively the traditions of murderous self-immolation that have come to mark our own time.

When I was seventeen I experienced a "teaching moment" that has marked the way I have viewed other cultures ever since. During my senior year in high school in the mid-1970s, my social studies teacher screened a film that had just won an Academy Award for best documentary: *Hearts and Minds*, directed by Peter Davis. The film offered a searing critique of the American foreign policy and cultural attitudes that had led to the war in Vietnam: Davis and his team made no pretense of evenhandedness, but unabashedly, relentlessly, and quite skillfully pieced together a mosaic of images that added up to a powerful indictment of the American involvement in Southeast Asia.

One of the sequences in this antiwar movie had to do with Western cultural stereotypes about Asians. I will never forget the impact of viewing that sequence: it impressed upon me, in a way that no amount of listening to lectures or reading books could have done, the deep wrongness of seeing other cultures through the simplifying lens of a blanket generalization. Five minutes of footage was worth a thousand hours of anthropology courses.

The film segment begins with tracer bullets and aerial bombardment, the rapid blasts of antiaircraft guns, followed by pictures of the smoking ruins of a hospital.[6] Dead children dressed in white funeral garments are lined up on the ground. A North Vietnamese man, about thirty years old, mourns for his family as he stands in the mud and devastation of a bombed-out village. He is dressed in white, and walks about ceaselessly as he speaks, his voice rising and falling, cracking with grief, his speech coming in short bursts, punctuated by stifled sobs. The English-language voice-over is measured and unemotional, the contrast only heightening the raw agony in the Vietnamese man's monologue:

> My eight-year-old daughter was killed. And my three-year-old son.
> Nixon, murderer of civilians.
> What have I done to Nixon so that he comes here to bomb my country?
> [*Points to a spot in the mud.*]
> My daughter died right here. She was feeding the pigs. She was so sweet.

She is dead. The pigs are alive.

[*Camera focuses on a child's comb in the mud.*]

My mother and my children took shelter here. Here they died.

The planes came from over there. No targets here. Only rice fields and houses.

[*Walks through mud.*]

I give you my daughter's beautiful shirt. Take it back to the United States. Tell them what happened here.

[*Looks into the camera.*]

My daughter is dead. She will never wear this shirt again.

[*He cries, his voice breaking, then stops himself, his face contorted.*]

Throw this shirt in Nixon's face. Tell them: she was only a little schoolgirl.

The scene abruptly shifts. A funeral; coffins lined up; military guards in a row, standing at attention. A South Vietnamese boy about nine years old, wearing a white funeral headband, his head leaning against one of the coffins, a low, moaning wail rising and falling from his chest. His fingers shake as he holds the funeral incense. His forehead gently touches the plain wood of the coffin.

He stands, holding a framed photograph of his father. The father is a young soldier, clean-cut, hatless, in a short-sleeve shirt. The boy moans, moans, his hands tremble as he holds the picture.

Uniformed South Vietnamese soldiers approach, line up, place their hands under the coffin. We see the boy from behind as he watches; they lift the coffin; he begins to shake, his tiny body jumping up and down in frantic denial; they walk past.

Graveside, the boy is standing, holding his father's picture. His little brother stands to one side, also wearing a white headband. The soldiers unfurl a flag over the coffin, a bugle sounds a short military salute.

The coffin is lowered into the muddy grave. Behind the heaped dirt stand the boy and his little brother, holding incense. The younger child does not cry; the older boy trembles violently, a low sound of desolation coming ceaselessly from him.

His grandmother, a wrinkled old woman dressed in black, is waiting by the mound of dirt, holding the folded flag under her arm. The soldiers look away for a moment: she crawls over the dirt and starts to climb down into the grave where her son's coffin lies. She wants to be buried with her son. The soldiers grab her; she sobs, her voice dry and harsh; they pull her out by force.

The burial is over. Dirt now fills the grave. The framed photograph stands propped on top. The boy sits nearby, holding his incense. Slowly he leans over to the picture of his father, speaking to the image up close, his voice coming through moaning sobs.

The scene shifts again. A handsome white man in a striped civilian suit, lean face and gray hair. The caption reads, "General William Westmoreland." In the background a bucolic scene, with a lake. Westmoreland begins to explain, in a calm, deliberate voice:

> Well, the Oriental doesn't put the same high price on life as does the Westerner. [*He pauses, looking into the camera.*] Life is plentiful, life is cheap, in the Orient. [*Long pause.*] As the philosophy of the Orient expresses it, life is not important.

As the opening quotation for this chapter suggests, Westmoreland was far from alone in holding this dehumanizing stereotype about Asian culture: Masanori Oshima, a Japanese scholar writing about his people's "national character" in 1947, concluded pretty much the same thing. Large numbers of Westerners had been voicing this kind of belief ever since the early colonial contacts in the 1800s: the Orientals, it was thought, simply lacked some of the basic capabilities, feelings, and values cherished by Occidentals.[7]

The idea that impressed itself upon me, after watching *Hearts and Minds*, was to look with suspicion on any statement about a nation, a people, a race, a very large group of human beings, that sought to characterize them all with some particular set of attributes. "Men are pigs." "Aryans are noble." "Italians like to sing songs while they work." "Jews are stingy." "Short people have a chip on their shoulder."

Sometimes widely held stereotypes are blatantly contradictory: "Mexicans are lazy." "You won't find a harder worker than a Mexican." The impulse to create these kinds of generalizations obviously runs deep, because virtually every known society appears to have produced them. "Athenians are cunning; Spartans are cruel." "Romans love order, but lack creativity."

How, then, are we to understand the phenomenon of the kamikaze, if we wish to avoid this kind of gross oversimplification? How to deal with Japanese attitudes toward death during World War II, without falling into the trap of perpetuating these intellectually disgraceful stereotypes? Let us begin by making four comparisons.

1. *Terrorists.*

The suicide attacks carried out against the United States on September 11, 2001, brought the image of the kamikazes quite vividly to the forefront of public awareness once again. Apart from the horror of the lives we knew were being lost, we also felt something else, as we watched, over and over again, the video footage of those planes gliding, under careful and deliberate control, into the side of those giant buildings. We felt a sense of deep discomfort at the thought that this was a kind of enemy we didn't know how to deal with: someone so desperate, so alien, that he was willing to kill himself in the act of taking out as many as he could of his declared foes. In the discussions that followed September 11, many of the same kinds of themes emerged in characterizing these Middle Eastern fanatics as had emerged in the wake of the kamikaze attacks of the Second World War.

But one important difference remained. The kamikazes went after military targets in wartime: troopships, aircraft carriers, destroyers, and cruisers. The September 11 terrorists attacked defenseless civilians in peacetime. No matter how fervently one might condemn the kamikazes' actions, this distinction placed a clear qualitative barrier between the two kinds of suicide assault. One group was extending the conduct of warfare to a new and disconcerting level of self-sacrifice; the other was engaging in a cowardly and criminal atrocity against noncombatants. The kamikazes, whatever they were, were not terrorists.

2. *Bravery against overwhelming odds.*

It is illuminating to compare the kamikaze attacks to certain episodes of extraordinary death-defying valor exhibited by Westerners. We have already described, in chapter 7, the self-sacrifice of the American torpedo squadrons in the Battle of Midway. Another famous example is that of the Charge of the Light Brigade during the Crimean War, celebrated by the poet Alfred, Lord Tennyson: 673 cavalry men were ordered, through a commander's error, to attack a heavily fortified Russian artillery position. Knowing full well that the maneuver stood virtually no chance of success, the men obeyed nonetheless, and were cut to pieces.

> *"Forward, the Light Brigade!"*
> *Was there a man dismay'd?*
> *Not tho' the soldier knew*
> *Some one had blunder'd:*
> *Theirs not to make reply,*
> *Theirs not to reason why,*
> *Theirs but to do and die:*
> *Into the Valley of Death*
> *Rode the six hundred.*[8]

A less famous example from the Second World War presents itself in the extraordinary story of a unit named Taffy 3, during the Battle of Leyte Gulf, in October 1944.[9] The American army was preparing a huge landing force for invading the Philippines, ready to come ashore on the eastern beaches of the island of Leyte. Offshore, the U.S. Navy under Admiral Halsey arrayed a large fleet to protect the landing ships from attack. The Japanese decided to try a complicated trick. They would send a major decoy fleet out into the Pacific, to the north. This would hopefully lure the impulsive Halsey away from his position, leaving the Leyte landing force weakly defended. At this point two powerful Japanese fleets would sneak in, from the south and northeast, and annihilate the American troopships as they prepared for their amphibious landing. It would be a disastrous defeat for the United States, with tremendous loss of life.

The maneuvers of the battle were long and intricate, but the Japanese plan actually worked. Halsey, partly through bad intelligence and partly through bad judgment, took the Japanese bait and sailed away into the Pacific in pursuit of the decoy fleet. Unbelievably, he took with him all his major warships. The only force he left behind to guard the vulnerable landing operation was a small group of five escort carriers—basically converted merchant ships—and their accompanying destroyers, under the command of Rear Admiral Clifton Sprague. Even the code name for this diminutive American flotilla conveys its weakness: it was called Taffy 3.

One of the two Japanese attack fleets was discovered by U.S. naval forces to the south, and successfully turned away. But the main Japanese fleet, under Admiral Takeo Kurita, slipped through the San Bernardino Strait during the night of October 24, and steamed south, ready to wipe out the American landing force. Nothing stood in its way—except Taffy 3.

Sprague saw the Japanese fleet coming: two super-battleships of the *Yamato* class, the most powerful warships in the world; two other battleships; eight heavy cruisers; and a swarm of destroyers. It was like a tiger bearing down on a mouse. Sprague decided that his only chance of stopping the enemy lay in a full-tilt frontal assault. Immediately he launched all the planes off his escort carriers, ordering them to concentrate their attacks on Kurita's four battleships. The planes were only equipped with antisubmarine bombs, but they let fly with these as best they could. At the same time, Sprague ordered his six destroyers to head straight for the advancing Japanese fleet, launching torpedoes.

The Japanese fired away with their massive guns, but they were hampered by the fact that they had to wheel wildly to dodge the torpedoes launched by Sprague's destroyers. To the amazement of the Americans, moreover, some of the Japanese armor-piercing shells, designed for large warships, simply passed through the thin walls of the American vessels without exploding—in one side and out the other. As the maneuvering went on, kamikaze planes based in the Philippines joined the attack against Taffy 3, sinking the escort carrier *St. Lô*.

Meanwhile, Taffy 3's torpedoes were taking a toll. They severely damaged three Japanese cruisers, forcing two to be abandoned and scuttled. The battle raged for more than two hours, with the Japanese ships weaving to and fro, firing their giant guns, while the American attackers desperately dodged and twisted to avoid annihilation. At one point Sprague ordered his ships to dive into a passing rain squall, to provide a momentary respite from the Japanese onslaught. Then he moved to the attack once again. To quote the Presidential Unit Citation awarded to Taffy 3 after the battle:

> With one carrier of the group sunk, others badly damaged and squadron air-craft courageously coordinating the attacks by making dry runs over the enemy Fleet as the Japanese relentlessly closed in for the kill, two of the Unit's valiant destroyers and one destroyer escort charged the battleships point-blank and, expending their last torpedoes in desperate defense of the entire group, went down under the enemy's heavy shells as a climax to two and one half hours of sustained and furious combat.[10]

In Kurita's mind, the fierce defense being put up by this American flotilla could mean only one thing: this must be an advance unit of Halsey's main task force of carriers and battleships, which must be about to arrive at any moment. At 10:30 a.m. Kurita made an astounding decision: instead of proceeding into Leyte Gulf, where General Douglas MacArthur's invasion fleet lay unprotected—where the guns of the Japanese battleships and cruisers could have methodically blown dozens of packed American troop-ships to smithereens—Kurita turned around and withdrew.

Sprague and his men watched the retreating Japanese ships, and slowly began picking up the pieces of their battered squadron. The mouse had bitten the tiger on the toe and made him run away. The bravery of Taffy 3, and the folly of Admiral Kurita, had saved the day for the Americans.

In all three cases—American torpedo planes at Midway, the British Light Brigade, and Taffy 3—a group of military men faced an enemy who overwhelmingly and unequivocally outgunned them. To attack such an enemy, by any reasonable assessment, was surely futile: yet in these situations the men defied the terrible odds, and (in two of the cases) held through to an unexpected victory. But it is precisely here that the difference from the kamikazes becomes clear: in all three of these cases the odds were very bad indeed—but they were still *odds*. A slim, outside chance of victory existed, and the individual men who went in for the attack could hold out a hope, however faint, of being among the lucky few who might survive the engagement.

Such was not the case, of course, with the kamikazes. The whole point of a kamikaze attack was to die in the act of exploding one's payload on an enemy target. The pilot and the bomb became one and the same device, and the only way a pilot could survive such an assault was through the total failure of his tactical mission.

Herein lies the feature of suicide attacks that leads most people around the world—including a great many Japanese—to recoil from them in abhorrence. The moral reasoning implicit here is best captured in the Kantian injunction never to consider a human being as a mere means toward an end, but always to treat a human life as an end in itself—something for which other things may be sacrificed, but which in itself must remain inviolable, and can never be reduced to mere instrumental value. To turn oneself into a weapon, in this sense, is to devalue the life of all humans, by making a human being into a mere instrument of warfare: according to the Kantian vision, humans can legitimately *bear* weapons and *use* weapons, under certain conditions, but they cannot reduce themselves to the degraded state of *being* weapons. Such an act, according to one of the core tenets of humanistic philosophy, violates the unique status of human beings as sources of value: by transforming a person into a mere tool, it irreparably degrades the very civilization on behalf of which the war is supposedly being fought.

Humans, according to this tradition of thought, can legitimately risk their lives in the name of defending themselves and other people, and of advancing certain ideals in which they believe. But they cannot in good conscience engage in outright suicide for the sake of achieving any ulterior goal. Suicide, by its very nature, can never be used as an affirmation of any "higher purpose"—because there is no higher purpose than that which derives from the infinite intrinsic value of a human life. This tenet, it is worth emphasizing, underlies not only the philosophy of secular humanism, but is embraced by the majority of religiously grounded philosophies as well, including most currents of Christianity, Judaism, Islam, and Buddhism. Suicide, according to virtually all these traditions, can be nothing but an act of ultimate desperation, of nihilistic destruction, and cannot legitimately become an instrument of any positive national policy.[11]

It is crucial to point out here that many Japanese shared this set of humanistic values, whether explicitly or tacitly, and therefore felt deeply uncomfortable about the kamikazes. Admiral Takajiro Ohnishi, the founder of the Divine Wind (kamikaze) Special Attack Corps, was widely regarded by his navy colleagues as a fanatic and extremist.[12] When Ohnishi informed Emperor Hirohito about the success of the first waves of kamikaze attacks, the emperor's response was revealing: "Was it necessary to go to this extreme? They certainly did a magnificent job."[13] Not surprisingly, Ohnishi was "completely upset" by the emperor's words, interpreting them as "criticism for the commander responsible for these tactics."[14] While most Japanese felt deeply moved by the idealistic spirit of self-sacrifice exhibited by the young men who volunteered for kamikaze missions, and considered them unequivocally as heroes, many harbored gnawing doubts about the wisdom, and morality, of this kind of warfare. Here is the conclusion reached by Rikihei Inoguchi, a Japanese officer who served under Ohnishi as an administrator of the kamikaze corps:

> The idea of systematically planned suicide attacks carried out over a period of months, while acceptable to the individuals concerned, seems to have been too much for the Japanese public. Thus the [kamikaze] system and its leaders came in for severe criticism from the home front.[15]

Admiral Kantaro Suzuki, the Japanese prime minister at the time of surrender, wrote after the war:

> The spirit and the deeds of the kamikaze pilots naturally arouse profound admiration. But, considered from the standpoint of strategy, these tactics are the product of defeat. An able commander would never resort to such extreme measures.[16]

The Zen Buddhist scholar Daisetsu Suzuki (no relation to the admiral) was still more blunt: "Far from being a matter of pride, it must remain a blemish on the people of Japan."[17]

3. *Self-sacrifice on the spur of the moment.*

Most societies do, however, recognize the act of suicidal self-sacrifice as a noble and awe-inspiring act—but only under certain conditions. For example, a significant proportion of the 3,500 persons who have received the

Congressional Medal of Honor, the highest award for valor bestowed by the United States, did so because they died in circumstances such as these:

- *Peleliu, 1944, Corporal Lewis Bausell:* "Swift to act, as a Japanese grenade was hurled into their midst, Cpl. Bausell threw himself on the deadly weapon, taking the full blast of the explosion and sacrificing his own life to save his men."
- *New Guinea, 1944, Second Lieutenant George Boyce:* "He was promptly met by a volley of hand grenades, one falling between himself and the men immediately following. Realizing at once that the explosion would kill or wound several of his men, he promptly threw himself upon the grenade and smothered the blast with his own body."
- *Iwo Jima, 1945, Corporal Charles Berry:* "When infiltrating Japanese soldiers launched a surprise attack shortly after midnight in an attempt to overrun his position, he engaged in a pitched hand grenade duel, returning the dangerous weapons with prompt and deadly accuracy until an enemy grenade landed in the foxhole. Determined to save his comrades, he unhesitatingly chose to sacrifice himself and immediately dived on the deadly missile, absorbing the shattering violence of the exploding charge in his own body and protecting the others from serious injury."[18]

These are all cases of suicide, but they differ from those of the kamikazes in two significant respects: they aimed at saving lives rather than killing; and they occurred in situations in which no time for reflection existed, but only time to make an instant decision and take action. The kamikazes, by contrast, volunteered for their special duty many months in advance, underwent systematic training in how to maximize the chances of blowing themselves up successfully, and had plenty of time to consider the choice they had made.

These two factors make all the difference, from a moral perspective. In these three examples the act of suicide does not devalue human life, because it is used as a vehicle for trading one life in return for the sparing of many: it is an affirmation of the sanctity of life, not a nihilistic destruction of one life in the act of destroying still more lives. Moreover, the fact that the kamikaze's suicide comes at the culmination of a long process of planning and training further underscores the instrumental calculus that lies at the heart of his deed: I, the suicide attacker, after careful deliberation, am turning myself into a tool of warfare. By contrast, the man who suddenly gives his life to save his comrades is acting as much out of emotion as rationality: the felt bond of comradeship probably compels the decision to take suicidal action more than any logical calculus about trading one life for many. There is simply no time for that kind of thought process to take place. Jumping on the grenade is an impulsive act of ultimate generosity, not a rational course of action following long preparation. Taken together, these two elements—the saving of lives, and the altruistic impulsiveness of the deed—transform the man's suicide into one of the most honorable acts a human can achieve.

4. *Scale of the program.*

Japan was not the only nation in World War II that created suicide squads. Germany, too, developed such a unit in November 1944, as the war situation grew increasingly desperate: the group, code-named KG200, included a squad of eighty men who had volunteered for *Totaleinsatz*, or "total effort"—meaning suicide attacks. Though they flew no actual missions, they were preparing for two types of assignments in the spring of 1945, as the end drew near: an attempt to assassinate Stalin, and the adoption of manned V-1 flights, which, instead of dropping randomly on cities like London or Rotterdam, could be directed to hit precise targets within enemy conurbations.[19] Soviet air force pilots, too, were known to have deliberately rammed incoming German aircraft when their own planes ran out of ammunition: some 270 instances of such (usually suicidal) rammings were officially entered in Soviet records.[20]

But Admiral Ohnishi's kamikaze corps clearly constituted an effort of a qualitatively different order of magnitude. All totaled, some 6,300 young Japanese pilots flew kamikaze sorties between October 1944 and July 1945; another 5,350 stood ready in August 1945 on the southernmost home island of Kyushu, where the American amphibious invasion of Japan was expected.[21] The Japanese in 1945 were developing special rocket-propelled planes specifically for this kind of mission; they also created a wide variety of nautical suicide vehicles: explosive-packed midget subs to ram incoming ships; 6,200 Shinyo suicide boats to hurl against troop transports; and last but not least, suicide swimmers in diving suits, ready to detonate mines under landing craft.

But Ohnishi was ready to go one considerable step further. On August 13, 1945—just days after the nuclear obliteration of Hiroshima and Nagasaki—the admiral joined a high-level meeting in Tokyo of army and navy leaders who were bitterly arguing over the terms of a possible surrender. Ohnishi interrupted them:

> Let us formulate a plan for certain victory, obtain the Emperor's sanction, and throw ourselves into bringing the plan to realization. If we are prepared

to sacrifice twenty million Japanese lives in a special attack [kamikaze] effort, victory will be ours![22]

Two days later, after the nation's surrender had been announced, Ohnishi went into the second-floor study of his home in Tokyo to commit hara-kiri. According to the historians Rikihei Inoguchi, Tadashi Nakajima, and Roger Pineau, who tell the story of the kamikazes in their book *The Divine Wind*, the admiral's own moment of self-immolation did not go well: the disemboweling cut across the abdomen "was cleanly done, but the following attempt by the Admiral to slit his throat was not so successful."[23] An aide came in to deliver the coup de grâce, but Ohnishi would have none of it: he insisted on lingering the entire day in agony, without medical assistance, until death finally came at six o'clock in the evening. Beside him lay a farewell note, which included the admonition: "I wish the young people of Japan to find a moral in my death. To be reckless is only to aid the enemy."[24]

The idealism of the young men who volunteered for these missions is perhaps their most salient—and moving—trait. To a man, they appear to have earnestly believed that they were not throwing their lives away, but were conducting powerful attacks that might yet contribute to a dramatic reversal of military fortunes. A few were highly trained pilots who had come through the aviation academy; most were reserve officers from civilian colleges and universities. All were volunteers: in fact, there were about three times as many volunteers for the kamikaze corps as there were slots available. Most of these young men had to wait several months before being assigned to a mission; thus, they had plenty of time to ponder their impending death. They read books, played cards, and wrote letters home.

- *Petty Officer Isao Matsuo (age twenty-three):* "Thank you, my parents, for the twenty-three years during which you have cared for me and inspired me. I hope that my present deed will in some small way repay what you have done for me. Think well of me and know that your Isao died for our country."

- *Cadet Jun Nomoto (age twenty-three):* "The first planes of my group are already in the air. These words are being written by my friend as he rests the paper on the fuselage of my plane. There are no feelings of remorse or sadness here. My outlook is unchanged. I will perform my duty calmly. . . .

"My last wish is that my brothers may have a proper education. It is certain that uneducated men have an empty life. Please see to it that their lives are as full as possible."

- *Ensign Ichizo Hayashi (a convert to Christianity, age twenty-three):* "Please do not grieve for me, mother. It will be glorious to die in action. I am grateful to die in a battle to determine the destiny of my country. . . .
  "From all reports it is clear that we have blunted the actions of the enemy. Victory will be with us. . . .
  "We live in the spirit of Jesus Christ, and we die in that spirit. This thought stays with me. It is gratifying to live in this world, but living has a spirit of futility about it now. It is time to die."

- *Ensign Teruo Yamaguchi (age twenty-two):* "Once the order was given for my one-way mission it became my sincere wish to achieve success in fulfilling this last duty. Even so, I cannot help feeling a strong attachment to this beautiful land of Japan. Is that a weakness on my part?
  "On learning that my time had come I closed my eyes and saw visions of your face, mother's, grandmother's, and the faces of my close friends. It was bracing and heartening to realize that each of you wants me to be brave. I will do that! I will! . . .
  "My greatest regret in this life is the failure to call you '*chichiue*' [revered father]. I regret not having given any demonstration of the true respect which I have always had for you. During my final plunge, though you will not hear it, you may be sure that I will be saying '*chichiue*' to you and thinking of all you have done for me."[25]

Looking back on the kamikazes from the perspective of hindsight, we tend to think of these young lives as an utter waste, carelessly thrown away by a nation that was already doomed to lose the war. But the Japanese did not see the war in this way at the time. Well into 1945, the overwhelming majority of the Japanese leadership earnestly believed that the war had not yet been lost. Although they did accept, by and large, that they would never gain the great Pacific empire they had once envisioned, they were far from believing that the war would necessarily have to end with the invasion or total devastation of Japan itself.

Indeed, a central facet of the Japanese strategy, after 1943, became precisely this: raise the cost so high for the Americans that they are forced to accept a compromise peace—one that preserves Japan's sovereignty and national honor. Make the Americans pay such a high cost, as they come closer to Japan, that they see no option but to accept that this war has been fought to a draw.[26]

This was, without doubt, a very unrealistic way of thinking: the Japanese leaders were badly deceiving themselves (and their own citizenry). Most observers around the world had come to assume, by 1944, the virtual inevitability of total Japanese defeat. But if we acknowledge the fact that the Japanese did not regard total defeat as inevitable, then, within this framework of assumptions, the kamikazes can actually be viewed as a rational use of dwindling national resources. Such a policy, though patently immoral by the standards described earlier in this chapter, might still be seen as a logically defensible option from a purely military standpoint.

Japan, by 1944, had lost most of its highly trained pilots: all it had were new recruits, who were being shot down in droves by seasoned American fliers. By that point in the war the Americans enjoyed dominance in virtually every significant category: superior planes, superior numbers, superior training and experience, superior logistical support. In the Battle of the Philippine Sea (June 1944), Admiral Raymond Spruance's carriers took on a large Japanese fleet in an engagement that lasted two days: the result was so lopsided that American sailors dubbed it "the Great Marianas Turkey Shoot"—123 planes lost for the Americans (with eighty of the pilots surviving to fight again) versus the destruction of three aircraft carriers and 395 planes for the Japanese.

Under these conditions, it is not surprising that some Japanese leaders should have said to themselves, Rather than waste the lives of our young men in futile conventional attacks against a superior foe, why not turn them into much more deadly and effective flying bombs? In this way, at least, their deaths will exact a high cost from the enemy in damage and casualties—and this, in turn, will greatly increase the likelihood of forcing the enemy to accept a compromise peace.[27]

Seen from this narrow military and strategic perspective, the results of the kamikaze campaign were impressive. In the Battle of Leyte Gulf, 12 kamikazes sank one American escort carrier, damaged two others, and killed a total of 131 Americans: a ratio of almost eleven to one. Off Lin-

gayen Gulf, Luzon, on January 6, 1945, 34 kamikazes killed a total of 167
Allied sailors and soldiers. In the battle for Okinawa, 1,900 kamikazes
attacked the Allied naval forces arrayed offshore: they killed a total of
3,389 men, sank 36 ships, and severely damaged 368 others.[28]

To an American military leader, the comparison of these statistics with
those from the preceding battles of the Pacific War cannot but have come
as a profound shock: overall, in most of the war's engagements, an average
of ten Japanese had died for every American death. Now, the ratio had been
skewed the other way: wherever the kamikazes came into play, an average
of 1.78 Americans died for every Japanese life lost.[29] These numbers, not
surprisingly, gave serious pause to U.S. military and civilian decision-
makers, and—as the historian Richard Frank has persuasively shown—
prompted a full-scale reassessment in Washington during June and July
1945 of the plans for invading the Japanese home islands.[30] Apart from the
kamikazes in planes and boats and subs, American leaders knew that the
invading Allied forces would face untold numbers of land-based suicide
attackers once they came ashore.

In this sense, the kamikaze campaign undeniably had the short-term
effect its leaders desired: it made the enemy wonder if a massive amphibious invasion of Japan was worth pursuing at all. What the Japanese leadership failed to understand, of course, was that the Allies had other options
open to them—options that would inevitably defeat the Japanese, with or
without an American invasion.[31] One such option was the continued naval
blockade and conventional bombardment of Japan, to be waged with increasing effectiveness and intensity as the months went by, until a sufficiently horrific number of its people had been incinerated or starved to
death. Another option was to bring the Soviet Union into a full-scale
ground assault on the Japanese home islands—for Soviet leaders had
fewer compunctions about throwing vast numbers of men into a pitched
battle, paying the necessary blood price for swift victory. The third option,
which the Japanese leaders could not know about, was the atomic bomb.

Seen from this broader perspective, therefore, the kamikaze campaign
violated two basic moral principles. First, it degraded human life, by turning persons into mere instruments of warfare. And second, it was a waste
of human life, because any reasonable person in 1944 and especially 1945
should have been able to see that Japan's defeat was inevitable. If Japan had
not been led by a group of fanatics, holding on irrationally to tendrils of
impossible hope, a great many young military men on both sides—and an
even greater number of Japanese civilians—would have lived on to see the
postwar world.

Let us return, in closing, to the question of Japanese attitudes toward life and death. Clearly, we must reject as a gross oversimplification the kind of view espoused by Masanori Oshima and William Westmoreland, namely, that the Japanese (or Asians) place a lower value on life than Westerners. This is crude, overgeneralized thinking used as a facile way to characterize someone or something not understood. Down that road lies racism, and the callous dehumanization of entire peoples.

But what are we to make of the overwhelming evidence that we have seen about Japanese behaviors in the 1930s and 1940s—the Rape of Nanking, the banzai charges, the widespread suicides, the systematic abuse and murder of POWs, the kamikazes, the mass murder-suicides of civilians on Saipan, the killing spree in Manila, the refusal by most soldiers to surrender on the battlefield, the equally stubborn refusal of the nation's leaders to give up when defeat was obviously unavoidable? Surely, all these behaviors add up to something, and that something requires *some* kind of explanation?

The explanation does not come from any blanket generalization about Asians, or from some kind of alleged "essential" quality to be found in the psyche of all Japanese. It comes from something far more interesting: the specifics of Japanese history. Japanese society in the 1930s and 1940s had fallen into a dangerous and self-destructive cultural pattern: one that fostered the dehumanization of foreigners, brutality toward people perceived as enemies (at home or abroad), fanatical submission to authority, severe conformism, uncritical acceptance of government propaganda, and wildly inflated nationalism. One could pin virtually every one of these attributes on Nazi Germany, and a good many of them on Mussolini's Italy and on Soviet society under Stalin.

The point here is that these are not "essential" qualities of all Japanese at all times (or of the Germans or Russians for that matter): they are temporally specific cultural attributes, arising out of particular historical processes. Any society is capable of degenerating into the atrocious behaviors shown by the Germans, Japanese, and Russians in the 1930s and 1940s, if the right historical ingredients come together—the kinds of factors discussed in chapters 2 and 3: the loss of a war, extreme economic hardship, foreign occupation, racist mentalities, dictatorial government, intense class conflict and social turmoil, chronic political instability, the embrace by many citizens of extremist ideologies, a perception of victimization or encirclement by hostile nations. What we see, in the history of

Japan leading up to World War II, is a tragic spiral of social and cultural forces at work, steadily building up the kind of attitudes, habits, and institutions that *did*, in fact, result in a lowering of the value placed on human life. Not all Japanese partook of this cultural degradation—some fervently resisted it, while others eyed it with sullen skepticism—but the overall cultural pattern was strong enough to impart an unmistakable tone of brutality to the nation's collective behavior. There was nothing eternal or "essential" about this; it did not "reveal" some atemporal quality of underlying "national character"; it was not "typical" of this nation's people, any more than it was irremediably "typical" of the Germans or Russians: it was a product of history, and like any such product, it could be made to fade away just as surely as it had arisen.

After the war, not surprisingly, the cultural pattern shifted dramatically. Both Japan and Germany underwent a prolonged period of national soul-searching, and confronted the task of rebuilding not just their shattered cities, but—more difficult still—their shattered traditions of democratic self-government, of civic decency and the rule of law, of humane values, and positive participation in the community of nations. The majority of Japanese and Germans categorically turned their backs from the ruthless ambitions and bestial deeds of their recent past, and sought, however falteringly, to start anew.[32] Most Japanese and Germans looked back with intense anger and revulsion at the militarism and fanaticism that had brought on the greatest catastrophe in their national histories—and that revulsion still persists today. Thus, the kamikaze attacks, like so many other life-denying practices of wartime, went into the history books—books written in the hope that another generation of young men might not forget, might come to understand how such calamitous inhumanity had taken over their country's past, might therefore possess the cultural and moral resources to affirm a different way of seeing.

And meanwhile, in other parts of the world, new ideologies of hatred and despair were already in gestation, ready to unleash other young men on their own deadly errands of clear-eyed self-immolation. The grim reality of suicide attacks surrounds us now: it forms part of the air we breathe. There is not much we can do about it as individuals—except perhaps to spread around, as best we can, the understanding we derive from the story of the World War II kamikazes: the powerful example of how utterly futile a fanatic's death can be.

Chapter Ten

THE DECISION TO DROP
THE ATOMIC BOMB
Twelve Questions

> If a man could write a book on Ethics which really was a book on Ethics,
> this book would, with an explosion, destroy all the other books in the
> world.
>
> —Ludwig Wittgenstein[1]

The American decision to drop the atomic bomb on Japan remains bitterly controversial even after all these years.[2] Was the United States right to use this powerful new weapon? Did American leaders make the proper choice? Or is it the case, as some have argued, that the atomic bombing of Hiroshima and Nagasaki was an unjustifiable act—an atrocity that darkens the history of the United States with a stain that can never be washed away?

Herein lies the core issue underlying the discussion that follows. Since the subject is complicated, let us break it down into twelve basic questions:

1. *Was it necessary to drop the bomb in order to get the Japanese to surrender?*
2. *Was this weapon qualitatively different from all the other weapons used during the war?*
3. *Did the use of the bomb speed up the Japanese surrender?*
4. *Were there plausible alternatives for achieving surrender without invading Japan or dropping the bomb?*
5. *Did the atomic bombing of Japan, by shortening the war, result in a net saving of lives?*
6. *Was the Nagasaki bomb necessary?*

WAR DEPARTMENT
OFFICE OF THE CHIEF OF STAFF
WASHINGTON 25, D. C.

25 July 1945

TO: General Carl Spaatz
     Commanding General
     United States Army Strategic Air Forces

1. The 509 Composite Group, 20th Air Force will deliver its first special bomb as soon as weather will permit visual bombing after about 3 August 1945 on one of the targets: Hiroshima, Kokura, Niigata and Nagasaki. To carry military and civilian scientific personnel from the War Department to observe and record the effects of the explosion of the bomb, additional aircraft will accompany the airplane carrying the bomb. The observing planes will stay several miles distant from the point of impact of the bomb.

2. Additional bombs will be delivered on the above targets as soon as made ready by the project staff. Further instructions will be issued concerning targets other than those listed above.

3. Dissemination of any and all information concerning the use of the weapon against Japan is reserved to the Secretary of War and the President of the United States. No communiques on the subject or releases of information will be issued by Commanders in the field without specific prior authority. Any news stories will be sent to the War Department for special clearance.

4. The foregoing directive is issued to you by direction and with the approval of the Secretary of War and of the Chief of Staff, USA. It is desired that you personally deliver one copy of this directive to General MacArthur and one copy to Admiral Nimitz for their information.

THOS. T. HANDY
General, G.S.C.
Acting Chief of Staff

Letter from General Thomas T. Handy to General Carl Spaatz authorizing the dropping of the first atomic bomb (July 25, 1945).

7. Was there a plausible alternative for achieving surrender with a lower loss of life, by using the bomb differently than the United States actually did?

8. Did the United States drop the bomb to intimidate the Soviet Union?

9. Did U.S. leaders rush to drop the bomb, in the hope of bringing about Japanese surrender before the Soviets could enter the Pacific War?

10. Was the bomb used out of racism?

11. Did the use of this weapon violate the basic principles of a just war?

12. Was the dropping of the atomic bomb justified? How to judge the morality of this act?

1. *Was it necessary to drop the bomb in order to get the Japanese to surrender?*

The answer to this question is clear. No, it was not necessary. The Allies were going to defeat Japan, with or without the bomb.

Some Manhattan Project scientists harbored real doubts about whether this complicated experimental machine—the bomb—would actually work as predicted. The United States government was by no means counting on the atomic bomb to win the Pacific War: by the summer of 1945, American leaders had a full-scale plan in place for the invasion of the Japanese home islands, and the assault fleets were already well on their way to a state of readiness.

The first phase of the planned invasion, code-named Operation Olympic, was set for November 1, 1945. It would involve a large amphibious assault, dwarfing even the D-Day operation of 1944 in France; the target would be the southernmost of the Japanese home islands, Kyushu. Once Kyushu had been seized by Allied forces, the plan called for this island to serve as a forward base for a second and definitive attack, code-named Coronet, scheduled for the spring of 1946. Coronet would entail a final push across the remainder of Japanese home territory, culminating in the imposition of terms on a prostrate nation sometime in 1946. The Allies had done this to Germany, and they were determined to do it to Japan as well.

The forces that the Allies could bring to bear in this effort so overwhelmingly outweighed those that the Japanese could muster in their own defense that any impartial observer in the summer of 1945 could clearly see Japan's defeat as inevitable. The problem lay in the fact that the Japanese government remained, perhaps not surprisingly, far from dispassionate on this issue. A majority of the Japanese Imperial Council, including

Emperor Hirohito, clung tenaciously to one final possibility through July and early August 1945. While they acknowledged that they could not win this war, they still held out hope that, through a combination of diplomacy and indomitable resistance, they could compel the Allies to accept a negotiated peace settlement rather than unconditional surrender.

The terms of this settlement, in the eyes of the Japanese hard-liners who dominated national policy, would have to include the following:

- a guarantee that Hirohito could remain on the throne;
- no occupation of the Japanese home islands;
- the Japanese government would control the postwar demobilization process; and
- all trials of military and civilian leaders would be held by Japanese courts.

Since the Allies deemed such conditions completely unacceptable, the stage was set for the war to continue until either one side or the other proved willing to budge. However, it would be a distortion of history to portray the situation in the summer of 1945 as a clear and unambiguous confrontation between the Japanese and Allied governments over the possible terms of surrender. The reality during those months was far messier and more fluid than that: the military situation shifted daily; both governments had numerous factions urging different policies on their own leaders; communication between the Japanese and Americans remained indirect and sporadic; and neither side had any clear sense of precisely how the war could be brought to an acceptable end. The phrase "the fog of war"—the unavoidable confusion and conflicting pressures that often characterize decision-making in the heat of ongoing battle—applies with particular force to the decisions made by the Japanese and American governments during the summer of 1945.

2. *Was this weapon qualitatively different from all the other weapons used during the war?*

The number of persons killed in Hiroshima and Nagasaki will never be exactly known, because the atomic weapons destroyed not only a large number of the cities' inhabitants, but much of the governmental and record-keeping infrastructure that might be used in making such an assessment. Estimates vary widely. The low range of the spectrum is 70,000 dead in Hiroshima and 40,000 in Nagasaki; the high range, which includes deaths from radiation sickness and other bomb-related causes in the years following 1945, is 200,000 in Hiroshima and 140,000 in Nagasaki.

These unimaginable numbers are not qualitatively different from the atrocious tally of persons killed in other major aerial bombing raids of World War II: Tokyo (100,000 killed), Dresden (60,000 killed), Hamburg (45,000 killed). All totaled, the Allied bombing campaign over Germany killed between 300,000 and 600,000 civilians. The nonnuclear bombing of sixty-six major Japanese cities, in the first seven months of 1945, probably killed between 200,000 and 300,000 civilians (though some estimates range as high as 900,000).[3]

If we put ourselves in the place of the Allied leaders in 1945, we have to make the leap into a very different mental world from that of today. We have already seen, in chapter 5, how the Allies gradually came to adopt the Orwellian logic of strategic incendiary bombing, in which the killing of masses of noncombatants could be rationalized as morally acceptable and even as "merciful," since it hastened the war's end and the earliest possible cessation of the carnage. The wartime context, moreover, was unequivocally one of brutalization, dehumanization of the enemy, racism, and hatred—on all sides. To lose sight of this fact is to miss one of the key realities of the Second World War: though most of the war's major decisions were certainly built on logical analysis, no judgment was made in a detached rational vacuum. On all sides, the wartime leaders could not help but make their decisions as human beings, subject to such emotions as outrage, fear, bitterness, and the desire for revenge. This is not to suggest that most of what they did was primarily motivated by such emotions: it was not. But it does call attention to the broader human context within which all wartime policies were unavoidably being shaped. This was a time of hard, cold, often grimly brutal resolutions, in which the deaths of large numbers of human beings had become commonplace, and in which the more humane considerations that normally characterize peacetime decision-making necessarily took a back seat.

Seen in this light, how different was the atomic bomb from the conventional ordnance that had already torched so many cities of Germany and Japan? When one focuses on the effects of such bombing, an argument could be made that it was not all that different. Here is a description of the effects of the British incendiary raid on Hamburg of July 27, 1943, one of the major firestorms of the war:

[A fifteen-year-old girl:]
Mother wrapped me in wet sheets, kissed me, and said "Run!" I hesitated at the door. In front of me I could see only fire—everything red, like the

door to a furnace. An intense heat struck me. A burning beam fell in front of my feet. I shied back but, then, when I was ready to jump over it, it was whirled away by a ghostly hand. I ran out into the street. The sheets around me acted as sails and I had the feeling that I was being carried away by the storm.

[A nineteen-year-old man:]

I struggled to run against the wind in the middle of the street but could only reach a house on the corner. . . . We got to the Löschplatz all right but I couldn't go on across the Eiffelstrasse because the asphalt had melted. There were people on the roadway, some already dead, some still lying alive but stuck in the asphalt. They must have rushed onto the roadway without thinking. Their feet had got stuck and then they had put out their hands to try to get out again. They were on their hands and knees screaming.

[The next day:]

Four-story-high blocks of flats were like glowing mounds of stone right down to the basement. Everything seemed to have melted and pressed the bodies away in front of it. Women and children were so charred as to be unrecognizable; those that had died through lack of oxygen were half-charred and recognizable. Their brains had tumbled from their burst temples and their insides from the soft parts under the ribs. How terribly these people must have died. The smallest children lay like fried eels on the pavement.[4]

Forty-five thousand persons died in this manner in Hamburg on that night and the following day.

Sometimes, as we engage in the intellectual exercise of trying to understand the complexities of the war, we can become inured to the underlying realities. This psychological distancing from our subject no doubt reflects, in a small way, the manner in which the wartime leaders themselves gradually became calloused to the dreadful acts that were being perpetrated all around them, and that they themselves were perpetrating. As we analyze the wartime decisions, we catch ourselves, to our shock, tossing around numbers of dead human beings—ten thousand here, a hundred thousand there—almost as unfeelingly as the participants themselves. This tendency toward psychological numbing is understandable and perhaps unavoidable, but we need to resist it as vigorously as we can. We must keep reminding ourselves what it really means, in practice, to speak the words "firestorm" or "Hiroshima." For hidden beneath the abstraction of the words—words grown customary from heavy use—lie the unimaginable cruelty and madness of what actually happened.

Here then is a glimpse of the reality under the word "Hiroshima." The excerpts are taken from Richard Rhodes's study *The Making of the Atomic Bomb.*

"Just as I looked up at the sky," remembers a girl who was five years old at the time and safely at home in the suburbs, "there was a flash of white light and the green in the plants looked in that light like the color of dry leaves."

[A series of official reports:]

Accompanying the flash of light was an instantaneous flash of heat. . . . Its duration was probably less than one tenth of a second and its intensity was sufficient to cause nearby flammable objects . . . to burst into flame and to char poles as far as 4,000 yards away from the hypocenter [i.e., the point on the ground directly below the fireball]. . . .

Because the heat in [the] flash comes in such a short time . . . there is no time for any cooling to take place, and the temperature of a person's skin can be raised [120 degrees Fahrenheit] . . . in the first millisecond at a distance of [2.3 miles].

Severe thermal burns of over grade 5 occurred within [0.6 to 1 mile] of the hypocenter . . . and those of grades 1 to 4 [occurred as far as 2 to 2.5 miles] from the hypocenter. . . . Extremely intense thermal energy leads not only to carbonization but also to evaporation of the viscerae.

People exposed within half a mile of the Little Boy fireball, that is, were seared to bundles of smoking black char in a fraction of a second as their internal organs boiled away.

At the same instant birds ignited in midair. Mosquitoes and flies, squirrels, family pets crackled and were gone. The fireball flashed an enormous photograph of the city at the instant of its immolation fixed on the mineral, vegetable and animal surfaces of the city itself. A spiral ladder left its shadow in unburned paint on the surface of a steel storage tank. Leaves shielded reverse silhouettes on charred telephone poles.

A human being left the memorial of his outline in unspalled granite on the steps of a bank. Another, pulling a handcart, protected a handcart- and-human-shaped surface of asphalt from boiling.

[A junior college girl:]

The vicinity was in pitch darkness; from the depths of the gloom, bright red flames rise crackling, and spread moment by moment. The faces of my friends who just before were working energetically are now burned and blistered, their clothes torn to rags; to what shall I liken their trembling appearance as they stagger about? Our teacher is holding her students close to her like a mother hen protecting her chicks, and like baby chicks paralyzed with terror, the students were thrusting their heads under her arms.

[Yoko Ota, the writer:]

I just could not understand why our surroundings had changed so greatly in one instant. . . . I thought it might have been something which had nothing to do with the war, the collapse of the earth which it was said would take place at the end of the world.

[A medical doctor, Michihiko Hachiya, and his wife:]

The shortest path to the street lay through the house next door so through the house we went—running, stumbling, falling, and then running again until in headlong flight we tripped over something and fell sprawling into the street. Getting to my feet, I discovered that I had tripped over a man's head.

"Excuse me! Excuse me, please!" I cried hysterically.

[A young woman:]

I heard a girl's voice clearly from behind a tree. "Help me, please." Her back was completely burned and the skin peeled off and was hanging down from her hips.

[One of Dr. Hachiya's visitors:]

There were so many burned [at a first-aid station] that the odor was like drying squid. They looked like boiled octopuses. . . . I saw a man whose eye had been torn out by an injury, and there he stood with his eye resting in the palm of his hand. What made my blood run cold was that it looked like the eye was staring at me.

There was a man, stone dead, sitting on his bicycle as it leaned against a bridge railing. . . . You could tell that many had gone down to the river to get a drink of water and had died there where they lay. I saw a few live people still in the water, knocking against the dead as they floated down the river. There must have been hundreds and thousands who fled to the river to escape the fire and then drowned.

[A history professor:]

I climbed Hikiyama Hill and looked down. I saw that Hiroshima had disappeared. . . . I was shocked by the sight. . . . What I felt then and still feel now I just can't explain with words. Of course I saw many dreadful scenes after that—but that experience, looking down and finding nothing left of Hiroshima—was so shocking that I simply can't express what I felt. . . . Hiroshima didn't exist—that was mainly what I saw—Hiroshima just didn't exist.

[Richard Rhodes concludes:]

Destroyed, that is, were not only men, women, and thousands of children but also restaurants and inns, laundries, theater groups, sports clubs, sewing clubs, boys' clubs, girls' clubs, love affairs, trees and gardens, grass, gates, gravestones, temples and shrines, family heirlooms, radios, classmates, books, courts of law, clothes, pets, groceries and markets, telephones, personal letters, automobiles, bicycles, horses—120 war-horses—musical instruments, medicines and medical equipment, life savings, eyeglasses, city records, sidewalks, family scrapbooks, monuments, engagements, marriages, employees, clocks and watches, public transportation, street signs, parents, works of art.

[The history professor who climbed Hikiyama Hill:]

Such a weapon has the power to make everything into nothing.[5]

From the perspective of the dead, perhaps, the difference between a firebombing and an atomic bombing is not very significant at all. Death is death. A German child lying "like a fried eel" on the pavement of Hamburg is not qualitatively different from a Japanese child lying "like a boiled octopus" in the first-aid station of Hiroshima. Nor, we should add, are these dead German and Japanese children qualitatively different from the broken body of a London child, killed by German rockets in 1944, or from the shattered form of a Shanghai child, killed by Japanese bombardment in 1937. In all these cases, a city's normal civilian life has been rapidly taken apart, and what remains are the dead, the maimed, the suffering beyond words, the wreckage of lives.

Nevertheless, there are two obvious differences. First, an atomic bomb goes on killing and maiming for years after it has been dropped. Unlike conventional explosives, it emits a powerful radioactive poison that insidiously, invisibly permeates the bodies of those who have survived the blast and heat from the initial detonation. Tens of thousands of Hiroshima's inhabitants who lived beyond August 1945 developed mysterious illnesses that slowly ate away at them, bringing on a wretched, agonizing death that contemporary medicine proved powerless to prevent. These people, known in Japanese as *hibakusha*, suffered a double ordeal in the years following the war: they not only had to contend with the myriad ailments brought on by radiation exposure, but also faced widespread social ostracism, since it was unclear both to themselves and to others whether their bodies might succumb at any moment to a mysterious disease. To be a young man or woman from Hiroshima or Nagasaki in the 1950s meant a virtual impossibility of finding a spouse, because no one wanted to take on the risk of having children with someone whose genetic constitution might have been damaged by radiation. In this sense, then, the bomb constituted a weapon of a uniquely cruel nature—a device that not only killed and harmed indiscriminately in the short term, but also cut deeply into the future lives of those who had seemingly emerged unscathed.[6]

The second qualitative difference of atomic bombs was one that most wartime leaders clearly recognized at the time. Hamburg was destroyed by 787 Lancaster, Stirling, and Halifax bombers, flying in from Britain to drop 1,000 tons of high-explosive bombs and 1,300 tons of incendiary bombs in a steady procession over the city that lasted for more than an hour. Hiroshima was devastated by a solitary B-29 bomber, carrying a single 5-ton bomb. The attack was over in just a few minutes.

What would happen when, in a single nighttime raid, 787 B-29 bombers dropped 787 of these new weapons on the cities of some future enemy nation? Even if only a quarter of the planes got through to deliver their bombs, what would be left of the society on the ground? What would a nation look like, when its two hundred largest cities and towns had been reduced to so many Hiroshimas and Nagasakis? And all in a single night?

This weapon was not just a new and more powerful piece of ordnance. It was a destroyer of societies. Its power crossed a clear qualitative threshold, and opened up a new era of history. And Allied leaders knew it at the time.

Henry Stimson, the U.S. secretary of war during World War II, was seventy-eight years old in 1945. He had fought in France in the field artillery during the First World War, served as governor of the Philippines and secretary of state under Herbert Hoover. As Roosevelt's secretary of war, he had presided over the Manhattan Project from its inception, and he knew the nature of the weapon the United States was creating. Stimson was not normally a man who used grandiose language. Here is what he wrote in his notes as he prepared for a secret top-level meeting in Washington to discuss the bomb on May 31, 1945 (a full six weeks before the device had even been tested):

> Its size and character
> We don't think it mere new weapon
> Revolutionary discovery of relation of Man to universe
> Great historical landmark, like gravitation, Copernican theory
> But: bids fair to be infinitely greater, in respect to its effect on the ordinary
>   affairs of man's life
> May destroy or perfect international civilization
> May be Frankenstein or means for world peace.[7]

Harry Truman, when interviewed after the war, claimed that he never lost a night's sleep over his decision to use the bomb against Japan. But his actions in the aftermath of Nagasaki are nonetheless revealing. On August 10, 1945, when his aides informed him of Japan's surrender offer, he immediately did two things. He directed that the strategic bombing of Japan continue, as a means of keeping pressure on the enemy until negotiations were finalized. And he ordered an immediate cessation of the atomic bombing. One member of his cabinet, Secretary of Commerce Henry Wallace, later described the president's decision: "The thought of wiping out another 100,000 people was too horrible. He didn't like the idea of killing 'all those kids.' "[8]

The historian Barton Bernstein notes the implicit significance of Truman's actions that day:

> Unlike Stimson, who had earlier agonized about the mass bombing of cities,
> Truman neither before nor after Hiroshima and Nagasaki seemed worried
> about such mass killings by conventional means. But before the Hiroshima
> bombing, in what can only be interpreted as self-deception, he had managed
> not to know that the A-bombs would slay many noncombatants.[9]

Now the president could no longer "manage not to know." The potency of the atomic bomb shattered the wartime rationalization, however tenuous, through which the killing of civilians had been sanitized thus far—the portrayal of noncombatant casualties as unfortunate but unavoidable "collateral damage" inflicted on the enemy while seeking to hit only factories and military installations with precision bombing. Hiroshima erased that fiction forever: it held up before Truman, in a way that could no longer be fudged or evaded, the true nature of modern warfare.

Today, of course, we know what grew out of that new weapon: the Cold War arms race, the nuclear balance of terror, the numbers of warheads in the tens of thousands. We know that the fear of this weapon may actually have contributed to stabilizing superpower relations during the tense years of standoff between the United States and the USSR. We know that it may actually have helped to avert a major war between great powers.

But we also know this: we came hair-raisingly close to unleashing the full fury of an intercontinental nuclear holocaust in the Cuban Missile Crisis of 1962. "At the end we lucked out," says Robert McNamara, U.S. secretary of defense during the Cuban crisis, in the 2004 documentary film *The Fog of War:* "It was luck that prevented nuclear war. Rational individuals came that close to total destruction of their societies."[10] One week after the Cuban crisis had passed, Soviet premier Nikita Khrushchev wrote a letter to the American scientist Leo Szilard, referring in a tone of awe to the "devastating thermonuclear war" that had just been averted. "During those days," Khrushchev wrote, "the world was practically on the brink of such a war."[11]

And the grandchildren of the World War II generation—German, Japanese, American, British, Russian, and all the others—must now grow up under the shadow of this very large question mark. For we know that if this weapon ever does get used again, on the scale that characterizes modern warfare, it holds the possibility for the kind of destruction that we cannot really imagine. The only word that comes to mind is one that melds together two existing words: ecology and genocide. To get: ecocide; the extermination of most forms of life on earth.

Having said this, however, we must be careful not to project backward onto the atomic bomb of 1945 all the imagery and knowledge that have come to be associated with it during the half-century that followed. The bomb, as it existed in 1945, was only *potentially* an ecocidal weapon, because just two specimens of such a device were available, and at most a dozen or so could be manufactured by the end of the year. The bombs that detonated over Hiroshima and Nagasaki released an explosive force equivalent to about 12,000 and 20,000 tons of TNT, respectively; the nuclear devices that were being built by the late 1950s positively dwarfed these weapons, releasing forces on the order of a million tons of TNT—a difference of two whole orders of magnitude.

Truman, Stimson, and the other 1945 leaders, both military and civilian, could undoubtedly intuit where this new weapon was headed in the years to come; they could sense that they were opening a Pandora's box. But they did not at the time invest the bomb with all the fear and opprobrium with which most people tend to view it today. They did not have lingering in their minds, as we do today, the images of the blasted cityscape of Hiroshima, the faces of the disfigured survivors; they were not (with a few exceptions like the Manhattan Project scientist Leo Szilard) placing the bomb in the mental framework of an all-out nuclear war that leaves behind it nothing but a world of radioactive rubble.

The Anglo-American leaders regarded the bomb from a position of cautiously optimistic pragmatism. They did not know for sure whether it would work, nor were they aware of precisely how destructive it would be if it did work (though the Alamogordo test certainly offered an impressive preview). Above all, they believed they had good reason to hope that this new weapon in the American arsenal might add a decisive factor to the array of pressures being brought to bear against Japan—this already defeated enemy that was stubbornly refusing to surrender. The bomb could be made to appear to the Japanese as a weapon that the United States possessed in sufficient quantities to produce one Hamburg, one Dresden, one Tokyo, every few days or even more frequently—until capitulation. The fact that this kind of nuclear destruction was actually not available to the United States in August 1945, because the new bombs could only be produced with a frequency of one every few weeks—remained a closely guarded secret. For the Allied leaders of 1945, therefore, the bomb was definitely not something to be dreaded; it was not an ecocidal weapon or a destroyer of nations. It constituted a possible trump card in an already strong hand, a potentially pivotal factor in the ongoing psychological game of getting the Japanese to admit defeat and lay down their arms.

3. *Did the use of the bomb speed up the Japanese surrender?*

The answer to this question is an almost certain yes. Nuclear weaponry constituted one of two factors that tipped the balance in the Japanese leadership, finally compelling them to open serious negotiations for surrender. The other factor was the Soviet entry into the Pacific War, which took place on August 8, two days after the bombing of Hiroshima and the day before the bombing of Nagasaki.

The Anglo-Americans issued their final ultimatum to Japan from the conference at Potsdam, Germany, on July 26. In this document, known as the Potsdam Declaration, they were careful to fudge some important issues. On the one hand, they did not want to be perceived by their own populations as retreating from the principle of unconditional surrender.

On the other hand, they did want to give the Japanese enough hope for the future so that they would perceive surrender as being clearly more advantageous than fighting on to the bitter end. The Potsdam Declaration was designed to appeal to those factions in the Japanese leadership who might be leaning toward surrender: it offered extensive assurances to the Japanese people and their country in the postwar period; and at the same time, it stated that Japan would have to return to real democracy in its postwar government, and that war criminals would be tried and punished for any atrocities they had committed.

Most important, the Potsdam Declaration deliberately left a somewhat vague spot in its language: it did not say that the emperor would have to give up his position, nor did it say that the postwar government would have to be a republic. The Allies knew that a majority of Japanese regarded Hirohito as semi-divine, and would have endured almost any sacrifice rather than watch him be killed or forcibly removed from power. This aspect of the declaration had been the subject of intense debate within the American government during the preceding months. Some officials, like Undersecretary of State Joseph Grew, had argued that offering an explicit promise of Hirohito's continuation on the throne would greatly increase the chances of Japan's accepting Allied terms. Others, like Assistant Secretary of State Dean Acheson, felt that this kind of imperial guarantee would amount to an unconscionable form of appeasement toward a regime that bore direct culpability for all manner of atrocities and aggression. The final wording of the Potsdam ultimatum, therefore, reflected a compromise between these factions—seeking to communicate a clear impression of continued Anglo-American resolve, while still keeping options open on the imperial question, so that the Japanese could see that surrender would not necessarily mean betraying Hirohito to the mercies of Allied justice. According to the historians Tsuyoshi Hasegawa and Richard Frank, the evidence we now have from Japanese archives shows that key members of the Japanese leadership indeed interpreted the Potsdam surrender terms as leaving open the continuation of the imperial dynasty.[12]

Why were the Japanese so reluctant to face the fact that they had lost the war? The answer lies partly in the highly militarized nature of Japanese society since the 1930s, and in the virtual stranglehold that the military leadership had on the government. Anyone who dared to voice counsels of caution, of reasonable doubt about the ultimate success of the war effort, ran the serious risk of being branded a traitor and either arrested or simply murdered outright.

Surrender was widely regarded by Japanese soldiers as the ultimate dishonor, a stain on a man's character to be avoided at any cost: the island campaigns in the Pacific had rendered this widespread mentality horrifyingly evident. Again and again, Japanese garrisons fought to the end, preferring almost any kind of death, including suicide, rather than facing the dishonor of being captured alive. The result was a recurrent fatality rate among the Japanese rarely before seen in the history of warfare: in the Gilbert Islands campaign, 99.7 percent killed; on Makin Island, 99 percent killed; in the Marshall Islands campaign, 98.5 percent killed; at Kwajalein, 98.4 percent killed; on Saipan, 97 percent killed.[13] Even when defeat became a virtual certainty, Japanese soldiers fought on, sometimes launching a final suicidal banzai charge, sometimes committing hara-kiri before capture. Even the wounded could not be counted on to give up: in many cases they turned themselves into human booby traps, detonating one last grenade as Allied soldiers prepared to take them prisoner.

Not surprisingly, this mentality applied to the defense of the home islands with an even greater conviction: for here the defense of territory constituted a direct effort in protection of Hirohito himself. Most Japanese leaders, and a majority of citizens, held to this view, and were therefore steeling themselves for a final series of battles that could end only in death or in a negotiated peace that preserved honor and emperor. The army and navy leaders, during the late spring of 1945, developed a detailed plan for this last-ditch defense of the homeland: they code-named it Ketsu-Go (Operation Decisive).

Their logic for Ketsu-Go was straightforward.[14] If we can convince the Allies that we will never give up, they will see no alternative but to launch a direct invasion of Japan, just as they did with Germany. And if we can render that invasion sufficiently bloody for them—costing them thousands and thousands of lives, day after day—then there is a good chance that at some point they will be forced to soften their terms, and will become willing to accept our conditions for a negotiated peace. Public opinion in the democracies will simply not abide the endless loss of young men that would be required for a full-scale conquest of Japan, fought against the implacably unyielding resistance we will lay out for them: We can play on this fact to extract a final set of concessions from the Allied governments. In the end, if Ketsu-Go succeeds, we will still have lost the war, but we will nonetheless emerge with our national polity intact, our emperor safe, and a set of relatively favorable peace terms.

Accordingly, preparations for Ketsu-Go received top priority in the Japanese war effort during the late spring and summer of 1945. Army and navy leaders accurately surmised that the first major Allied thrust would aim at Kyushu, and they accordingly began building up troop concentrations, war supplies, and multiple lines of fortifications along all the likely landing points. They also started training the civilian population—both on Kyushu and on the other Japanese home islands—to participate directly in the coming military operations, thereby effectively turning millions of former noncombatants into a vast guerrilla force to bleed the invading enemy. Such hastily trained and scantily equipped partisans would clearly pay an extremely high blood price in their confrontation with the heavily armored and mechanized Allied armies, but this price was evidently acceptable to the Japanese government. Finally, there were the kamikazes, who would be brought out in unprecedented numbers, with orders to aim at both the Allied ground troops and the ships assembled offshore.

The numerical dimensions of Ketsu-Go, exhaustively compiled by the historian Richard Frank, are sobering, to say the least. In the first six months of 1945, the Japanese boosted their manpower on Kyushu from 150,000 troops to 545,000; fighter aircraft available for Ketsu-Go by July 1945 numbered about 5,000, while the aircraft available for kamikaze strikes numbered about 5,400. Overall troop strength on all the home islands had more than doubled since January 1945, as military leaders brought them back from outlying theaters for the war's final phase: active troops numbered about 1.9 million by midsummer. Japanese leaders were, in effect, banking on the bloodbath that would engulf Kyushu that fall as their best point of leverage for securing a negotiated peace. As in the game of chess, when one sees defeat looming and sacrifices one's queen to end the game in a draw, the leadership chose to make a climactic sacrifice of their own people so as to have a chance of ending the war on acceptable terms.

Emperor Hirohito, it should be emphasized, unequivocally supported this policy until mid-June 1945, and he acquiesced to it—albeit with increasing reluctance—right through the first week of August 1945.[15] The emperor, along with several key moderates among the leadership, did not share the recklessly defiant attitude of the army and navy brass, and felt certain that the war was irretrievably lost. Nevertheless, both Hirohito and these moderate figures continued to hold out hope, through early August 1945, that the evolving military and diplomatic situation might still present an opportunity for obtaining a negotiated peace.

The Japanese government therefore responded to the Potsdam Declaration with icy reserve. Although the leaders agreed that it would be impolitic to reject outright this major Allied declaration, they nonetheless wanted to make it clear both to the Allies and to their own population that the Potsdam terms were unacceptable. On the morning of July 28, Japanese newspaper headlines unambiguously proclaimed that Japan was rejecting the ultimatum. The article on the subject in *Asahi Shimbun*, for example, led with the headline LAUGHABLE MATTER, then reported that the government deemed the Potsdam ultimatum "a thing of no great moment."[16] No official of the Japanese government issued any denial or correction of these reports. Then, on the afternoon of July 28, Prime Minister Kantaro Suzuki held a press conference. "The government," he stated, "does not regard [the Potsdam Declaration] as a thing of any value; the government will just ignore [*mokusatsu*] it. We will press forward resolutely to carry the war to a successful conclusion."[17]

The word *mokusatsu* literally means "kill with silence," but it could be broadly construed as conveying a range of connotations: "ignore," "treat with silent contempt," or the more neutral "refrain from comment." Some observers have argued that the government, in choosing the word *mokusatsu* to characterize its stance, was actually engaging in a subtle form of deliberate ambiguity, and was trying to leave the door open for further negotiations over the possible acceptance of the Potsdam terms.[18] The historian Richard Frank, however, argues persuasively that—regardless of the issue of how to translate *mokusatsu*—the intention of the Japanese government in late July and early August, as revealed by documentary evidence, was to continue prosecuting the war while preparing for Ketsu-Go and simultaneously seeking to enlist Soviet assistance in negotiating a favorable peace.[19] The Allies, not surprisingly, interpreted Suzuki's *mokusatsu* as a flat-out rejection: this was reasonable, given that the prime minister had sandwiched this ambiguous word between a sentence that dismissed the Potsdam Declaration as valueless, and a sentence that promised to continue "pressing forward" with the war.

The Japanese diplomatic démarche toward the Soviet Union, in these closing months of the Pacific War, rested on a mixture of desperation and highly unrealistic hope. Japanese leaders, from Hirohito on down, evidently believed that a vague promise of postwar territorial concessions in Asia might pry the Russians loose from their British and American allies.[20] In this belief they were gravely mistaken. The Soviets had already announced in April 1945 that they would not renew their 1941 nonaggression treaty with Japan. Now, in July and early August, they responded noncommittally to the Japanese diplomatic overtures, and instead began rapidly building up their troop concentrations all along the Chinese border.

The days went by after the proclamation of the Potsdam ultimatum.

The killing continued. On July 26, the American heavy cruiser *Indianapolis* delivered Little Boy, the first of two atomic bombs, to the Pacific island of Tinian, where the United States had built an enormous airbase for B-29 bombers. Three days later, the Japanese submarine *I-58* found the *Indianapolis* in the Philippine Sea, and sank it with a salvo of six torpedoes. Of the 1,199 men on board, some 350 were killed outright or went down with the ship; another 850 jumped overboard and watched their ship sink in a mere twelve minutes. Through a series of negligent mistakes at the ship's destination, Leyte, no one in the U.S. Navy even knew that the ship had been hit. For three days and nights the men of the *Indianapolis* floated, sinking slowly deeper as their life jackets became waterlogged—blinded by sunlight during the day, dying of thirst, hallucinating, raving in the darkness at night, the helpless prey of repeated shark attacks.[21] When an American PBY floatplane discovered them, purely by chance, on August 2, only 318 remained alive to be rescued.

On August 6, at 8:15 a.m., the B-29 bomber *Enola Gay* dropped the first atomic bomb on Hiroshima. At first the news filtering into Tokyo was sketchy or contradictory; then, by the morning of August 7, the situation became clearer. Japanese radio began picking up President Truman's announcement about the atomic bomb early in the morning, and a scientific team was dispatched to Hiroshima to verify the American claims. Prime Minister Suzuki called a cabinet meeting on the afternoon of August 7, but the Japanese government took no immediate action other than to lodge a formal protest through the International Red Cross about the American use of this cruel new weapon. Ongoing discussions among the members of the Imperial War Council—the Big Six, as they were known—revealed a complete deadlock between moderates and hardliners: the three moderates (Suzuki, Shigenori Togo, Mitsumasa Yonai) urged acceptance of the Potsdam terms with the sole condition that the emperor be allowed to stay on the throne; the three diehards (the army and navy chiefs Korechika Anami, Yoshijiro Umezu, Soemu Toyoda) argued that this new weapon was not qualitatively different from the firebombs, that the Americans could not have very many of these weapons, and that Japan must fight on until the Allies accepted all four Japanese surrender terms.

Then, during the night of August 8, the news broke that the Soviet Union had just launched a massive surprise attack against Japanese army units in Manchuria and Outer Mongolia. Soviet forces advanced rapidly, overrunning the unprepared Japanese, taking hundreds of thousands of prisoners. Starting in the early morning of August 9 the Big Six began holding continuous meetings to deal with the double crisis that now confronted them. At midmorning their discussions were interrupted by the news that the Americans had just dropped a second atomic bomb on the city of Nagasaki. Preliminary reports indicated extensive damage, but considerably lower casualties than at Hiroshima. Yet still the top leadership could not reach agreement on what to do: they remained hopelessly deadlocked, three to three.

Late that night Emperor Hirohito summoned the Big Six for a meeting in his presence. Surely now, the moderates argued, anyone could see that the situation was completely hopeless. The combined armies and navies of the United States, Britain, China, and the Soviet Union were closing in. American ships and submarines had imposed a nearly impenetrable blockade on the home islands, and very little food, oil, or men could be brought in to sustain the war effort. Stockpiles were already dangerously low. Atomic bombs had just leveled two entire cities. The strategic bombardment was continuing.

But the three diehards on the council insisted that unconditional surrender remained out of the question. Only if the Allies accepted the four basic conditions would the fighting men of Japan lay down their arms. And the hard-liners warned the moderates: Even if we generals and admirals in this room were to accept unconditional surrender, we cannot guarantee that this dishonorable solution might not result in an insurrection or even a coup d'état by the armed forces.

At 2:00 a.m. Prime Minister Suzuki turned to the emperor, bowed, and apologized for the council's inability to reach agreement. Emperor Hirohito stood up and began speaking. Tradition held that the emperor's role in these kinds of deliberations would entail nothing more than a ritualistic acceptance of the consensus among the council members: but Hirohito could plainly see that the discussion was going nowhere. For the first time in eighty years, a Japanese emperor intervened directly to break an impasse among the leadership. Hirohito quietly chastised the military leaders for their persistence in offering unrealistic appraisals of Japan's war prospects. Then he told the stunned council that it was time to "bear the unbearable" and accept the Allied terms along the lines suggested by the three moderates.[22]

The next day, August 10, the Tokyo government communicated its reply to the Allies: We agree to surrender, as long as the imperial institutions will be allowed to remain. The Allied response came back promptly with an artfully ambiguous reply: "The authority of the Emperor and the

Japanese government shall be subject to the Supreme Commander of the Allied Powers." In other words: Yes, you can keep your emperor, but he will be subject to the authority of our occupation forces. This formula proved acceptable to Hirohito, who once again overruled some of his hard-line subordinates who wanted to reject it.

Hirohito recorded a speech to be broadcast on the radio, addressing his people throughout the Japanese empire. This, too, was a first: most Japanese had never heard his voice. In his recorded speech he said that the enemy's terrible new weapon meant that it was time to give up.[23] He explained to his people that Japan's national honor actually required surrender now, because by surrendering the nation would bring a halt to this devastating war, and hence would be seen by the rest of the world as sacrificing itself in the name of peace.

Hirohito's speech made a big impression on the Japanese armed forces, scattered all over the country and the rest of Asia and the Pacific. The emperor sent out personal envoys to assure the main military commanders in the field that it was truly his wish that they surrender. But in the following days many militarists still refused to give up. Some committed suicide. Another group started preparing a military coup against the emperor—a move that was discovered and quashed by the majority who still accepted his authority.

Even in Hiroshima itself, capitulation remained an unspeakable word. One of the doctors in the main hospital, Michihiko Hachiya, recorded the reaction among the wounded and those tending them, after they had heard the emperor's announcement:

> Like others in the room, I had come to attention at the mention of the Emperor's voice, and for a while we all remained silent and at attention. Darkness clouded my eyes, my teeth chattered, and I felt cold sweat running down my back. . . . By degrees people began to whisper and then to talk in low voices until, out of the blue sky, someone shouted: "How can we lose the war!"
>
> Following this outburst, expressions of anger were unleashed.
>
> "Only a coward would go back now!"
> "There is a limit to deceiving us!"
> "I would rather die than be defeated!"
> "What have we been suffering for?"
> "Those who died can't go to heaven in peace now!"
>
> The hospital suddenly turned into an uproar, and there was nothing one

could do. Many who had been strong advocates of peace and others who had lost their taste for war following the *pika* [atomic blast] were now shouting for the war to continue. . . .

The one word—surrender—had produced a greater shock than the bombing of our city.[24]

The bomb had, in effect, shattered the main piece of logic to which the Japanese leadership still clung in the summer of 1945: that of Ketsu-Go. If the Americans could keep wiping out Japanese cities with atomic blasts, one after another, then they would never need to launch an invasion on the ground. They could simply continue as they had done with Hiroshima and Nagasaki, methodically annihilating one piece after another of the Japanese nation until nothing remained but radioactive rubble. As if this were not bad enough, moreover, the Soviet Union's entry into the war had simultaneously destroyed any prospect, however tenuous, of securing a negotiated settlement through Russian mediation. For the Japanese leaders, the possibility suddenly loomed that the imperial government might be overthrown, not by invading Americans, but by their own enraged population, rising up against a regime that was insanely squandering their lives in its blind refusal to admit defeat.

One Japanese scholar, Sadao Asada, has argued that the bomb gave the moderates in the Japanese government a veritable "gift from heaven" because it so clearly and overwhelmingly undermined all the arguments of the diehards for continuing the war.[25] Indeed, Asada argues, the bomb paradoxically rendered capitulation considerably more palatable for the Japanese military as well. It was one thing to have to admit being bested by an enemy who had squared off with you on a level playing field, using the same types of weapons as you did: such a humiliation was simply too much to contemplate. But it was quite another thing to yield to an enemy whose weaponry summoned up the very innermost forces of nature. To admit defeat by such a foe was, in effect, akin to admitting defeat by a typhoon or an earthquake. There could still be some honor in surrendering to science itself.

4. *Were there plausible alternatives for achieving surrender without invading Japan or dropping the bomb?*

Four possible courses of action lay open to the Allies.

• *Option 1.* Let go of "unconditional surrender" and offer the Japanese a more flexible set of terms.

Franklin Roosevelt had first announced the Allied demand for unconditional surrender at the Casablanca Conference of January 1943. The doctrine had three main purposes: to prevent Nazi or Japanese leaders from seeking to split the Allies by offering separate peace terms to one of the Big Three; to reassure the Soviets that the Anglo-Americans would stay in the war all the way to complete victory; and to avoid the sort of problem that had arisen after the First World War, in which the defeated German army claimed that it had not really been vanquished on the battlefield, but had been "stabbed in the back" by traitorous German civilian leaders who had called for an armistice sooner than necessary. The 1943 doctrine of unconditional surrender meant that, this time around, when Germany finally gave up, all Germans would clearly understand that their Wehrmacht had been incontrovertibly crushed.

The problem with applying this doctrine to the Pacific War lay in the fact that most Japanese interpreted "unconditional surrender" as delivering their emperor into the vengeful hands of the enemy—an act they perceived as an unthinkably disgraceful dereliction of duty. Therefore, some historians have argued that, in the interest of ending the war quickly and bringing a halt to the bloodshed on both sides, the United States should have abandoned the formula of unconditional surrender, and given explicit assurances to the Japanese that they could keep their emperor if they laid down their arms.

This line of argument has three major weaknesses—one political, one moral, and one purely pragmatic. First, it ignores the American political context of the year 1945. Americans, civilians and military alike, had been waging war for several years with the words "unconditional surrender" as the stated goal of their nation's war policy. Japanese atrocities, both against Americans and against other Asians, had been well documented and repeatedly publicized. Under these conditions, any perception that Allied surrender terms were suddenly being softened would have proved completely unacceptable to a majority of the American people. In a June 1945 opinion poll, Americans were asked if they would accept a compromise peace with Japan as a way to shorten the war and avoid a bloody push into the Japanese home islands: they rejected the idea by a margin of nine to one.[26] The historian John Dower has exhaustively documented the thirst for revenge that characterized significant portions of the American citizenry: in wartime opinion polls, he notes, 10 to 13 percent of Americans

consistently supported the "annihilation" or "extermination" of the Japanese as a people, while a comparable percentage were in favor of severe retribution after Japan had been defeated. . . . A poll conducted by *Fortune* in December 1945 found that 22.7 percent of respondents wished the United

States had had the opportunity to use "many more [atomic bombs] before Japan had a chance to surrender."[27]

In this political climate, it is reasonable to assume that, if President Truman had offered concessions to the Japanese in 1945, an enraged American populace would have vehemently turned on him, accusing him of appeasement, of another Munich, of caving in unnecessarily to an enemy who was on the verge of defeat.

But let us suppose for a moment that Truman had decided to brave the wrath of the American electorate, and offer Hirohito an explicit guarantee. From a moral point of view, such an act could be construed in two different ways. From one perspective, it could be viewed as a courageous gesture of magnanimous statesmanship; yet from another, it could equally plausibly be seen as allowing a war criminal—the leader of a truly bestial regime—not only to avoid prosecution for his crimes, but to remain in power indefinitely. Herein lies the second main weakness of the "flexible surrender terms" argument. At a deeper level, the doctrine of unconditional surrender was not just about forcing the enemy to give up, but about the basic Allied aim of *remaking* Germany and Japan into peaceful and democratic societies after the war was over. One way of redeeming the wartime suffering and bloodshed would be to know that these two nations, once defeated, would be placed under completely new leadership, infused with a radically different set of values, and firmly channeled down a path of civic and moral transformation.[28] Unconditional surrender, in other words, was not just a brash wartime slogan, but a code word for precisely the kind of unequivocal and decisive military victory that would be needed to pave the way for a deep reordering of the aggressor societies. Hence, from a moral point of view, a softening of "unconditional surrender" to allow the retention of the emperor could be seen as fatally undermining this long-term political goal, by leaving in place the very government that had launched this bloody mess in the first place.[29]

Finally—and most important of all—we have good reason to believe that, from a purely practical point of view, such a policy might have brought about the opposite effect from the one intended. Knowing as we do now the arguments being made by the diehards in the Imperial Council during the summer of 1945, it is easy to imagine how they would have interpreted a sudden Allied retreat from the principle of unconditional surrender: they would have argued that the Allied populations were succumbing to war-weariness now that the European War was over; that the bloody battle for Okinawa had frightened the Americans into stark awareness of the casualties that lay ahead; and that Japan should therefore fight on harder than ever, holding out adamantly for favorable peace terms. Unfortunately, the mentality of the Japanese militarists was one that could never see an easing of Allied terms for what it would have been—a reasonable and magnanimous offer from a powerful victor. To them, such an act could only spell weakness, and would most likely have emboldened them to hold out even more tenaciously than before. The historian Tsuyoshi Hasegawa concludes that, even if the Americans had included an imperial guarantee in the Potsdam terms, "it is doubtful that Japan would have capitulated before the atomic bomb was dropped on Hiroshima and the Soviet Union entered the war."[30]

• *Option 2.* Bombard and blockade Japan into submission.

Japan was in appallingly bad shape in the summer of 1945. The Allied campaigns of bombardment and naval blockade were taking a terrible toll, and they would have become ever more effective as the months went by into the fall of 1945 and (perhaps) the spring of 1946. It is quite possible, then, that the combined impact of blockade and bombardment would have eventually brought the nation to surrender—without an invasion, and without the dropping of atomic bombs. The key question, from a moral point of view, is whether such a path would have been more or less humane than the one actually taken.

By the beginning of August 1945, sixty-six of Japan's largest cities had been blasted from the air, in a crescendo of attacks that had killed some 300,000 persons and left about 8 million homeless. The United States had more than a thousand B-29 bombers on hand for the pummeling of Japan, and more were on the way. As the bombings went on, the number of fighter planes and antiaircraft guns that the Japanese could bring to bear in their own defense was steadily dwindling—as was the fuel for the planes and the ammunition for the guns themselves. Losses to American flight crews over Japan were accordingly going down.

At the same time, the blockade imposed by Allied navies had just about sealed off Japan's access to foodstuffs, oil, and raw materials from outside the home islands. American submarines were sinking Japanese merchant ships at devastating rates; American mines blocked the major straits and channels of Japan's Inland Sea; and American carrier-borne aircraft patrolled Japan's seashores at will. Food rationing in Japan had begun early in the war, and had set the average intake of a Japanese citizen at 2,000 calories daily; this number had been gradually cut as the war went on, to 1,900 calories in 1944, and 1,680 calories in 1945. The Japanese, in short, were moving down a path that led to death by starvation.

But the situation was about to get much worse. General Curtis LeMay issued an order to his B-29 bombers on August 11, 1945, that would have temporarily focused the rain of airborne destruction primarily on Japan's transportation infrastructure. The nation's mountainous terrain and island geography meant that a large part of its transportation needs in peacetime had been met by ships carrying freight along shoreline routes: this mode of transport had been virtually obliterated by submarine and naval attacks. What remained was the nation's relatively flimsy network of railroads, concentrated in a few main lines that ran down the island valleys, and linked to small trunk lines that were already grossly overburdened. The destruction of these railroads in August 1945 would have forced key aspects of the Japanese economy back to the level of medieval times—but with a modern population of 70 million to feed and supply.

How many Japanese would have had to die—of starvation, of malnutrition-related disease, or through aerial bombardment—before the government finally acknowledged that the survival of Japan itself as a viable society lay at stake? Might the Japanese people have mounted an insurrection against their own government as their suffering reached intolerable levels? No one can be sure, of course. But we do know that as late as May 1946, a full nine months after the war, the effects of wartime destruction on Japanese food production and distribution were still getting worse: the average citizen's daily nutritional intake in Tokyo continued to fall through the winter of 1945–1946, to a remarkable 800 calories, and General Douglas MacArthur had to order 800,000 tons of food brought in during 1946 to avert a general famine. One Japanese scholar reported that estimates of likely deaths in such a famine ran to 10 million persons.[31]

The historian Richard Frank maintains that this option—continued blockade and bombardment instead of invasion—was in fact being considered with growing seriousness by key American military leaders such as Admirals Ernest King and Chester Nimitz in the summer of 1945.[32] Throughout June and July, the decryption of high-level Japanese radio communications was revealing to American leaders the massive Japanese defensive buildup on Kyushu, exactly where the main thrust of Operation Olympic was scheduled to go in. As it dawned on American leaders that the amphibious assault would face forces two to three times as large as originally estimated, they began questioning the wisdom of the Olympic plan and started reassessing other options—with the "siege and bombardment" strategy prominent among them. In the end, as we know, the atomic bomb and Soviet entry into the war brought about Japan's surrender more quickly than anticipated, and Allied leaders were spared the grimly medieval scenario of having to systematically starve millions of Japanese men, women, and children into submission.

• *Option 3.* Demonstrate the atomic bomb on an uninhabited target other than a city.

Here's the idea: Invite a group of Japanese military and political leaders to observe a detonation of one of the American atomic devices on a deserted Pacific island. Construct a scale model of a Japanese city on the island, with various kinds of buildings, including perhaps a realistic replica of the kind of bomb shelter used by Emperor Hirohito. Then retreat to an observation ship offshore, and allow the most senior Japanese official to push the button himself. After watching the explosion, go back ashore (presumably waiting a few hours for things to cool off) and let the Japanese representatives take a walk around. Let them inspect the devastation, then report this back to Tokyo, with the message: Surrender now or we'll do this to your cities.

To counter this idea, defenders of the bomb's use on populated cities offer several arguments.

First, they contend that, if the demonstration device had been a dud, then this would have proved acutely embarrassing to the United States and would have further strengthened Japanese resolve. But this is, quite frankly, a very silly argument. A demonstration of such a devastating weapon is a serious matter, if it holds the real possibility of saving tens of thousands of human lives by bringing about prompt surrender: to refuse such a demonstration because of a fear of embarrassment seems acutely disproportional to the matter at hand. Besides, the device had already been tested once, at Alamogordo, and had worked better than expected: there was no reason to expect a technical failure in a demonstration. Even in the unlikely event of technical failure, nothing would have prevented the Americans from swiftly diagnosing and fixing any technical glitches and scheduling another demonstration.

Second, the defenders of the bomb's use on cities argue that only an actual combat release, with huge numbers of civilian casualties in a real city, would have the shock effect required to push the Japanese leadership toward surrender. This argument has merit, but it assumes that a demonstration on an uninhabited target would inevitably fail to produce such a shock. There was no way to know this for certain, of course, until such a demonstration had been attempted.

Third, the defenders of the bomb's use on cities maintain that the United States only had two operational bombs in August 1945, and that it would have taken several weeks to build more. (The official estimate at the time was that one new bomb could be manufactured every few weeks, yielding a total of seven more atomic bombs by November 1.) Thus, if an August 1945 demonstration failed to bring about surrender, the United States would have wasted half its existing atomic arsenal. And meanwhile, American soldiers would be continuing to die all over the Pacific, in the ongoing battles that raged every day.

All three of these arguments are heavily outweighed by the moral advantage that the United States would have gained if it had carried out a demonstration on an uninhabited target. At least, afterward, the Americans could say that they were *forced* to nuke a city, because the Japanese simply would not accept a harmless demonstration. This would have strengthened the American moral position considerably.

Within the U.S. government, the responsibility for this decision rested primarily with a body known as the Interim Committee.[33] When Truman became president, he asked Henry Stimson, the secretary of war, to convene a top-level group of military and civilian officials who would provide the president with concrete recommendations about the use of the atomic bomb. The Interim Committee met several times in May and June 1945; its members included such respected figures as James Conant, the president of Harvard; Karl Compton, the president of MIT; Manhattan Project scientists Robert Oppenheimer, Enrico Fermi, and Ernest Lawrence; and the incoming secretary of state, James Byrnes. In its lengthy deliberations, the Interim Committee never seriously contemplated nonuse of the bomb, and only very briefly discussed (and dismissed) the option of a noncombat demonstration. Oppenheimer framed the question as follows, envisioning a demonstration of the bomb by means of an airburst over an uninhabited site in Japan:

> You ask yourself would the Japanese government as then constituted and with divisions between the peace party and the war party, would it have been influenced by an enormous nuclear firecracker detonated at a great height doing little damage and your answer is as good as mine. I don't know.[34]

Byrnes, for his part, found two reasons for rejecting such a demonstration:

> We feared that, if the Japanese were told that the bomb would be used on a given locality, they might bring our boys who were prisoners of war to that area. Also, the experts had warned us that the static test which was to take

place in New Mexico, even if successful, would not be conclusive proof that a bomb would explode when dropped from an airplane.[35]

On June 1, 1945, the committee's report advised Truman that the United States should drop the bomb, without prior warning, on inhabited cities possessing important military and industrial assets—since this manner of use would be most likely to shock the Japanese into surrender.

Today, of course, from the perspective of hindsight, we know that even the atomic bombing of Hiroshima failed, in itself, to secure surrender. The Japanese Imperial Council remained deadlocked over possible surrender terms between August 6 and August 9, which resulted in practice in a policy of continuing the war. Therefore, a fortiori, we can be just about positive that a harmless demonstration of the bomb's effects on an uninhabited site would not have produced the desired surrender.

From the moral perspective, however, the crucial point still remains: the U.S. government did not know, *before* the bombing of Hiroshima, that the Japanese would subsequently refuse to surrender. Therefore, a noncombat demonstration would still have constituted a reasonable and humane alternative. Though American leaders could not know for sure how many people the bomb would kill when dropped on a city, they could safely assume that the number would be at least in the tens of thousands, and would include a great many noncombatants. By deliberately ignoring (or overriding) this consideration, the United States was in effect choosing to target large numbers of noncombatants for destruction, without giving a serious chance to an alternative course of action that might possibly have rendered the atomic bombing of a city unnecessary.

The objections to a demonstration of the bomb, as laid out by Oppenheimer and Byrnes, seem grossly disproportional to the possible benefit in human lives saved that would have resulted if the demonstration had succeeded. Oppenheimer himself admitted that he did not know for sure—that a *possibility* existed that a demonstration might work. "Your answer is as good as mine. I don't know." This seems a terribly thin thread on which to hang a decision that consigns tens of thousands of noncombatants to incineration.

What would it really have cost the United States to give this option a try? One atomic bomb would have remained, to be dropped on a city like Hiroshima if the demonstration failed. A third bomb (of the more powerful Fat Man design used on Nagasaki) would have been ready on approximately August 21.[36] How the war would have ended under this scenario is a matter for speculation, which we duly take up in a separate section below. But one cannot help being left with a strong impression that American leaders missed a major opportunity here. Their attitude toward the prospect of using the bomb on an inhabited city seems to have been cavalier and callous. This missed opportunity arguably qualifies as one of the more serious moral failings of the Anglo-American war.

• *Option 4.* Adopt a combination of the above-mentioned strategies: modified surrender terms, continued blockade and bombardment, and noncombat demonstration of the bomb.

Barton Bernstein has argued that, while any one of the three strategies we have just discussed did not have a large chance of success if adopted by itself, the three of them together might have stood a very good chance of bringing about Japan's surrender. Why then was such a combination not attempted? Bernstein believes that a widespread fallacy comes into play here, having to do with how we think of the aims and intentions of American leaders in 1945. We tend to project backward onto those men the mentality of today, which (understandably) regards the bombing of Hiroshima and Nagasaki with horror: we assume, therefore, that those men would have been anxiously and energetically casting about for alternatives—*any* viable alternative—to using the bomb.

But this is completely mistaken, Bernstein argues.[37] American and British leaders regarded the bomb as one important element alongside many others in a broad array of pressures and inducements that they were bringing to bear on Japan so as to end the war as quickly as possible, in a manner consistent with long-standing Allied war aims. These pressures and inducements included:

• Soviet entry into the war against Japan;
• intensive aerial bombardment;
• naval blockade;
• threat of an amphibious invasion of Japan's home islands;
• offering Japan assurances for a generous postwar peace;
• fudging on the retention of the emperor in the Potsdam Declaration; and
• the atomic bomb.

According to Bernstein, American and British leaders in 1945 certainly recognized the revolutionary nature of the weapon they had created, but they did not regard its use against a city as being qualitatively different, from a moral standpoint, than the firebombing that had been visiting destruction on cities like Hamburg, Dresden, and Tokyo since 1943. Thus, they were not particularly interested in finding ways to avoid using the bomb; rather, they were interested in finding the most efficient way to shock the Japanese into accepting defeat in the most orderly manner possible. Any combination of the above factors that would achieve this goal swiftly, and with a minimum of Allied casualties, struck these leaders as the most humane and moral way to bring the war to an end.

In this sense, to speak of an Allied "decision" to drop the atomic bomb in 1945 can be somewhat misleading. If it implies that the leaders were agonizing over whether or not to use the bomb, and were anxiously seeking alternatives to such use, then we are dramatically out of touch with the realities of wartime decision-making in London and Washington. It is more accurate to say that the leaders hoped that the bomb would work, and were earnestly trying to figure out the most effective way to put it to use, as part of a broad, multipronged strategy for ending the war. Only a small minority of scientists in the Manhattan Project, and an even smaller minority (if anyone at all) in the U.S. and British governments, ever seriously considered relinquishing the bomb as an instrument of warfare.

Leo Szilard was such a man, but the majority of other Manhattan Project scientists, including Robert Oppenheimer, strongly disagreed with him.[38] The British government (which had been intimately involved in the Manhattan Project from its inception) gave American leaders its formal assent to the use of the bomb at the Potsdam Conference. Franklin Roosevelt had never shown the slightest qualms about the prospect of using this new weapon once it became available.

Overall, what the historians of the atomic bomb have shown us is a story in which the powerful momentum of the Manhattan Project, coupled with the extraordinary pressures of wartime, overwhelmingly stacked the deck in favor of a combat use of this radical new weapon. President Truman, in theory, could have said no to the dropping of the bomb: he certainly possessed the legal authority to do so. But in order to make such a decision he would have had to step completely out of the context of 1945, casting aside the entire body of assumptions and practices that had been built up by his government since 1941. He would have had to fly in the face of the overwhelming majority of his military and civilian advisors, and unilaterally countermand the policies bequeathed to him by his illustrious predecessor. In the words of General Leslie Groves, the military man in charge of the Manhattan Project, Truman's "decision was one of non-interference—basically, a decision not to upset the existing plans."[39]

The space for human agency is always a rather dicey matter, even for a sitting president of the United States. Truman possessed real power, and his choices certainly shaped the war's concluding months and the history that followed. But in the end, his power was also limited, because he made his decisions within a broader context of accumulated policies already established by his predecessors, accumulated moral and political assumptions already entrenched by wartime practice, and accumulated technological and bureaucratic processes already firmly in place when he assumed office. It is only in this rather constrained sense that we can say that Truman "decided" to drop the atomic bomb in 1945. And it is only with this context as our backdrop that we can accurately assess the possible alternatives to the bombing of Hiroshima and Nagasaki.

Having said this, we can still ask the question: what might have resulted if the Allies had tried a combination policy that entailed four powerful elements working in synergy?

- Offering modified surrender terms that included a guarantee of the emperor's position;
- continued naval blockade and conventional aerial bombardment;
- demonstrating the atomic bomb on an uninhabited target; and
- the Soviet attack that started on August 8.

No one can say for sure, of course. It seems highly unlikely that, under this scenario, the Japanese government would have capitulated as rapidly as it did in the wake of the Hiroshima and Nagasaki bombings, because these four factors (even taken together) did not possess the kind of extreme urgency conveyed by the threat of further atomic attacks on cities. How long the Japanese would have held out before surrendering is a matter open to speculation. One cannot easily imagine the militarist diehards on the Imperial Council suddenly waxing reasonable and conciliatory under the new pressure of Soviet intervention: the actual record of their arguments in the daylong meetings of August 9, after the Soviet attack in Manchuria, reveals that they still adamantly rejected surrender. Among these three fanatics, the logic of extracting favorable peace terms through the threat of a monstrous bloodbath still remained intact. Thus, it is likely that, in the name of saving national honor, the diehards probably would have insisted on a policy of writing off the military losses to the Soviets in China, while reinforcing both Kyushu and the possible Soviet landing sites on the island of Hokkaido.

As for the atomic bomb, the psychological impression made by a non-combat nuclear demonstration might have been significant at first, but it would have diminished substantially with the passing of time, once the Japanese realized that the United States was not following up with atomic bombardment of cities. (For the purposes of this scenario, we are assuming that the U.S. government has made a decision not to use atomic bombs against enemy population centers unless all other options have failed.) Meanwhile, the ongoing naval siege and conventional aerial bombardment would certainly be taking an awful toll among the Japanese population, but the fact remains that the Japanese had been enduring these pressures for more than eight months, on a colossal scale, without showing signs of a significant collapse of morale. Finally, the explicit guarantee of the emperor's position might have substantially strengthened the hand of the moderates in the Imperial Council—but one can argue with equal plausibility that the council could have read it as a sign of weakening Allied resolve, to be met by stiffened demands for further concessions.

It is useful here—and sobering—to note the actual words spoken by one of the Japanese moderates on the council, in the wake of the Potsdam Declaration. On July 30, Prime Minister Kantaro Suzuki held a meeting of his Cabinet Advisory Council, during the course of which one of his aides informed him that the nation's leading businessmen had "urged that Japan accept the Potsdam terms." Suzuki replied as follows:

For the enemy to say something like that means circumstances have arisen that force them also to end the war. That is why they are talking about unconditional surrender. Precisely at a time like this, if we hold firm, they will yield before we do. Just because they have broadcast their Declaration, it is not necessary to stop fighting. You advisers may ask me to reconsider, but I don't think there is any need to stop [the war].[40]

This was a moderate member of the Imperial Council. If even he, at this stage of the war, could interpret the Potsdam Declaration as a sign of weakness—indicating that the Allies might yield if Japan held firm—then it seems far-fetched to argue that the Japanese government stood poised on the verge of surrender at the beginning of August 1945. The leadership, in reality, was divided among those who wanted to hold out to the death, those who wanted to hold out for as long as necessary to get favorable peace terms, and those who stood ready to accept surrender on condition of an imperial guarantee. A great deal more blood would have to flow before that balance of views would shift appreciably.

In the end, it seems reasonable to conclude that this fourfold combination strategy might well have ultimately resulted in a Japanese surrender (without the need for an invasion or for the atomic bombing of cities)—but that the process might have required anywhere between one and six months to bear fruit.[41] The emperor would play a crucial role in such a course of events, of course, since the final decision to accept surrender undoubtedly lay with him. But Hirohito had carefully avoided, throughout the war, any direct interference in the deliberations of the Imperial Council: his intervention to break the deadlock on the night of August 9 constituted a unique event, precipitated by the dire extremity of the atomic emergency that faced his nation. Over the closing months of the war, Hirohito's views had largely paralleled those of the moderates on the council: accepting the inevitability of defeat, but holding out steadfastly for favorable peace terms—and for the decisive military operation (Ketsu-Go) that might secure those terms. It seems most plausible to conclude that Hirohito's own thinking would have steadily evolved, as the weeks went by after Soviet entry into the war, toward accepting the need for surrender. But it remains unlikely that he would have intervened directly in voting for such a policy, as he did on the night of August 9: he would probably have operated more subtly from behind the scenes, waiting for the balance of opinion among his subordinates to tilt significantly toward an acceptance of capitulation. Either way, this process of assembling a sufficient consensus within the Japanese leadership would have taken time. It is highly unlikely that the fourfold combination strategy would have brought about a Japanese surrender, on terms acceptable to the Allies, before mid-September at the earliest.

And there's the rub: for how many lives would have been lost, in the meanwhile? How many Japanese, American, Chinese, and Soviet soldiers—and how many civilians both in Japan itself and throughout Asia—would have had to die before the Japanese leadership finally made up its mind? It is to this complex issue that we now turn.

5. *Did the atomic bombing of Japan, by shortening the war, result in a net saving of lives?*

This is undoubtedly the most vexing question surrounding the morality of the atomic bomb's use in 1945: it has formed the subject of acrimonious controversy for decades. Part of the problem lies in the fact that answering this question inevitably takes us into the domain of making guesses and estimates and extrapolations. We have to hazard all kinds of assumptions, and this leaves plenty of room for various kinds of bias to distort what we end up thinking we see. But it is a fair conclusion that the bomb's use probably saved an enormous number of lives—far more Japanese than Allied.

The key to addressing this question lies in how we assume the war would have gone, in the absence of the atomic bombing of Hiroshima and Nagasaki. Three scenarios seem most plausible in this regard:

• The "Soviet shock" scenario. Here we assume that, even without the bomb, the sheer shock of Soviet entry into the war forces Japanese capitulation before the start of Operation Olympic on November 1. The deadlock in the Imperial Council is finally broken by the devastating losses experienced by Japanese armies in China, coupled with the threat of simultaneous invasion of the northern home island of Hokkaido by the Soviets and of the southern home island of Kyushu by the Anglo-Americans.

• The invasion scenario. Here we assume that Soviet entry into the war proves insufficient to force surrender, and that Operation Olympic consequently proceeds on schedule.

• The "siege and bombardment" scenario. Here we assume that the Anglo-Americans, having taken stock of the massive Japanese buildup on Kyushu, cancel or postpone Operation Olympic and instead pursue a strangulation policy, while the Soviets methodically smash the trapped Japanese armies in China.

Of these three scenarios, the first is similar to the "fourfold combination strategy" described above—but without the added pressure brought to bear by the factors of a noncombat nuclear demonstration and the modified surrender terms. We have seen how this scenario, while it certainly could have resulted in an eventual capitulation, would have required the passing of a significant amount of time in order for the Japanese leadership to reach a sufficient consensus on accepting the Allied terms.

The second scenario—the launching of Olympic against southern Kyushu—might well have become a reality. Although some American leaders, like King and Nimitz, were having misgivings about the invasion, others, like Marshall and MacArthur, appeared strongly determined to forge ahead with it if necessary. Certainly the preparations for this assault were already well under way: Marshall even ordered a feasibility assessment, in July 1945, of using atomic bombs as tactical weapons to obliterate the Japanese armies massing on Kyushu three days before the start of Olympic.[42] Such was the grim resolution in Washington, as the war's finale approached.

The third scenario—long-term strangulation and pulverization from the air—also stood a good chance of taking place. If King and Nimitz had ultimately prevailed in the behind-the-scenes struggle in Washington over Olympic, then Truman might have canceled the invasion or postponed it until the spring, preferring instead to let the bombers and navies do their deadly work on the islands, while the Soviets chewed up the Japanese armies on the mainland.

In all three of these scenarios, the possibility for loss of life (on all sides) appears extremely high. The first scenario ("Soviet shock") would be the cheapest in blood price for the Anglo-Americans, but one would have to assume that large numbers of Soviet and Japanese soldiers would have perished in the pitched battles on the China front. The number of Chinese civilians caught in the crossfire of this warfare is hard to estimate, but could conceivably prove enormous as well: when the defeated Japanese withdrew from Manila, they indulged in an orgy of vindictive violence against the local inhabitants, leaving some 100,000 dead amid the rubble of the shattered city. The imagination pales at the thought of what the retreating Japanese legions might have wreaked upon the citizens of China. In any case, the sheer scale of these Soviet-Japanese battles cannot but give pause to the historical observer: Japanese forces in China numbered some 1.2 million troops, while the Soviets had around 1.5 million. In the first six days of conflict, between the Soviet attack on August 8 and the cessation of hostilities after August 14, approximately 84,000 Japanese and 12,000 Russian soldiers were killed in combat. During the weeks that followed, the Soviets took prisoner some 2.7 million Japanese nationals residing in occupied China: of these, about 350,000 are known to have perished in Soviet captivity.[43]

Finally, we need to take into account the ongoing deaths among Allied POWs and among the vast numbers of Asian laborers forcibly conscripted into serving the Japanese throughout the far-flung lands still under Japanese occupation. The death rates among both these groups were appallingly high because of the barbarous treatment they received at the hands of their keepers. We must also consider the ongoing deaths by starvation among Asian civilians in those lands where the Japanese armies were forcibly requisitioning food supplies, in disregard for the famines that resulted.[44] After a meticulous analysis of the subject, the historian Richard Frank concludes that "the minimum plausible range for deaths of Asian noncombatants each month in 1945 was over 100,000 and more probably reached or even exceeded 250,000."[45]

Thus, even if we assume a relatively early Japanese surrender date of September 15 under this "Soviet shock" scenario, a conservative estimate of the resultant death toll would run something like this: another 30,000

Japanese civilians killed through conventional bombardment of the home islands; 500,000 Japanese soldiers killed in China; 70,000 Soviet soldiers killed in battle; 100,000 Chinese civilians killed in the crossfire or through war-related actions; 100,000 Asian noncombatants outside China (including a smaller number of Allied POWs) dying through maltreatment under Japanese occupation; another 50,000 Japanese dying in Soviet captivity. The total adds up to about 850,000 lives (of which a significant portion would be civilians)—and this is erring considerably on the low side of the plausible.[46]

The second scenario, the Allied invasion of Kyushu, has formed the subject of particularly intense controversy over the years. After the war, Stimson and Truman wrote articles and gave interviews in which they claimed it was reasonable to believe that Operation Olympic would have cost between 500,000 and a million Allied casualties: in their view, therefore, dropping the bomb undoubtedly saved those lives. These estimates subsequently acquired something of a talismanic status in discussions of the Pacific War, particularly among the U.S. servicemen who were boarding troopships in Europe in 1945 for transfer to the Pacific Theater. Then, in the 1960s and 1970s, a new generation of American historians issued a challenge to this orthodoxy: their research, they argued, suggested that Allied casualties in Olympic would have been much lower (on the order of from 20,000 to 100,000 men, including both dead and wounded), that the Japanese were on the verge of surrender anyway in 1945, and that dropping the bomb had therefore constituted an unnecessary and atrocious act.[47] In response, defenders of the orthodox position have claimed that these revisionists were unjustifiably downplaying the number of invasion casualties, and systematically overestimating Japan's readiness to surrender.[48]

Estimating casualties for Operation Olympic, in other words, is a very touchy subject. But after surveying six decades of debates in the literature, it seems reasonable to conclude that the estimate of half a million Allied casualties has been completely discredited by the thorough research of a wide array of historians: the number is far too high, and it is time to put that myth to rest once and for all.[49] On the other hand, the most persuasive casualty estimates for the Japanese side are truly hair-raising in their implications: here, the numbers on the order of a million do ring true. Thus, if we are counting not just Allied lives, but *human* lives, it is reasonable to conclude that the invasion of Kyushu would have resulted in one of the most horrific bloodbaths of World War II.

Richard Frank provides the most exhaustive and up-to-date overview in his 1999 book, *Downfall*. He points out that there are numerous ways to estimate the casualties in a battle, and that most of these were actually tried by American planners as they prepared for Olympic. At the crudest level, one can simply compare the average statistics from previous engagements—so many attackers against so many defenders yielding so many casualties—and plug in the numbers for Olympic. A more sophisticated approach involves tailoring the formula to the specific terrain, types of troops, and conditions of attack, before running the numbers.[50]

Okinawa offers a good point of comparison with the projected battle for Kyushu. In both cases, we have Japanese garrisons ready to fight to the end; we have large numbers of kamikazes to factor in; we can assume American superiority in overall firepower. Although the terrain on Kyushu was less mountainous than that of Okinawa, thus giving the Allies greater room for maneuver, this advantage would be offset by the fact that substantial portions of Kyushu's civilian population had been trained for guerrilla operations against advancing Allied troops.

On Okinawa, the defending Japanese garrison numbered 110,000; of these, about 95 percent, or 104,000, were killed. The civilian population totaled 400,000; about 25 percent of these, or 100,000, died in the battle. The attacking Allied naval and ground forces added up to 170,000; of these, about 7 percent, or 12,000, were killed.

On Kyushu, the defending Japanese garrison numbered 545,000; the civilian population was 10 million (with 3 million living in the areas directly targeted for the American landings); the Allies had 766,000 soldiers poised to strike on November 1. If we simply apply the Okinawa percentages to Kyushu, we get 517,000 Japanese soldiers killed; 750,000 Japanese civilians dead; 53,000 American troops and naval personnel killed. A total of 1.3 million dead.

Richard Frank offers a more conservative assessment, based on an analysis that takes into account such important intangibles as the degradation of American combat effectiveness caused by the reshuffling of fighting units after European demobilization. In the end, he estimates, at least 200,000 Japanese soldiers and 380,000 civilians would have died, while American battle deaths would lie in the vicinity of 33,000. A total of 613,000.[51]

But these numbers, of course, yield a tally only for the Kyushu operation itself, through late November or early December 1945. By that point in time, however, most of the deaths incurred in the "Soviet shock" scenario would also have taken place: indeed, that gruesome figure would most likely be still higher by late November. Thus, if we take Frank's conservative estimate and couple it with the other deaths likely to have occurred in Japan, China, and the rest of Asia by the end of 1945, we get an absolute minimum number that stands in the vicinity of 1.4 million lives lost.

The third scenario—cancellation of Olympic and intensive blockade and bombardment of Japan—has already been described above in the section on alternatives to dropping the bomb. It is hard to estimate how many would have died under such an outcome, because we have no clear idea how long it would have taken for the Japanese government to face the facts and capitulate. If its leaders had held out into the spring of 1946, then the naval blockade, coupled with continued bombardment and the near-total destruction of the nation's transportation infrastructure, would probably have resulted in a famine of catastrophic proportions, in which estimates of deaths run as high as 10 million (one-seventh of Japan's population).[52] Thus, if we conservatively estimate the starvation deaths at only 10 percent of this number (i.e., 1 million), and couple that number with those killed in the "Soviet shock" scenario, we have a final tally on the order of 1.8 million dead.

So we come to our cruel bottom line. The highest estimates for lives lost in the bombing of Hiroshima and Nagasaki stand at 340,000. By comparison, the three nonnuclear scenarios we have just described yield conservatively estimated totals on the order of 850,000, 1.4 million, and 1.8 million, respectively. By this arithmetic, the atomic bombs probably resulted in the saving of at least half a million, and perhaps as many as 1.5 million lives.

In reaching this final judgment, we have dealt heavily in speculative reasoning, basing our conclusions on distinct sets of concatenated assumptions to construct the most plausible scenarios we could for an ending to the war without atomic weapons in play. It is still possible, of course, to imagine a much happier outcome: the swift capitulation of Japan's government without any need for either Hiroshima, invasion, or bloody battles in China—followed by prompt and orderly compliance of the country's far-flung military garrisons in laying down their arms. But this relatively felicitous outcome, as we have seen, is the least plausible of all: most of the available evidence points dramatically in the opposite direction.

Indeed, it is worth underscoring that the three scenarios depicted above are based on a systematic effort to err on the side of conservative assumptions and the lower end of statistical estimates. It is quite possible that the numbers of dead, down any one of those three paths, could have been far higher. Therefore, it is with a fairly high level of confidence that we can reach this conclusion: dropping the bomb in 1945 (coupled as it was with the Soviet attack in Manchuria) significantly shortened the war, and thereby probably saved an extremely large number of human lives.

6. *Was the Nagasaki bomb necessary?*

The basic question here is whether the Japanese leadership stood poised on the verge of surrender on August 9, after Hiroshima and the Soviet attack in China, and would have tendered its August 10 capitulation offer anyway, regardless of the news coming in to Tokyo about the atomic blast at Nagasaki. Should the United States have waited longer, giving the Japanese more time to absorb the full impact of Hiroshima, before unleashing the nuclear holocaust on a second city?

We now have a detailed picture, from the research of both Japanese and American historians, of what was going on in the highest levels of the Tokyo government between August 6 and August 10. The emperor, in the aftermath of Hiroshima and the Soviet attack in China, had rapidly come around to the view that the war was hopeless, and that the army and navy leaders were not behaving rationally in their insistence on keeping up the fight. Thus, it is probable—although not certain—that Hirohito's mind was already made up for surrender by the morning of August 9, and that the bad news from Nagasaki only reinforced, but did not substantially alter, his position.[53]

But the Nagasaki bomb did have one important effect within the Imperial Council: it dramatically undermined the position of the hard-liners in their ongoing struggle with the moderates. Admiral Toyoda, a key figure among the diehards, had argued emphatically on August 7 that the obliteration of Hiroshima was probably unique—that the Americans could not have produced more than a few such bombs, and that, even if they did possess an ample supply of nuclear weapons, they would not dare to keep dropping them for fear of being branded as war criminals by world opinion.[54] The news from Nagasaki on August 9 effectively destroyed this argument: the Americans, apparently, had both the weapons and the will to keep using them indefinitely.

This, it turns out, is precisely the psychological effect that the U.S. leadership hoped the second bomb would have. Originally, the dropping of Fat Man had been scheduled for August 11, but weather reports on August 8 forecast increasing storms and clouds over southern Japan starting on August 10 and continuing for several days—which would have delayed the dropping of the second bomb until August 15. The result was a frantic rush on the island of Tinian to prepare Fat Man for immediate loading on a B-29, so that the bombing run could take place right away. As one member of the bomb assembly team put it: "The sooner we could get off another mission, the more likely it was that the Japanese would feel that we had large quantities of the devices and would surrender sooner."[55]

We cannot know, of course, what would have happened if the Nagasaki bomb had not figured into the top-level Japanese debates of August 9–10. We can, however, hazard two tentative conclusions. First, the Nagasaki bomb probably facilitated the surrender decision, by simultaneously weakening the position of the diehards and strengthening the resolve of the moderates on the Imperial Council. Second, the Nagasaki bomb most likely helped to mitigate the resistance that some diehards (both inside and outside the Imperial Council) put up in the aftermath of the emperor's decision to capitulate. Faced with the Americans' seemingly unlimited supply of this supreme weapon, some of the diehards may have resigned themselves to surrender in a way that they would not otherwise have done. This was important, because the compliance of the nationalist zealots—not just those in the Imperial Council but also those scattered throughout the officer corps of the Japanese army and navy—was crucial to ensuring a smooth transition into peace. If these fanatical leaders had not been persuaded about the hopelessness of Japan's cause, then far more of them might have refused to accept the surrender order, taking up arms in rebellion against a government they now considered dishonored by capitulation.

In the end, it seems reasonable to conclude that the primary blame for the dead in Nagasaki should rest squarely on the shoulders of the Japanese army and navy militarists on the Imperial Council. It was they who refused to face reality on the morning of August 7, after the nature of what had happened to Hiroshima the day before had become abundantly clear. It was they who clung blindly to irrational shards of hope, after the Soviet entry into the war on August 8. If they had been less fanatical in their intransigence, less willing to brush aside the suffering of their fellow citizens, Japan's surrender could have been communicated to Washington with plenty of time to stop Fat Man from flying.

7. *Was there a plausible alternative for achieving surrender with a lower loss of life, by using the bomb differently than the United States actually did?*

Let us suppose that the United States had attempted a harmless demonstration of the bomb on a desert island, sometime around August 6—while formally giving the Japanese three days to accept the Potsdam terms. We have reason to believe that this demonstration would have failed to make a sufficient impression on the Japanese leadership to secure a prompt surrender. But it is worth exploring at greater length the question that follows from this: what might have happened next?

The Soviet Union launched its onslaught against Japanese forces in China two days later, on August 8. Let us suppose that the United States, having allowed the three-day period to pass, had sent the *Enola Gay* on its mission against Hiroshima on August 9. It is plausible to argue that this sequence of actions—demonstration of bomb, Soviet attack, Hiroshima—might have decisively tipped the scales toward capitulation. By first demonstrating the atomic bomb and then following up promptly with the nuclear destruction of a city, the United States would have brought immense pressure to bear against the Japanese government. The Japanese could not know that the United States had used up its nuclear arsenal, and that a third bomb would not be ready for dropping until August 21. A powerful impression would have been created that the Americans possessed an unlimited supply of nuclear weapons, as well as the resolve required to use them against cities. Indeed, this impression would arguably have been all the stronger, precisely because the Japanese leadership would have had to admit to themselves the following disturbing fact: the United States evidently felt sufficiently well stocked with nuclear bombs that it could afford to use one on a harmless warning shot.

Given the actual historical record of the Imperial Council's decisions, it is reasonable to assume that a vote taken on August 9 or 10, in the wake of such a sequence of events, would have resulted (once again) in a three-to-three deadlock. Everything hinges, then, on the attitude of the emperor. What would Hirohito have done?

A strong argument can be made that the emperor would have found himself in a very similar frame of mind to the one that impelled him, in actual fact, to intervene personally and break the deadlock in the council with a decision for surrender. For almost two months—since mid-June—his outlook on Japan's prospects had been steadily growing more pessimistic. Although he had not yet made this bleak assessment explicit in his statements to the council, Hirohito had begun to voice grave doubts to his aide and confidant, Marquis Kido.[56] As August 1945 opened, his final hopes for a negotiated peace lay with playing the Soviet card through a last-ditch effort at secret diplomacy. Now, in the wake of August 8, that hope, too, would have been dashed. And then, on August 9, the Americans demonstrate all too vividly that they not only possess a revolutionary new weapon, but are capable of using it to destroy Japanese cities at will. To Hirohito, this could plausibly appear as the beginning of a terrible sequence of atomic warfare against his country: first an ultimatum (Potsdam), then a nuclear demonstration shot fired as a final warning, then the actual obliteration of an entire city.

There is a significant possibility that Hirohito—with no grounds whatsoever left for hope, and strong reason to believe the Americans could continue waging atomic warfare indefinitely—would have made up his mind that it was time to surrender. If this had happened, then the war might have ended in mid-August without the need for a nuclear attack against a second Japanese city. Tens of thousands (or more) of Japanese noncombatants might have been spared. The final death toll for the war's closing act, along this path, would have stood at around 200,000—the long-term result of the sole nuclear attack on Hiroshima.

Of course, it is also possible to imagine a very different outcome to this speculative scenario. If Hirohito had not, in the end, made up his mind to break the council's deadlock after the nuclear destruction of a single city, and the war had therefore dragged on, then the number of additional dead in the overall Pacific Theater would have very rapidly surpassed 200,000. We can assume that the Soviet-Japanese confrontation in China would have proceeded apace, that the ongoing loss of life in Japan's occupied territories would have gone on, that the pummeling of Japanese cities by B-29s would have continued—and finally, that another atomic bomb would probably have been dropped on a Japanese city around August 21. At what point the emperor would finally have decided to give up, under such a scenario, is hard to tell.

On balance, the chances of this path leading to a surrender by mid-August are quite significant—significant enough to outweigh the countervailing possibility of even worse loss of life than the toll reached in Hiroshima and Nagasaki. This assessment of the odds, while necessarily highly speculative, underscores once again the judgment that U.S. leaders missed an important opportunity when they decided against a noncombat demonstration of the bomb. We cannot be sure, of course; but it is at least plausible to argue that the war might have ended without the need for the nuclear annihilation of a second Japanese city.

8. *Did the United States drop the bomb to intimidate the Soviet Union?* During the 1960s and 1970s, a group of American revisionist historians put together a new and highly critical interpretation of the history of American foreign policy. In this interpretation, responsibility for the Cold

War lay not just with Stalin, but equally with the United States. Revisionist history works portrayed the United States as an aggressive, neo-imperialist power, imposing its own political and economic system on countries and peoples all over the globe—by military force if need be.

According to some revisionists, particularly the historian Gar Alperovitz, American political leaders in 1945 regarded the bomb as an excellent way to keep the Soviets in a relatively docile and subordinate role during the postwar decades. If the Russians didn't behave themselves, and it came to conflict, we had the bomb and they didn't. According to this interpretation, therefore, the United States leadership fully realized that the Japanese were on the verge of capitulation in the summer of 1945, but insisted on dropping the atomic bombs anyway because of the powerful impression this would make on the Soviets. The bombs, in other words, were not militarily necessary, but were primarily intended as tools for gaining postwar political leverage: President Truman and the other U.S. leaders accepted the sacrifice of two Japanese cities as a way to play a strong hand in the ongoing struggle for power with the USSR.[57]

The evidence presented by this group of historians is quite solid, but does not justify their full argument. What they show, without a doubt, is that the Anglo-American leaders fully appreciated the postwar implications of the bomb, as a device that immeasurably strengthened Western governments in dealing with the Russians. Henry Stimson referred to the bomb in May 1945 as the "master card" in the ongoing American relationship with the Soviet Union.[58] The British chief of staff, Field Marshal Alan Brooke, wrote in his diary at the Potsdam Conference on July 23, 1945, that the successful test of the atomic bomb in New Mexico had changed everything: "We now had something in our hands which would redress the balance with the Russians."[59] Truman, too, acutely felt the diplomatic impact of the new weapon he wielded, as the following entry from Stimson's diary at Potsdam makes plain:

> [Churchill] told me that he had noticed at the meeting of the [Big] Three yesterday that Truman was evidently very much fortified by something that had happened and that he stood up to the Russians in a most emphatic and decisive manner. . . . When he got to the meeting after having read this report [on the Alamogordo test] he was a changed man. He told the Russians just where they got on and off and generally bossed the whole meeting.[60]

Nevertheless, few historians have accepted Alperovitz's thesis that the main motivation for dropping the bomb was political rather than military, and that a determined and pervasive effort to intimidate the Soviet Union outweighed all other considerations regarding atomic weapons in 1945. Most have concluded, rather, that American leaders primarily regarded the bomb as a military device that might contribute to ending the war swiftly and decisively, with a minimum loss of Allied troops—and that only as a *secondary* consideration did some American leaders view it as a political cudgel for the postwar era, to keep the Soviets in line.[61] Other American leaders saw things very differently, moreover—to the point that they seriously considered the possibility, after 1945, of handing over control of atomic technology to the newly created United Nations.[62]

9. *Did U.S. leaders rush to drop the bomb, in the hope of bringing about Japanese surrender before the Soviets could enter the Pacific War?*

The historian Tsuyoshi Hasegawa argues in his book *Racing the Enemy* that a key factor motivating President Truman and his secretary of state, James Byrnes, during the turbulent weeks of July and early August 1945, was a growing fear of Soviet expansion into East Asia. The American leaders distrusted Stalin, and felt certain that he would use the excuse of the war against Japan as a way of securing major territorial gains and postwar political leverage in the region. Therefore, Hasegawa maintains, Truman and Byrnes executed a nimble diplomatic about-face at Potsdam: whereas the United States had been pressuring the Soviets for two years to enter the Pacific War once Hitler was defeated, now the Americans did all they could to sideline the Russians and to position themselves for conquering Japan without Soviet participation. The successful test of the atomic bomb on July 16, according to Hasegawa, convinced American leaders that they might be able to bring Japan to capitulation through atomic warfare alone, and without the need for Russian involvement.

Hasegawa makes a compelling case for this interpretation of the Pacific War's climax. He demonstrates that Stalin indeed harbored extensive expansionist designs in the East Asian region; that the Soviets urgently moved up the date of their attack in Manchuria, with the intent of becoming major players in the defeat of Japan; and that in the aftermath of Japanese surrender they aggressively maneuvered to extract the maximum territorial and political gain from their brief participation in the Asian war. Truman and Byrnes, in other words, had been essentially correct in their reading of Soviet intentions.

It would be a mistake, however, to conclude from Hasegawa's analysis that Truman's *primary* aim, in dropping the bomb, was to forestall Soviet entry into the Pacific War. Hasegawa presents a far more nuanced and complex picture than that: the Soviet factor was only one among many in the American motivations for resorting to atomic weapons. Foremost in Truman's mind was the desire to save American lives;[63] but he also wanted to break the power of the Japanese government in a decisive manner that would pave the way for a thoroughgoing postwar reconstruction of the nation's polity; he believed that the Japanese deserved strong retribution for their attack against the United States and their barbaric conduct during the war; he wanted to avoid appearing weak before the American electorate; and finally he wanted to keep East Asia as free as possible from undue Soviet influence in the postwar peace. All these factors, according to Hasegawa, pointed toward the use of the atomic bomb as a powerful tool for bringing a speedy and decisive end to the Pacific War.[64]

Toward the end of his book Hasegawa expresses his hope that the analysis he presents will help dispel the multifaceted myth that still surrounds the use of the atomic bomb in American culture—a myth that "serves to . . . ease the collective American conscience."[65] Contrary to what many Americans believe, he maintains, the bomb did not by itself provide "the knockout punch to the Japanese government"; rather, it only did so in conjunction with the Soviet attack of August 8.[66] The bomb was not dropped by the United States with great reluctance, as an absolute last resort after all other alternatives had been exhausted; rather, American leaders eagerly embraced it as a promising means of securing Japan's swift surrender. Finally, the bomb was not dropped solely to save Allied lives; it also served an important political purpose in forestalling the need for a Soviet invasion and occupation of Japan.

10. *Was the bomb used out of racism?*

In the years between 1942 and 1944, Japanese-Americans in the United States were rounded up and herded into detention camps; no such large-scale camps were ever set up for Italian-Americans or German-Americans. Hatred of the Japanese, according to the historian John Dower, ran deeper in American wartime culture than hatred of the Italians and Germans: it was based on rage over Pearl Harbor, and on a wide array of dehumanizing racial stereotypes that pervaded wartime America from top to bottom. These well-documented realities of World War II prompt the historical observer to ask, If the bomb had been ready for use before V-E Day, would the United States have considered dropping it on Munich or Hamburg? Or was this sort of treatment reserved solely for America's Asiatic enemy?

The problem with this hypothesis is that no evidence has emerged suggesting that the United States would have refrained from using atomic bombs against Germany, had the military need arisen. The atomic bomb was conceived, at its inception, as a specifically anti-German weapon: it was developed because the world's best physicists persuaded American leaders that Germany might be building a nuclear device of its own. To preempt this development, or at the very least to ensure that the Allies could equal this threat from Germany, the United States and Britain built the bomb. In the end, of course, it turned out that the European War ended before the weapon was ready. Nevertheless, if the European War had dragged on for very long without showing signs of a decision in the Allies' favor, and atomic weapons had become available, it is far from inconceivable that such bombs might have been brought into play against Nazi Germany.

The best way to think about this issue is to compare the types of non-nuclear bombing that the Allies were willing to undertake against Germany and Japan. What we see is that there was virtually no difference: Allied aircraft carpet-bombed and firebombed the cities of both nations with equal and impartial destructiveness. Allied attacks massacred both German civilians and Japanese civilians, by the hundreds of thousands: there is no reason to believe that attitudes governing the use of atomic bombs would have been any different.

Without a doubt, racial dehumanization did play a major role in the day-to-day conduct of the Pacific War at the tactical level—on the Japanese side as well as the American. It pervaded practices regarding the taking of prisoners, and ran deep into the motivations of many fighting men. Nevertheless, there is no evidence suggesting that racist impulses governed the key Allied strategic decisions that ultimately shaped the Pacific War: from the "Europe First" policy, to the planning of major land or seaborne operations, to the guidelines governing aerial bombardment, to the drafting of reconstruction blueprints for the postwar period. We have little reason to believe that racism constituted a salient factor in the decision to drop the atomic bomb.

11. *Did the use of this weapon violate the basic principles of a just war?*

Over the past two millennia, since the early Middle Ages, Christian church leaders and Western moral philosophers have struggled to define a doctrine for what constitutes a just war.[67] When is it morally acceptable for people to take their swords or guns or cannons and start killing large numbers of other people? And what rules should govern this violence once it has started?

The first of these issues, generally referred to as *jus ad bellum*, concerns the initial decision to go to war, and has usually entailed the following five principles:

- *Just cause.* The war must have a legitimate purpose, such as defending against unprovoked aggression or protecting the weak.
- *Legitimate authority.* Only governments, and not private individuals, can legally go to war.
- *Last resort.* The war must constitute the option of final resort, to be embarked upon only after all peaceful alternatives have been exhausted.
- *Probability of success.* The war must have a reasonable prospect of success, and not squander human life in senseless violence.
- *Proportionality of goals.* The human and economic costs incurred by the war must be proportionate to the good expected by taking up arms.

The second issue, generally referred to as *jus in bello*, concerns the conduct of warfare after the violence has commenced. Its principles have generally entailed the following two elements:

- *Proportionality of means.* The destructive devices and practices used in warfare must be proportionate to the overall aims of the warring parties.
- *Sparing noncombatants.* Innocent civilians and noncombatants should never become the direct targets of warfare; only military personnel and installations can be legitimately attacked.[68]

Needless to say, Western history is replete with conflicts in which some or all of these moral constraints were deliberately violated. The siege of a city in the Middle Ages, for example, often violated the principle of shielding noncombatants, since it aimed at subduing an entire population through starvation. The carnage of the First World War, by contrast, generally respected the sanctity of noncombatants, but it arguably violated the principle of proportionality, since it is hard to see how the changes brought about by this conflict could be worth 8 million human lives.

Some political theorists have maintained that the concept itself of "justice" in warfare is irrelevant: once the state-to-state violence starts, the domain of justice is left irrevocably behind, and only force matters, until a new power equilibrium is reached, and on its foundation the domain of peacetime justice is then reestablished. According to this position, therefore, winning is everything: any and all means that can get you to victory are valid, and moral qualms represent only a needless distraction from the grim business at hand. Nevertheless, as philosophers like Michael Walzer have persuasively argued, the moral ideals of justice in warfare—though often ignored or violated—still bear great significance in human affairs.[69]

Human beings are always moral agents, and cannot simply shuck off their moral nature when war is declared: they take their intuitions about fairness and justice with them even into combat. Mercy and honor on the battlefield have always made up a large part of the story of human conflict; nor should we underestimate the powerful restraints that these moral principles have placed on the historical conduct of warfare.[70] This restraint that humans have shown, even in the way they wield violence against one another, not only constitutes an important part of what makes us civilized beings: it is an outgrowth of the deepest moral qualities that render our lives meaningful, worth living.

How, then, does the destruction of Hiroshima and Nagasaki figure into this tradition of thought? The answer is more complex than one might think at first glance. Dropping atomic bombs on these two cities egregiously violated the principle of sparing noncombatants; it partially violated and partially satisfied the principle of proportionality; and it fully satisfied the criterion of probability of success.

It doesn't take a great deal of imagination to realize that nuclear weapons are profoundly indiscriminate devices. They make possible the kinds of devastation that ultimately sweep away all distinctions: defense and aggression, innocent or culpable, military or civilian, bystander or active participant. With nuclear weapons, everyone becomes a participant. Amid the rubble of Hiroshima and Nagasaki, after August 9, lay the remains not only of Japanese old women and toddlers, mentally handicapped persons and Buddhist monks, but of Korean laborers pressed into service in those cities, as well as several dozen American, British, and Australian POWs—all equally reduced to ashes by the pitiless impartiality of the nuclear flash. There is no escaping this conclusion: according to one of the core traditions of Christianity and of Western moral thought, the use of nuclear weapons against civilian population centers is an inherently unjust form of warfare, because it inevitably slaughters vast numbers of helpless noncombatants. It is, by the very standards of ethics that have undergirded American civil society since its founding, utterly barbaric. The United States, by using such a weapon of indiscriminate mass destruction to annihilate a city, committed a clearly immoral act.

Our second criterion, the principle of proportionality, holds that the amount of destructive force we use in warfare must be commensurate with the threat we face and with the aim we are trying to achieve. In the Bible it says, "an eye for an eye." In concrete terms, the principle of proportionality stipulates that if you attack my city, using cannons and infantry, saying that you want to enslave me and my people, I am justified in counterattacking, using cannons and infantry of my own. It is also morally justifiable for me to build a better cannon, if I can do this.

But if I develop totally new weapons, so that you are helpless before me, and I chase you down and destroy your army, and kill every one of you, and then I kill all your wives and children and grandchildren, and then I wipe your city off the face of the earth, and then I destroy every city you have ever lived in, poisoning the ground where all those cities lay, so that nothing can ever grow there again for hundreds of years—then, according to the moral doctrine on just wars, this would violate the principle of proportionality because my counterattack is not commensurate with the threat posed by your initial attack. My "self-defense" is seen as going too far.

At one level, the atomic bombs dropped on Hiroshima and Nagasaki were extremely "unproportional" devices, because they obliterated not only the military garrison and war-related industries of these cities, but the entire cities themselves. They destroyed, in other words, not only the cities' contribution to the Japanese war effort, but their whole social order from top to bottom. Total destruction of this magnitude was hugely disproportional to the attack that the Japanese had leveled against the United States.

At another level, however, the atomic bombing of these two Japanese cities *did* satisfy the criterion of proportionality, because it did not eliminate Japanese society in its entirety, but only threatened to do so through a graduated and continued use of these weapons. Although the destruction of the two targets themselves was close to total, the impact of these attacks on the Japanese nation as a whole remained proportionately limited: even after suffering this terrible blow, Japan could go on existing as a viable polity. Thus, precisely because the American attack came at the dawn of nuclear technology, and hence remained unavoidably constrained by the short supply of these horrific new weapons, it did not yet partake of the ecocidal quality that this technology would later acquire. The atomic bombing of 1945 was still relatively limited in scope—it was not yet an "instantaneous destroyer of entire nations"—and could therefore legitimately claim an element of measure, of proportionality, as an instrument of warfare.

In brandishing this extreme threat of destruction, moreover, the United States did succeed in achieving its immediate aim, which was to persuade the Japanese to surrender. The means—destruction of two cities—was arguably proportional to the vitally important goal of bringing the war to a swift end. This brings us in turn to our third just-war criterion, the principle of probability of success. The Japanese leaders were egregiously violating this principle in the summer of 1945, by fanatically continuing to prosecute a war that they were doomed to lose. They seemed willfully blind, or in some cases even indifferent, to the bloodshed that their policies were causing. Dropping the atomic bombs brought this senseless squandering of human lives to a rapid and decisive end. Seen in this light, therefore, the destruction of two cities, cruel as it was, could be construed as a morally justifiable act because it probably resulted in a net saving of human lives on an immense scale.

What we have here, then, is a classic instance of a mixed verdict. According to the tradition of just-war theory, the atomic bombing of Hiroshima and Nagasaki was unequivocally bestial, unconscionable, barbaric; yet it shortened the war and thereby probably saved a tremendous number of lives.

12. *Was the dropping of the atomic bomb justified? How to judge the morality of this act?*

In evaluating any moral decision, we need to take into account three basic factors: context, intention, and consequences. The broader context of the Second World War, as we have seen, firmly situates the atomic bombing of Japan within an escalating pattern of atrocious practices: the maltreatment or massacre of civilians on the part of the Japanese and Germans, the mass killing of prisoners of war by the Russians, Japanese, and Germans, the barbaric practices of area bombing and firebombing on the part of the Anglo-Americans. Well before Hiroshima, the human species in World War II had already stained itself with cruelty and butchery on a scale that was arguably unprecedented in history. Of course, this wider pattern of behavior in no way excuses what was done to the people of Hiroshima and Nagasaki. But it does put these acts into their wartime context: this was a time of desperate struggle for survival, a time in which horrendous loss of life filled the news on a daily basis, a time of extremes. The atomic bombings were unfortunately far from unique in their atrociousness: rather, they fit squarely into the generalized barbarization of human behavior in the war. While this broader wartime context does not in the slightest way legitimize any of the crimes that were perpetrated, it does help us to understand how seemingly ordinary people could have proved capable of unleashing such breathtaking cruelty. The situation itself had become far from ordinary, and human beings (on all sides) proved all too malleable, all too amenable, in adapting themselves to the war's vicious pattern.

The intentions of the Allied and Japanese leaders must occupy a central place in our assessment. A heavy burden of responsibility lies on the shoulders of Hirohito and his Imperial Council: if they had been willing to face the reality of defeat when it became undeniable in the early months of 1945, they might have spared their nation (and many other nations) untold suffering. Defiance in the face of unfavorable odds can be seen as bravery; but protracted defiance in the face of impossible odds is nothing but a senseless waste. There is no honor here, but only an irrational stubbornness and an appalling disregard for human life.

As for the Anglo-American leaders, their primary intention in dropping the bomb was to end the war quickly and decisively, with as few casualties on their own side as possible. Their decision, as we have seen, was not motivated by racism, nor was it primarily motivated by any ulterior political motive such as intimidating the Russians or forestalling Soviet entry into the Pacific War (though these political considerations did count as significant secondary motivating factors). Their refusal to back down from unconditional surrender in the war's final months can be soundly justified on both moral and pragmatic grounds: an offer of peace negotiations would probably have strengthened the determination of the diehards on the Imperial Council to hold out even longer. Moreover, the way the Allied leaders fudged this issue in the Potsdam Declaration, and then partially yielded on it in the touchy give-and-take between August 10 and August 14, should be recognized as adroitly pragmatic statesmanship: it skillfully trod a delicate line between breaking the emperor's power and keeping him in place as a figurehead to ease the transition into a postwar occupation.

Where the Allied leaders arguably fell grievously short was in their failure to consider with sufficient seriousness the enormity of the device that they were introducing into human affairs. The fact that they never formally discussed the possible nonuse of the bomb is simply astounding, and inexcusable. Once it became clear in 1944 that Germany was headed toward inevitable defeat, and that no German nuclear weapons would likely come into play (which Allied leaders knew by November 1944),[71] the most urgent rationale for developing atomic weapons faded away. The bomb was being built as a deterrent to counterbalance the possibility of German nuclear weaponry; now that this threat was gone, it was time to step back and reevaluate the implications of the Manhattan Project under the new strategic circumstances. But no such reassessment took place in the spring of 1945: the giant project went rolling on, like a technological juggernaut outside human control. Even the wise and experienced public servant Henry Stimson, who recognized the bomb as a potential "Franken-stein," capable of "destroying international civilization," never brought up before the Interim Committee, which he chaired, the possibility of refrain-ing from using this new weapon. Even if the committee's decision had ulti-mately come out in favor of using the device, it remains appalling that the U.S. government never gave this momentous question the consideration it deserved.

One rejoinder to this line of criticism might run as follows: You are for-getting that we were at war. With every passing day, Americans (and Japanese) were dying in large numbers. In such a situation, it is unreason-able to expect American leaders to have seriously considered relinquishing a potentially war-winning weapon. To judge them negatively for failing to do so is to apply an unfair form of 20-20 hindsight to the decisions made in a historical context of all-out war. What mattered was *winning*, quickly and decisively, and dropping the bomb held out the very real possibility of furthering that aim.

There is considerable validity to this line of argument: it embeds the decision-making process of the Allied leaders within the wartime context of 1945, and thereby helps us to understand how decent men could have gone forward so straightforwardly with the assumption that the bomb should be used. But this argument does not, in itself, justify the way they reached their decision. They knew (from the Alamogordo test) the magni-tude of this weapon's destructiveness; they knew it would indiscriminately kill a huge number of noncombatants; they knew it would bring about a revolution in the nature of warfare: we have clear documentary evidence of the fact that the Allied leaders understood the grave consequences of unleashing this new weapon. It is not unreasonable, therefore, to expect them to have carefully weighed all their options, including nonuse of the bomb, before giving the green light. Even in the dire circumstances of wartime—indeed, especially in those circumstances—it was incumbent on the nation's leadership to weigh very deliberately and soberly the possible short-term and long-term consequences of their actions.

Much the same can be said—but even more emphatically—for the option of demonstrating the bomb on an uninhabited target. Even though we can be almost certain, given what we now know in retrospect, that such a demonstration would have failed to compel a prompt Japanese surrender, this simple act would have considerably strengthened the American moral position in the final phase of the war. Such a demonstration, followed by the Soviet attack in China and by the atomic bombing of Hiroshima, could conceivably have resulted in a swift surrender, thereby sparing Nagasaki (or some other city) from nuclear incineration. But the U.S. government dismissed the possibility of demonstrating the bomb, after giving the idea only cursory consideration. It thereby cast an indelible shadow over America's handling of the war's final act. The nuclear era could have opened with a gesture of courageous magnanimity—a warning shot across the bow of Japan, a harmless demonstration of the bomb on an uninhabited site. Instead, it opened like a blind step off a precipice.

Finally, we come to the retrospective assessment of consequences. The bombing of Hiroshima and Nagasaki killed between 110,000 and 340,000 people; as we have seen, the three most plausible scenarios for the war's ending without nuclear weapons yield conservative estimates of deaths between 850,000 and 1.8 million. Can the logic of the lesser of two evils apply to events of such enormity, in which the loss of human life is so high? We have no alternative but to answer yes. If these were indeed the only realistic scenarios for ending the war—kill 340,000 or kill 850,000—then we are morally bound, in retrospect, to recognize the relative legitimacy of the path that resulted in the lower loss of life.

The United States has to bear the moral responsibility for the gap between the path it actually followed in ending the war and the nuclear demonstration path that might plausibly have spared the lives of 100,000 or more noncombatants. Nevertheless, the argument remains intact that the atomic bombing of at least one Japanese population center was necessary for a speedy end to the war. We still arrive at the conclusion, in other words, that atomic weaponry significantly shortened the war, and thereby probably saved a great many lives.

We must exercise caution in saying this, however. To argue that the atomic bombs "ultimately saved lives" can lead us to slip all too easily into a retroactive blanket justification of the entire process through which the United States went about ending the Pacific War. But this is actually a far from straightforward matter. We have to make a clear distinction between the intention of the Allied leaders in 1945, which was primarily to save Allied lives by ending the war swiftly, and the retrospective conclusion that dropping the bomb also probably ended up saving an even larger number of Japanese lives. These are two separate moral considerations.

Of course, the consequences of Hiroshima and Nagasaki extended well beyond the year 1945. They ushered in the era of nuclear arms races, of Mutually Assured Destruction, of terrorists potentially wielding WMD (weapons of mass destruction). They opened up a Pandora's box that can never be closed again: human beings now know how to build these weapons, and have established the precedent of using them on one another.

These are heavy consequences indeed, but it is not reasonable to impute them entirely to the bombing of two Japanese cities in World War II. Sooner or later, these kinds of weapons would undoubtedly have emerged in our industrial civilization, regardless of the particularities of the war. Even if the Manhattan Project had never taken place, the science was there, waiting, and the human impulse to build ever more potent weapons would unquestionably have taken civilization down the nuclear path. Regardless of Hiroshima, we would no doubt live today in an age of atomic killing machines. World War II merely hurried the process along.

Was the dropping of the atomic bomb justified? This question cannot be answered in a straightforward way, with a clear-cut yes or no. Too many important contradictory factors come into play for that: either a pure yes or a pure no would force us to ignore or override extremely compelling arguments on the other side. The morality of the atomic bombing of Hiroshima and Nagasaki cannot but remain profoundly ambiguous.

Those who consider the dropping of the bomb an absolute evil usually rest their case on the horror of what happened to hundreds of thousands of helpless noncombatants on the ground. If this is not pure evil, they ask, then what in the world is? This judgment, however—while understandable—fails to address one key point: the war had to end, somehow. In one way or another, the Japanese had to be brought to accept the need for surrender. Therefore, if we conclude that dropping the bomb was absolutely wrong, we are unavoidably affirming that one of the nonnuclear paths to surrender would have been morally preferable—even though, as we have seen, it is probable that all those paths would have exacted a much higher blood price than the path that led through Hiroshima and Nagasaki. This is, without a doubt, a deeply problematic position to take.

But the alternative is equally troubling. If we conclude that dropping the bomb probably resulted in a net saving of human lives, and therefore constituted the lesser evil among many terrible options, we are in effect saying that there can be such a thing as a "justifiable" atrocity. It is one thing to speak of the lesser of two evils when we are assessing something like the amputation of a gangrenous limb as a way of saving a person's life. It is quite another to use this logic, when the "items" being weighed in the scale are hundreds of thousands of human beings. Logic is logic: it is indifferent to the scope of the factors being considered. But the full human reality in this case entails more than cold logic: we cannot help being brought up short by the sheer awfulness of *all* the courses of action we are comparing.

William Styron, in his novel *Sophie's Choice*, depicts a situation in which an SS man at Auschwitz forces a Polish woman to choose which one of her two young children will go to the gas chambers, and which will be spared. If she does not choose, he tells her, both children will go to the gas immediately.[72] In a sense, the culmination of the Pacific War in August 1945 places all of us—as we look back in retrospective judgment on those momentous deeds—in an analogous position. We are presented with an impossible decision among courses of action that are all totally abominable. Either way we choose—kill 200,000, kill 340,000, kill 850,000, kill 1.8 million—we are in effect giving our assent to an abomination, in which hundreds of thousands of innocents will suffer and die. Either way we choose, we cannot but be morally lessened, spiritually wounded, by the choice. Despite our undeniable moral obligation to opt for the lesser among several terrible evils—despite the unavoidable need to adopt *some* course of action that would bring swift termination of a brutal war—this still does not take away the sense of stain that lingers from our decision. We are running, here, against the very outer limits of moral reasoning itself.

It would be a strange conscience indeed that could rest easy with this kind of choice. How could we ever reach a clear and "comfortable" conclusion regarding this atrocity that probably saved a vast number of lives? How can we possibly frame a moral response to the story of these two Japanese cities, without having profound misgivings, without agonizing and faltering in rendering judgment?

[A grocer in Hiroshima:]

The appearance of people was . . . well, they all had skin blackened by burns. . . . They had no hair because their hair was burned, and at a glance you couldn't tell whether you were looking at them from in front or in back. . . . They didn't look like people of this world.

[One of Dr. Hachiya's visitors:]

I came onto I don't know how many, burned from the hips up; and where the skin had peeled, their flesh was wet and mushy.

And they had no faces! Their eyes, noses and mouths had been burned away, and it looked like their ears had melted off. It was hard to tell front from back.[73]

When a moral choice entails using weapons of such cruelty, when it confronts us with loss of life on this scale, when all the options are so patently unspeakable, our moral faculty understandably cracks and groans under the pressure.

If it doesn't, there is something wrong.

PART THREE

LONG-TERM CONSEQUENCES OF THE WAR

On March 9, 1974, the last soldier of World War II finally surrendered on the Philippine island of Lubang. He was a Japanese army lieutenant named Hiroo Onoda. For thirty years, Lieutenant Onoda had been holed up in a series of damp caves hidden deep in the island's remote jungle. Initially he had been part of a platoon of four men, but, one by one, they had all died except him. They had been told to stay at their posts until relieved. Neither surrender nor suicide were acceptable options, their officers had emphasized.

And orders are orders.

They subsisted on bananas, coconuts, breadfruit, fish, the occasional wild pig. From time to time after 1945 efforts were made by Japanese government officials and by the men's relatives to contact them: in 1949 and again in 1952, Japanese planes dropped leaflets over the Lubang jungle saying, in effect, "You can come out now. The war is over." But the men regarded these as cunning ploys by the enemy to flush them out of hiding. They refused to budge.

In 1965 Onoda and his sole surviving companion, Kinshichi Kozuka, managed to steal a transistor radio from a farming village near their jungle. They found Japanese-language broadcasts from Australia, and listened, wide-eyed, as the world events of 1965 unfolded before them. Finally they concluded that these broadcasts, too, were nothing but a devilishly clever ploy by American disinformation units to trick the Japanese soldiers into revealing their location.

"When you think of it, the Americans are really pretty good at this, aren't they?" said Kozuka.

"Yes," Onoda replied. "They have to take out anything they don't want heard and then rebroadcast it in almost no time. They must have managed to gather together a bunch of very smart people. Just one slip, and the whole thing would sound fishy. I take off my hat to them. It must be very tricky work!"[1]

Back to their cave they went.

Kozuka died after a skirmish with Filipino police near a farming village in 1972. For the last year in hiding Onoda carried on alone.

Finally, early in 1974, a young Japanese adventure seeker named Norio Suzuki decided he would hike into the Lubang jungle and find out if the rumors about World War II holdouts in there were true. Suzuki eventually found Onoda—or, to be precise, Onoda found *him*—and the two had a long conversation.

"What could I do to persuade you to come out of the jungle?" Suzuki finally asked.

"Major Taniguchi is my immediate superior," replied Onoda. "I won't give in until I have direct orders from him."[2]

Suzuki went back to Japan and ascertained that Taniguchi was, fortunately, still alive. Together the two of them traveled back to Lubang. They met Onoda at a prearranged location on the jungle fringe. Taniguchi saluted Onoda and formally delivered to him his orders from the Special Section of the Chief of Staff's Headquarters. Onoda later recalled the scene:

Major Taniguchi slowly folded up the order, and for the first time I realized that no subterfuge was involved. This was no trick—everything I had heard was real. . . .

We really lost the war! How could they have been so sloppy?

Suddenly everything went black. A storm raged inside me. I felt like a fool for having been so tense and cautious on the way here. Worse than that, what had I been doing for all these years?

Gradually the storm subsided, and for the first time I really understood: my thirty years as a guerrilla fighter for the Japanese army were abruptly finished. This was the end.

I pulled back the bolt on my rifle and unloaded the bullets.[3]

It was March 9, 1974. Hiroo Onoda was fifty-two years old. When he returned to Japan two weeks later he was hailed as a national hero: banquets, TV appearances, press conferences, speeches. He wrote a memoir of his jungle experiences that quickly became a best seller, earning him a sizable fortune.

But he was terribly disappointed to see what Japan had become. Was this what he had fought for, what he had held out all those long years to see? His beloved homeland, Westernized, commercialized, eagerly devoted to making TVs and cars to sell to the great new protector and client, the United States? Utterly disgusted, Onoda did not stay long in Japan. He moved to Brazil, where he bought a large tract of rural land and 1,800 cattle, and became a rancher.[4]

Hiroo Onoda had, in effect, traveled through a sort of time warp, from World War II into a future thirty years removed—a future in which the long-term effects of the war had had enough time to manifest themselves. It proved too much for him to bear: the transformation of his homeland, and of the surrounding world, was simply too deep and far-reaching to comprehend. In this sense, the shock experienced by Lieutenant Onoda, and his great disillusionment with the Japan of the 1970s, powerfully underscore the magnitude of the changes that the war brought on— changes that continued to unfold decades after 1945.

One of the more serious mistakes we commonly make about World War II is to think of it too narrowly as a mainly military event that culminated in the surrender of Nazi Germany and Japan. We need to understand that the defeat of the aggressor nations—however important in itself— merely constituted the short-term effect exerted by this war. Seen from a broader perspective, the Second World War was the single greatest catalyst of change in the twentieth century, bringing about (or sharply accelerating) deep transformations in virtually every domain of human life, from geopolitics to social movements, from economies to high culture. Put all the pieces together, and you have a historical watershed of the first magnitude—like the French Revolution—one of those markers we tacitly use in delimiting the major eras of history.

World War II brought an end to the old multipolar order of the preceding centuries: for the first time, global politics became overwhelmingly bipolar. European power suffered a relative decline, from which it has not yet fully recovered. A new force in world politics, the Third World, slowly began to coalesce; but its potential remained largely untapped, held back by internal ethnic and religious divisions and by persistent economic woes. This left two new superpowers to call the shots in the postwar era: their rivalry shaped the next half-century.

The war powerfully lifted the world out of the Great Depression. In some nations, like Nazi Germany, this had already happened during the 1930s. But for the most part, the global economy in 1939 had still been mired in a miserable cycle of protectionism, mass unemployment, closed businesses, weak trade, tight belts, and failing hopes. The war quickly and decisively changed all that.

The United States emerged from the war as the world's number one power—relatively unscathed by wartime damage, its factories booming, its population flush with cash, its prestige higher than ever before in its history—and with a monopoly on atomic weapons. A profound change in American attitudes had come about after Pearl Harbor. Most citizens now became convinced that America's traditional isolationism was like the strategy of the proverbial ostrich, hiding its head in the sand. In a world made smaller by technology, only an active policy of engagement and involvement, on a global scale, would suffice to protect the United States' national interest in the future. Of all the long-term effects exerted by the war, this was to prove one of the most significant.

World War II also brought about dramatic social transformation in the countries that experienced it. Each national case possessed its own unique character, of course, but all shared the quality of swift, profound—and in many cases unintended—upheaval. In the United States, two particularly salient aspects of such social change were the transformed status of African-Americans and of women. Feminism and civil rights had both existed as social movements before the war; but the war gave them a strong boost, propelling them into a new era of escalating struggle and achievements. In Britain, the rigid old class structure began to break down dramatically: elites and commoners drew closer together, their backs having been forced to the same wall by the Nazi threat. Winning World War II bestowed enormous legitimacy on the Soviet regime—both in the eyes of the Russian people and more broadly in other parts of the world—thereby giving that regime the prestige and stability it needed to endure for four more decades. Germany and Japan underwent drastic social reform under the firm tutelage of Allied occupation authorities. China suffered through four more years of civil war after 1945; when that struggle ended with the victory of Mao Zedong's forces in 1949, the nation experienced the sweeping transformation of communist rule. Apart from the problematic status of Hong Kong and Taiwan, China was now more truly unified than it had been in half a century.

In Western Europe, North America, and most of the world's emerging industrial democracies, the sphere of politics underwent dramatic change in the wake of this war. The horrors perpetrated by the Nazis changed the face of right-wing politics well beyond the borders of Germany. Conservatism since 1945 has tended for the most part to back away from the aristocratic, authoritarian, and anti-democratic values that it held so dear before the war. In the space of a few years, the right wing came to be firmly anchored to the parliamentary, democratic tradition: it moved solidly into the political mainstream, and shared many basic assumptions with its political rivals on the moderate left.

Wartime also gave people a taste of what they could achieve through government, wielding these instruments of public policy that had shown themselves so effective in mustering national energies for the military effort. After 1945, central governments began to play an unprecedented role in areas once considered beyond their purview: funding scientific research, promoting and overseeing education, regulating and fine-tuning the national economy, guaranteeing public health and social welfare, launching major technological enterprises—not to mention the symbiosis of government with defense industries that President Dwight Eisenhower dubbed "the military-industrial complex." One could already observe elements of this trend before 1939, but the war greatly accelerated the process. Even though some leaders like Margaret Thatcher and Ronald Reagan later did their best to push back the advancing steamroller of state intervention, the overall trend since World War II has remained clear: state powers have come to be widely accepted as viable and appropriate instruments for shaping a nation's social and economic system in fundamental ways.

Well before the twentieth century, the idea had been slowly dawning on thoughtful people that science and technology constituted crucial factors in determining a nation's rank in the global power hierarchy. But in World War II it became obvious to everyone: science and technology were *the* name of the game. It is only after 1945 that we see the rise (in virtually all major nations) of the massive scientific-research establishments with which we are familiar today—institutions both public and private, in universities and in corporations—thousands of men and women in lavishly funded laboratories, the new intellectual armies determining the shape of the future. The Second World War took science and technology and elevated them to a level of prestige and power that they had never dreamed of possessing before—a stature that has only increased as the decades have gone by.

It should be clear, from this short overview, how much more this war brought about than the mere military defeat of Germany, Italy, and Japan. International relations, economic forces, social patterns, politics, science and technology: in each of these domains, World War II precipitated deep and enduring change. If we stand back, taking all these elements together, what we see is one of the great tectonic shifts in the history of the modern world.

The three chapters that follow focus on the moral aspects of this epochal transformation: the war's long-term impact on international law and human rights; its radical redefinition of the quest for peace; its intractably controversial place in public memory and national identity.

- Global law and the practice of international justice underwent a veritable revolution in the late 1940s, through the postwar trials of Nazi and Japanese war criminals; but it was also a revolution that went on developing and deepening over the subsequent decades, profoundly recasting the way we think about national sovereignty and basic human rights.

- The advent of nuclear weapons in 1945 marked the beginning of a new period in human history: the era of warfare as the instantaneous incineration of large civilian populations. In this sense, the doomsday shadow cast by World War II over the subsequent half-century has constituted one of its most salient moral legacies. How we think about peace and war will never be the same again.

- Over the decades following the Allied victory, all the major belligerent nations have experienced bitterly divisive "memory wars" over how to transmit the story of World War II to the new generations. Was this truly the "Good War" that some make it out to be? Monuments, historical textbooks, museum exhibits, war movies and novels—wherever the meaning of national honor lies at stake, citizens have confronted the inherent tension between celebratory commemoration on the one hand, and historical accuracy on the other.

In all three of these cases, it is only by taking a long view, casting our regard over six decades of events since 1945, that we can appreciate the war's full historical impact and moral significance.

Chapter Eleven

JUSTICE FOR THE UNSPEAKABLE?

The Enduring Legacy of the War Crimes Trials at Nuremberg and Tokyo

In his last meeting with Stalin, Churchill had remarked that whenever they captured one of the Nazi bigwigs, he ought to be summarily shot. With that, Stalin announced sanctimoniously, "In the Soviet Union, we never execute anyone without a trial." Churchill responded, "Of course, of course. We should give them a trial first."
> —From an account given by Samuel Rosenman,
> chief speechwriter for Franklin Roosevelt,
> of a conversation he had with Churchill in 1944[1]

Individuals have international duties which transcend the national obligations of obedience imposed by the individual State.
> —Judgment of the International Military Tribunal,
> Nuremberg, October 1946[2]

It was not until about halfway through the war that the Allied leaders began seriously considering a trial for the Nazi archcriminals in the wake of victory. Until that point, both Roosevelt and Churchill had leaned toward summary execution. But gradually, between 1942 and 1944, Roosevelt's thinking on the subject changed completely, ultimately coming around to an adamant insistence on dealing with the vanquished enemies through due process of law. Within the Roosevelt administration, this decision reflected the final outcome of a long and fierce bureaucratic battle between the secretary of the treasury, Henry Morgenthau, who advocated harsh vengeance against the German people, and the secretary of war, Henry Stimson, who argued that such a vindictive policy would not only violate the values that underpinned American democracy, but would breed

Defendants' dock in the Nuremberg trials (1946). Seated in front row, from left to right: Hermann Göring, Rudolf Hess, Joachim von Ribbentrop, and Wilhelm Keitel. Seated in second row, from left to right: Karl Dönitz, Erich Raeder, Baldur von Schirach, and Fritz Saukel.

more enmity and violence among the Germans for decades to come.[3] Roosevelt ultimately found Stimson's logic more persuasive; the president prevailed upon Churchill to accede to this policy, and at Yalta in February 1945 the Big Three formally announced their intention to hold a major trial.

It was, admittedly, a risky business. The American and British leaders were determined that this should *not* take the form of a mere show trial, echoing the rigged travesties of interwar Nazi justice (and Soviet justice): the defendants would be given a fair chance to plead their cases, aided by well-qualified defense lawyers, with full acquittal as a possible outcome. That was one risk. A real danger existed, moreover, that the Nazi officials, speaking from the prisoner's dock, would use the trial as a platform for Hitlerite propaganda or self-exculpatory lies; nor was it clear exactly what kind of legal framework Allied jurists could bring to bear in judging the actions of the accused. Anthony Eden, the British foreign secretary, had even argued in 1942 that "the guilt of such individuals [as Hitler and

Himmler] is so black that they fall outside and go beyond the scope of any judicial process."[4] But in the end, Roosevelt and Churchill concluded that anything less than a fair trial would amount to a betrayal of the very liberal ideals for which they had fought the war: in their moment of military triumph, they would not dispense "victor's justice," but would inaugurate the transition into peacetime by returning to the rule of law.

In a sense, one might think it should have been a cinch for the prosecution. Here in the prisoner's dock sat a group of men who had presided over one of the most heinous series of crimes in all history, ranging from genocide to enslavement, from medical experiments on prisoners of war to the killing of civilian hostages. Just their names, by themselves, had already become synonymous worldwide with gruesome atrocities: Hermann Göring, Rudolf Hess, Joachim von Ribbentrop, Albert Speer, Ernst Kaltenbrunner, Hans Frank. The challenge, however, lay in presenting the evidence against these men in a way that the German people themselves would find irrefutable and compelling—and to do so through legal procedures that not even the craftiest of defense lawyers could portray as biased or unfair. In a larger sense, therefore, the Nuremberg trials were an attempt to do properly what had been so badly botched in 1919: assigning war guilt to a defeated nation, in a way that would resonate with the people of that nation itself.[5]

The trials took place in two phases. From November 1945 to October 1946 a group of twenty-two prominent Nazis faced a panel of judges from the four main Allied victors, Britain, the United States, France, and the Soviet Union. (Hitler himself, of course, along with Heinrich Himmler, Joseph Goebbels, and several other top figures, had removed themselves from the hands of justice by committing suicide.) Then, from late 1946 until the spring of 1949, a second series of trials was held at Nuremberg under the sole jurisdiction of the United States: here a total of 185 lesser-known defendants faced a wide array of charges, ranging from mass murder to the use of slave labor, from illegal confiscation of Jewish property to conducting medical experiments on human beings.

The twenty-two defendants in the first trial faced four principal counts. Count One, "Conspiracy to Commit Aggressive War," relied on a concept of American jurisprudence that had been successfully used in the 1930s to prosecute elusive gangsters and racketeers: it aimed to hold individual German leaders responsible for working together over a sustained period of time with an avowed intention to violate international laws. Count Two,

"Crimes Against Peace," related to the specific acts of aggression committed by the German government in the 1930s and during the war. Count Three, "War Crimes," covered violations of internationally accepted norms in the conduct of warfare, such as shooting prisoners of war or attacking civilian populations. Count Four, "Crimes Against Humanity," embodied a concept created by the Allied jurists to deal with the unprecedented nature of the Nazi campaign against the Jews and other defenseless European populations.

From the start, the trials produced high drama: Hermann Göring, the number two man in the Third Reich, delivered an unexpectedly self-confident performance, adroitly playing the four judges against one another, and passionately portraying himself as a German patriot whose primary motivation had been to save his country from the evils of communism. He had already sensed the emergent tensions of the Cold War world, and astutely sought to position himself as a prescient defender of the West against Soviet aggression. (At that point in the trial, however, the prosecution screened a movie graphically showing the carnage in several extermination camps, and Göring's carefully scripted self-portrayal came apart: "And then," he wrote in his notes, "they showed that awful film, and it just spoiled everything.")[6] Ernst Kaltenbrunner, the highest-ranking SS man on trial, astounded the court with his coldly unrepentant acknowledgment of his wide-ranging brutal deeds. Albert Speer, Hitler's economic prodigy, chose the opposite path: he not only admitted the prosecution's claims against him, but denounced his own wartime behavior as unjustifiable, claiming that he bore the sole responsibility for having swallowed Nazi ideology as uncritically as he had (the judges ultimately rewarded his stance by sentencing him to twenty years' imprisonment instead of execution).

In October 1946 the judges delivered their verdict in the first trial. Three prominent figures in the Third Reich were acquitted: Franz von Papen, the Weimar politician who had handed over power to Hitler in 1933; Hjalmar Schacht, the financial genius behind Germany's stunningly successful economic recovery during Hitler's first three years in power; and Hans Fritzsche, one of Goebbels's lieutenants in the Nazi propaganda machine. All three were deemed to have been morally culpable for the evils of Nazism, but the judges decided that their misdeeds did not fall within the legal purview of the Nuremberg Charter. Twelve prominent Nazis received the death sentence: the political leaders Göring, Ribbentrop, Wilhelm Frick, Alfred Rosenberg, Julius Streicher, Martin Bormann (in absentia), and Arthur Seyss-Inquart; two top Wehrmacht officers, Wilhelm Keitel and Alfred Jodl; and three administrators of the death camps and slave labor camps, Kaltenbrunner, Frank, and Fritz Saukel. Seven others, including Admirals Karl Dönitz and Erich Raeder, and the Nazi Party boss Rudolf Hess, received sentences ranging from fifteen years' imprisonment to life. Hermann Göring managed one final *coup de théâtre* a mere two hours before his scheduled execution on October 15, 1946: he committed suicide in his prison cell by swallowing a cyanide capsule concealed in one of his teeth. Wilhelm Frick's last act, as he approached the gallows, was to shout out "Long Live Eternal Germany!"[7] It formed a neat piece of historical symmetry: Frick had been one of the chief architects of the Nuremberg racial laws of 1935.

The second series of trials ultimately resulted in acquittal for thirty-five defendants, death sentences for twenty-four, life sentences for twenty, and eighty-seven sentences of prison terms for varying lengths of time. Many of those imprisoned, however, found that the changing political climate of the 1950s worked in their favor: with a new West German republic formed in 1949, and the growing tensions of the Cold War increasingly diverting the public's attention, the Allies chose to ignore the decision of the West German government to reduce the sentences of many former Nazis and begin releasing them back into civilian life. By 1966, two of the most famous Third Reich personalities, Speer and Dönitz, had both served their sentences and were discharged from jail; they lived on peaceably as retirees until their deaths in the 1980s (enjoying handsome royalties from the publication of their memoirs). Thousands of lesser Nazi officials and party members served much shorter prison terms, then returned without further ado to their old prewar professions: teacher, farmer, civil servant, politician, banker.

In the Potsdam Declaration of July 1945, the Allies had promised to mete out "stern justice" to all Japanese war criminals: the instrument of this justice was a tribunal closely modeled on the Nuremberg precedent, convened in the old Imperial Army Ministry building in Tokyo between May 1946 and November 1948. Eleven justices sat on the bench, each representing one of the nationalities claiming a grievance for Japanese aggression: the United States, the Soviet Union, Britain, France, China, Australia, New Zealand, India, Canada, the Netherlands, and the Philippines. In the dock sat twenty-eight Japanese military and civilian leaders, the most famous of whom were Hideki Tojo, the general and former prime minister, and Yosuke Matsuoka, the hawkish foreign minister who had done so much to prod the Japanese government toward war in 1941. They faced a set of criminal counts that deliberately echoed the principles concurrently in use at Nuremberg: crimes against peace ("conspiracy" and "aggressive war"), war crimes, and crimes against humanity. The war crimes count also formed the primary judicial basis for a long series of secondary tribunals, convened outside Japan in various nations where Japanese military officers had surrendered at war's end.

Perhaps the most significant feature of the Tokyo trial was the glaring absence in the dock of Emperor Hirohito. Douglas MacArthur, the new shogun of occupied Japan, had decided (with the full concurrence of the Truman administration) that the United States stood to lose far more in prosecuting this man than it would gain by using him as a transitional figure, softening the humiliation of defeat for the Japanese people: the tacit "deal" was that the Japanese would get to keep their beloved emperor, and in exchange would accept a far-reaching set of social, economic, and political reforms under American tutelage. Institutional continuity under the emperor, in other words, would help to legitimize the process of radical Americanization that the occupation forces were busily carrying out: from women's suffrage to land reform, from educational restructuring to breaking up the prewar industrial conglomerates. But in order for this trade-off to work, Hirohito had to be made to appear before world opinion as a mere figurehead leader, a man who bore no direct responsibility for any of the bestial policies pursued in his name during the preceding two decades. Such became the official American position on the emperor's role—and as it turned out, this stance coincided perfectly with the ardent wish of virtually all the defendants who testified in the Tokyo trial: to protect their emperor from any suggestion of guilt by systematically minimizing his role in the direction and conduct of the war. Hirohito, therefore, sat quietly in his palace while the trial went on, powerfully shielded by the convergent complicities of his disgraced Japanese subordinates and his new American mentors.[8]

Tojo, like his counterpart Göring, gave the most impressive performance of the trials: proud, unrepentant, crisp and terse in his statements, he claimed that Japan's resort to war had been purely defensive in nature— a response to European and American imperialism in general, and to the draconian American, British, and Dutch economic sanctions of 1941 in particular. His broad array of arguments sufficiently impressed three of the judges—Radhabinod Pal of India, Henri Bernard of France, and B. V. A. Röling of the Netherlands—that they ultimately dissented from the court's majority verdict of guilty in November 1948.[9] Nevertheless, the eight remaining judges concurred in pronouncing a death sentence for seven defendants (Tojo included) and life sentences for sixteen others, and lesser terms for the remaining five. Meanwhile, the war crimes trials conducted in various Allied nations for captured Japanese officers went on with their work; in the end (by 1951), 5,700 individuals had been tried; some 2,000 were given long prison terms, and approximately 1,000 were executed.

Here, however, as in the case of West Germany (but with a notably greater degree of insouciance), the hand of justice was soon restrained by the more forceful hand of political expediency. Japan returned to full sovereignty and self-government in 1952: a nascent economic powerhouse, it quickly became the primary ally and agent of American anti-communist policy in Asia during the Cold War. Under these changed circumstances, no Western outcry ensued when the Japanese government, in 1958, issued a blanket pardon to all the convicted war criminals who still remained in prison: they were released and returned to civilian life.[10] "In this milieu of willful forgetting," writes the historian John Dower,

> the years that followed [the verdict of 1948] witnessed the almost wholesale rehabilitation of . . . war criminals. . . . Defendants who had been convicted and sentenced to imprisonment became openly regarded as victims rather than victimizers, their prison stays within Japan made as pleasant and entertaining as possible. Those who had been executed, often in far-away lands, were resurrected through their own parting words. One remembered the criminals, while forgetting their crimes.[11]

Despite the good intentions of the Allies in choosing due process of law rather than summary execution for their vanquished enemies, most historians and legal scholars concur today that the postwar trials of the Japanese and German leaders egregiously violated numerous fundamental principles of judicial fairness. Here are some of the main objections they have raised.

1. *Retroactivity.*

A basic principle of legal practice is *nullum crimen sine lege:* in order for any deed to count as a crime, that deed must violate a legitimately established law that is already on the books. The defense lawyers in both Nuremberg and Tokyo maintained that their clients were being tried for deeds that—however gory or immoral—had not been defined as crimes until after the fact. No statute of international law existed before 1945, for example, to define genocide and to establish punishments for it. The Allied prosecutors realized all too well that this constituted a serious weakness in their case: they sought to work around it by weaving together a tissue of legal precedents from existing laws and treaties that might plausibly apply to the atrocities committed during the war.

The first international treaty to set formal limits on the conduct of warfare had been the Geneva Convention of 1864, organized by the founder of the Red Cross, Henri Dunant: it established rules for the treatment of the enemy sick and wounded during war. A second Geneva Convention came into effect in 1899, banning the use of asphyxiating gases and dumdum bullets on the battlefield; a prohibition on bacteriological warfare followed in 1925. In 1929 a third Geneva Convention established basic rules for the decent treatment of prisoners of war; this latter agreement had been formally signed by forty-six nations, including Japan and Germany.[12]

Equally as important as the Geneva Conventions were the Hague Conventions of 1899 and 1907, which together established numerous formal rules of humane conduct during wartime. One clause in particular, known as the Martens Clause after the Russian jurist Fedor Martens, who drafted it, stated that even in cases not explicitly covered by the Hague restrictions, the "belligerents remain under the protection of . . . the principles of the laws of nations, as they result from the usages established among civilized peoples, from the laws of humanity, and the dictates of public conscience."[13] Here, according to the Allied prosecutors at Nuremberg, lay a solid legal precedent for the modern concept of "crimes against humanity." All that the Nuremberg judges had to do, they argued, was interpret this existing law as it applied to the misdeeds of the various Nazi defendants.

The judges, as we know, agreed. But most legal scholars believe that this reading of the existing laws was dubious at best: the Martens Clause had certainly constituted a major step forward in establishing basic principles of international criminality, but its extremely vague language, and the fact that it had never been backed up by formal enforcement procedures, severely weakened it as a legal precedent. The Nuremberg judges were certainly *establishing* such a precedent by convicting the Nazi leaders under these principles, but they were doing so by stretching existing laws well beyond the customary limits.[14]

2. *Double standard.*

The defense lawyers at both Nuremberg and Tokyo argued that numerous military and civilian officials of the Allied nations had themselves committed many of the same types of acts—or comparable acts—for which the defendants were now being tried. This, they claimed, violated the basic principle of fairness known as *tu quoque:* "You did it too!" Had not the Anglo-Americans deliberately killed hundreds of thousands of noncombatants with their bombardment of enemy cities? Had not Allied submarines sunk the ships of the enemy and refused to rescue survivors? Had not hundreds of thousands of German POWs died through deliberate maltreatment in Soviet camps? Had not the Russians killed thousands of captured Polish officers in cold blood during the Katyn Forest massacres in 1940?

One can imagine the unease of the Allied judges, because every one of these accusations was straightforwardly and undeniably true. (The furious Russian judge vehemently denounced the German claim that the Katyn murders had been committed by Soviet agents: the issue remained controversial until Mikhail Gorbachev formally acknowledged Soviet responsibility in 1989.) Faced with this line of argument, therefore, the Nuremberg judges had no choice but to rule summarily that any such *tu quoque* defense would simply be deemed out of order. Somewhat lamely, they lectured the defendants: "We are not the ones on trial here. The aim of this tribunal is to establish whether you did or did not commit such acts."

One does not have to be a Nazi apologist to regard this kind of ruling as grossly unfair. In the eyes of many postwar Germans and Japanese, it constituted the single most obvious reason for dismissing the trials as victor's justice.

3. *Tenuous conspiracy.*

The thrill of nabbing bootleggers and mobsters in gangland America had given the United States juridical team at Nuremberg an unshakable confidence in the power of the "conspiracy" count: but in the end this concept proved ill-suited to the complexities of international politics. Demonstrating that Hitler's Germany had engaged in wanton and unprovoked aggression was one thing; showing that a large number of German officials and military men had engaged in a conspiracy to commit such aggression—a conspiracy dating back to 1933 or even earlier—turned out to be entirely another matter. Defense lawyers detailed the many iniquities of the Versailles treaty; they quoted British criticisms of the 1923 French invasion of the Ruhr; they cited Hitler's speeches, many of which had been ostensibly directed at achieving peace; they pointed to the abject failure of the 1932 World Disarmament Conference, in which no nation proved willing to reduce its weaponry; they offered documents from Hitler's military advisors counseling him to avoid military action; they described in detail the long-running disagreements and bureaucratic struggles among Nazi leaders over foreign policy; they challenged the prosecution to show any tangible evidence of a concerted and long-term plot among the German leadership to commit aggressive war.

In retrospect, it is easy to see why the prosecution failed in this effort: there was no such conspiracy. German foreign policy in the 1930s—like any other nation's foreign policy—resulted from a complex nexus of causal factors: bureaucratic struggles, ideological shifts, rivalries between individuals, opportunistic responses to international events. To reduce this complicated interweaving of factors to a clear and linear story line—a bunch of bad guys meeting in smoky rooms to plot bad deeds—could not help but result in a ridiculously oversimplified and distorted account of the interwar years: it was like trying to explain the workings of an airplane cockpit by using the schematics of a kitchen stove.

In the end, the Nuremberg count of "conspiracy to commit aggressive war" proved the weakest of the four charges: it resulted in fourteen acquittals and only eight guilty verdicts—and even those required a stretching of the available evidence. In the Tokyo trial, the conspiracy count yielded twenty-three guilty verdicts and two acquittals: this lopsided outcome so outraged the French, Indian, and Dutch judges that they openly declared the tribunal to be engaging in a travesty of justice. No high-level and sustained conspiracy in Japanese ruling circles had been remotely proven, they argued: this simplistic and highly partial reading of the run-up to war amounted to little more than victor's vengeance cloaked in judicial language. Most historians and legal experts who have studied the trials concur.[15]

Few (if any) historians would want to deny that the Germans and the Japanese engaged in acts of unprovoked aggression against their neighbors during the 1930s; but pursuing this charge through the legal concept of conspiracy was a serious mistake. By setting out to prove a grossly simplistic version of history, it significantly undermined the legitimacy of the tribunals.

4. *Procedural iniquities.*

Both trials—but especially the Tokyo tribunal—engaged in a wide array of irregular or questionable judicial practices that would disqualify any normal tribunal.[16]

- Though able and experienced defense lawyers were provided to most of the defendants, the prosecution was allowed to draw on a much larger set of resources: more lawyers, research personnel, secretaries, archivists, paralegals.

- Some of the judges should have been barred from serving. The Soviet judge at Nuremberg distinguished himself for his frankness: "The whole idea is to secure quick and just punishment for the crime. . . . If . . . the judge is supposed to be impartial, it would only lead to unnecessary delays."[17] In the Tokyo trial, the Chinese judge had never served as a magistrate before; the Soviet judge spoke no Japanese or English (the official languages of the court); and the Philippine judge was himself a survivor of the Bataan Death March.[18]

- The selection of defendants gave a marked impression of arbitrariness, particularly in the Tokyo trial. The prosecution arraigned a total of 250 Japanese military and civilian officials, but decided to try only 28—a group that would constitute a "representative sample of the country's prewar and wartime leadership."[19] The remaining 222 individuals were simply released from custody in 1948 without undergoing trial at all.

- One of the concepts adopted at the Tokyo tribunal was that of "negative criminality": a military officer could be held responsible for failing to prevent his men's misdeeds, even if the prosecution could not demonstrate that the officer in question had any knowledge of those misdeeds being perpetrated.[20]

- The judges at the Tokyo tribunal regularly allowed the prosecution to present hearsay evidence against the defendants, often accepting this highly questionable source at face value.[21]

5. *Political interference.*

In too many instances, the trials gave way to political pressures from one or another of the Allied powers, thereby resulting in a blatant miscarriage of justice. At Nuremberg, for example, the Anglo-American judges ultimately chose to maintain an embarrassed silence over the Nazi-Soviet Pact of 1939 and over the question of responsibility for the Katyn massacres. But the most troubling example of political interference undoubtedly arose in the context of the Tokyo trial: the case of Shiro Ishii and his biological warfare research team known as Unit 731.

Ishii, a Japanese medical doctor, had begun work on biological weapons as early as 1932, establishing his base of operations near the city of Harbin in Japanese-occupied Manchuria—far from the eyes of journalists and other outsiders. After the outbreak of World War II, Ishii received authorization (and lavish funding) from the Japanese government to expand his research efforts, creating a top secret facility in the Manchurian countryside at a place called Pingfan.[22] Here, over the following four years, Ishii and his team conducted experiments on several thousand human subjects, most of them Chinese civilians arrested for various forms of resistance to the Japanese occupation. Some of the experiments involved animal-to-human blood transfusions, or freezing the limbs of individuals to investigate the most effective ways of treating extreme frostbite. Bubonic plague and other diseases were deliberately released in the surrounding Chinese villages, the deadly effects carefully recorded by Japanese observers as the villagers succumbed over several weeks. Inside the research facility, the Japanese team injected plague, anthrax, cholera, malaria, beriberi, tuberculosis, glanders, typhoid, and several dozen other exotic pathogens into the bodies of their prisoners, meticulously chronicling the fatal course of disease. In most cases, the infected prisoners were dissected while still alive, since this afforded researchers better insight into the progression of the infection and its effect on the subjects' internal organs. Here is how one of Ishii's technicians, a young man named Yoshio Shinozuka, later recalled his role:

> I still remember vividly the first vivisection I participated in. I knew the Chinese individual we dissected . . . because I had taken his blood once for testing. At the vivisection I could not meet his eyes because of the hate he had in his glare at me. This intelligent-looking man was systematically infected with plague germs. As the disease took its toll, his face and body became totally black. Still alive, he was brought on a stretcher by the special security forces to the autopsy room. Transferred to the autopsy table, the chief pathologist ordered us to wash his body. I used a rubber hose and a deck brush to wash him. Since this was my first vivisection, I think I was somewhat sloppy in washing him. I remember feeling somewhat hesitant in using the brush on his face. Watching me, the chief pathologist, with scalpel in hand, impatiently signaled me to hurry up. I closed my eyes and forced myself to scrub the man's face with the deck brush. The chief pathologist listened to the man's heartbeat with his stethoscope and then the procedure started. The man's organs were methodically excised one by one and I did as I was ordered to. I put them in a culturing can we had already prepared.[23]

In August 1945, after hearing Hirohito's surrender speech on the radio, Ishii ordered the destruction of the Pingfan facility and hastily returned to Japan, taking with him his most essential laboratory records (along with a good deal of stolen cash). After successfully evading the American occupation authorities for several months, he was finally apprehended by United States military intelligence (G-2) operatives and placed under house arrest.

The G-2 agents soon realized that this man possessed a veritable treasure trove of information on biological warfare—a research area that the United States had been pursuing at its facility in Fort Detrick, Maryland. During 1946 and 1947, G-2 officials repeatedly interviewed Ishii and several of his close subordinates: Ishii played his cards like a master, each time offering the Americans more detailed and more comprehensive experimental data.

But time was running out: several left-wing publications in Japan began airing testimonials by repentant former employees at the Pingfan facility about Unit 731's activities; they called for Ishii and his men to be handed over to the Tokyo tribunal for trial as war criminals. The American officials responded swiftly: in great secrecy, they granted full immunity from prosecution to Ishii and his entire team, in exchange for their continued cooperation in furnishing biological warfare data exclusively to their American handlers. Douglas MacArthur himself lent his authority to this move: in a secret radio message to Washington, transmitted on May 6, 1947, he explained, "Exemption [from prosecution] requested. Information about vivisection useful."[24] It remains unclear to this day exactly how the U.S. military intelligence officers exerted pressure on the multinational Allied prosecution team in Tokyo, but the result was that neither Ishii nor any of his subordinates in Unit 731 ever faced trial for their deeds. Dr. Shiro Ishii lived peacefully as a free man until his death in 1959.

The United States, in this episode, disgraced itself in two ways. First, it deliberately circumvented and undermined an international judicial process in which its own jurists were playing a central role: by shielding Ishii, it cynically cheated justice. And second, in the name of pursuing its own national security, it eagerly seized upon that most heinously tainted of scientific data, the laboratory and field records derived from deadly experiments on unwilling human subjects. The irony, according to one scholar, is that American experts on biological warfare later came to deem the information retrieved from Unit 731 as being "at best of minor significance."[25] But even if the data had proved excellent in quality, the entirety of it should have been swiftly destroyed. Any information gleaned from the torture and murder of helpless people is not science: it is an abomination, and can never be legitimately put to use in any way. There are certain lines that no self-respecting scientist should ever cross, and that no self-respecting government should ever allow its agents to cross: never, no matter what the reason. The United States crossed that line in the Ishii case: this despicable chapter in American history has still not been clearly acknowledged or confronted by the U.S. government.

The foregoing catalogue of serious judicial flaws makes it hard to avoid the conclusion that the Nuremberg and Tokyo trials did in the end amount to a form of victor's justice. The ex post facto nature of some of the trials' legal judgments; the double standard of trying Axis leaders for some deeds that had also been committed by the Allies; the inappropriateness of the conspiracy count; the multitude of procedural irregularities; and the clear-cut influence of political pressures on the final outcome—all these defects might lead one to conclude that the trials were a failure, a mistake. Might it not have been better, in the end, simply to apprehend and execute the Axis leaders, forthrightly and honestly, without going through an elaborate and potentially problematic judicial process?

In order to sustain such a position, however, one would have to ignore the very significant positive features of the trials—features that far outweigh even the most serious defects witnessed at Nuremberg and Tokyo. For all their flaws, the trials constituted a historic turning point in international affairs, and the Allied insistence on conducting them has been more than vindicated in the decades that followed. Here are the major reasons why.

1. *These were not mere show trials.*

Let us imagine for a moment that the war had ended differently, and that it was triumphant Germans and Japanese who were sitting in judgment in 1945 on men like Stalin, Zhukov, Eisenhower, Nimitz, Churchill, Eden, Truman, Harry Hopkins, and Henry Ford. Would they even have bothered with a trial? And if they had, can we expect that such a trial would have been any different than the cynically rigged proceedings that characterized the *Volksgericht* in Nazi Germany during the 1930s? A series of screamed indictments, a laborious brow-beating by party-certified jurists, a few photos for propaganda purposes—and off to the firing squad or gallows.

This was very far from being the case at Nuremberg and Tokyo: the most convincing proof lies in the significant number of acquittals and relatively tempered prison sentences that resulted from both tribunals. A man like the banker Hjalmar Schacht, for example, who had done so much to advance Hitler's economic agenda between 1933 and 1936, was allowed to walk, because the judges determined that his deeds had not constituted crimes suitable for conviction under the specific four counts of the trial. A man like Albert Speer, who showed sincere remorse and who argued convincingly that his intentions had not been genocidal in nature, received a mitigated sentence. A man like the former Japanese foreign minister Mamoru Shigemitsu, who had intervened on the side of the moderates during the Imperial Council's debates over surrender in August 1945, received from the Tokyo tribunal a relatively modest sentence of seven years' imprisonment.

These trials, in short, fell somewhere between the full standard of due process that one would expect in the courtroom of a Western democracy, and the thoroughly sham justice that characterized the Nazi (or Soviet) tyrannies. The Nuremberg and Tokyo judges systematically made the kinds of nuanced distinctions that gave an innocent man, or a manifestly less culpable man, a very real opportunity to make his case. While imperfect, these two tribunals still conducted their business according to identifiable standards that limited the discretion of the judges and that gave the defendants a legitimate chance of establishing their innocence.

2. *The proportionality of atrocious crimes.*

Hermann Göring argued, in effect, that the Nuremberg trials were illegitimate because all sides in the war had committed atrocities, and therefore all sides were equally culpable. It was a logic that exerted a strong appeal for many Germans and Japanese in the postwar years: they claimed that they were being singled out unfairly for condemnation, when in fact they had only done what everyone else had also done. Bad things had happened on all sides: the Anglo-Americans had killed hundreds of thousands of civilians with their bombardment of cities; the Russians had killed hundreds of thousands of German POWs through starvation and neglect. Why should Germany and Japan have to suffer the sole opprobrium for the gross evils perpetrated by all sides in the war?

One lasting achievement of the Nuremberg and Tokyo tribunals was to demolish this argument, showing it clearly for the casuistry it was. The documentation presented at the trials demonstrated conclusively that the Germans and Japanese had committed a series of crimes of a historically unprecedented nature—crimes that crossed a qualitative threshold, into a new level of evil. For Göring to have made the "*tu quoque!*" argument with any degree of persuasiveness, he would have had to show that various Anglo-American and Russian policies were morally just as bad as the methodical extermination of 6 million Jews. This is a judgment that most historical observers are understandably unwilling to make. Soviet abuse of German POWs could be at least partially (though not wholly) explained as the result of dire supply shortages in a country whose entire population was suffering terribly because of an unprovoked attack by the Germans. The Anglo-American policies of area bombing and firebombing cities, as we saw in chapter 5, were undeniably atrocities, but they could not be placed on a par with the slaughter of the European Jews or the Japanese rampages in cities like Manila. Strategic bombing—even in those clearly unjustifiable cases when it needlessly slaughtered noncombatants—still formed part of a military campaign aimed at destroying the German and Japanese ability to wage war. By contrast, the Nazi death camps and the Japanese massacres of civilians yielded no military advantage whatsoever. They amounted to nothing more than gratuitous murder on a colossal scale.

This is by no means to minimize the very real burden of guilt borne by the Anglo-Americans and Russians for the brutality that characterized some of their wartime policies: but it does help us to gain a sense of proportion for the *tu quoque* claim that is sometimes raised by right-wing nationalists in Germany and Japan. The trials established, through massive and incontrovertible evidence, that in World War II the Germans and Japanese had descended several steps further into barbarism than the other nations of the world: they had distinguished themselves as perpetrators of uniquely heinous acts.

3. *Judicial sentence versus summary execution.*

The suicides of people like Hitler and Himmler leave us with a somewhat empty feeling: for death, by itself, offers no moral judgment. Everybody dies, sooner or later. In a somewhat similar way, a firing squad, a summary execution of Axis leaders at war's end, might well have given the victims of German and Japanese aggression some sense of closure; but it could not have provided a larger sense of real justice being served.

What the Nuremberg and Tokyo trials offered, by contrast, was the spectacle of the criminal being confronted with his deeds: Göring having to watch "that awful film," staring into the eyes of his victims. It presented before world opinion a detailed and reasoned explanation of what the defendants had done, why they had done it, whom they had harmed, and why this was wrong. It gave the defendants a chance to explain their actions; it gave the victims (speaking on behalf of countless others) a chance to explain the suffering they had endured.

In the end, the tribunals restored some compass of moral meaning to the nihilistic acts committed during the war. A summary execution of Axis leaders in 1945 would have vindicated that nihilism, showing to the world the naked triumph of superior force, the loser crushed beneath the heel of the winner's boot. But when individuals like Kaltenbrunner and Tojo went to the gallows as tried and convicted war criminals, their deaths meant something more. These men had not merely failed to win the war: their actions, their choices, had debased the image that humankind could hence-forth have of itself. Through the medium of the tribunals, their deaths became not merely a question of winning and losing, but of multileveled shame: the shame of individuals, of perpetrator nations, and of bystander nations. The two tribunals, for all their failings, took the deaths of these men and inscribed them into history with the full measure of indelible dis-honor they deserved.

4. *Thwarting the Holocaust deniers.*

Periodically, on university campuses or in the mass media, one encoun-ters the passionate debates stirred up by groups of individuals who have come to be known as Holocaust deniers. Their organizations appear to be rather small and marginal in nature: two of the better-known ones are the Institute for Historical Review and the Committee for Open Debate on the Holocaust.[26] Their approach varies from episode to episode, but the under-lying message remains essentially the same: the Nazi gas chambers were not really used to kill millions of Jews; the attempted genocide of Euro-pean Jews never happened (some Jews were killed, yes, but never in the systematic way that historians claim); the National Holocaust Museum in Washington, D.C., is putting out a false and manipulative message.[27] In short, the Holocaust is a hoax that has fooled the overwhelming majority of historians since World War II.

Who perpetrated the hoax, and who is still actively promoting it? Here the Holocaust deniers remain rather unclear. But the underlying point is that the hoax benefits the state of Israel, and Jews in general, because the sufferings of the (alleged) Holocaust have generated enormous sympathy for Jews all over the world. The Holocaust deniers' tactic is simple: they take advantage of the high value we place in our society on free speech; they appeal to our sense of open-mindedness and fair play, the obligation to hear out all points of view, no matter how different from our own.

One of the lasting effects of the Nuremberg trials is that the Holocaust deniers have very little purchase for their anti-Semitic propaganda. The prosecution team at Nuremberg wisely decided to build its case primarily on the basis of documentary evidence, supplemented by the testimony of several hundred firsthand witnesses. The German government, it turned out, had kept extremely detailed records of the bureaucratic apparatus and physical plant required for carrying out the transportation and murder of its millions of victims; a surprisingly large portion of those records sur-vived the war and fell into Allied hands. They filled literally hundreds of boxes: official correspondence, government memoranda, lists of prisoners, receipts for delivery of poison gas canisters, photographs, personal letters, soldiers' diaries, blueprints for crematoria, medical records, budgetary ledgers, railroad schedules for the deportation trains, telegrams among government ministries. These mountains of documents were carefully sorted by the prosecution team, then brought powerfully to bear in the trials, supplemented by oral testimony and sworn affidavits from German officials, death camp guards, camp survivors, and other direct participants in the Holocaust.[28]

To deny that the Holocaust happened, in the face of the evidence accumulated at Nuremberg, is just about like denying today that the First World War happened—that the whole thing, the assassination in Sarajevo, trench warfare, the Battle of Ypres, the Red Baron, and so on, is all just a devilishly clever fabrication. To be sure, historians have gathered together still more evidence concerning the Holocaust in the decades since 1946—an overall amount outweighing the trove assembled at Nuremberg. But it was the Nuremberg prosecution team that laid the foundation for that subsequent scholarship, piecing the evidence together into the first systematic portrait of the Nazi genocide—laying it out in detail for all the world to see. In this sense, one of the important legacies of the Nuremberg trials has been to keep the Holocaust deniers on the fringe of contemporary society.

Among the positive achievements of the Nuremberg and Tokyo trials, however, the one that future historians will probably consider most significant lies in the area of international law. The trials need to be understood not just as the concluding acts of World War II, but as the catalysts of a revolutionary shift in the defense of basic human rights. Bringing men like Göring and Tojo to justice was vitally important, but more important still was the laying of legal and institutional foundations for dealing with the crimes of future Görings and Tojos who might arise in later generations. Herein lies the trials' real historical (and moral) legacy: they constituted a qualitative leap toward a truly global system of justice.

In order to appreciate what a major development the trials represented in the advance of international law, we need to survey the overall trajectory of that process as it has unfolded from the late 1800s to the early 2000s. States have established bilateral and multilateral treaties and other legal arrangements for dealing with one another since ancient times, but it was only toward the end of the nineteenth century that the notion of creating an international tribunal began to gather serious momentum. Growing technologies of communication and transportation were bringing people from the farthest corners of the globe increasingly into contact (and conflict) with one another; growing technologies of military destruction were rendering clashes among states increasingly bloody and costly; and so the concept of creating a permanent body for international arbitration and jurisprudence began to strike many late-nineteenth-century statesmen as an eminently sensible "next step" in the evolution of human civilization. Theodore Roosevelt, for one, became a passionate advocate of the idea.[29]

The first faltering moves in this direction accordingly took place at the Hague Conferences of 1899 and 1907, when some forty-six nations (including an American delegation dispatched by Roosevelt) agreed on the goal of establishing a world court that would possess binding authority over its members. But when it came to the moment of actually handing over sovereignty to such a body, the delegates balked: they squabbled over procedures for selecting judges, they bickered over the wording of the treaty, and in the end inserted so many loopholes into the proposed legislation that it became practically meaningless.[30] Nevertheless, the delegates did agree to proceed with the construction of a building to house the new international tribunal: Andrew Carnegie provided the cash, and the magnificent Peace Palace at The Hague duly opened its doors—in August 1913. History, unfortunately, is all too rich in such piquancies.

The bloodletting of World War I forcefully concentrated minds once more; and again the United States played a key leadership role, this time incarnated in the driving personality of Woodrow Wilson. The League of Nations, as Wilson envisioned it, would not only arbitrate disputes among states, but would also possess the authority to enforce its decisions by levying economic sanctions against recalcitrant nations. In addition, the League would perform vital administrative functions at the global level: regulating labor practices, promoting public health, and seeking to alleviate poverty. It was a heady vision, but it proved too advanced for its time: the isolationist U.S. Senate broke Wilson's heart by refusing to allow the United States to join the new organization.

As we saw in chapter 3, the League lacked the means to deal effectively with the combined crises of a severe economic depression, coupled with the rise of fascism and communism in the political sphere. In 1929 France and the United States launched a quixotic endeavor to "outlaw war as a means of resolving international conflicts." The resultant Kellogg-Briand Pact was solemnly signed by sixty-two nations, including Germany; it became risibly irrelevant over the coming decade as the European peoples lurched spastically toward war. A similarly idealistic impulse resulted in the World

Disarmament Conference of 1932, held under the auspices of the League of Nations at its offices in Geneva: once again, the nations all agreed that disarmament lay in everyone's best interest; but they balked when it came to actually laying down arms. Hitler astutely used the failure of this conference to justify German rearmament in violation of the Treaty of Versailles.

The Hague Conferences, the Geneva Conventions, and the League of Nations: these were the principal entities humankind had been able to create, in the effort of building international legal institutions, during the first half of the twentieth century. Their abysmal inadequacy convinced a new generation of leaders, in the wake of World War II, that it was time to push much further—all the way into a qualitatively different system. The central problem, they concluded, lay in the concept of national sovereignty itself: the stubborn refusal by virtually all national governments to hand over real decision-making powers and judicial authority to a body higher than themselves. Now, at war's end, with the imagery of Auschwitz and Hiroshima still fresh in their minds, the world's leaders launched a three-pronged attack on the principle of national sovereignty:

- the Nuremberg and Tokyo judicial processes (1946–1951);
- the United Nations (1945);
- and a bevy of new international treaties focusing on human rights, most prominent among them the Universal Declaration of Human Rights, or UDHR (1948); the Convention Against Genocide (1948); and the Fourth Geneva Convention (1949).

All three of these undertakings rested on a firm rejection of the notion, once held sacrosanct, that a national government's right to self-determination—to do as it pleases within its own territory—is absolute. No longer: the Nuremberg trials established a solid precedent that certain misdeeds would henceforth be punishable through the instruments of a higher law than that of the mere nation-state. The UDHR, the Convention Against Genocide, and the Fourth Geneva Convention spelled out the details of that higher set of laws with great precision; and the United Nations provided an instrument for enforcement, using economic sanctions and its own military corps to do so when necessary. This revolutionary shift in the nature of international politics—a major step beyond the principles of untrammeled state sovereignty and competitive balance of power—can only be understood as a vehement reaction to the horror that had just laid half the globe to waste. It was a reaction shared by virtually all the world's peoples with an unprecedented degree of unanimity.

And once again—as with the Hague Conventions, the League of Nations, and the Kellogg-Briand Pact—it was the United States that stepped forward as a prime mover in the creation of this new order. American diplomacy spearheaded the establishment of the United Nations; American leadership saw through the Nuremberg and Tokyo tribunals to fruition; American jurists helped to draft the UDHR and the Convention Against Genocide. Those who argue, today, that supporting the United Nations is "un-American" need to sit down for a few hours with a good history textbook: the building of international bodies for peace and justice reflects a long tradition of American foreign policy, a tradition reflecting the convictions held by some of the most eminent Republican and Democratic statesmen of the past 120 years.[31]

This is not to deny, of course, that United States foreign policy over the past century has also exhibited an equally significant tradition of reluctance to engage in foreign entanglements: examples include the isolationism of the interwar years; the growing distrust of the United Nations as U.S. dominance in that organization began to fade after the 1950s; the long hesitancy (until 1988) in ratifying the U.N. convention on genocide;[32] and the more recent withdrawal from such international treaties as the Kyoto Protocol on climate change. The point here is twofold: First, American history reflects a fundamental tension between these two impulses, the internationalist and the nationalist, both of which have played strong roles in determining how American power came to be applied at different times. And second, the decade following World War II undoubtedly marked one of the all-time high points of United States internationalism: not only the government leadership under Truman and Eisenhower, but the broader citizenry, overwhelmingly embraced the idea that American interests required vigorous international institutions and active American leadership through those institutions.

Nevertheless, the principle of national sovereignty refused to give up easily: it did not "go gentle into that good night." The rubble of World War II had barely begun to cool when the first signs of East-West tension began to manifest themselves; by 1949 the United Nations found itself completely hamstrung by the mutual antagonism and suspicion between the two rival blocs of the Cold War. For the next four decades, until the collapse of the Soviet empire in 1989, the world lived in the polarized force field of these two economic and military colossi. International organs of justice, and the good offices of the United Nations, would register few significant achievements during those decades.[33] Only in those rare instances when both superpowers happened to agree on a major issue—such as the reckless illegality of the Anglo-French-Israeli incursion into the Suez in 1956—was the U.N. able to take prompt and effective action. (On that particular occasion the U.N. General Assembly, backed by strong support from Washington and Moscow, peremptorily ordered the Anglo-French-Israeli forces to return home; they immediately obeyed; and a U.N. peace-keeping force moved in to stabilize the situation on the ground.)

A second reason for the slow progress of international law during the Cold War years lay in the drastically limited powers of the U.N.'s primary judicial arm, the International Court of Justice at The Hague. The ICJ was an almost comically impotent institution, crippled by the restrictions imposed on its rules of procedure at its founding in 1946. It could not try individual persons, but only national governments; and any government brought before it had to consent to the court's jurisdiction before legal action could proceed. This was, in the words of one scholar, tantamount to "requiring an accused murderer to give his consent before he could be tried."[34] For example, when Nicaragua sued the United States at The Hague in 1984 for having mined its harbors, the United States simply withheld its consent to ICJ jurisdiction and walked away: not a particularly edifying moment in the conduct of international jurisprudence.

The near-paralysis of the U.N. abruptly ended after Mikhail Gorbachev's reforms in the Soviet Union spun out of control and brought about the implosion of one of the two Cold War rivals. Suddenly, amid talk of a "new world order," the U.N. began taking action once again—sometimes successfully, sometimes more hesitantly and fecklessly. When Saddam Hussein's Iraq invaded Kuwait in 1990, a potent U.N. coalition (led by the Americans but broadly supported and financed by most other great powers) moved in swiftly and expelled the Iraqis; U.N. officials imposed a tough regime of sanctions and weapons inspections on the aggressor government. When Yugoslavia slid into civil war in the early 1990s, however, the U.N.'s response proved less impressive: it dithered until the violence had degenerated to genocidal levels, then delegated NATO forces to clean up the mess. When a civil war tore apart the African nation of Rwanda in the mid-1990s, the U.N. once again failed to intervene promptly enough to stop a genocide in progress: some 800,000 civilians perished before peacekeepers finally moved in.[35]

The Yugoslavian and Rwandan genocides, however, did prompt a decisive return to the judicial precedent of the Nuremberg and Tokyo trials. By the late 1990s, two U.N. tribunals had convened at The Hague: the ICTY (International Criminal Tribunal for the Former Yugoslavia) and ICTR (International Criminal Tribunal for Rwanda). (Anyone who deals even briefly with the United Nations soon learns that its institutions thrive, perhaps unavoidably, within an A.R.E. [acronym-rich environment].) The Serbian statesman Slobodan Milosevic, one of the most cynical instigators of the Yugoslavian nightmare, soon found himself hauled before a U.N. judge in the Netherlands to answer for his many misdeeds; Jean Kambanda, the prime minister of Rwanda when that country's civil war took place, pled guilty at The Hague in 1998 to six counts of genocidal crimes.[36]

Building on the success of the tribunals for Yugoslavia and Rwanda, U.N. jurists moved in 1998 to create a permanent International Criminal Court (ICC).[37] This new tribunal, however, would possess several key differences from its predecessor, the irretrievably wimpy International Court of Justice: it would be the real thing. The ICC would try individual persons, not national governments; its jurisdiction would be universal, applying to all member states and their citizens without need for prior consent; it would be empowered to initiate prosecutorial action rather than waiting for aggrieved parties to present cases before it. This court, in other words, would function in much the same manner as the ad hoc tribunals for Yugoslavia and Rwanda, but on a permanent basis and with a global mandate. Like its predecessors, it would be housed at The Hague; but unlike its predecessors it would operate independently from the United Nations, rigorously insulated from the political maneuvering in the Security Council and General Assembly. Its legal authority would focus on four categories of crime that transcend national jurisdictions: genocide, crimes against humanity, war crimes, and aggression.[38] Nothing like it had ever existed before.

After several years of international negotiations, the court's statute officially went into force in 2002: sixty nations, including the United States and most of its closest allies, had ratified the transfer of sovereignty to this pioneering judicial body. This time around, however, the role played by the United States was much more openly ambivalent than in the past: influential groups of American conservatives had come to regard any transfer of sovereignty to this kind of international tribunal as unacceptable. They feared that American soldiers might someday find themselves summoned to The Hague to stand trial as war criminals, simply for participating in military actions that their own government had sent them to perform. In May 2002 the new administration of President George W. Bush formally withdrew the United States from membership in the ICC.

Nevertheless, the International Criminal Court now existed, its role powerfully backed by a remarkable array of the world's nations. By 2005 these included ninety-nine countries: all the member states of the European Union, twenty countries from Latin America, fifteen from Eastern Europe, twelve from Asia, and twenty-seven from Africa—over half the membership of the U.N.[39] Henceforth, when a future Saddam Hussein or Slobodan Milosevic decides to initiate policies involving serious violations of human rights, they will have to do so knowing that a court is sitting in The Hague, open for business, closely monitoring their actions, and ready to pursue them as individuals and try them for their deeds. To quote from the ICC's Web site:

> This is the first-ever permanent, treaty based, international criminal court established to promote the rule of law and ensure that the gravest international crimes do not go unpunished. . . . Anyone who commits any of the crimes under the Statute after [July 1, 2002] will be liable for prosecution by the Court.[40]

From The Hague, 1907, to The Hague, 2002: the principle of international criminal justice came a long way during the arc of the twentieth century. Most probably, it was the very nature itself of that century—its breathtaking cruelties, its terrifying weaponry—that prodded the process along. The reflex of national sovereignty dies hard, and it took extraordinary sufferings and dangers to move the world's peoples toward an acceptance of supranational legal structures. But the movement is there, plain to see, if one stands back from the past hundred years and assesses the overall thrust of the achievements that have marked human endeavors in this domain. The progress is slow, faltering, punctuated by periodic setbacks—but unmistakable.

Nuremberg and Tokyo constituted the chronological halfway mark; but from a qualitative point of view, they clearly amounted to much more than that. For all the flaws we have laid out in the foregoing discussion, these trials took humankind over the threshold of a new era—one of universal human rights, enshrined in written laws, protected by a court whose jurisdiction is global. The trials took a very bad business—genocide, hatred, nihilism—and used it as a springboard for something constructive, the solid foundations of a future hope.

Chapter Twelve

GENERATIONS UNDER A SHADOW

The Challenge of Peace Since Hiroshima

Either war is finished or we are.
—Herman Wouk, *War and Remembrance*, 1978[1]

War is a part of God's creation.

—Helmut von Moltke, 1880[2]

World War II forever changed the moral stakes surrounding the challenge of global peace. In the aftermath of Hiroshima, peace was no longer merely a worthy goal for statesmen to pursue, but became a question of long-term survival for all of civilization. We have come to think of the period since 1945 as the nuclear era, and this terminology explicitly reflects the fact that we live in a qualitatively different world from that which came before. Among the many moral dimensions of the Second World War, this one cannot be ignored: because of the way this conflict played itself out, all of us must now live, day by day, with the knowledge that our civilization is mortal, and that we ourselves may be the instruments of its passing.

But there is also hope in this new awareness. The horrors of the war provided an impetus for bold experimentation in the quest for peace during the postwar decades, resulting in a wide range of pathbreaking endeavors all over the planet—undertakings not only of thought and imagination, but also of concrete practice carried out on the ground. World War II certainly did present the world with a terrible problem—the danger of nuclear annihilation. But it would be misleading simply to leave the issue there: we must also recognize the real progress people have made in addressing that threat, charting a course toward a more irenic global sys-

United Nations flag waves over crowd in Taegu, Korea, after U.N. vote for direct military intervention in the Korean conflict (July 30, 1950).

tem. Even during the bleakest years of the Cold War—indeed, precisely because the outlook in those years often seemed so bleak—human beings struggled to gain a better understanding of the nature of peace, and sought to enshrine that understanding in new international institutions and practices.

Both peril and hope without precedent: this dual nature of the war's legacy was already clear to some observers within a few months of the Japanese surrender. On October 16, 1945, at a ceremony in Los Alamos, New Mexico, Robert Oppenheimer accepted a certificate of appreciation from the War Department on behalf of all the men and women who had built the atomic bomb. The speech he gave was characteristically short.

> It is our hope that in years to come we may look at this scroll, and all that it signifies, with pride.
>
> Today that pride must be tempered with a profound concern. If atomic bombs are to be added as new weapons to the arsenals of a warring world, or

to the arsenals of nations preparing for war, then the time will come when mankind will curse the names of Los Alamos and Hiroshima.

The peoples of the world must unite, or they will perish. This war, that has ravaged so much of the earth, has written these words. The atomic bomb has spelled them out for all men to understand. Other men have spoken them, in other times, of other wars, of other weapons. They have not prevailed. There are some, misled by a false sense of human history, who hold that they will not prevail today. It is not for us to believe that. By our works we are committed, committed to a world united, before the common peril, in law, and in humanity.[3]

This chapter focuses on the radical transformation wrought by World War II in the domain of global politics: the challenge that Oppenheimer so clearly articulated, of creating "a world united . . . in law, and in humanity" under the shadow of the mushroom cloud.[4] Will humankind have to keep muddling through indefinitely on the knife edge of arms races, weapons of mass destruction, and "security" enforced by intercontinental suicide pacts? Or might it be possible to move our species—gradually, incrementally, but decisively—toward a more cooperative and effective system of conflict resolution? And what might such a system realistically look like? These questions, and the myriad global efforts they encapsulate, arguably constitute the most significant moral legacy of World War II. It boils down, in the end, to our long-term prospects for avoiding World War III.

Let us start with something very concrete and specific: the story of what has happened to the relationship between France and Germany over the past sixty years. It is an extraordinary account, partly because it appears so mundane that we tend to take it for granted. Yet, when one stands back from it, looking at it from the long view of the historian, what we see is nothing less than amazing. As a direct result of the trauma of World War II, these two hardened enemies committed themselves to an ambitious and multifaceted process of reconciliation; through the decades that followed, they gradually succeeded in undoing deeply entrenched patterns of hostility and distrust, and in building an exceptionally strong partnership. Their postwar story holds out a powerful example to the rest of humankind: stable peace, it turns out, is not necessarily the utopian goal that many tend to assume.

The enmity between the French and German peoples goes back for centuries, dating even to a time before there was such an entity as "Germany." The French statesman Cardinal Richelieu made a point of fostering disunity among the German statelets and principalities during the seventeenth century, cynically prolonging the Thirty Years War because the resultant German division and weakness left the field of European politics open for French power. Napoleon's armies trampled through the divided German states in 1806, thereby igniting the first significant fires of German national feeling. These patriotic sentiments culminated six decades later in the German unification wars of the 1860s, the final act of which was consummated when the Prussians trounced the French in a short war in 1870. Otto von Bismarck (in one of history's least tactful gestures) formally announced the creation of a united German nation in the Hall of Mirrors at Versailles, the royal palace of a defeated and occupied France. Adding injury to insult, he also lopped off two of France's northeastern provinces, Alsace and Lorraine, and annexed them to Germany. The French vowed revenge: over the following decades (and particularly after Bismarck's retirement in 1890), they gradually pieced together a web of alliances with the British and Russians, surrounding Germany with a ring of potentially hostile armies. In World War I the Germans almost succeeded in defeating all three of these combined enemies, but the arrival of United States forces in 1917 decisively tipped the balance against them. The French savored the moment: at the Peace of Paris in 1919 they took back Alsace and Lorraine; they called for the forcible dismemberment of the remainder of Germany into several small states (a policy that Wilson and British prime minister David Lloyd George sensibly vetoed); they demanded harsh reparations payments (on an installment plan that extended into the 1980s); they rammed the punitive Treaty of Versailles down the throat of their now helpless neighbor.

The furious Germans refused to comply: they cheated on reparations payments and then deliberately wrecked their own economy, allowing it to go into a tailspin of hyperinflation. The French responded in 1923 by invading the Ruhr with their army, importing French laborers to run the German factories and extract the reparations by force. The young agitator Adolf Hitler had a field day with these events, vowing he would make the French pay dearly someday: it became one of the major sources of his appeal among the German electorate. After Hitler came to power in 1933 and launched rearmament, the French knew they would sooner or later bear the brunt of the German grudge: they built the Maginot Line along their border with Germany, one of the greatest (and most expensive) fixed fortification networks of all history—like a modern Wall of China, to keep out the barbarian hordes. It did no good: the Germans nimbly got around it in 1940 and smashed the French army in a mere six weeks. Hitler, ever one to savor historical turns, forced the French generals to sign the surrender document in the same railroad car—sitting on the exact same spot in a clearing of the Compiègne Forest—where the humiliating German surrender had been signed in 1918. "For the next four years," observes the French historian Alain Beltran, "we lived day-to-day with the very real possibility of ceasing to exist as a national unit, of being dismembered whenever our new masters might wish it."[5] The Germans imposed a puppet dictator on France; they forced French workers to labor in German factories; they massacred the populations of French villages suspected of aiding the anti-fascist Resistance.

As the dust settled in 1945, therefore, one could hardly pick two nations less likely to inaugurate an enduring peace between themselves. Like the Hatfields and McCoys, like the Montagues and Capulets, the Germans and the French had established a multigenerational track record of unjust and cruel deeds perpetrated against each other. They hated and feared each other, passionately, reciprocally—and with good reason.

And yet, sixty years later, the border between France and Germany has become very much like the border between Canada and the United States: it is a nonborder, a flimsy imaginary line separating two neighbors between whom war is virtually unthinkable; two neighbors who constitute each other's largest trading partners; two neighbors who, despite occasional tensions and disagreements, work together through close and fruitful partnership. France and Germany, in short, now enjoy a relationship of stable peace: they have succeeded in "breeding lilacs out of the dead land."[6]

How did this happen? The answer is that it didn't "just happen": the Franco-German peace was built, like an edifice, one stone at a time, through deliberate planning, and through the patient, unrelenting efforts of statesmen and common citizens on both sides.[7] The key lay in the powerful array of convergent political interests that these two peoples came to see themselves as sharing. Both wanted to avoid another bloodbath like the one they had just survived. A majority of both populations wanted to avoid Soviet hegemony over their country. Both—mainly the French at first, but later the Germans as well—hoped to avoid inordinate American influence over their affairs.

Complementing these shared interests were two asymmetrical national interests that (fortunately) happened to dovetail splendidly with each other. The French feared, with good reason, that Germany would someday recover from its prostrate and divided state: they decided that the best way to control renascent German power was to submerge that power within a new supranational European entity—an entity in which France would play a leading role. The Germans, for their part, wanted to end as quickly as possible their status as international pariahs: they decided that the best way to bring this about was to submerge the German recovery within a strong network of alliances—a close transatlantic partnership with the Americans, a close partnership with the French in building a united Europe.

These convergent interests provided the driving force behind the Franco-German reconciliation process that unfolded over the postwar decades. To be sure, French and German citizens did not immediately artic-ulate these interests in such straightforward terms in 1945; rather, these guiding principles only gradually emerged and became clearer as the years went by. The French, during the 1950s, responded to memories of the traumatic defeat of 1940 by building their own nuclear arsenal, the Force de Frappe, as a sort of ultimate insurance policy for guaranteeing their national security; it became operational in 1962, and was steadily enhanced by French governments of both left and right over the ensuing years. The Germans, on the other hand, had been forbidden by the victorious Allies from ever acquiring nuclear arms—nor did they want such weapons. Their people had been too badly burned by the Hitler experience, and now adopted a resolutely internationalist stance that emphasized achieving security only through alliances with other like-minded nations, and never again through unilateral military action. Once more, the asymmetry between the French and German stances offered an incentive for coopera-tion: French nukes, it was thought, would contribute potently to the defense of Western Europe (including Germany), aiding in the deterrence of Soviet aggression or intimidation; German economic power would provide the foundation of prosperity for sustaining Western European dynamism and independence.

Without a doubt, economic integration constituted the leading edge of Franco-German peace-building. Spurred by the visionary leadership of the Frenchman Jean Monnet, the two nations joined four others (Italy, Bel-gium, the Netherlands, and Luxembourg) in fusing their coal and steel industries under a supranational governing body in 1951. From there the European integration process unfolded, gradually expanding both its membership and its power—by fits and starts but making steadily recog-nizable progress—over the next five decades. And as it went, it littered the European landscape with a whole slew of new acronyms: European Coal and Steel Community (ECSC) in 1951; European Economic Community

(EEC) in 1957; European Parliament (EP) in 1979; European Union (EU) in 1992; European Monetary Union (EMU) in 2002. Throughout this process, scholars agree, the Franco-German partnership has constituted the solid backbone of the integration movement. When the French and Germans squabbled, the European integration process slowed or bogged down; when the French and Germans worked together, the process moved forward.

Today the French and German economies are so profoundly interwoven with each other (and with those of their European neighbors) that the observer is hard-pressed to tell where one economy ends and another begins. Workers move freely among the twenty-five member nations, taking jobs and paying taxes as if in a single country; they enjoy comparable health care and retirement benefits across borders; they operate under common safety and environmental laws; they vote for a common parliamentary body that oversees legislation binding on every citizen of every member state; many of them use the same currency; they increasingly speak a common second language (English); more and more, they live and experience a distinctively "European" identity that complements their individual national traditions.

But this broader European process of economic integration should not mislead us: for the French and Germans have also worked with equal alacrity on the special bilateral relationship between their two countries. In 1963, German chancellor Konrad Adenauer and French president Charles de Gaulle signed a Franco-German friendship pact, known as the Elysée Treaty, which laid out the framework for an unprecedented effort of political cooperation and popular reconciliation. The treaty mandated regular meetings between French and German leaders: every six months for the heads of state, every three months for the defense ministers, and every two months for the military chiefs of staff. Both parties pledged to consult with the other before launching any major new initiative in foreign policy; both agreed to work closely on harmonizing their defense policies.

In addition, the Elysée Treaty created a lavishly funded body dedicated to encouraging direct contacts between the French and German peoples— particularly among the nations' youth—so that they could get to know each other better. In the forty years that followed, this exchange program resulted in more than 7 million French and German citizens conducting extended visits (up to several months long) to each other's countries, their travel and accommodations heavily subsidized by their respective governments.[8] The citizens of France and Germany established "twin town" relationships between some seven hundred pairs of their municipalities, with all the official and unofficial exchanges that accompany such liaisons.[9] A joint coordinating committee, the Working Circle of Franco-German Societies, oversaw the pullulating activity of more than a hundred local or special-interest groups seeking to promote amity between the two nations: church groups, both Protestant and Catholic, established formal ties with their homologues across the border; trade unions sent fact-finding missions to each other's cities; ex-soldiers' associations sponsored meetings between French and German war veterans.[10]

Last but not least, de Gaulle and Adenauer agreed in 1963 that military cooperation between France and Germany should receive the highest priority.[11] Over the years that followed, as French and German defense ministers and military officers conducted their regular meetings, they laid out a framework for an increasingly close partnership: in 1986 French and German troops conducted joint military maneuvers; in 1990 a Franco-German brigade was born, comprising 4,700 troops under the alternating leadership of officers from both countries; in 1995 this brigade was expanded into the Eurocorps, consisting of 45,000 troops from France, Germany, Belgium, Spain, and Luxembourg; and in 1999 the Eurocorps was in turn subsumed into a European Rapid Reaction Force, a body of 60,000 troops drawn from all EU member states.[12] Not surprisingly, the military sphere—the cornerstone of national sovereignty—has been the slowest to yield to the decades-long process of European integration. Nevertheless, the overall pattern in this domain remains clear: Franco-German military cooperation has been steadily advancing since the 1960s.

"The peoples of the world must unite, or they will perish." With the trenchant clarity of a physicist laying out a mathematical proof, Robert Oppenheimer summed up for his Los Alamos audience the challenge facing humankind in this new era of history—the era those men and women had all played a direct role in bringing into being. One can imagine the thoughts running through the minds of the Manhattan Project scientists, technicians, and administrators who heard his words. "Yes, but how?" "Will we be able to succeed now, when so many in the past have failed to achieve this?"

The postwar story of the Franco-German reconciliation directly addresses these kinds of skeptical (and entirely reasonable) questions. Three general principles can be discerned in that story—and all three apply (with modifications) to the broader problems of world politics, the fundamental long-term problems of aggression, injustice, and conflict resolution among humankind as a whole.

1. *Deep transformation is achievable.*

Two peoples who are at each other's throats can, over the space of a half-century, relinquish their hatred, break the cycle of violence and counterviolence—and make an enduring peace. The conditions have to be right, and they have to actively *want* peace; but this possibility is no mere pipe dream, because we have now seen the French and Germans accomplish it. As the peace researcher Kenneth Boulding was fond of saying: "If it exists, then it must be possible."[13]

Humans—both as individuals and as national collectivities—can change their behavior patterns significantly, given the will, the incentives, and a sufficient amount of time. They can move from a long-standing pattern of distrust, resentment, threats, and violence, to a pattern of trust, compromise, and active partnership in which violent solutions have become taboo.

2. *Peace and war are not all-or-nothing conditions, but graded elements along a spectrum.*

When Admiral Karl Dönitz signed the surrender document at the end of World War II, a state of war ceased to hold between the French and German peoples. However, this does not mean that anything like an enduring peace had automatically come into being. Many Germans still hated the French as much as ever. Most French citizens harbored not only anger against Germany, but a deep fear for what the age-old enemy would be up to twenty years down the road. This state of affairs, which arguably prevailed well into the 1950s, might be more aptly described as "unstable peace"—an absence of fighting, to be sure, but also a state in which the two peoples stood a very real chance of sliding back at some point into all-out war.

In order for that unstable peace to become stabilized and solid, a multifaceted transformation had to take place.[14] Gradually, over the years, the pattern of behaviors between the French and the Germans shifted along a spectrum: large-scale violence in 1944; tense and suspicious hostility in the late 1940s; tentative joint projects launched in the early 1950s; growing confidence in the late 1950s as the projects succeeded; further initiatives in the 1960s, including a major escalation of partnership and reconciliation efforts; relative prosperity blossoming in both nations, a direct and tangible "peace dividend" to reward them for cooperation; new institutions emerging in the late 1970s and mid-1980s, linking the two peoples through their economies and political ventures; successful compromises reached even where seemingly intractable disagreements divided the two partners; popular contacts in full swing, contributing to a further shift in mutual perceptions; further growth in supranational institutions during the 1990s, resulting in still more intensive cooperation; and on into the mature, enduring partnership of today.

Peace, therefore, can best be understood as a relative quality: it can grow stronger or weaker over time, depending on the nature of the institutions, perceptions, and behavior patterns that underpin it. Kenneth Boulding, in his pathbreaking writings on the subject, likened peace to a building: as with any man-made structure, he argued, a state of international peace can possess varying degrees of tensile strength and structural integrity. If properly put together, with the right materials, even the most violent storms will not break it down; if flimsily constructed, on the other hand, even a relatively mild stress will shatter it.[15] Working for peace, in this sense, is not really about "abolishing war": that is much too simplistic a conceptualization of the problem. Rather, it requires a sustained effort along all the gradients we observed in the Franco-German reconciliation process: economic, political, social, cultural, and military. Working for peace is about gradually, incrementally strengthening the structure of all these interlocking pieces, so that the resulting edifice is more likely to resist the stresses that history brings.

3. *Stable peace requires redefining the concept of national interest.*

Politics among nations has almost always been a nasty, selfish business: I look after my own, I push as hard as I can to grab the largest slice of the pie for my nation; and to hell with everyone else. Niccolò Machiavelli, Camillo Cavour, Otto von Bismarck: this tradition of thought, commonly known as realpolitik, has argued that a national leader's primary duty consists in pursuing unilateral gain for his or her own country. In the zero-sum game of international politics, any major gain by one group is likely to derive from a commensurate loss by someone else's group. We may not like it, argue the realpolitikers, but that's the way the world works; any attempt to make it operate differently is wishful thinking; and wishful thinking is always dangerous. Sometimes, the realpolitikers admit, two or more nations can also benefit by going beyond unilateral action and cooperating with each other; but such cooperation must always remain subordinate to the ultimate value in state politics, which is the self-interest of the home nation.[16]

The French and the Germans, in the decades since World War II, did not depart altogether from this tradition of thought: they have consistently continued to identify and pursue their own national interests. What has happened, however, is that these two peoples have also increasingly come to perceive their interests as being intertwined. Their relationship has moved beyond a zero-sum game, because the partnership they have established has shown, again and again, that a gain for one side can also result directly in a gain for the other; conversely, a loss for one side often yields direct negative consequences for the other. A prosperous Germany means monetary stability for France; the massive May 1968 strikes in France sent a tremor through the Frankfurt stock market; rising German labor costs raise the price of component parts for the French auto industry; travails of French farmers result in higher food prices for German consumers; French nuclear-generated electricity helps reduce Germany's oil dependency; strict German environmental regulation benefits French forests. The list of such interlinked causal relationships could go on and on: it constitutes the most tangible sign of the blurred national interests that exist not only in the rhetoric of French and German statesmen, but in the all-pervasive details of life's daily business in both countries.

Six decades of growing partnership have created a situation between France and Germany that can best be described as a "positive-sum game"—a relationship in which a win-win outcome is often achievable.[17] Such a game requires a very different logic from the players: any unilateral gain by one side that significantly weakens the other side is only the illusion of a gain: in the long run, such a lopsided outcome will produce a whole slew of unwanted side effects. By weakening my partner, I ultimately weaken myself; worse still, such a narrowly selfish act cannot help but undermine the close relationship of trust and cooperation that binds our two countries together: as a result, our partnership will bear fewer fruits, and both countries will lose.

The Franco-German peace, in other words, has grown out of a partial redefinition of the word "us." We must be careful not to overdramatize or idealize this point: most French or German citizens today still identify quite strongly with their own national traditions—Paris, Molière, Pasteur; Berlin, Beethoven, Goethe. Nevertheless, beyond these age-old reflexes, a new set of supranational allegiances has also come into being—a clear-eyed understanding of being in the same boat with the other peoples of Europe, and especially so with the former enemies on the other side of the Rhine.

Clearly, it would be a mistake to transfer the lessons drawn from the Franco-German peace directly and uncritically to the global arena, which is more complex by several orders of magnitude. At the global level, states-men face the problem of reconciling the sharply divergent economic inter-ests of nations ranging from Switzerland to Bangladesh. Global leaders have to find ways to bridge the gaps between Islamic fundamentalists and Swedish atheists, Chinese communists and Colombian conservatives, Sri Lankan separatists and Japanese internationalists. Amid such diversity, finding an acceptable ground on which to articulate common goals and shape collective policies unavoidably constitutes an especially daunting challenge. The sheer complexity of the power relationships at the global level, the shifting dynamics of alliances and alignments among 190 nations, present the world's statesmen and diplomats with a much more compli-cated challenge than the one facing Paris and Berlin. Finally, any discussion of conflict resolution at the global level has to take the possibility of war seriously into account, offering plausible mechanisms for stopping aggres-sion and making sure that violations of the peace do not go unpunished.

Nevertheless, despite these significant differences, the case of France and Germany does offer at least one important insight that applies directly at the global level. The main reason why these two peoples succeeded in building a stable peace between themselves is because it was manifestly in their interest to do so. They did not build peace merely because it was nicer, or more neighborly, or morally the right thing to do. They did it pri-marily because peace offered tangible and immediate rewards, whereas a return to a relationship of rivalry and hostility promised to bring them nothing but grief. The realpolitikers are dead right on this issue: people cannot always be counted on to do what is morally right; but they can, for the most part, be counted on to do what they perceive as being clearly in their interest.

Do the world's peoples, at the global level, have a similar set of conver-gent interests driving them in the direction of building a stable peace? The answer to this question is yes. One of the most important features of con-temporary global politics is the growing interdependence of peoples: the increasingly dense web of connections (and shared vulnerability) linking humans across boundaries of nation, race, cultural identity, or degree of wealth.[18] More and more, what happens to a complete stranger on another continent can no longer be a matter of indifference for me: his or her fate impinges on my life; it influences the fate of my children. If the govern-ment of Brazil decides to default on its national debt, that move can trigger a chain of bank collapses in the United States that shakes my livelihood to its foundation. If a Thai chicken farmer gets sloppy with his animals, he can unleash a strain of avian flu that winds up killing people in Montreal, Paris, Rio de Janeiro. If the Indians and Pakistanis go to war, armed as they both are with nuclear weapons, their conflict can spread radioactive poison over much of the Northern Hemisphere. If the Chinese refuse to curb their emissions of chlorofluorocarbons, the resultant fraying of the earth's ozone layer can cause skin cancers in Cancun or California. If an underpaid Russian nuclear scientist sells a few pounds of uranium to an Islamic fanatic, dirty bombs can start going off in London or New York. It does not matter that I live in the world's sole surviving superpower: in all these ways, I am equally as vulnerable to these kinds of global threats as is a starving beggar in Calcutta. My government cannot protect me; the U.S. Marines cannot protect me; my high standard of living cannot protect me.

World politics, in short, is becoming strikingly similar in some ways to the positive-sum game that we described in the case of France and Germany. What happens on the other side of the Rhine (or Pacific, or Atlantic) directly affects my security and prosperity here at home in the United States—and vice versa. If I can find a way to help increase the job stability and wages of that Russian nuclear scientist, so that he does not need to sell uranium on the side just to feed his family, I am tangibly increasing the security of my own family as well. If I can help build an effective international system for regulating poultry farmers from Thailand to North Carolina, then I am significantly reducing the likelihood that my own children may catch avian flu. Conversely, if the Chinese government cooperates with my government in restricting emissions of chlorofluorocarbons, then my government becomes more likely to favor increased trade with China: the result is greater prosperity for Chinese citizens. In all these cases, we have an outcome in which *everybody wins*. The positive-sum game means that we possess strong incentives for increased cooperation, and strong reasons to avoid unilateral actions aimed at short-term gains for one nation by itself.

This growing condition of global interdependence has not come about as a result of deliberate governmental policies aimed at making it happen. Rather, it has emerged as the unintended side effect of a much broader trend in world history: the technological and economic shifts that we associate with the Industrial Revolution. As technologies for transportation and communication grew cheaper and more effective, markets for goods slowly spread out beyond national and regional boundaries. As military technologies increased in destructive potency, the global ramifications of distant quarrels grew proportionately. As industrializing economies impinged ever more massively on the natural environment, serious problems began to manifest themselves at the planetary level. These global-scale interconnections have been intensifying, along a steep gradient, over the past two centuries; they have deepened and proliferated even more rapidly since 1945.

The broad contours of this new global reality were already becoming apparent to some far-sighted observers within months of the bombing of Hiroshima.[19] On October 29, 1945, George Marshall was invited to present his ideas on "the future peace" at the Herald Tribune Forum in New York. In characteristic fashion, he got quickly to the point.

> For centuries man has been seeking, I believe, to extend [political order] to the level of the entire planet. There are two ways in which this has been manifest: we might say one is by way of *cooperation* and the other by way of *operation*. Hitler, whether he knew it or not, sought to establish one kind of order in the world when he precipitated the recent holocaust.
>
> This would be by way of operation. The League of Nations, on the other hand, sought to establish a global order by cooperation. . . . It would appear that one or the other of these methods will prevail. Time and space have been so shrunken that the world must, I believe, establish definite global rules. Community and national rules no longer suffice. They by themselves are no longer realistic.
>
> Basically then, the question in my opinion is, which one of the two methods is to prevail—global order by cooperation or by operation? Since the United States is one of the senior partners in this world, we have a powerful interest in the formulation of these rules. That is how I would define our responsibility of the victory. . . .
>
> We and our Allies have recently advanced the structure of the United Nations organization as a vehicle to promote the cooperative idea of global order. Nations which subscribe to this principle, this system, do not propose to establish order by conquering everybody else as Hitler did, nor do they propose to control for their own profit the domestic affairs of the other peoples of the earth. What they do propose is a set of rules for global conduct, principally rules against aggression or international violence. They themselves are to resort to violence only to enforce these rules, just as does the State of New York, and every other state in this nation, to enforce its rules. . . .
>
> I personally am convinced that the [United Nations] organization has not

even a remote chance of success unless it is nourished by the strength and fiber of the United States.[20]

Marshall was not the kind of man who could be accused of being a woolly-headed idealist who indulged in wishful thinking. He was among the chief architects of Allied victory, and he now cast a sober eye on the war's aftermath and the predicament that humankind faced. The future peace, he concluded, would require a radically new system of international conflict resolution, centered on the United Nations. The core premise of traditional realpolitik—a world of independent nations pursuing their own distinctive interests in isolation from one another—had become in many ways a thing of the past. That state-centered logic was "no longer realistic," in Marshall's view: only global rules, complementing and in some ways superseding national power, would suffice. Marshall regarded the creation of this new planetary order as the primary moral and political challenge that had emerged out of World War II: it was "our responsibility of the victory."

What might these new global rules look like? Marshall did not spell them out explicitly. But the successful example of the Franco-German reconciliation does suggest the following rough outlines of such a new realpolitik for the nuclear era:

1. *Promote multilateral, multinational tools of military security; adopt an ethic of restraint in foreign policy.*

World War II, from one perspective, can be plausibly seen as a colossal—and ultimately successful—exercise in collective security. Germany, Japan, and Italy, through their acts of aggression in the 1930s and early 1940s, ultimately compelled many of the other peoples around the world to join forces against them; the "United Nations" was a defensive military alliance binding twenty-six countries before it became an even larger political institution in 1945.

The underlying principle of collective security is straightforward in nature (even if the practical challenge of implementing it is not). Someone violates the peace; most everyone else agrees the action is unjustified; a warning is issued; and then the nations come together, preferably through a body like the League of Nations or the United Nations, using their conjoined military force to compel the aggressor to back down. If these conditions applied to all of the world's deadly quarrels, then the challenge of keeping global peace would be relatively manageable; but unfortunately such favorable conditions often do not hold. The mechanism of U.N.-sanctioned collective security cannot work, for example, to compel compliance from a nuclear-armed great power, because such a nation can threaten to unleash a holocaust if attacked; the mechanism also tends to fail whenever the decision-making bodies of the U.N. prove incapable of reaching consensus.

The future confronts humankind, therefore, with two basic categories of international armed conflict: those for which the mechanism of U.N.-sanctioned collective security stands a good chance of working, and those for which it doesn't. Strengthening the edifice of peace, under these conditions, requires a commensurately two-pronged strategy over the long haul. In situations similar to Japan's conquest of Manchuria in 1931, or Italy's incursion into Ethiopia in 1935—situations exemplified in the postwar period by Iraq's invasion of Kuwait in 1990—the world's nations should always seek to use the diplomatic and military tools of the U.N. to reverse the act of aggression; they should, whenever possible, avoid unilateral military action that lacks the imprimatur of a U.N. mandate.

Thus, for example, when Great Britain warred with Argentina in 1982 over the Falkland Islands dispute, the U.N. issued a resolution calling for Argentina to withdraw its invasion forces from the islands; but rather than waiting for the laborious United Nations process to work its way through to a solution, the British simply went ahead and retook the islands by trouncing the Argentines using exclusively British military forces. This resulted in a short-term political gain for British prime minister Margaret Thatcher, who soon thereafter rode to a reelection victory on a wave of nationalistic fervor; but the atavistic British response did a serious disservice to the long-term health of the U.N., which found its authority circumvented and its role as a peace broker undermined. A wiser British policy, aimed at strengthening the long-term prospects of global peace, would have been to work patiently through the U.N., building a coalition to compel Argentine withdrawal using the mechanism of collective security. Such a policy would have stood an excellent chance of success, because in this case both superpowers and many of the world's leading nations were resolutely aligned against the initial Argentine aggression.[21]

In all those situations, by contrast, where the U.N. finds itself deadlocked or otherwise stymied, the world's nations should adopt foreign policies that emphasize great restraint of means, and multilateral rather than unilateral solutions to conflicts whenever possible. Strengthening the edifice of peace, in these kinds of cases, means working through broad alliances, taking time to build diplomatic consensus for one's initiatives abroad, engaging in compromise and trade-offs with many other nations in the pursuit of national goals.

The Berlin Airlift of 1948 provides a good example of such a foreign policy: here we get a concrete sense of what George Marshall meant when he referred to new "global rules" (he was serving as U.S. secretary of state when the Russians made their surprise move). On June 24, 1948, Soviet military forces abruptly closed down all land-based transportation links into the contested city of Berlin. American leaders knew that no U.N.-sanctioned mechanism of collective security could be realistically brought to bear in this case: the USSR was not only a permanent Security Council member but also wielded the overwhelming power of the Red Army. Instead, confronted with this unilateral act of aggression, the United States responded in a measured and highly creative manner: studiously avoiding direct military engagement, it nonetheless neutralized the Soviet blockade by flying a steady stream of planes into the encircled city, twenty-four hours a day over many months, thereby keeping West Berlin provisioned and functional within the Soviet zone. At the same time, the United States wove together a strong defensive alliance against further acts of Soviet aggression (NATO), and stepped up its Marshall Plan aid to West European nations, thereby stabilizing their economies and undermining the influence of communist parties among their populations. This combination of resolve, restraint, and multilateralism paid off handsomely, as the Soviets eventually backed down and reopened the roads into Berlin; in the long run, this far-sighted policy laid the foundations for the close U.S. partnership with the West European nations that endures today.

Strengthening the edifice of peace will require that more and more nations, particularly the most powerful ones, accept the military consequences that flow from global interdependence and shared vulnerability. Deadly quarrels and armed conflict will no doubt remain basic facts of life in world affairs for the foreseeable future—but how we handle those clashes can make a tremendous difference for the chances of peace. Foreign policies that flow out of the unilateralist and nation-centered logic of yesteryear offer a grim prospect of continued tensions, crises, and hair-raising risks. Foreign policies of genuine multilateralism and restraint, by contrast, are likely to fashion a world characterized by increasingly dependable mechanisms of collective security. Such policies will yield greater stability and safety over the long haul.

2. *Promote the institutions of international law.*

For all the importance of multilateralism and restraint in handling military matters, the real cornerstone of stable peace lies in the institutions of the law. The peace that obtained between France and Germany did not really become stable until these two nations had gradually created higher, supranational structures of arbitration and coordination whose authority they accepted as binding upon both of them. Peace, after all, requires far more than a mere absence of armed conflict: it requires effective tools for handling the inevitable disputes that arise from time to time among sovereign nations.

This is, ultimately, what a state of international law accomplishes: it sets rules that the partners accept in advance; it establishes institutions for interpreting and applying those rules; and it offers each participant a guarantee that all the other participants will continue to play by those rules even under circumstances disadvantageous to one or more of the players. Instead of relying on ad hoc arrangements hastily thrown together to meet the demands of a particular crisis or dispute, a state of international law creates a system already in place for resolving conflicts before they spin out of control.

Strengthening the edifice of peace, therefore, means vigorously continuing the pioneering work that commenced during the twentieth century: building an international legal system that the world's nations can regard as impartial and effective, and whose authority they can willingly accept. Here, once again, the logic of a revised realpolitik is clear: as long as individual states use the concept of national sovereignty as an excuse for rejecting the authority of international law, the opportunities for arbitration and compromise at the global level will remain limited and sporadic at best. But if the world's peoples come to recognize the benefits that flow from such supranational legal structures, and prove willing to nurture their growth, then the practice of cooperative conflict resolution can become a regular and reliable feature of global politics. As in the case of France and Germany, a peace that was initially rather precarious in nature could progressively evolve into something solid and secure. Unstable peace rests on the implicit threat of armed force; stable peace can only rest on a foundation of law.

3. *Work to reduce global economic disparities.*

No peace at the global level can be considered truly stable as long as large numbers of human beings live in conditions of wretched poverty, their children dying of preventable diseases, while others elsewhere enjoy high levels of affluence and conspicuous consumption. If we are indeed persuaded that world politics is becoming more and more a positive-sum game, then it follows that the economic hardship endured by large portions of humanity will increasingly come to undermine the security of the better-off populations as well. Their diseases will become our diseases;

their political instability will heighten the stress on the international system; their wars will unleash deadly poisons and hordes of refugees; their environmental disarray will harm our planet; their desperate emigrants will clamor at our gates and infiltrate our borders. Their suffering, in short, will rock our boat.

Strengthening the edifice of peace, therefore, will require assigning this problem a much higher priority in world affairs than it has tended to receive thus far: it should rank alongside military security, economic stability, and public health on the agendas of the world's nations. A revised realpolitik requires that we become our brother's keeper: not in the sense of giving him handouts and charity, but in the sense of embarking on a concerted campaign to change the basic structural features of the world economy that perpetuate poverty on so vast a scale.[22] This will not be easy: it will require sacrifices, ingenuity, patience, and intensive effort sustained over many years. It will no doubt necessitate significant adjustments of behavior and attitudes on the part of the rich as well as the poor. We should get going with it nonetheless—not only because it is morally the right thing to do, but also because it is the smart thing to do, from the perspective of our long-term self-interest. We will not have stable peace and security until this problem can be brought under control.

4. *Promote an ethic of tolerance, of resistance to dehumanizing the "other."*

In every conflict that crosses the threshold into violence—whether at the level of individuals or of entire peoples—a crucial step must first have been taken: one or more of the disputants must have dehumanized those on the other side, casting a mental image of the "other" that invests their identity with all manner of abstract negative qualities. In that act of abstraction lies the key to most violence: we no longer see the man or woman before us as a whole human being, an evolving individual of unfathomable complexity, but reduce the person to a mere symbol of certain bad characteristics, a carrier of certain evil purposes. Only then, when the person is no longer a person, can we step forward and strike them down.

Most of the world's major religions emphatically make this point, urging us to resist the temptation to demonize our opponents in a dispute; paradoxically, it is often in the name of religious identity that human beings go furthest in dehumanizing one another. Strengthening the edifice of peace, in this sense, requires from each of us a kind of ongoing reeducation of our emotional impulses: learning how to recognize within ourselves the reflex of abstraction that leads to dehumanizing other people—and countering it with an active effort of empathy and humane imagination, remaking the other back into a person once again.[23]

The French and the Germans, over several decades, gradually came to perceive each other less and less as abstractions, whose character and intentions could be subsumed under a single slogan or concept ("barbarians," "baby-killers," "treacherous bastards"). On the opposite side of the Rhine lived some individuals worthy of admiration, some worthy of scorn, some whom one liked and others whom one disliked—which was exactly the way one would feel about people on this side of the Rhine. Over time the dehumanizing abstraction disintegrated: the rich complexity of reality took its place.

This internal psychological struggle within each of us may seem quite far removed from the broader problems of international peace and armed conflict, but in fact it is not. By reeducating ourselves in this way—making the ongoing effort to resist dehumanizing our opponents—and by seeking to propagate this kind of reeducation among other people, we are laying the only practical foundations on which cooperative conflict resolution can thrive. Stable peace certainly does require large-scale institutional changes at the level of nation-states, but it also begins here at home, inside the mind and feelings of each of us.

In February 1957, Winston Churchill wrote an epilogue to his six-volume memoirs of the Second World War, which had won the Nobel Prize for literature in 1953. Churchill closed by reflecting on the war's historical impact, the Cold War rivalry that divided the world of the 1950s, and the long-term prospects for avoiding another catastrophe like the one he had narrated. "I do not intend to suggest," he wrote,

> that all the efforts and sacrifices of Britain and her allies . . . have come to nothing and led only to a state of affairs more dangerous and gloomy than at the beginning. On the contrary, I hold strongly to the belief that we have not tried in vain. Russia is becoming a great commercial country. Her people experience every day in growing vigour those complications and palliatives of human life that will render the schemes of Karl Marx more out of date and smaller in relation to world problems than they have ever been before. . . . And when war is itself fenced about with mutual extermination it seems likely that it will be increasingly postponed. Quarrels between nations, or continents, or combinations of nations there will no doubt con-

tinually be. But in the main human society will grow in many forms not comprehended by a party machine. As long therefore as the free world holds together, and especially Britain and the United States, and maintains its strength, Russia will find that Peace and Plenty have more to offer than exterminatory war. The broadening of thought is a process which acquires momentum by seeking opportunity for all who claim it. And it may well be if wisdom and patience are practised that Opportunity-for-All will conquer the minds and restrain the passions of mankind.[24]

Churchill, like Marshall, believed that military force would continue to play a key role in world politics for the foreseeable future; both men maintained that the best way to avoid war with the Soviet empire was to present it with a strong and united front in the West, making it abundantly clear that there would never be another Munich in the postwar era. But the two men also shared several other beliefs: they argued that new international instruments for wielding military force had to be created and sustained; and that an ethos of deep restraint had perforce to characterize international affairs in the nuclear era. Both men affirmed, finally, that humankind was not necessarily doomed to self-destruction, and that a new kind of peace might emerge from the ashes of the recent world conflict. When George Marshall was awarded the Nobel Peace Prize in 1953, the speech he gave did not mince words on this issue:

> For the moment the maintenance of peace in the present hazardous world situation does depend in very large measure on military power, together with Allied cohesion. But the maintenance of large armies for an indefinite period is not a practical or a promising basis for policy. We must stand together strongly for these present years, that is, in this present situation; but we must, I repeat, we must find another solution.[25]

Thus spoke the man who, perhaps more than any other, had organized the American military effort in World War II. Some might conclude, in looking back over the foregoing discussion, that this quest for "another solution" is hopelessly utopian—that stable peace demands too radical a social and moral transformation for ordinary humans to tackle with any realistic chance of success. But this impression is mistaken. All we have to do is look at France and Germany: they have built stable peace between themselves, and yet (as far as we can tell) they are still just people like the rest of us—no more virtuous or nasty than any of the other populations of the world. They did not have to become nations of saints: they merely had to alter how they conducted their relationship with each other. They did not have to give up anything except certain ingrained modes of thinking and behaving: what they got in return was prosperity, stability, and security.

A skeptic might still argue that the Franco-German case is a rare exception, and that the odds operating at the global level are stacked against us. Perhaps this is true. The tools at our disposal are, admittedly, imperfect ones, and long-term success is far from guaranteed. The United Nations—this instrument bequeathed to us by the victors of World War II—is an ungainly contrivance, too often bogged down in bureaucratic infighting, cynical political maneuvering, or feckless dithering (the same might be said, of course, for our national governments). Individual nations sometimes get in the way, stubbornly blocking progress just at the moment when many other states seem ready to take a common step forward. International laws and courts remain in their infancy, and will no doubt register many demoralizing defeats in the years to come. Catastrophic war remains a very real possibility, and it is likely that this will continue to be the case for a long time.

Nevertheless, the evidence presented in this chapter, hinging on the story of the Franco-German reconciliation, does suggest one intriguing conclusion. Building peace revealed itself to be a gradual and cumulative process, advancing through countless intermediary steps; it required great perseverance on the part of those carrying it forward. But the obverse of this fact is that even relatively small advances, yielding a slightly more effective system of conflict resolution, are well worth pursuing (and worth celebrating when they happen). Every partial success in strengthening the edifice of peace constitutes a tangible improvement in the odds of our long-term survival.

Humankind, in other words, does not have to make it all the way into a full-fledged system of stable international peace in order to begin enjoying the rewards that peace offers: those rewards are incremental in nature, and the changes they bring can start rendering our lives more prosperous and secure immediately. Cooperative conflict resolution pays off quickly, in direct proportion to the depth of the effort it reflects. And each successful exercise of cooperative politics, in turn, can help embolden people to push still harder, thus paving the way for intensified efforts and further achievements down the road. Little by little, the horizon of the possible can shift outward: and how far it shifts is entirely up to us.

Chapter Thirteen

THE POLITICS OF MEMORY
Remembering and Unremembering Wartime

The past is never dead. It's not even past.
> —William Faulkner, *Requiem for a Nun*[1]

I n 1995 one of the most venerable museums in the United States, the
Smithsonian, attempted to put on an exhibit of the *Enola Gay*, the
B-29 bomber that had dropped the atomic bomb on Hiroshima.[2] It seemed
at the time like a reasonable undertaking: fifty years had passed since the
nuclear blast over the Japanese city; the Cold War had ended, prompting
widespread reflection about the future role of nuclear weapons in world
politics. But the exhibit became a disaster. Long before the scheduled opening date, a powerful alliance of veterans groups and conservative journalists and politicians assailed the script for the proposed exhibit, claiming it
was intolerably biased, and would bring dishonor on the brave men who
had sacrificed so much in the Pacific War. The proposed exhibit, they
argued, was blatantly anti-American: it made the dropping of the bomb
seem like a gratuitous act of aggression, rather than a decisive military act
that brought the ordeal of war to a swift end and thereby saved countless
Allied lives.[3]

The Smithsonian's team of historians and curators seemed taken aback
at first by the furor: they revised the script several times, seeking to find a
compromise that would satisfy the critics. But this in turn prompted a
backlash from a variety of other groups, who claimed that the heavily
revised script was now "sanitizing" the past to fit an uncritically celebratory version of the American role in World War II. The *Enola Gay* exhibit,
in short, had fallen afoul of the culture wars that pitted left against right in
contemporary America. The shiny aluminum frame of the B-29 bomber,

B-29 bomber Enola Gay *on exhibit at the National Air and Space Museum, Smithsonian Institution, Washington, D.C. (1995).*

sitting in its hall at the museum, had become a symbolically charged focal point for a much wider struggle—the struggle to define America's historical identity and self-image.

In the end, the Smithsonian's director decided he had no choice but to abort the proposed exhibit: some members of Congress had begun darkly hinting that the museum's funding might be cut drastically if the project went ahead as planned.[4] In August 1995, the *Enola Gay* was unveiled, newly restored, in its Smithsonian hall: but the rest of the surrounding exhibit had been axed. Anything that might serve to elaborate on the broader significance of the aircraft had been removed: the only information deemed permissible was a technical history of the plane's development, coupled with a terse statement that it had flown the mission that dropped the atomic bomb. No details, no context, no artifacts, no nothing: just the barest bones of bland information.

Half a century after August 6, 1945, it turned out, Americans proved incapable of agreeing on even the most basic narrative of what had happened on that date. Instead of shedding light on the past, the exhibit had only brought about a cacophony of ugly and intemperate political name-calling. Both sides in the controversy blamed each other for the debacle.

Each regarded the other as being, in a deep way, un-American—as standing for values that ran counter to the nation's most cherished cultural and political traditions.[5]

Seen from a broader international perspective, the controversy in the United States over the *Enola Gay* exhibit was by no means exceptional: it echoed, in its own distinctively American idiom, the fierce battles that every major nation has experienced when it comes to handing down the memory of World War II to the next generation. What should we remember about our past, and what should we allow to fade into oblivion? In what kind of light should our nation's past deeds be portrayed? Who decides, and how? What does it mean to have a constructive and honest relationship with our past?

Japan

The historian John Dower argues persuasively in his book *Embracing Defeat* that most Japanese have had a very difficult time facing the full implications of their wartime past. They have tended to view World War II through a distorting lens that deemphasizes the atrocities committed by their armies throughout Asia, and that highlights instead the suffering endured by the Japanese people as a result of the war.[6] Most Japanese in the postwar decades have earnestly believed that they were victims, in a double sense, during the 1930s and 1940s: victims of a militarist clique of national leaders who forced them down a path of overseas aggression; victims of exceptionally cruel violence in wartime, symbolized by the atomic bombing of Hiroshima and Nagasaki.[7] The propagation of this "victim consciousness" has rendered it difficult for many Japanese to come to grips in an honest way with their own individual and collective responsibility for the deeds their nation committed during the war.

An illustrative case in point is the way the Japanese have tended to remember the Rape of Nanking. Intense debate still continues today over how to teach Japanese schoolchildren about the events of 1937.[8] Some school textbooks persist in presenting the event in a whitewashed way, as part of a defensive action by the Japanese military, with no mention of the massacres. Right-wing politicians have successfully pressured the Ministry of Education to censor textbooks that told the story accurately. "In Japanese schools," reports the writer Ian Buruma, the controversy is officially killed by silence. All it says in a typical textbook for high school students is: "In December [1937] Japanese troops occupied Nanking." A footnote explains: "At this time Japanese troops were reported to have killed many Chinese, including civilians, and Japan was the target of international criticism." This is all. But even this was too much for some conservative bureaucrats and politicians, who wanted the passage deleted altogether.[9]

In teaching my undergraduate course on World War II, I have encountered college-level Japanese exchange students who tell me—wide-eyed and amazed—that they have never heard of this massacre in all their years of schooling.

Some Japanese, to be sure, have vehemently questioned both the "victim consciousness" of their compatriots and the "killing with silence" (*mokusatsu* once again) that tends to surround controversial aspects of the national past. One such man was the Japanese army veteran Shiro Azuma, who served in Nanking at the time of the massacre.[10] Azuma kept a diary during the six-week rampage in China, and managed to get it past official censors when he returned to Japan. The diary sat in a closet in Azuma's house until 1987, when he was approached by curators who were putting together a new war museum in Kyoto: would he be willing to make his diary public? Azuma handed the diary over, and its detailed descriptions of atrocities by Japanese soldiers promptly became the object of a nationwide furor. Right-wing nationalist groups accused him of deliberately propagating lies in order to defame his country's honor. The veterans association to which he belonged expelled him. Two of his former comrades-in-arms sued him for defamation.

Azuma was taken aback at first, then became increasingly outraged as the campaign against him mounted. He had always been an ardent patriot, and had never questioned the rationale for Japan's military campaigns during the 1930s and 1940s. "I always believed it was a just war," he told a journalist. "But the threats, the abusive phone calls, the letters, they made me furious. I was just telling the truth. And they wanted to stop me. I was damned if I couldn't tell the truth!"[11]

Azuma also received mail that enthusiastically supported him in his quest to tell the story accurately: he drew strength from these letters, and decided—at the age of eighty-five—that he simply could not back down. He wrote a book based on his diary, but publication was blocked by the courts because of the pending defamation lawsuit. When that lawsuit ended with a ruling against him, Azuma appealed to Japan's Supreme

Court in 1995.[12] When the Supreme Court ruled against him in 1998—prompting an outcry in China and widespread criticism of Japan from abroad—Azuma still did not give up. In April 2000 he took his case before the United Nations Human Rights Commission, calling on the commission to force the Japanese government to allow dissemination of his book; the case is still pending.[13] Meanwhile, in January 2000, a group of right-wing activists convened a seminar at the Osaka International Peace Museum: it was titled "The Biggest Lie of the Twentieth Century: Documenting the Nanking Massacre."[14]

The struggle, in short, goes on. Some recent opinion polls show significant numbers of Japanese citizens accepting the reality of the Nanking massacre, and supporting the idea of offering an official apology to the Chinese (along with monetary compensation to the surviving victims);[15] but so far the policy of the Tokyo government remains what it has always been: evasive, reticent, and stubbornly noncommittal. The controversy constitutes an exceedingly sore point in contemporary Sino-Japanese relations, and appears set to continue that way for a long time to come.

Germany

By most accounts, the Germans have done a far better job of confronting their wartime past than the Japanese.[16] The Holocaust forms a major subject in German secondary education; the German government has paid out some $84 billion in reparations payments to Holocaust survivors and in aid to the state of Israel (compared with just $4 billion paid by the Japanese to various Asian nations);[17] legions of German historians have explored the criminal behaviors of the Nazi era with great dedication, honesty, and thoroughness.

Nevertheless, it is hardly surprising that the subject of the Third Reich and its place in German national identity remains as controversial today as it was six decades ago. The historian Roderick Stackelberg identifies four basic phases in German attitudes toward the Nazi past:[18]

- *1945–1960:* most Germans ardently denounce Nazism, but place primary blame for the catastrophe on the shoulders of Hitler and his top leaders; this demonization of the National Socialists allows many Germans to avoid feeling personal responsibility for the crimes of the Third Reich.
- *1960s–1970s:* following the 1960s countercultural revolt, a mordantly self-critical interest in the Nazi era emerges; many of Germany's left-liberal historians and intellectuals earnestly explore the question of the

German citizenry's responsibility for the Holocaust and other Nazi crimes; major trials of former Nazis in German courts take place during this period.

- *1980s:* a neoconservative backlash against the left-liberal stance emerges; conservative historians, intellectuals, and politicians argue that German "self-flagellation" over the Nazi past is dangerously debilitating, and weakens West Germany in its Cold War struggle against the communist threat; these figures advocate moving beyond national guilt and toward a more positive sense of German historical identity.

- *1990s–2000s:* in the wake of German reunification, the issue of the communist threat recedes from view; but intensive debate continues between conservatives who argue that the Nazi era was merely a tragic parenthesis in an otherwise honorable national history; and left-liberals who claim that an acute awareness of the horrors of the Nazi past is essential to maintaining a vibrant commitment to democratic principles in the present.

Perhaps the most provocative reappraisal of the Third Reich came from the prominent historian Ernst Nolte, who had made his name in 1963 with a widely respected scholarly work, *Three Faces of Fascism*. In that book Nolte had maintained that the Holocaust should be regarded as a unique event, "both as to scope and to intention"—a crime whose monstrous nature set German history apart from that of other nations.[19] But by 1986 Nolte had apparently changed his mind. In the summer of that year he published an article entitled "The Past That Will Not Pass" in the prestigious newspaper *Frankfurter Allgemeine Zeitung*—an article that read like a manifesto for a resurgent German nationalism. Nolte lamented the fact that Germany continued to be seen, both at home and abroad, as an "abnormal" nation: he argued that it was time to let go of the "bugaboo" of the Nazi past and cast off the guilt that still afflicted so many Germans.[20] The Holocaust was far from unique, he maintained: countless other genocides had been perpetrated by many other peoples throughout history. What was more, the Nazi genocide could be interpreted as a *defensive* move on the part of the German people—a preemptive strike against Soviet communism, which had already revealed its own genocidal nature in the early 1930s, and which could be reasonably expected to have turned this genocidal intent against the German people if unopposed.

Did the National Socialists or Hitler perhaps commit an "Asiatic" deed merely because they considered themselves and their kind to be potential victims of an "Asiatic" deed? Was the Gulag Archipelago not prior to Auschwitz? Was the Bolshevik murder of an entire class not the logical and factual precedent for the "racial murder" of National Socialism?[21]

In Nolte's view, in other words, the Germans had been provoked into committing the crimes of the Nazi era by the looming communist evil in the east; it was time now to put aside the paralyzing guilt over those deeds and to stand tall once again—ready to wield great force in the ongoing crusade against the ever-resurgent Soviet menace.

Perhaps if this newspaper article had been an isolated phenomenon, most Germans might have dismissed it as yet another rant from a Nazi apologist spewing venom on the extremist fringe. But the *Frankfurter Allgemeine* was one of Germany's most respected newspapers; Nolte was a well-known and distinguished historian; and he was not alone. A sizable group of other conservative intellectuals and politicians had been voicing congruent views in recent months about the need for a prouder, more confident form of national identity. The article generated a furor that polarized German public life over the following year, as journalists, historians, intellectuals, and politicians wrangled over the meaning of the Nazi legacy.[22]

In the end, this *Historikerstreit*, or "historians' controversy," as the debate came to be called, resulted in a smoldering standoff—overshadowed eventually by the hoopla over national reunification that commenced three years later. But the crux of the matter remained manifestly unresolved as the new millennium opened: Is German national identity strengthened or weakened by the ongoing acknowledgment of past misdeeds? What kind of national self-image is best suited for Germany's constructive participation in world affairs? A stance of brash self-confidence that deliberately de-emphasizes the dark periods of the nation's past? Or one of chastened self-awareness, tenaciously holding on to the vivid admonitory presence of a "past that will not pass"?[23]

The Soviet Union

The "Great Patriotic War," as most Russians call World War II, was a sacred topic in the Soviet era and still remains one in post-Soviet Russia today. Any "revisionism" about the war has come mostly from military historians who have been gradually unearthing evidence of even more dramatic suffering on the part of the Soviet people than the communist regime had been willing to admit—along with some major Soviet military defeats deleted from history by Communist Party officials because they made the Red Army look bad.[24]

But the man who ran World War II for the Russians, Joseph Stalin, has undergone a veritable tempest of revisionism: indeed, it is fair to say that the debate over Stalin's legacy ultimately became one of the key factors in the democratic reform process that ended with the collapse of the Soviet empire. The stakes, in other words, could not have been higher: questioning Stalin's image was tantamount to questioning the legitimacy of the entire Soviet system; when a majority of Russians could openly say that Stalin was a criminal, the empire he created did not survive long.

The struggle to come to grips with Stalin's legacy waxed particularly intense during two major periods of reform within the Soviet system. Nikita Khrushchev, the Soviet premier between 1956 and 1964, launched the first critical reassessment of Stalin at the Twentieth Party Congress in 1956—only three years after Stalin's death.[25] In a secret speech before the assembled leaders of the world's communist parties, Khrushchev submitted his former boss, under whom he had served as a close subordinate, to a withering array of criticisms, arguing that it was time for the Soviet Union to move beyond the one-man dictatorship and police terror that had come to prevail under Stalinism. The foundations of the communist system were sound, Khrushchev maintained—the one-party state, centralized economy, and class-based ideology—but it was time to reform this system, removing the excessively harsh and arbitrary features of Stalinist rule. Khrushchev's speech sent shock waves through the communist world, well beyond the USSR: later that year the Hungarians, taking Khrushchev's call for reform as a signal of greater pluralism, attempted to shake free from their status as a Soviet satellite state—and discovered, under a hail of gunfire from Soviet tanks, that genuine pluralism remained quite far from Khrushchev's mind. Three thousand Hungarians perished in the Soviet clampdown, resulting in a wave of outrage among many ardent communists: more than a quarter of them around the world left the party in protest. Khrushchev had learned that criticizing Stalin's legacy— even in a carefully scripted and circumscribed manner—carried powerful consequences.

Eight years later Khrushchev was overthrown in a bloodless Kremlin coup, and his successor, Leonid Brezhnev, soon moved to rehabilitate Stalin's image: statues, party conferences, and countless articles and books placed the "Man of Steel" back on the pedestal of historical infallibility. There he remained for the next twenty years, until a new Soviet leader, Mikhail Gorbachev, came to power in 1985. Gorbachev, like Khrushchev, had a reforming agenda; but he was willing to go much further than Khrushchev in probing the limits of political and economic change. He began signaling, both in his speeches and through his actions, that certain highly sensitive issues—such as the state of the economy, the performance of the bureaucracy, or the legacy of Stalin—would no longer be off limits for frank public discussion: this came to be known as glasnost, the policy of openness.[26]

Timidly at first, then with increasing boldness, Soviet citizens began testing the waters of public debate: when they discovered that the KGB was truly no longer punishing those who dared to speak their minds, the gates of criticism opened wide. For the first time in their long history, Russians enjoyed the heady experience—and the chaotic energy—of untrammeled civic freedom. One of the first places they turned was to the legacy of the Stalinist era, focusing particularly on the immeasurable human cost of Stalin's policies. Those who had lost relatives in the purges; those whose parents or grandparents had disappeared into the Gulag; those whose ancestors, serving in the Red Army during the war, had been arbitrarily executed by the NKVD; those non-Russians, like the Poles, Ukrainians, or Lithuanians, whose relatives had been massacred by the NKVD—all these victims of Stalin's regime came forward, seeking a just accounting for the criminal past.

Not surprisingly, this reappraisal of Stalin's memory during the Gorbachev years met with anything but approval from a great many Soviet citizens, high and low, who still felt a strong allegiance to the existing system. Some Communist Party bureaucrats did their best to block access to Soviet archives and public records; they suppressed journals that published critical articles and exposés; they sent police to harass and break up public meetings where the Stalinist past was being discussed. One group of neo-Stalinist citizens formed a grassroots organization, Pamyat ("Memory"), to orchestrate a campaign in defense of Stalin's legacy and of the communist system. A chemistry teacher, Nina Andreyeva, stirred up a nationwide debate in March 1988 when she published a letter in the journal *Sovetskaya Rossiya*, denouncing the reformers and their glasnost policy, and calling for a return to Stalinist values. "Our media are lying about Stalin now," she told an interviewer.

> They are blackening our history and erasing the world of millions of people who were building socialism in terrible conditions. . . . Our lives [under Stalin] were hard, but everyone had the belief that we could live better and our children and grandchildren would live better still. People with nothing

could achieve something. And now what? Now do we have such trust and faith in the future? I think in the four years of *perestroika* [economic reform under Gorbachev], they have undermined the trust of the working people—I emphasize working people, decent, normal people—because they have spit on our past.[27]

In the end, as we know, it was Gorbachev's vision that prevailed; Andreyeva and her associates had no choice but to look on as his reforms unleashed uncontrollable social and political forces that ultimately led to the implosion of the Soviet Union. To some, Gorbachev was truly "spitting on the past"—and the price he eventually paid for it was his own fall from power as well as the breakup of a great and once proud nation. To others, Gorbachev was finally allowing his fellow citizens to make an honest reckoning with their own history—and the imperial collapse that resulted constituted a necessary step toward building a stronger, more democratic Russian nation in the future. The debate hinged, in the final analysis, on what one meant by "greatness": a nation of ironclad social and political discipline, inspiring fear in its neighbors through tremendous military might; or a nation built on the more unruly and unpredictable forces of democracy and human rights, a country learning to deal with other countries on a basis of diplomacy and accommodation. How one saw the past depended, not surprisingly, on what values one held dearest in the present.

France

Let us sketch three important episodes in the French experience of World War II; then we will follow the trajectory of these episodes as they lived on in postwar French culture.[28]

• *The Vel d'Hiv.* On the morning of July 16, 1942, several hundred French police officers fanned out among the various districts of Paris, arresting Jewish families whose names and locations had been carefully catalogued in advance. In the two days that followed, French officials were able to capture 12,884 Jews; they assembled them at an indoor sports arena known as the Velodrome D'Hiver ("Vel d'Hiv" in common parlance). The captured men, women, and children were kept under awful conditions for five days, then shipped off by German authorities on a journey that was eventually to lead most of them to the death camps. To what extent did the Vichy officials know the fate to which they were condemning these people? After the war, they claimed that they had believed these Jews were being sent away to work camps in Poland, or to populate a new Jewish state that the

Nazis intended to establish on the island of Madagascar. Mostly, they avoided confronting the difficult question of their complicity in the Holocaust. By agreeing to a limited collaboration with the Nazis in the roundup of Jews, they argued, they were doing their best to shield the remaining non-Jewish population of occupied France. Overall, the Vichy regime was directly instrumental in rendering the deportation of 75,000 Jews from France a relatively effective operation for the Nazis.

• *The Plateau Vivarais-Lignon.* Since there is a detailed overview of this story in chapter 6, here the account will be brief. From 1940 to 1944, the villagers of Le Chambon-sur-Lignon and the surrounding Plateau Vivarais-Lignon in south-central France systematically harbored Jewish refugees, hiding them from the Nazis and from the Vichy French police, and aiding them in their efforts to escape from France. This was a fairly isolated case, attributable to the inspirational leadership of the region's Protestant pastors, who were able to mobilize their parishioners around a simple and heartfelt interpretation of Christianity: that loving one's neighbor, in evil times like these, could mean risking one's own life so as to save the lives of other innocent people. Approximately five thousand refugees were saved by the courageous villagers during the course of the Second World War.

• *Oradour-sur-Glane.* On June 10, 1944, a unit of the Waffen-SS moved into the village of Oradour-sur-Glane, near Limoges in west-central France, and quickly sealed it off. They assembled women and children in the town church, and men and teenage boys in several haylofts around town. Then the Germans machine-gunned all the men and teenage boys to death; they locked the church and set it on fire, burning alive all the people inside. Six hundred forty-two persons were killed—almost the entire population of the village. The SS did not publicly explain their deed, but everyone understood their intent: to terrorize the region's population into withholding support from the Resistance, which had been staging a widespread series of attacks in coordination with the recent Allied invasion in Normandy.[29]

How did the French people, and the French government, commit these three chapters of their history to memory? The first two episodes, at the Vel d'Hiv and on the Plateau Vivarais-Lignon, fell fairly rapidly out of the French public consciousness—or perhaps it is more accurate to say that they never really came into the public consciousness. In the decades following 1945, the roundup of Jews at the Vel d'Hiv was commemorated primarily by the French Jewish community, as part of its broader rituals of remembrance surrounding the Holocaust. As for the events on the Plateau Vivarais-Lignon, they remained virtually unknown outside the region's villages. The only reason we know what happened there is because two Americans, the philosopher Philip Hallie and the filmmaker Pierre Sauvage, researched the region's wartime history and produced powerful narratives of it that subsequently drew international attention.[30]

The Vel d'Hiv story raised far too many troubling questions about shades of complicity among the broader population; most French citizens evidently preferred not to be reminded of such things in the aftermath of 1945. But even the story of the Plateau Vivarais-Lignon, in which French men and women had risked their necks to save Jews, had its problematic side: for this episode inevitably raised disturbing questions about the broader Vichy context in which the sheltering of Jews had taken place. Why had the rescue efforts undertaken on this remote plateau been so exceptional? And what had been happening to Jews throughout the rest of France?

Oradour-sur-Glane was different, however. What had happened to this village during the war apparently resonated within the experience of a very broad spectrum of French citizens. On the center and right, the followers of General de Gaulle could recognize in Oradour a symbol of the Nazi oppression from which they had liberated France. The communists, on the other side of French politics, regarded Oradour as a symbol of the sacrifices of the French Resistance, in which they had played a significant role (at least, after Hitler's betrayal of Stalin in 1941). Whatever their political orientation, French citizens could see Oradour as epitomizing the sufferings of innocent men and women during the German occupation. The French government, therefore, swiftly allocated substantial funds for the preservation of Oradour in the exact conditions in which the Nazis had left it. It was to become the most important commemorative site in France—an entire town designated as a national monument. The term used in French was *village martyr*, village of martyrs. In the early 2000s, visitors to Oradour still numbered in the hundreds of thousands per year.[31]

For about twenty years after 1945, the dominant image of World War II in France was that of the Resistance, of the Maquis. It was personified by General de Gaulle; it was deeply enmeshed as a theme in postwar French literature; and it can even be seen in such popular comic books as the *Astérix* series, in which a small village of Gauls resists tenaciously against the pressures of the encroaching Roman empire. In this picture, the story of Oradour fit perfectly: French citizens, in World War II, had been the innocent victims of Nazi barbarism.

Then, in the late 1960s and early 1970s—just as in West Germany—

the war years began to undergo public scrutiny in a much more open and self-critical light. In 1971, the filmmaker Marcel Ophuls produced his remarkable documentary on the Vichy period, *The Sorrow and the Pity*— a trenchantly frank account of the occupation years that called into question many of the comfortable assumptions about French innocence and resistance.[32] Weaving together a meticulous and nuanced montage of original wartime footage and several dozen riveting interviews, Ophuls's film offered a startling new perspective on the French experience of World War II: the Vichy regime had enjoyed widespread popular support; those who had actively resisted the occupation had been distressingly few in number; vast numbers of French men and women who had done nothing directly to aid the Germans or their Vichy puppets had nonetheless compromised themselves in countless small, but still morally significant ways. The film proved so controversial, and so disturbing to many of its viewers, that it was banned from French television until 1981—but it heralded a major shift in attitudes toward World War II, a far greater willingness to take a hard look at the issues of collaboration and Vichy's role as an ancillary player in the Holocaust.

The issue attained renewed prominence in 1992, as the fiftieth anniversary of the Vel d'Hiv roundup approached. A committee responsible for the commemoration of the Vel d'Hiv issued a public appeal to French president François Mitterrand to attend the ceremony on July 16 and give a speech that openly acknowledged the role played by the French government in that sordid episode.[33] Mitterrand responded with a spectacularly ambivalent gesture: he was willing to attend the ceremony, he said, but he would not give such a speech. The French state, he claimed, was not responsible for the deeds perpetrated by an illegitimate regime foisted on France at gunpoint by the Germans: he could not, and would not, apologize in the name of France for its actions. This was, to say the least, a disingenuous response from a man like Mitterrand, who had himself, at the age of twenty-six, served as a junior official in the Vichy government.[34] The Vel d'Hiv committee retorted, with understandable bitterness, that the Vichy regime had been "served by French administrators, French magistrates, and French police," and had enjoyed the strong support of a large part of the French population. The well-publicized exchange ignited an acrimonious nationwide controversy: on July 16 the ceremony took place, with Mitterrand sitting stonily in the audience, amid whistles, jeers, and occasional shouts of "Send Mitterrand to Vichy!"[35]

It was not until three years later, in 1995, that this particular ghost was finally laid to rest. A new French president, Jacques Chirac, attended the ceremony marking the fifty-third anniversary of the Vel d'Hiv roundup: he gave a short but decisively clear speech, in which he assumed full responsibility, in the name of the French nation, for the disgrace perpetrated a half-century before:

> There are, in the life of a nation, times that are painful for memory and for the idea that we have of our country. . . . It is hard to speak of these times because these dark hours have forever fouled our history, and are an insult to our past and our traditions. Yes, it is true that the criminal insanity of the occupying forces was backed up by the French people and the French state. . . . France, land of the Enlightenment and of human rights, land of hospitality and of asylum, France, on that day, committed an irreparable act. It failed to keep its word and delivered those it was protecting to their executioners. . . .
>
> In witnessing again and again, in acknowledging the sins of the past, and the sins committed by the State, in covering up nothing about the dark hours of our history, we are simply defending an idea of humanity, of human liberty and dignity. We are fighting against the forces of darkness which are constantly at work. This endless combat is mine as much as it is yours.[36]

The speech was met, not surprisingly, by vituperation from France's extreme right-wing parties, which denounced it as "fraudulent exploitation of the Shoah against French honor."[37] But among the moderate parties of center-left and center-right—the great majority of French citizens—Chirac's forthright reckoning with the past received strong approval.

Nine years later, in 2004, the story came full circle: President Chirac traveled to Le Chambon-sur-Lignon and gave another landmark speech. He called the attention of his fellow citizens to the heroic deeds carried out by the Chambonnais six decades earlier, but he also frankly acknowledged the exceptional nature of what those villagers had achieved: he did not, in other words, seek to elevate the heroism of the Chambonnais into an occasion for national complacency or self-flattery. On the contrary, he devoted the majority of his speech to a denunciation of the rash of racist hate crimes that had been plaguing French cities—crimes against Jews, Muslims, and other foreigners, which he described as "unworthy of France," and which he vowed to combat implacably with all the resources of the French state.[38] The example of the Chambonnais during World War II, Chirac argued, offered the French citizenry of today a powerful source of inspiration as they struggled to face the ever-resurgent forces of xenophobia, racism, and intolerance that still afflicted their society.

Chirac's speeches at the Vel d'Hiv and Le Chambon—and more importantly, the favorable reaction they elicited among a majority of French citizens—suggest that the ghosts of Vichy have truly begun to be laid to rest in contemporary France. To be sure, one would not want to go too far with this positive assessment, for these issues still elicit harsh controversy in French society, and will no doubt continue to do so for the foreseeable future. Still, the French president's speeches offer an encouraging example of how a nuanced and self-critical vision of the national past can be constructively brought to bear in the moral and political struggles of the present day.

Britain

For the British, the story of World War II remains an understandable source of national pride even to this day. Between June 1940 and June 1941, after all, they stood completely alone against the seemingly unstoppable Axis onslaught, refusing to lose heart despite the grimmest of odds; then after 1941 they continued the struggle alongside their powerful allies, ultimately winning through to the greatest victory in their long history.

The only cloud on this sunny horizon was the strategic bombing campaign. In the late summer of 1945, as the war drew to an end, the British leadership gathered round for some well-deserved mutual congratulations: every major branch of the military services received its own special campaign medal, while their top brass were given peerages and inducted into the House of Lords. Every branch and every leader, that is, except one: the RAF's Bomber Command and its chief, Sir Arthur Harris. The men of Bomber Command were awarded nothing more than a generic medal, common to all the armed services; Harris received a private letter of thanks from Winston Churchill.[39] When Harris bitterly complained about this unequal treatment, he was quietly promoted to a higher rank in 1946 and offered a lesser title of nobility—which he indignantly refused, publicly proclaiming that he would never accept any such title until his men had been given the distinctive campaign medal they had earned, alongside all the other branches of military service. Deeply aggrieved, he moved to South Africa and took up a job as an administrator of a shipping company; though he later returned to England and participated in an official capacity in many commemorative events, he never forgave the British government for what he described to the end of his days as the disgracefully shabby treatment that Bomber Command had received.[40]

The policy of strategic bombing had been hotly debated within the British government at various points during the war, and Arthur Harris had emerged as its most vigorous and outspoken proponent. Through all these debates, however, that policy had never been repudiated either by Churchill or by the British wartime cabinet (which included Churchill's successor, Clement Attlee). On the contrary, Churchill and the rest of the British leadership had consistently given Harris the authorization and the wherewithal to conduct the bombardment of Germany on a steadily mounting scale: they had known as well as anyone what was happening on the ground in those German cities that were being plastered night after night with British bombs.[41] But when victory came, the British leaders suddenly grew skittish at admitting publicly (and perhaps even to themselves) how central a role the bombing campaign had played in Britain's war—in *their* war. The slaughter of helpless women and children did not sit comfortably with the glorious imagery of a national moment of triumph. After V-E Day, accordingly, both the British people and their leaders quietly distanced themselves from Bomber Harris and from the men who had flown his planes. Here is how the British historian John Keegan sums up this turn of events:

> [The strategic bombing] campaign, though it gave a dour satisfaction to the majority of the British people in the depths of their war against Hitler, never commanded the support of the whole nation. Its morality was publicly questioned in the House of Commons by the Labour MP Richard Stokes, more insistently in the Lords by Bishop Bell of Chichester and in private correspondence by the Marquess of Salisbury, head of the leading Conservative family in Britain. All made the point, to quote Lord Salisbury, "that of course the Germans began it, but we do not take the devil as our example." . . . With their backs to the wall the British people had chosen not to acknowledge that they had descended to the enemy's level. In victory they remembered that they believed in fair play. Strategic bombing, which may not even have been sound strategy, was certainly not fair play. Over its course and outcome its most consistent practitioners drew a veil.[42]

Some 55,000 British men had lost their lives in the strategic bombing campaign against Germany. Even though the campaign's efficacy in contributing to Germany's defeat was already controversial in 1945, and still remains controversial today, those men had undeniably answered the summons of their country and fought skillfully and bravely. Was it fair to deny them full recognition for their sacrifice? And yet, how to honor their memory without at the same time seeming to endorse the undeniably atrocious mission on which they had been sent? This tough conundrum had been successfully evaded by the British people and their government in the aftermath of war, through the simple expedient of pretending it didn't exist. But the matter finally came to a head in 1992, when a group of RAF veterans and officers arranged for a bronze statue of Arthur Harris to be erected in front of the RAF chapel in central London, St. Clement Danes.

The statue's unveiling took place on June 1, 1992. Upon hearing of plans for a statue for Bomber Harris, the mayors of Dresden and Cologne publicly called on the British government to block the event from going forward; German demonstrators took to the streets in both cities to protest the initiative. Prime Minister John Major, caught between his commitment to a uniting Europe and the sensibilities of the RAF, finessed the issue by declaring that since this was a private and unofficial ceremony, he could not intervene.[43] Despite this disclaimer, however, the Queen Mother herself gave a short speech as the statue was unveiled, and former prime minister Margaret Thatcher sat prominently among the assembled audience of veterans and RAF supporters. Behind them stood the church of St. Clement Danes, a quaint seventeenth-century structure designed by Christopher Wren, which had been gutted by German bombs in 1941 and restored in 1955 with RAF funds.

As the Queen Mum began to speak, a crowd of 250 demonstrators loudly heckled from across the road, shouting "Shame!" and "Harris was a war criminal!" When they lobbed cups of red paint at the statue, various groups of veterans, most of them in their seventies or older, burst out of their seats and attacked the demonstrators, shouting insults in return. Police made nine arrests. The Queen Mother, ninety-two years old herself, hesitated for a moment, then calmly went on with her speech, asking for remembrance "for those of every nation and background who suffered as victims of the Second World War."[44]

Not all the demonstrators fit the "peacenik" stereotype. One of them, an elderly man named Denis Bols, had served as a flight navigator with Bomber Command: he told a reporter it was "disgraceful that we honor a psychopath, a murderer, and a megalomaniac who killed women and children."[45] On the other side of the police barricade another veteran—a former flight engineer named Kenneth James—said the statue "was long overdue in recognition of a very courageous man who did an extremely difficult job."[46] Above the fray stood the Bomber Harris statue itself, its legs set apart in a stance of defiant determination, its eyes looking ahead in cool disregard of all the controversy—much as the man himself had done in his prosecution of the war.

The foregoing vignettes of the politics of memory in various nations suggest three general observations.

1. *Historical memory is unavoidably interpretive.*

In speaking of the past, and of our relationship to it, we need to make a clear distinction between "the past" (the totality of what has happened before now), and "history" (our evolving understanding of what happened in the past). This epistemological point often gets lost in debates over historical memory: people speak of the past as if it were displayed before us, fixed and inert, accessible to us humans in a definitive form, comprehensible once and for all in a clear and self-evidently accurate way.

But this is not the way our knowledge works at all. Even supposing that we could gain access to the totality of facts about the past (which we can't), we would never be able to hold that totality in our minds: there is simply too much for us to grasp. Therefore, we narrow the field, focusing our attention on specific events and problems. We ask questions of the past, seeking answers to particular issues that concern us—and leaving aside countless other issues that we regard as irrelevant to the matter at hand. Out of the mass of information, we gradually piece together a particular story—our own interpretation of one small segment of what happened.

This may seem obvious, but it has profound implications. Every year I ask my students to try to envision a better way to have handled the *Enola Gay* exhibit, so that it would not end in the miserable way it did. Invariably, some students return to me with the following conclusion:

> A museum exhibit should be objective, neutral. It should not try to convince the viewer one way or the other about the decision to drop the bomb. The exhibit should only lay the facts out on the table, and let the viewer decide for himself or herself.

This is an admirable sentiment. But it fails in one key respect: it assumes that someone could put together an assembly of bare facts in a perfectly neutral way, without engaging in any interpretation of those facts. This, it turns out, is impossible.

It is true that facts exist; but whenever you start to weave facts together to tell a story, you are inevitably picking and choosing which facts to include, which facts to exclude, and how to portray the facts that you do include. In other words, you are thereby *interpreting*. Once you go beyond simply stating a single fact in isolation, you can't help but add your own selections and assumptions and wording as you paint the broader picture that gives your bare fact meaning.

Thus, it is a fact that the atomic bomb was dropped, and many people died. But when we try to assess the historical significance of this fact—its causes, its consequences, its moral aspects, the context in which it occurred, the intentions of the main actors involved—we inevitably pass into the domain of interpretation.

Some interpretations, of course, are demonstrably more accurate than others. Over the centuries historians have developed clear criteria for judging one another's interpretations, comparing them to decide which one is most persuasive. These criteria include cogency of argument, comprehensiveness of scope, attention to the full range of available evidence, conceptual clarity, and a compelling defense of the ways in which this particular interpretation diverges from other relevant historical accounts. The result, not surprisingly, is a great deal of ongoing debate: for it is often far from easy for historians to agree on what constitutes a truly persuasive interpretation of a particular historical event or process.[47]

To some of my students, this is deeply frustrating. They seek, from a professional like me, the closest thing possible to a "definitive" account. When they go to the doctor, they do not want an agonizing assessment of the pros and cons of various antibiotics: they want a clear and straightforward prescription for the best remedy available. Quite understandably, they look for the same kind of thing from me. But the study of history does not work like this (and some doctors would no doubt say that medicine does not really work so straightforwardly either). When I, the professor of history, tell them that all I can offer is my own provisional conclusion, based on where the ongoing debates currently stand, they look at me in dismay. But there is no other way: our historical knowledge is irreducibly interpretive. If students come through their undergraduate education in the field of history with a clearer understanding of this epistemological reality—and with a more sophisticated set of tools for judging the conflicting interpretations they will encounter beyond college—their teachers should be well satisfied.

2. *The past is fixed, but historical memory is not.*

If the past is only accessible to us as a series of interpretations, then it follows that as we ourselves change, so will our picture of the past. The physical evidence from the past does not change; what changes is our understanding of what happened, why it happened—and what it meant. The books, documents, and stone tablets grow older and more dusty, continuing forever to say the same things. What shifts, what is continually open to revision, is our understanding.

We saw this very clearly in the vignettes presented above. In postwar France, for example, the Vichy past itself did not change; but the meaning of that past underwent a steady evolution, as three generations of French citizens looked back on World War II, each generation animated by its own distinctive questions, perplexities, and priorities. The stories of Vichy shifted subtly—and sometimes not so subtly—as different generations searched through the archives with their own particular concerns. Yet, at the same time, this perpetual rereading of the past remained far from arbitrary: it was always constrained by the existing evidence, and by the existing range of accepted interpretations. Historical memory, in other words, is indeed a fluid construct; but there is always a limit to the elasticity of that construct, as each generation renegotiates it anew.

3. *Historical memory is shaped by the psychological attitude through which we hold our identity and self-image in the present.*

Whether in Japan, Germany, the Soviet Union, France, Britain, or the United States, the battles over memory all had one feature in common: they turned on such words as "pride" and "shame," "national honor" and "national disgrace." Again and again, those citizens who sought to bring out into the open the nastier aspects of the national past faced accusations of wanting to besmirch the good name of their country; of dwelling too much on guilt; of systematically downplaying the great achievements made by earlier generations; of demoralizing the citizenry of today (whether intentionally or unwittingly) through a morbidly negative view of the national track record. In all these cases, ultimately, the debates turned on one central question: What constitutes a "healthy" sense of national identity? Should we deliberately deemphasize the more unsavory episodes of our past, in the interest of bolstering our self-confidence and willingness to take strong action in the present? Or should we place heavy emphasis on those unsavory episodes, keeping our awareness of them alive and vivid, so as to reduce the chances of our ever repeating the errors of judgment made by our ancestors?

The neo-Stalinists like Nina Andreyeva (who insisted that Gorbachev was "spitting on the past") had one important characteristic in common with the French right-wingers who denounced Chirac for "smearing French honor." From opposite ends of the political spectrum, these two groups both articulated a form of national identity that was Manichaean and harshly judgmental in nature—a psychologically primitive stance that painted honor and dishonor as pure absolutes: "I am either good or bad. I am either proud or disgraced." Coming from such a stance, it was understandably rather hard for these people to deal with any shameful or morally ambiguous moments in the deeds of yesterday; they found it impossible to rest easy with a mixed historical track record. The result, accordingly, was an effort to rewrite the past, selectively editing it and touching it up to lend bygone choices a retroactive clarity that they had never possessed at the time. Moral ambiguity, for them, was psychologically unbearable: the thought that national greatness might coexist with significant episodes of grievous moral failure was simply too threatening to entertain. A nation could only be great if it had a pure, clean past; the duty of a true patriot was to stand guard over the nation's historical memory, defending the purity of the past from those who would taint it with striations of gray.

President Jacques Chirac, by contrast, exemplified a much more sophisticated psychological attitude in the speeches he gave at the Vel d'Hiv and Le Chambon. His conception of national identity was simultaneously critical yet constructive in nature: it rested on the ability to see past crimes as serious moral transgressions that nonetheless formed part of a broader historical learning process. In this sense, it is not surprising that he repeatedly emphasized the Enlightenment heritage of the French national identity he sought to affirm: for it was only on the basis of that relatively optimistic vision of long-term social and political progress that he could ground his hopes for a more tolerant, more fraternal future. National honor, as articulated by Chirac, was not a static absolute that a country either possessed or lost; rather, it was a more nuanced quality that grew out of a long story of moral deepening—an ongoing collective struggle on the part of the French people to come to terms with their failings and limitations, and to grow beyond them. In that learning and gradual self-transformation lay the real meaning of honor.

In Chirac's conception of historical memory, then, the human suffering caused by the Vichy regime could never be undone, nor even fully atoned for; but it would be partly redeemed, nonetheless, if French citizens of today could achieve an honest and balanced reckoning with their collective past. This would mean, at the very least: forthrightly acknowledging the complexities and moral ambiguities of their history; celebrating the memory of those few, like the Chambonnais, who had stood up well to the moral trials of wartime; taking full responsibility for the crimes committed by a collaborating nation against the Jews; and using the resultant knowledge to guide them in building a more humane social order in the present.

Historical memory, then, is unavoidably interpretive; it is a fluid construct, disciplined by the twin constraints of evidence and public debate; and it is profoundly shaped by the psychological attitude through which we hold our identity and self-image in the present. How might these three observations help us shed light on the Smithsonian Museum's ill-fated exhibit of the *Enola Gay*? In retrospect, the Smithsonian's curators made two primary mistakes when they set about designing their display of the historic plane. First, they failed to take sufficiently into account the distinction between a commemorative presentation—a war memorial staged on the fiftieth anniversary of the Hiroshima bombing—and a regular museum display; by confusing the two, they were asking for trouble. Second, they assumed that they could produce a sufficiently judicious and balanced synthesis of perspectives on the *Enola Gay*'s mission to satisfy all sides in the ongoing debates—a laudable goal, but a naïve one, given the profoundly contested nature of the topic.

The first of these two mistakes boiled down to a simple matter of timing. By choosing to display the *Enola Gay* in the summer of 1995, on the fiftieth anniversary of the Second World War's ending, the curators were invoking (whether intentionally or not) a major trope in civic discourse: the trope of the war memorial. Perhaps even more than the centenary (when most of the original participants will inevitably have died off), the fiftieth anniversary is usually set aside, through a widely accepted cultural convention, as an especially poignant and symbolically charged occasion for remembrance. The Smithsonian's curators did not intend to stage a war memorial: they appear to have honestly believed that they could put on a regular museum exhibit that happened to coincide felicitously with a fifty-year anniversary. But this was a big mistake. From the very start, because of its timing, their exhibit would automatically—and understandably—summon up a long tradition of rites and rhetorical customs associated with reverence for the wartime dead. Framed in this anniversary context, the shiny B-29 fuselage took on the kind of meaning associated with memorial services, battle monuments, war cemeteries, and all the other fora where citizens pay homage to surviving veterans and to the memory of the soldiers killed while serving their country.

This confusion of representational tropes placed the Smithsonian in an impossible bind. Its mission, as a museum, was primarily educational rather than commemorative: to prepare rich and complex exhibits that reflected the full range of ongoing scholarly research on a particular topic, giving visitors a better sense of the history of science and technology in their evolving social context.[48] But this educational mission clashed irreconcilably with the required reverential spirit of a commemorative event. One does not, after all, apply the scholarly standards of critical objectivity and balance in crafting someone's funeral oration:

> John Smith was at times warm and generous, but also on occasion quite aloof and even downright nasty. His relatives all claim that they will miss him terribly—though past experience suggests that as time goes by they will think of him less and less often.

To many war veterans and other observers, the proposed script for the *Enola Gay* exhibit read in precisely this fashion, as an unconscionably inappropriate and insulting way to portray the self-sacrifice of an entire generation. Their expectations had been cued by the powerful symbolism of the fiftieth anniversary—a memorial occasion that called for homage and gratitude, not for hedged scholarly judgments over the possible atrociousness of the war's closing act.

Were the veterans' expectations unreasonable? Not at all. The soldiers of World War II deserved a memorial ceremony in 1995—a big one, commensurate with the sacrifices they made and with the immeasurable benefits they thereby bestowed on the generations that followed. In a time of deep crisis they had answered the call of their country and given up years of their lives—or their very lives themselves—in defense of our liberties. When they died on the battlefield, or struggled to save a dying comrade lying before them, they had given their all: we should give our gratitude to them in the same way. Wholeheartedly.

The citizenry of today, therefore, needs to make a clear distinction between two equally important aspects of the year 1945:

- This was the year when the terrible struggle against fascism finally came to an end, with a victory that cost millions of Allied lives;
- This was the year of Hiroshima, the first combat use in history of a nuclear weapon of mass destruction, a wartime act of annihilating violence against a civilian population center, a deed that has remained deeply controversial ever since.

There is no reason why we cannot keep this distinction in our minds as we look back on the ending of World War II. There is a time for expressing our gratitude to the veterans, and a time for critical reflection on the profoundly troubling manner in which the war ended: these two very different things should not be confused with each other.

In retrospect, then, the solution to this aspect of the Smithsonian's *Enola Gay* fiasco would have been relatively simple: move the exhibit to another year—one unburdened by the heavy symbolism of a major anniversary occasion. As an additional precaution, one could also have scheduled the opening of the display in December or January, so as to further dissociate it from any commemorative connotations. The exhibit's title, moreover, could have explicitly underscored the fact that this was not a war memorial, but rather an educational display designed to shed light on a pivotal moment in world history in all its complexity. Under these changed circumstances, it would have been entirely appropriate for the exhibit to confront—without pulling any punches—the deeply controversial nature of the Hiroshima attack.

One of the few incontestable facts about the atomic bombing of Hiroshima is that people still disagree vehemently about this event, six decades after it happened: common citizens, veterans, politicians—and, not surprisingly, professional historians as well. The divisions cut across all social groups and professional categories. The points of contention range from basic matters of fact (such as the number of people killed by the blast and radiation) to the intentions of the major participants; from key speculative matters such as casualty estimates or alternative courses of action, to the moral implications of the actions actually taken. The story of the Hiroshima bombing, in other words, is fraught with interpretive ambiguity: it presents historical observers with all manner of occasions for reasonable disagreement.[49]

For any historian writing a book or essay on this subject, therefore, a key goal must be to come to grips with all these conflicting interpretations of what happened, adjudicating among those divergent perspectives in order to reach some kind of synthesis or conclusion—however provisional or tentative in nature that bottom-line judgment may be. For the curators of a public museum, however, the challenge is necessarily rather different. Unlike a single author, who can take personal responsibility for any conclusions reached, a museum like the Smithsonian is a collective and semi-official entity whose exhibits are tacitly understood as "speaking for" the entirety of the broader national society. Its perspective, therefore, should not predominantly reflect the views of any single individual, social group, or partisan ideological constituency, but should give voice in a balanced manner to a representative sampling of the major schools of thought. The museum's curators articulated this goal explicitly in their script for the *Enola Gay* exhibit, in which they pledged to offer visitors "as objective and balanced a presentation of these issues as possible."[50]

Unfortunately, however, they went about pursuing this laudable goal the wrong way. Their exhibit should have spoken with many voices, accurately reflecting the full range of conflicting opinions on the subject; instead, it spoke with one basic voice, just as if it were the product of a single scholar's research and reflections. To be sure, the voice it adopted was a measured and judicious one, carefully taking into account the findings of a broad range of scholarship on the subject, and weaving it into a single broad narrative. But this was manifestly inadequate. No single story line, no single synthesis—no matter how scrupulously fair-minded or even-handed—could possibly do justice to the welter of competing and conflicting perspectives on the bombing of Hiroshima. Why? Because a good many of those perspectives were simply irreconcilable. To someone who believes that massacring helpless civilians is always an absolute evil, under any circumstances, the notion that the A-bomb saved Allied lives will ring hollow. To someone who had fought in Europe and was about to be transferred to the Pacific in 1945 to join the invasion of Kyushu, the notion that strategic bombing of cities is always evil will ring equally hollow. These perspectives are not open to negotiation or arbitration: they reflect totally divergent lines of argument, based on incommensurable assumptions and priorities. One cannot do justice to them by seeking some kind of Olympian synthesis that would somehow adjudicate between them from a putatively "objective" standpoint: no such standpoint exists. The only way to do them justice is to give them a space in which to speak for themselves, frankly presenting the museum visitor with the irreducible divergence that they embody. And at that point, of course, the visitor will have to figure out for himself or herself what to do with that information.

The Smithsonian's curators did acknowledge forthrightly that their exhibit covered many areas of ongoing controversy, and they duly noted those areas throughout their script. But in the end the script always returned to its core narrative voice in laying out the fundamental story of the *Enola Gay*'s mission and its implications—a voice that claimed final authority (as far as the exhibit was concerned) in pronouncing its verdict on history. This type of blandly univocal epistemological stance might work well for a display on the history of kitchen tools or comic books, perhaps, but it was bound to cause serious trouble for an exhibit on one of the most intractably controversial topics in American history. Inevitably, some social constituents who regarded themselves as stakeholders in the exhibit complained that their own perspective was being suppressed or distorted by the Olympian synthesis of the Smithsonian's script. Equally inevitably, when the curators sought to placate those disgruntled stakeholders by modifying the script, this resulted in a hue and cry from other constituents who regarded the modifications as doing violence to *their* position. Precisely because the topic at hand was so profoundly contested in nature, no single synthesis could ever hope to satisfy all the various groups of clamoring stakeholders—and the end result was the collapse of the exhibit itself.

The only solution to this problem would have been to abandon altogether the unrealistic goal of reaching consensus—of crafting, through a kind of endlessly patient negotiation, a single common narrative that would satisfy everybody. Rather, the sole legitimate meaning of the words "objective and balanced," in this context, is to tell the story through the lens of controversy itself, emphasizing the intensely problematic nature of the major issues at stake, and giving ample space for all the most significant contending perspectives to have their full say. The fact itself of intractable disagreement and debate needed to lie at the heart of the *Enola Gay* exhibit: its title should have been something like "The Atomic Bombing of Hiroshima: Six Decades of Controversy."

Such an exhibit would have needed to incorporate the perspectives of specialized military historians, veteran memoirists, veterans groups, Japanese historians, survivors of the atomic bombings, moral philosophers, peace advocacy groups, along with the wide-ranging scholarship of a variety of academic experts on twentieth-century U.S. history. The goal should have been to give each point of view a concise and vivid airing—and to lay out these conflicting (and overlapping) interpretations side by side, so that their divergences and convergences might appear clearly to the museum visitor.

One potential drawback of this approach, of course, is that it could be misread as implying a stance of moral and epistemological relativism. The absence of a conclusive judgment underpinning the exhibit might prompt some museum visitors to assume that no basis existed at all for making such a judgment—that there was simply no way to adjudicate the relative strengths and weaknesses of the competing perspectives on display. This issue would have to be addressed explicitly within the exhibit itself— perhaps in the form of a brief movie explaining why the museum, which is a public and semi-official space, cannot offer a final judgment on a controversy that still remains fundamentally unresolved within the nation's civic discourse. The movie would need to emphasize the fact that this "unresolved" nature of the ongoing public controversy should not preclude individual citizens from assessing the persuasiveness of the various competing perspectives, and from reaching their own conclusions about their relative merits.

Would such a multivoiced exhibit fare any better, in the real world, than the one attempted by the Smithsonian in 1995? It is hard to know. Some stakeholders might claim that the museum's curators had a hidden agenda, and were slanting the exhibit (whether intentionally or not) toward one side or another; but this kind of objection could perhaps be neutralized (or at least mitigated) by offering the various stakeholders early versions of the script for commentary and feedback. At another level, however, some stakeholders might consider the very idea itself of a multivoiced exhibit intrinsically offensive and preposterous. One group of congresspersons, for example, wrote an irate letter to the Smithsonian's director in 1995, claiming that there was "no excuse for an exhibit which addresses one of the most morally unambiguous events of the twentieth century to need five revisions."[51] These kinds of stakeholders, apparently, could only envision one interpretation—their own—as having any legitimacy; to them, the deeds of August 6, 1945, spoke in such clear, ringing terms of moral righteousness that they should be self-evidently obvious to all persons of goodwill. Anyone who saw things differently was, by definition, misguided or ill-intentioned. To such individuals, needless to say, an *Enola Gay* exhibit that emphasized controversy—methodically laying out the wide-ranging variety of opinions on the subject—would in itself constitute an outrage. They might do their best, once again, to shut it down.

But these kinds of people do not reflect the enduring spirit of American democracy, which rests on the principle of pluralism—the right of individuals to make up their own minds after reviewing the full range of alternatives. They stand more in the tradition of the neo-Stalinists like Nina Andreyeva, or the French neo-fascists, who simply could not bear to entertain the possibility of their country having a morally complex past. Such people, with their "My Way or the Highway" attitude, are not doing their country a service when they seek to force public reflection to stay within certain "approved" lines of interpretation. Their stance should be unequivocally repudiated by all Americans who value our long and precious traditions of liberty.

CONCLUSION

What Would Be the Opposite of Hitler's World?

In the Northwest territories of Canada, two Eskimo villages raised
$7,000 for Ethiopian relief.

—*Newsweek* (November 26, 1984)[1]

Adolf Hitler killed himself in a bunker below the Reich Chancellery building in Berlin during the night of April 30, 1945. The crash and thud of Russian artillery surrounded him outside. He had lost the war, in the most utterly clear-cut way a war could be lost: his country completely ravaged, his people at the mercy of enraged occupying armies, and his own body felled by a simultaneous dose of cyanide and a self-inflicted pistol shot to the head.

Hitler's situation on that day constituted the full fruition of his view of what human life is about.[2] Life, for Adolf Hitler, was fundamentally about competition and domination—ruthless competition for scarce resources, ineluctable domination of the strong over the weak. Like a logical syllogism, this worldview had now revealed its ultimate consequences. Utterly alone, he made a final pathetic gesture of marrying his longtime mistress, Eva Braun. Deeply embittered, he blamed the Jews, the Slavs, the British, his generals, his closest associates, and the weakness of the German people for the catastrophe that surrounded him: he blamed anyone but himself. Gaunt and wasted from years of unrelenting pressure, his body was a trembling wreck, mirroring the ruin of the German nation outside. Even if he had wanted redemption, it is hard to see from where in his life's deeds and beliefs it might have come—but in fact he did not want redemption. He chose instead the flailing, snarling gesture of berating all those who had populated his life's story, whether as his opponents or as his closest

*Rowboat and rifle left on the beach of Cap Bon, Tunisia, by retreating
German forces (May 1943).*

allies. In the end, he became nothing more than a singularly vivid portrait
in failure—probably one of the most pervasive and total failures of any
human life ever lived. The fact that he could not see or acknowledge his
own responsibility for that failure only rendered it all the more complete.

In 1950 my father, Donovan Bess, visited the German city of Hamburg. He
was an expatriate Yank, working as a reporter for the Reuters news agency
in London, and had been sent over from England to see how the Germans
were faring with their postwar recovery and reconstruction efforts. What
he found impressed him. Generous British aid in 1945 and 1946, and still
more generous Marshall Plan aid after 1947, had been put to excellent use
by the Germans. Hamburg was booming: the rubble had been cleared,
cranes filled the sky as new buildings went up, the economy was growing
robustly, public confidence was high, the fledgling institutions of the
brand-new Federal Republic of Germany were humming along like a
Mercedes-Benz on the autobahn.

Having done his research and filed his story, my father was getting
ready to return to London the next morning. He stopped at a restaurant

near his hotel that evening for one last fancy meal: London, five years after the war, was still on a comprehensive regimen of rationing, from food to gasoline to all manner of consumer goods. He perused the ample menu, and ordered a large steak. The waiter, a middle-aged man, took his order, giving him a peculiar look as he walked away. A little later he returned with a handsome slab of broiled meat. He asked my father where he was from, and they chatted awhile. Then the waiter said, casually, "You can't get a steak like that in London these days, can you?"

"No, you certainly can't," my father replied.

The waiter gave him a cold smile and leaned down a little closer. "Who won the war?" he asked.

It's an interesting perspective. The three nations with the fastest economic growth rates after 1945 were Germany, Japan, and Italy. This was partly due to ample aid from the victors, partly to the fact that these three devastated nations had to start from scratch, and hence built up new industries with the latest technology. Partly it was due also to the fact that none of these three nations had large expenses for postwar military purposes, as did France, Britain, the United States, and the Soviet Union. Most of all, of course, the three former Axis powers did very well after the war because they had completely new leadership, new economic and social systems, and a radically new attitude among their populations.

But the story of the Hamburg waiter also makes you pause for a moment.

Did these people really learn anything, underneath? More broadly, did humankind as a whole learn anything from this orgy of bloodletting? Did all the suffering really cause an enduring change of heart among the world's citizens—the winners as well as the losers? Did we learn anything?

One of the most profound legacies of World War II lies in the mythology that still surrounds this conflict sixty years later, in films and novels, in popular understanding, in public memory, in the rhetoric and assumptions of diplomats and statesmen. This mythology, in a nutshell, is about powerful action against uncomplicated evil—the triumph of righteous military force in an overwhelmingly just cause. When George Lucas wanted to grab his audience in the *Star Wars* films with a viscerally satisfying confrontation between good and evil, he drew copiously from the imagery of World War II—the helmets, the marching ranks, the nihilistic power-lust of the imperial leadership, the freedom fighters flying small fighter craft against giant enemy battle stations.

The irony, of course, is that this kind of war imagery became hopelessly obsolete even before the war itself had ended. On August 6, 1945, the world was introduced to a new mode of combat, and a new era of history: a solitary plane flies in at high altitude, well above the range of most antiaircraft guns and enemy fighters, and releases a single device that obliterates a city. "Surrender now, or we'll do this to your whole country." Advanced technology replaces valor; indiscriminate mass destruction replaces the age-old drama of man-to-man warfare. Within ten years, by the late 1950s, the confrontation between good and evil had become a deadly technological standoff, with both sides locked in the embrace of a mutual suicide pact. The *Star Wars* films, in other words, were a carefully crafted fantasy, harking back nostalgically to an era in which men and women could still put their lives on the line in the just cause of an all-out war against evil. But that era was irrevocably gone: World War II itself had traced a stark demarcation line across history. All-out war, on this side of that line, has become unthinkable, the ultimate human folly, a destroyer of worlds, a disgrace.

It is time to bring our mythology up to date. We can and should honor with fervor the memory of the people who sacrificed so much in that last great military cataclysm of world history; but it is time to let go of our nostalgia for that era. Nostalgia for World War II will not serve us well as a moral compass for working our way through the conflicts that lie ahead in the century to come. The rules of the game have changed too drastically for that: precisely because of the way the Second World War played itself out, the fundamental premises of international relations have shifted profoundly, and forever. We have to find new ways of resolving our conflicts— and a revised mythology to sustain us in that quest.

What might such a new mythology of warfare look like? The arguments presented in this book suggest the following three elements as a starting point.

1. *Justice and ambiguity in coexistence.*

There is such a thing as a just war; but significant evil deeds and good deeds can often still be observed on all sides. The Allied nations have much to be proud of, as they look back over World War II: the Allied cause in this war was a just cause—defense against unprovoked aggression by tyrannical nations. Our soldiers exhibited extraordinary bravery and self-sacrifice, across the whole broad canvas of the war over six years and countless theaters of combat. Where Anglo-American armies marched in, they arrived as liberators, and treated the local populations with decency and propriety. In victory, the British and Yanks showed remarkable generosity toward the defeated peoples; in the aftermath of war, they paved the way for a major resurgence of democratic practices and values in many parts of the world.

But we have also seen, in the foregoing stories, a more complicated picture emerging. Racism was not a monopoly of the Axis powers: it pervaded the thinking and the conduct of warfare in the Allied nations as well. The monstrous deeds perpetrated by the Germans and Japanese should never be forgotten; but the Allies, too, must honestly confront those aspects of the war around which controversy understandably still swirls. We did not do nearly enough to aid the victims of Nazi oppression in the 1930s. We killed hundreds of thousands of helpless civilians with our strategic bombing campaign: this aspect of the war was not nearly as straightforward, from a moral point of view, as some would have us believe. We won the war through an alliance with a vicious regime, Stalin's USSR; and although this alliance was justified by the dire exigencies of warfare, we need to include it among the morally ambiguous aspects of our victory. Even though dropping the atomic bomb probably resulted in a major net saving of human lives, we should have resorted to it only after a much more thorough process of deliberation; and we should definitely have given the Japanese a demonstration of it before annihilating one of their cities.

My point, in laying out this brief balance sheet, is that World War II was a morally complicated event. Even though we can wholeheartedly affirm, in the end, that it was indeed a just war—a war that needed to be fought—this should not prevent us from paying close attention to the conflict's many important gray areas. Our mythology of warfare needs to move beyond the *Star Wars* imagery of pure goodness confronting pure evil in a pure contest with a pure outcome: such rectitude exists only on movie screens, not in the real world where we all live our daily lives.

2. *We cannot afford another war like this.*

The new mythology of warfare cannot but draw heavily from the imagery of suicide—the swift and irretrievable self-destruction of an entire civilization. In World War II it was still possible to launch globe-spanning coalitions of nations headlong into unrestrained collision with each other. Today that has become sheer insanity: all-out war among great powers is no longer viable as a means of resolving deadly quarrels. If we wish to look to the popular movies of Hollywood for our imagery, then we must put aside the *Star Wars* series as a totally unrealistic fantasy, and look instead to a different futuristic film like *The Terminator* for our inspiration: for in that movie we find depicted (in all its gritty reality) the tragic stupidity of our nuclear predicament. We take our wonderful planet, our cities, our daily lives, and we blow them to radioactive smithereens out of sheer pigheadedness and a failure to imagine alternatives. Senseless waste, criminal folly: that is the admonitory image we need in our minds as we look to the future—for that image, and not the quaint nostalgia of *Star Wars*, is the one that more accurately captures the all too real dangers of our military technologies in today's world. The new mythology of warfare must remind us vividly, relentlessly, of Herman Wouk's conclusion at the end of his epic World War II novel, *War and Remembrance:* "Either war is finished or we are."

3. *Heroism is still needed.*

Chapter 12 showed that powerful forms of conflict resolution, using fair and effective tools other than military force, are already available to us today: over the coming century we can build a world of increasingly stable peace in which all-out war becomes less and less likely. It follows that among the most important heroes of today's world we should now include all those who—in countless ways, at all levels of society—advance the cause of stable peace. They are the "fighters" whose efforts and sacrifice are analogous, in today's context, to the struggle waged by the Allied fighters in the 1940s. The enemy this time around is not Nazism or Japanese imperialism, but war itself: the obsolete system of militarized security arrangements that promises to bring us nothing but grief over the long haul.

This struggle for stable peace, on the surface of it, is not nearly as glamorous as the struggle waged with B-17 bombers and Sherman tanks against the Nazi legions. Blowing things to bits, unfortunately, is inherently more exciting (at least, to a great many people) than building things up. Here, too, then, our mythology must change. We need new heroes whose deeds are suited to guide and inspire us in our new struggle: figures like Gandhi, King, Mother Teresa, and Mandela, to be sure, but also more ordinary individuals like the Chinese man who stood before a tank in Tiananmen Square in June 1989, laying his body and his conscience across the path of a totalitarian regime wielding brute military force. Or the Canadian general Roméo Dallaire, who desperately tried to stop the carnage in the Rwandan civil war of 1994, leading his outnumbered team of U.N. soldiers on an impossibly difficult mission in which his own life and that of his men lay at constant risk. Or the Burmese woman Aung San Suu

Kyi, who in 1988 gave up her family life in England in order to lead a non-violent democracy campaign against the military junta that tyrannized her native land. Or the Eskimo villagers in the opening quotation for this chapter: taking up a collection among themselves to send money to starving Africans, complete strangers on the other side of the world.

We also must remember that 90 percent of the deeds done in World War II were themselves far from glamorous in nature. Driving trucks laden with supplies down long muddy roads, well away from the fighting; planning the D-Day attack, pushing mountains of paperwork for more than fourteen months at Dwight Eisenhower's staff headquarters in the run-up to June 1944; working in factories to manufacture jeeps and planes and ammunition; swabbing decks on an aircraft carrier; spending thousands of hours at a desk trying to decode enemy communications; ferrying aircraft across the South Atlantic to Africa, far from the combat theaters; cooking meals, tending to the wounded, burying the dead—these were the kinds of activities that most people experienced in "fighting" World War II. The glamorous, exciting stuff was the rare exception.

Winning World War II, in short, required immense patience and perseverance on the part of millions of ordinary individuals, each contributing his or her own small (but cumulatively important) element to the broader struggle. Building a more stable peace over the coming century will require the same kind of commitment, sustained over a much longer span of time: 10 percent heroism, 90 percent small steps, taken by each of us in the course of our daily lives, patiently pressing for a transformation. This, too, needs to become part of our new mythology of warfare.

"Who won the war?" asked the waiter in Hamburg. The story of that encounter is disheartening, because it forces us to acknowledge that despite the shattering defeat of the Nazis, their underlying mentality lived on. That sour fellow had learned nothing from the calamity of war: he remained unrepentant, firmly wedded to the narrow vision of arrogant chauvinism that had brought on this disastrous conflict.

What would it mean, then, for Hitler's worldview truly to be defeated? Not just for Hitler and the Nazis to be squashed, like some ugly bug, but for the ideas they promoted, the values they embodied, to become weak, marginal, insignificant? What would it take for us to really win the Second World War, in this deeper sense?

The answer may be lying right there in the history itself, for this was the very question that the anti-fascist Resistance fighters of World War II asked themselves. Sitting around their campfires at night, holed up in the hills of Norway or Italy, France or Yugoslavia, freezing in some ditch waiting for an airdrop, hiding in a cellar waiting for nightfall: they asked themselves not just "What are we fighting against?" but mainly: "What are we really fighting *for*? What do we want to make of the world, once this bloody mess is over?"

They were an extremely motley bunch, these Resistance men and women: from hard-core communists to Christian conservatives; from illiterate migrant laborers to university professors; from well-to-do doctors to wretchedly poor factory hands—all thrown together by their common repudiation of fascism and their desire to liberate Europe. But even across their wide-ranging backgrounds and political ideologies, many of them (though not all) were able to agree on certain basic principles for the future.[3]

In the end, the Resistance fighters told themselves, these are the beacons by which we must set our bearing, if we want this war truly to be won: whereas fascism glorified the state, we place our emphasis on the intrinsic dignity and value of the individual. Fascism rested on the *Führerprinzip*, an ethos akin to a military chain of command; we will build our new society on critical thinking, open-mindedness, and grassroots democracy. The fascists organized their polity through privilege, hierarchy, domination, exclusion; ours will offer equal rights and equal opportunities for all citizens. Fascist ideology was nihilistic at its core, embracing brute force and deception as the tools of power; our ideals will be those of civic duty, honesty, transparency, and taking responsibility for everyone in our community. The fascists believed in expansionism and war; we will find ways to build cooperation among peoples. This way lies the opposite of Hitler's world.

It should be plain that this deeper struggle—this moral and political dimension of the great anti-fascist campaign—could never have ended with the surrender formalities of V-E Day and V-J Day. This was not the kind of struggle that one ever "wins" definitively: it was more like a long-term orientation, a direction into which one could launch one's postwar life. And the key to this vision lay in its emphasis on individual moral responsibility. Though these men and women certainly hoped to build a radically different social order in the fighting's aftermath, most of them clearly understood that the foundation of all their hopes lay in the choices made by each of them as individual citizens. The real transformation, they believed, would only come about if they each asked themselves, every morning anew: what is the opposite of Hitler's world, and what does it mean to incarnate this vision in a single day of one person's life?

Their legacy, looking back over the past sixty years, has not surprisingly been mixed. Many of the Resistance fighters became deeply disappointed by the shape that the postwar world took: by the mid-1950s, as the Cold War gripped Europe, they felt that their wartime ideals had been betrayed, that the great potential for a moral renovation had been lost.[4] But this is an excessively pessimistic reading of postwar history. When we look at Europe today, we certainly do not find a utopian society, but we do see a social and political order in which many of the Resistance ideals still live and flourish—albeit in understandably imperfect, incomplete form. These are free societies, in which representative democracy and civil liberties are not only thriving, but are actually expanding their reach. Europe boasts the most advanced welfare states of the modern world—a perpetually negotiated balance between left and right, resting on commonly accepted principles of equity and social solidarity. Europeans are among the world's leaders in the campaign for human rights, both at home and abroad; and they give a significant portion of their wealth every year for aid to less prosperous countries. The chauvinistic nationalism of the interwar era has given way to a more open, cosmopolitan form of cultural identity that bridges traditional boundaries of nation, language, and customs.

None of these positive features, to be sure, can be mentioned without a need for careful qualification. Racism, authoritarianism, poverty, corruption, the will to dominate—these still play a very real role in shaping Europe's history today. The struggle continues: after all, these are human beings we are describing here, not angels or saints. But it would be a mistake to underestimate the progress that has been made since the harrowing decade of the 1930s. The ideals of the anti-fascist Resistance, though only imperfectly realized, still constitute the foundation, the moral bedrock, of contemporary European society.[5]

To view World War II in this way—as a deeper moral and political struggle on behalf of a particular set of values—is to realize that this conflict is not just a piece of our history, a thing of the past. Today, as we look at the world around us, we cannot help but recognize that the great struggle of the 1940s still remains dramatically unresolved, the verdict as yet unclear. In some respects the long-term outcome of the war has been a major advance for the rule of law, equal opportunity, human rights, and humane social values—in a great many parts of the planet. In other respects, it is equally true to say that these ideals remain appallingly immature, unfulfilled, in contemporary global society. We are all, in this sense, not just the descendants of the World War II generation, but also the inheritors of the campaign on which those people embarked, and in which they made such impressive progress. Today that moral and political contest continues, played out under different banners and among different historical actors. But the underlying stakes have not changed.

The implication is rather startling: we are still fighting to win World War II. The responsibility rests on our shoulders now, and it is our generation that must take up the question: what is the opposite of Hitler's world, and what does it mean to incarnate this vision in a single day of one person's life?

Here, then, is another story, one that reflects this deeper dimension of the Second World War. It comes from Studs Terkel's collection of oral histories: a terse account, narrated almost in passing by a medical doctor from Southern California who served in the battle for Europe. He was a young army surgeon named Alex Shulman.

I was in Belgium at the time of the Bulge. Winter, '44. I was doing neuro-surgery, head surgery. This German youngster was brought in. He was fourteen, fifteen. Looked like a lost little boy. Hitler was takin' the kids and the old men. This kid was cut off from his outfit several weeks before, and he hid in a barn. He was a sad, dirty-looking kid, with a terrible gash in his head. It was actually a hole through his scalp and his skull.

When I first saw him, he was covered with old straw and manure and blood, and it was all caked together. I didn't know what to do with him. What is his injury? We always pictured Germans as having short-cropped hair. It was the GI's who had short-cropped hair. The German boys had long hair, long before our boys did. So did this kid, and his hair was matted together.

As I took him to the operating room, he started to cry. A little kid. I said, "Stop crying." I could speak a little bit of German, and a little bit of Yiddish helped. All I did was get a basin of hot water and some soap and washed his hair. Here was a captain in the United States Army washing the hair of a little German boy. I finally cleaned him up and looked at the wound. It wasn't bad. Nature had done quite a job healing it.

Then he really started to cry. I said, "What are you crying about?" He said, "They told me I'd be killed. And here you are, an American officer, washing my hands and face and my hair." I reminded him that I was a Jewish doctor, so he would get the full impact of it.[6]

A day in the winter of 1944, amid the turmoil of the battlefield, with people still killing one another all around: the moment passes, simple, like taking a breath. One man, refusing to hate. Fully cognizant of what he is doing—of the relation between himself, a Jew, and this young German before him—he chooses an act of kindness. For the medic Alex Shulman, the real contest of World War II was already won.

NOTES

Introduction

1. Czeslaw Milosz, "Flight," in *Czeslaw Milosz: The Collected Poems* (Ecco, 1988), 75.

2. Thucydides, *History of the Peloponnesian War,* trans. Rex Warner (Penguin, 1972), 402. Since the various translators of Thucydides have worded this passage rather differently from one another, I have settled here on a somewhat modified version of Warner's wording. Warner's original reads as follows: "The strong do what they have the power to do and the weak accept what they have to accept."

3. On the concept of justice in warfare, see Jean Bethke Elshtain, ed., *Just War Theory* (New York University Press, 1992); J. Glenn Gray, *The Warriors: Reflections on Men in Battle* (Harper & Row, 1959); Michael Howard, ed., *Restraints on War: Studies in the Limitation of Armed Conflict* (Oxford University Press, 1979); John Keegan, *The Face of Battle* (Penguin, 1995); Richard Overy, "Evil Things, Excellent Things: The Moral Contest," in *Why the Allies Won* (Norton, 1995), 282–313; Michael Walzer, *Just and Unjust Wars: A Moral Argument with Historical Illustrations* (Diane, 1977).

4. Ronald Schaffer, *Wings of Judgment: American Bombing in World War II* (Oxford University Press, 1985), Chapter 5.

5. Studs Terkel, *The "Good War": An Oral History of World War Two* (Ballantine, 1984).

6. Nancy Arnot Harjan, quoted in ibid., 560–63.

7. Tom Brokaw, *The Greatest Generation* (Random House, 1998), xviii.

8. For an excellent discussion of *Saving Private Ryan*—a discussion considerably more detailed (and more critical) than my own in this chapter—see John Bodnar, "*Saving Private Ryan* and Postwar Memory in America," in Gordon Martel, ed., *The World War Two Reader* (Routledge, 2004), 435–48.

Chapter One: A Wide World of Racisms

1. Quoted in Morton Grodzins, *Americans Betrayed* (University of Chicago Press, 1949), 20.

2. See Mike Hawkins, *Social Darwinism in European and American Thought,*

1860–1945: Nature As Model and Nature As Threat (Cambridge University Press, 1997).

3. Adolf Hitler, quoted in Hugh Trevor-Roper, *The Last Days of Hitler* (Pan, 1952), 88.

4. Eberhard Jäckel, *Hitler's World View* (Harvard University Press, 1981), Chapters 2 and 3. See also Ian Kershaw, *Hitler, 1889–1936: Hubris* (Norton, 1999); and *Hitler, 1936–1945: Nemesis* (Norton, 2001).

5. Scott Dickers, ed., *Our Dumb Century* (Three Rivers, 1999), 58.

6. John Dower, *War Without Mercy: Race and Power in the Pacific War* (Pantheon, 1986), Chapter 10.

7. Andrew Gordon, *A Modern History of Japan* (Oxford University Press, 2003), 211.

8. Detailed statistics on the forced labor practices are given in Dower, *War Without Mercy*, 47–48.

9. For fuller accounts of these atrocities, see Yuki Tanaka, *Hidden Horrors: Japanese War Crimes in World War II* (Westview, 1998); Arthur Zich et al., *The Rising Sun* (Time-Life Books, 1977), Chapter 5; and Dower, *War Without Mercy*, especially Chapters 3 and 10.

10. Carlos Romulo, quoted in Dower, *War Without Mercy*, 45.

11. I rely heavily in this overview on the account by David M. Kennedy, *The American People in World War II* (Oxford University Press, 1999), especially Chapter 8.

12. Clayborne Carson, "Japanese-Americans," in I. C. B. Dear and M. R. D. Foot, eds., *The Oxford Companion to World War II* (Oxford University Press, 1995), 632–34. See also Peter Irons, *Justice at War: The Story of the Japanese Internment Cases* (University of California Press, 1983).

13. Walter Lippmann, quoted in Kennedy, *The American People in World War II*, 326.

14. For online access to the extensive photo collections on Japanese internment in the National Archives, see the Central Photographic File of the War Relocation Authority, located at http://www.archives.gov/research/arc/topics/ww2 .html#wra.

15. Kennedy, *The American People in World War II*, 329.

16. An overview of the legal aspects of the internment policy, as well as the relevant portions of the justices' opinions, are reproduced on http://usinfo.state.gov/usa/ infousa/facts/democrac/65.htm.

17. Estelle Ishigo, quoted on "Exploring Japanese American Internment," at http://www.jainternment.org/camps/end.html.

18. Kennedy, *The American People in World War II*, 344.

19. Clayborne Carson, "African-Americans at War," in Dear and Foot, eds., *The Oxford Companion to World War II*, 6.

20. Bill Horton, "Just a Negro Soldier," in Fred Stanton, ed., *Fighting Racism in World War II* (Pathfinder, 1980), 324.

21. Gerhard Weinberg, *A World at Arms: A Global History of World War II* (Cambridge University Press, 1994), 488.

22. Joe W. Wilson Jr. et al., *The 761st "Black Panther" Tank Battalion in World*

War II (McFarland, 1999); Neil Wynn, *The Afro-American and the Second World War* (Elek, 1976).

23. The citation for Ruben Rivers is reproduced on http://www.army.mil/cmh-pg/mohiib1.htm#Rivers.

24. Alfred Duckett, quoted in Terkel, *The "Good War,"* 369–70.

Chapter Two: Causes of the Pacific War

1. Matsuo Taseko, a "woman who produced silkworms in the Ina Valley in mountainous central Japan" in the 1860s, quoted in Gordon, *A Modern History of Japan*, 51.

2. I draw heavily in this account on the excellent survey of Japanese history by Gordon, *A Modern History of Japan;* and on Akira Iriye, *The Origins of the Second World War in Asia and the Pacific* (Longman, 1987). See also John Benson and Takao Matsumura, *Japan, 1868–1945: From Isolation to Occupation* (Pearson, 2001); and Ronald Spector, *Eagle Against the Sun: The American War with Japan* (Vintage, 1985).

3. Gordon, *A Modern History of Japan*, 50. Emphasis in original.

4. Ibid., 175–81.

5. Ibid., 175.

6. See the discussion in ibid., 180.

7. For a detailed account of the massacre, see Iris Chang, *The Rape of Nanking* (Penguin, 1997).

8. For an overview of the historiographical and public debates over the massacre, see Yang Daqing, "A Sino-Japanese Controversy: The Nanjing Massacre as History," *Sino-Japanese Studies* 3 (November 1990), 14–35; and Ian Buruma, *The Wages of Guilt: Memories of War in Germany and Japan* (Meridian, 1994).

9. Dower, *War Without Mercy*, 43.

10. Did FDR know that the Pearl Harbor attack was coming, and yet deliberately allow it to take place because he felt that this was the only way to get the isolationist American public sufficiently aroused to enter World War II? This conspiracy theory continues to emerge as a staple of World War II lore, despite the lack of even a scrap of reliable evidence to support such a hypothesis. Historians have effectively demolished this theory over the years: see, for example, Gordon Prange, *At Dawn We Slept* (Penguin, 1982); and Roberta Wohlstetter, *Pearl Harbor: Warning and Decision* (Stanford University Press, 1962).

Chapter Three: Causes of the War in Europe

1. Sir Nevile Henderson, *Failure of a Mission: Berlin, 1937–1939* (Putnam, 1940), 158.

2. Fritz Fischer, *Germany's Aims in the First World War* (Norton, 1968).

3. See, for example, Anthony Adamthwaite, *The Lost Peace: International Relations in Europe, 1918–1939* (St. Martin's, 1981); E. H. Carr, *The Twenty Years' Crisis, 1919–1939: An Introduction to the Study of International Relations* (Pal-

grave, 2001); Winston S. Churchill, *Memoirs of the Second World War*, one-volume abridged ed. (Houghton Mifflin, 1959); Keith Eubank, *World War II: Roots and Causes*, 2nd ed. (Heath, 1992); Ian Kershaw, *The Nazi Dictatorship: Problems and Perspectives of Interpretation*, 4th ed. (Arnold, 2000); Laurence Lafore, *The End of Glory: An Interpretation of the Origins of World War II* (Waveland, 1970); Richard Overy, *The Road to War* (Penguin, 2000); A. J. P. Taylor, *The Origins of the Second World War* (Simon & Schuster; rpt. 1996); Donald Cameron Watt, *How War Came: The Immediate Origins of the Second World War, 1938–1939* (Pantheon, 1989); Gerhard Weinberg, *The Foreign Policy of Hitler's Germany*, 2 vols. (Prometheus, 1994).

4. Taylor, *The Origins of the Second World War*.
5. William Manchester, *The Last Lion: Winston Spencer Churchill: Alone, 1932–1940* (Little, Brown, 1988), 349.
6. For a lucid discussion of these assumptions, see Robert O. Paxton, *Europe in the Twentieth Century* (Harcourt Brace Jovanovich, 1975), 417–18.
7. For a discussion of these frantic but ultimately doomed endeavors in France, see Michael Bess, *Realism, Utopia, and the Mushroom Cloud: Four Activist Intellectuals and Their Strategies for Peace* (University of Chicago Press, 1993), 8–10.
8. Adamthwaite, *The Lost Peace*, xv.
9. Overy, *Why the Allies Won*, 286.

Chapter Four: Bystanders

1. Elie Wiesel, "Foreword," in Carol Rittner and Sondra Myers, eds., *The Courage to Care: Rescuers of Jews During the Holocaust* (New York University Press, 1986), x.
2. Leni Yahil, *The Rescue of Danish Jewry: Test of a Democracy* (Jewish Publication Society, 1969). See also Milton Meltzer, *Rescue: The Story of How Gentiles Saved Jews in the Holocaust* (Harper & Row, 1988).
3. Susan Zuccotti, *The Italians and the Holocaust* (Basic Books, 1987); and Ivo Herzer, ed., *The Italian Refuge: Rescue of Jews During the Holocaust* (Catholic University of America Press, 1989).
4. Zuccotti, *The Italians and the Holocaust*, 219; see also http://www.raoulwallenberg.net/?en/saviors/others/palatucci/1340.htm.
5. The text of the Vatican document, *We Remember: A Reflection on the Shoah*, is available online at: http://www.bc.edu/bc_org/research/cjl/Documents/We%20Remember.htm.
6. Franz von Papen, quoted in Sergio I. Minerbi, "Pius XII," in Israel Gutman, ed., *Encyclopedia of the Holocaust*, vol. 3 (Macmillan, 1990), 1135.
7. Minerbi, "Pius XII," in Gutman, ed., *Encyclopedia of the Holocaust*, vol. 3, 1135.
8. See Victoria Barnett, *For the Soul of the People: Protestant Protest Against Hitler* (Oxford University Press, 1992); and Victoria Barnett, *Bystanders: Conscience and Complicity During the Holocaust* (Greenwood, 1999).
9. For a thoughtful overview of the literature from an author sympathetic to the

pope, see Kenneth D. Whitehead, "The Pope Pius XII Controversy," *The Political Science Reviewer* 31 (2002), available online at: http://www.catholicleague.org/pius/piuswhitehead.htm. For a measured argument by an author who is on balance critical of the pope, see Susan Zuccotti, *Under His Very Windows: The Vatican and the Holocaust in Italy* (Yale University Press, 2002). For an account that unabashedly condemns the Vatican's role, see Daniel Goldhagen, *A Moral Reckoning: The Role of the Catholic Church in the Holocaust and Its Unfulfilled Duty of Repair* (Knopf, 2002).

10. Gordon Thomas, *Voyage of the Damned* (Fawcett, 1976).
11. The poll is cited in "Voyage of the St. Louis," an article on the Web site of the United States Holocaust Memorial Museum: http://www.ushmm.org/wlc/article.php?lang=en&ModuleId=10005267. See also Samantha Power, *"A Problem from Hell": America and the Age of Genocide* (Perennial, 2003).
12. I draw this arresting image of the lights of Miami from the article "Slamming the Doors Shut" on http://www.eugenics-watch.com/roots/chap04.html.

Chapter Five: Bombing Civilian Populations

1. W. B. Yeats, "Lapis Lazuli," in *The Collected Poems of W. B. Yeats* (Macmillan, 1965), 338.
2. In framing my arguments in this chapter, I rely heavily on Overy, *Why the Allies Won;* and Schaffer, *Wings of Judgment*.
3. See Walter Boyne, *The Influence of Air Power upon History* (Pelican, 2003); Alan J. Levine, *The Strategic Bombing of Germany, 1940–1945* (Praeger, 1992); Sven Lindqvist, *A History of Bombing* (New Press, 2001); Stewart H. Ross, *Strategic Bombing by the United States in World War II: The Myths and the Facts* (McFarland, 2003); Schaffer, *Wings of Judgment;* and Michael S. Sherry, *The Rise of American Air Power: The Creation of Armageddon* (Yale University Press, 1989).
4. Quoted in Lindqvist, *A History of Bombing*, 33.
5. Yuki Tanaka, "Firebombing and Atom Bombing: An Historical Perspective on Indiscriminate Bombing," on http://japanfocus.org/282.html.
6. See, for example, John Keegan, *The Second World War* (Penguin, 1989), 102.
7. Adolf Hitler, quoted in Richard Hough and Denis Richards, *The Battle of Britain* (Norton, 1989), 244.
8. Schaffer, *Wings of Judgment*, Chapters 4 and 5.
9. Ibid., Chapter 5.
10. R. A. C. Parker, *The Second World War: A Short History* (Oxford University Press, 1989), 164–65.
11. Quoted in Richard Rhodes, *The Making of the Atomic Bomb* (Simon & Schuster, 1986), 471.
12. Curtis LeMay, quoted in Kennedy, *The American People in World War II*, 420. Also see Thomas M. Coffey, *Iron Eagle: The Turbulent Life of General Curtis LeMay* (Random House, 1986); Robin Neillands, *The Bomber War: Arthur Harris and the Allied Bomber Offensive, 1939–1945* (John Murray, 2001); and Henry

Probert, *Bomber Harris: His Life and Times—The Biography of Marshal of the Royal Air Force Sir Arthur Harris, the Wartime Chief of Bomber Command* (Greenhill, 2003).

13. Schaffer, *Wings of Judgment,* Chapters 2, 5, and 8.

14. One particularly prominent exponent of this opinion was Colonel Richard D. Hughes, the chief target selection officer for the USAAF. See ibid., 74–79.

15. "Bombs," in Dear and Foot, eds., *The Oxford Companion to World War II,* 150–52.

16. See Daniel Green's informative Web site at: http://www.ww2guide.com/bombs .shtml.

17. Rhodes, *The Making of the Atomic Bomb,* 597.

18. "Bombs," in Dear and Foot, eds., *The Oxford Companion to World War II,* 151.

19. LeMay, quoted in Mark Selden, "The United States, Japan, and the Atomic Bomb," in Kyoko Selden and Mark Selden, eds., *The Atomic Bomb: Voices from Hiroshima and Nagasaki* (East Gate, 1989), xxvii–xxviii.

20. See Overy, *Why the Allies Won,* Chapter 4.

21. For a detailed articulation of this argument see ibid., Chapter 4. See also the similar conclusion reached in Williamson Murray and Allan R. Millett, *A War to Be Won: Fighting the Second World War* (Harvard University Press, 2000), Chapter 12.

22. Overy, *Why the Allies Won,* 131.

23. All totaled, the Allied bombing campaign over Germany killed between 300,000 and 600,000 civilians. The nonnuclear bombing of sixty-six major Japanese cities, in the first seven months of 1945, probably killed between 200,000 and 300,000 civilians (though some estimates range as high as 900,000). For a discussion of these statistics, see Richard Frank, *Downfall: The End of the Imperial Japanese Empire* (Penguin, 1999), Chapters 1 and 10.

24. Elshtain, ed., *Just War Theory,* Chapters 5 and 7; Walzer, *Just and Unjust Wars;* and Howard, ed., *Restraints on War.*

25. Whether the attacks on Schweinfurt were worth the exceptionally large number of American deaths they incurred among bomber crews is an entirely separate moral issue.

26. Schaffer, *Wings of Judgment,* 131–32.

27. Curtis LeMay, quoted in ibid., 152.

28. Schaffer, *Wings of Judgment,* 137.

29. See, for example, the arguments pro and con in Keegan, *The Second World War,* Chapter 22; Schaffer, *Wings of Judgment,* Chapters 4–8; Overy, *Why the Allies Won,* Chapter 4; Murray and Millett, *A War to Be Won,* Chapter 12; A. N. Frankland, Richard Overy, and Stanley L. Falk, "Strategic Air Offensives," in Dear and Foot, eds., *The Oxford Companion to World War II,* 1066–79; R. A. C. Parker, *The Second World War,* Chapter 10; and Neillands, *The Bomber War.*

30. Overy, *Why the Allies Won,* 125.

31. See the succinct discussion of this point in Weinberg, *A World at Arms,* 580–81.

32. Robert Oppenheimer, quoted in Rhodes, *The Making of the Atomic Bomb,* 647.

Chapter Six: Deep Evil and Deep Good

1. Quoted in Christopher Browning, *Ordinary Men: Reserve Police Battalion 101 and the Final Solution in Poland* (HarperCollins, 1992), 73.
2. Browning, *Ordinary Men.*
3. In my discussion in this chapter I avoid reference to Daniel Goldhagen's book *Hitler's Willing Executioners: Ordinary Germans and the Holocaust* (Vintage, 1997), which I find one-sided and unpersuasive.
4. Quoted in Browning, *Ordinary Men*, 73.
5. I am indebted to Nelly Trocmé Hewett, the daughter of André Trocmé, for providing me with invaluable firsthand information about the wartime story of the Plateau Vivarais-Lignon. She repeatedly emphasized the key roles played in the rescue operation by villages throughout the region other than Le Chambon, and by men and women other than her father. I also draw heavily on Patrick Henry, "Banishing the Coercion of Despair: Le Chambon-sur-Lignon and the Holocaust Today," available at http://people.whitman.edu/~henrypg/banishing.htm. Henry underscores the importance of recent research on rescue efforts in the Vivarais-Lignon area, assembled in Pierre Bolle et al., eds., *Le Plateau Vivarais-Lignon: Accueil et Résistance, 1939–1944* (Le Chambon-sur-Lignon: Société d'Histoire de la Montagne, 1992). Other key sources for this chapter are Philip Hallie, *Lest Innocent Blood Be Shed: The Story of the Village of Le Chambon and How Goodness Happened There* (Harper, 1979); and Pierre Sauvage, *Weapons of the Spirit* (Los Angeles, Friends of Le Chambon, 1987), VHS tape, 91 minutes. See also the forthcoming book by Patrick Henry, *We Only Know Men: The Rescue of Jews in Le Chambon-sur-Lignon and on the Plateau Vivarais-Lignon*. I am indebted to my colleague John Compton for pointing out Henry's work to me.
6. Sermon quoted in Henry, "Banishing the Coercion of Despair."
7. Quoted in ibid.
8. See, for example, Barnett, *Bystanders;* Inga Clendinnen, *Reading the Holocaust* (Cambridge University Press, 1999); Peter Haas, *Morality After Auschwitz: The Radical Challenge of the Nazi Ethic* (Fortress, 1988); Raul Hilberg, *Perpetrators, Victims, Bystanders: The Jewish Catastrophe, 1933–1945* (HarperCollins, 1992); Michael Marrus, *The Holocaust in History* (University Press of New England, 1987); John J. Michalczyk, ed., *Resisters, Rescuers, and Refugees: Historical and Ethical Issues* (Sheed & Ward, 1997); Helmut Walser Smith, *The Butcher's Tale: Murder and Anti-Semitism in a German Town* (Norton, 2002); and Ervin Staub, *The Roots of Evil: The Origins of Genocide and Other Group Violence* (Cambridge University Press, 1989).
9. Browning, *Ordinary Men*, 165.
10. Stanley Milgram, *Obedience to Authority: An Experimental View* (Harper & Row, 1974).
11. By contemporary ethical standards, the Milgram experiments would clearly be considered unacceptable as psychological experiments on human subjects, because of the psychic stress and potential damage to the long-term self-esteem of the subjects resulting from the experiments.

12. Milgram, *Obedience to Authority*, 56.

13. Ibid., 75–76.

14. Ibid., 6.

15. See, for example, Gray, *The Warriors*, Chapter 2.

16. Slide 4, "The Stanford Prison Experiment," on http://www.prisonexp.org/slide -4.htm.

17. Slide 18, "The Stanford Prison Experiment," http://www.prisonexp.org/slide -18.htm.

18. Slide 31, "The Stanford Prison Experiment," http://www.prisonexp.org/slide -31.htm.

19. Slide 38, "The Stanford Prison Experiment," http://www.prisonexp.org/slide -38.htm.

20. See, for example, the discussion in Barnett, *Bystanders*, 30–31.

21. René Girard, cited in ibid., 150.

22. Hallie, *Lest Innocent Blood Be Shed*, 92.

23. Milgram, *Obedience to Authority*, 50–52.

24. Clendinnen, *Reading the Holocaust*.

25. I came to this conclusion through a series of long conversations with Beverly Asbury, the former Vanderbilt University chaplain. Asbury founded the Holocaust Lecture Series at Vanderbilt some twenty-five years ago, and has devoted much of his career to advancing the cause of Holocaust education in the United States. I would also like to thank my colleague Helmut Smith for helping to deepen my understanding of this point.

Chapter Seven: Decisions at Midway, 1942

1. Mitsuo Fuchida and Masatake Okumiya, *Midway: The Battle That Doomed Japan* (Ballantine, 1955), 12.

2. Raymond A. Spruance, "Foreword," in ibid., 8.

3. In piecing together this account of the battle, I have drawn primarily on the following books: Stephen Budiansky, *Battle of Wits: The Complete Story of Codebreaking in World War II* (Free Press, 2000); Fuchida and Okumiya, *Midway*; Walter Lord, *Midway: Incredible Victory* (Harper & Row, 1967); Gordon Prange, *Miracle at Midway* (Penguin, 1982); Herman Wouk, *War and Remembrance* (Little, Brown, 1985); and Zich et al., *The Rising Sun*, Chapter 6. The novelist Wouk, in particular, has produced an overview of the battle that is unsurpassed in its clarity and insight; my narrative in this chapter is heavily influenced by his analysis.

4. George C. Marshall, *Biennial Reports of the Chief of Staff of the United States Army to the Secretary of War: 1 July 1939–30 June 1945* (Center of Military History, U.S. Army, 1996), 107.

5. On the broader historical context of the battle see, for example, Edwin P. Hoyt, *How They Won the War in the Pacific: Nimitz and His Admirals* (Lyons, 2000); Yoshida Mitsuru, *Requiem for Battleship Yamato*, trans. Richard Minear (Uni-

versity of Washington Press, 1985); Samuel Eliot Morison, *History of United States Naval Operations in World War II*, 15 vols. (Book Sales, 2001); Spector, *Eagle Against the Sun;* and H. P. Willmott, *The War with Japan: The Period of Balance, May 1942–October 1943* (Scholarly Resources, 2002).

6. Churchill, *Memoirs of the Second World War*, 410.
7. Keegan, *The Second World War*, 269–70.
8. See the vivid account in Budiansky, *Battle of Wits*, 1–24.
9. Ibid., 11.
10. Joseph Rochefort, quoted in Peter Azzole, "Rochefort on the Making of a Cryppy," located on http://www.usncva.org/clog/cryppy.html.
11. Joseph Rochefort, quoted in Budiansky, *Battle of Wits*, 11.
12. Budiansky, *Battle of Wits*, 16.
13. William Halsey, quoted in Dower, *War Without Mercy*, 85.
14. Thomas B. Buell, *The Quiet Warrior: A Biography of Admiral Raymond A. Spruance* (Little, Brown, 1974).
15. Zich et al., *The Rising Sun*, 179; Fuchida and Okumiya, *Midway*, 134.
16. Lord, *Midway*, 96.
17. Ibid., 125.
18. Prange, *Miracle at Midway*, 231.
19. Zich et al., *The Rising Sun*, 181.
20. Wouk, *War and Remembrance*, 413.
21. Wade McClusky, account reproduced on the Web site *"USS Enterprise CV-6,"* at http://www.cv6.org/company/accounts/wmcclusky/.
22. Wouk, *War and Remembrance*, 414–17.
23. Ibid., 409.
24. This is the conclusion reached by Fuchida and Okumiya in their analysis of the battle. *Midway*, 203.
25. This scene is ably described in Lord, *Midway*, 222–23.
26. Yamamoto's reasoning is set forth in Wouk, *War and Remembrance*, 424–26; Prange, *Miracle at Midway*, 299–304; and Lord, *Midway*, 216–17.
27. Lord, *Midway*, 228.
28. Ibid., 227–28.
29. Raymond Spruance, quoted in ibid., 228.
30. Spruance's reasoning is laid out in detail in Prange, *Miracle at Midway*, 301–5; and in Wouk, *War and Remembrance*, 424–28.
31. Prange, *Miracle at Midway*, 154.
32. Raymond Spruance, quoted in a speech by Herman Wouk, "Sadness and Hope: Some Thoughts on Modern Warfare," delivered in 1980 at the Naval War College. The speech text is available on http://www.nwc.navy.mil/press/Review/1998/winter/art13w98.htm.
33. Isoroku Yamamoto, quoted in Fuchida and Okumiya, *Midway*, 184.
34. Raymond Spruance, quoted in Wouk, *War and Remembrance*, 428.
35. See for example the Web site of the Surface Navy Association at http://www.navysna.org/awards/Hall%20of%20Fame%20Write%20Ups/Spruance.htm.

Chapter Eight: Tyranny Triumphant

1. Harry Truman, quoted in David McCullough, *Truman* (Simon & Schuster, 1992), 262.

2. Stephen Ambrose, *Citizen Soldiers: The U.S. Army from the Normandy Beaches to the Bulge to the Surrender of Germany* (Simon & Schuster, 1998), 473.

3. Demaree Bess, "Can We Live with Russia?," *Saturday Evening Post* (July 7, 1945), 10.

4. Earl Ziemke, "German-Soviet War," in Dear and Foot, eds., *The Oxford Companion to World War II*, 434; and David M. Glantz and Jonathan M. House, *When Titans Clashed: How the Red Army Stopped Hitler* (University Press of Kansas, 1995), 282–84.

5. Glantz and House, *When Titans Clashed*, 284. "German armed forces' losses to war's end numbered 13,488,000. . . . Of these, 10,758,000 fell or were taken prisoner in the East."

6. I draw the idea for this comparison of distances from the excellent article by Benjamin Schwartz, "A Job for Rewrite: Stalin's War," *New York Times* (Feb. 21, 2004), A17, A19. I have changed the places to which Schwartz refers in his comparison, so as to parallel more precisely the diagonal nature of the Soviet north-south front and the German eastward penetration into the USSR.

7. Glantz and House, *When Titans Clashed*, 165. Richard Overy gives notably lower totals of 2.3 million in his book *Why the Allies Won*, 90.

8. Keegan, *The Second World War*, 473.

9. Glantz and House, *When Titans Clashed*, 288–89.

10. Warren Kimball, "Lend-Lease," in Dear and Foot, eds., *The Oxford Companion to World War II*, 681.

11. See the discussions in Glantz and House, *When Titans Clashed;* Keegan, *The Second World War;* and Murray and Millett, *A War to Be Won*.

12. See, for example, Isaac Deutscher, *Stalin: A Political Biography* (Oxford University Press, 1967); Herbert Feis, *Churchill, Roosevelt, and Stalin: The War They Waged and the Peace They Sought* (Princeton University Press, 1957); Sheila Fitzpatrick, *Everyday Stalinism: Ordinary Life in Extraordinary Times—Soviet Russia in the 1930s* (Oxford University Press, 2000); Ian Kershaw and Moshe Lewin, eds., *Stalinism and Nazism: Dictatorships in Comparison* (Cambridge University Press, 1997); Arthur Koestler, *Darkness at Noon* (Bantam, 1984); Leszek Kolakowski, *Main Currents of Marxism* (Oxford University Press, 1981); George Lichtheim, *Marxism: A Historical and Critical Study* (Routledge, 1964); Martin Malia, *The Soviet Tragedy: A History of Socialism in Russia, 1917–1991* (Free Press, 1995); and Simon Sebag Montefiore, *Stalin: The Court of the Red Czar* (Knopf, 2004).

13. See the discussions in Glantz and House, *When Titans Clashed*, 17–18; and Keith Sword, "The Katyn Massacre," in Dear and Foot, eds., *The Oxford Companion to World War II*, 644–46.

14. Glantz and House, *When Titans Clashed*, 213.

15. Ibid., 214. See also the similar conclusion reached in Murray and Millett, *A War to Be Won*, 451–52.

16. Antony Beevor, *The Fall of Berlin 1945* (Penguin, 2003), 434.

17. Antony Beevor, quoted in Daniel Johnson, "Red Army Troops Raped Even Russian Women As They Freed Them from Camps," *Daily Telegraph* (January 24, 2002), available online at http://www.telegraph.co.uk/news/main.jhtml?xml=/news/2002/01/24/wbeev24.xml&sSheet=/news/2002/01/24/ixworld.html.

18. Antony Beevor, *Stalingrad: The Fateful Siege, 1942–1943* (Penguin, 1998); and Alan Clark, *Barbarossa: The Russian-German Conflict, 1941–1945* (Harper & Row, 1985).

19. Beevor, *Stalingrad*, 174; Clark, *Barbarossa*.

20. Prime Minister Winston Churchill's broadcast on the Soviet-German War (London, June 22, 1941), reproduced on http://www.ibiblio.org/pha/policy/1941/410622d.html.

21. Winston Churchill, quoted by John Colville in Winston S. Churchill, *The Second World War*, vol. 3, *The Grand Alliance* (Cassell, 1950), 331.

Chapter Nine: Kamikaze

1. Masanori Oshima, quoted in Rikihei Inoguchi, Tadashi Nakajima, and Roger Pineau, *The Divine Wind: Japan's Kamikaze Force in World War II* (Greenwood, 1959), 177.

2. William Halsey, quoted in Desmond Flower and James Reeves, eds., *The War: 1939–1945: A Documentary History* (Da Capo, 1997), 744.

3. Dower, *War Without Mercy*, 97.

4. Ibid., 144.

5. See, for example, Albert Axell and Hideaki Kase, *Kamikaze: Japan's Suicide Gods* (Longman, 2002); Haruko Taya Cook and Theodore F. Cook, *Japan at War: An Oral History* (New Press, 1992); Dower, *War Without Mercy*; Frank, *Downfall*; Inoguchi, Nakajima, and Pineau, *The Divine Wind*; and Mitsuru, *Requiem for Battleship Yamato*.

6. Peter Davis, *Hearts and Minds* (Criterion Collection, 1974; DVD reissue, 2002).

7. See, for example, Edward W. Said, *Orientalism* (Vintage, 1979).

8. Alfred, Lord Tennyson, "The Charge of the Light Brigade," reproduced on http://eserver.org/poetry/light-brigade.html.

9. The most incisive narrative I have found of the battle is the one given by the novelist Herman Wouk in *War and Remembrance*, Chapters 86–92. See also the shorter accounts in Weinberg, *A World at Arms*, 842–58; Murray and Millett, *A War to Be Won*, 362–70; Kennedy, *The American People in World War II*, 396–403; and Keegan, *The Second World War*, 554–60.

10. Presidential Unit Citation, awarded to Task Unit 77.4.3 (Taffy 3), reproduced on http://www.bosamar.com/citation.html.

11. See the discussion in M. Pabst Battin, *Ethical Issues in Suicide* (Prentice-Hall, 1995).

12. Inoguchi, Nakajima, and Pineau, *The Divine Wind*, 165–72.
13. Emperor Hirohito, quoted in ibid., 72.
14. Inoguchi, Nakajima, and Pineau, *The Divine Wind*, 73.
15. Ibid., 174.
16. Kantaro Suzuki, quoted in ibid., 174.
17. Daisetsu Suzuki, quoted in ibid., 176.
18. From citations for the Congressional Medal of Honor, at the following Web site: http://www.cmohs.org/recipients.htm.
19. "KG200," in Dear and Foot, eds., *The Oxford Companion to World War II*, 649.
20. Johnnie Johnson, "Fighters," in Dear and Foot, eds., *The Oxford Companion to World War II*, 362.
21. Frank, *Downfall*, 178–83.
22. Takajiro Ohnishi, quoted in ibid., 311.
23. Inoguchi, Nakajima, and Pineau, *The Divine Wind*, 161.
24. Takajiro Ohnishi, quoted in ibid., 162.
25. Quotations taken from letters reproduced in Inoguchi, Nakajima, and Pineau, *The Divine Wind*, 180–89.
26. See the more detailed discussion of this logic in Chapter 10.
27. Inoguchi, Nakajima, and Pineau, *The Divine Wind*, Chapter 9.
28. I draw these statistics from Frank, *Downfall*, 178–83; and Kennedy, *The American People in World War II*, 408.
29. Frank, *Downfall*, 182.
30. Ibid., Chapter 13.
31. I discuss these options in detail in Chapter 10.
32. See John Dower, *Embracing Defeat: Japan in the Wake of World War II* (Norton/New Press, 1999); Buruma, *The Wages of Guilt;* and Yoshikuni Igarashi, *Bodies of Memory: Narratives of War in Postwar Japanese Culture, 1945–1970* (Princeton University Press, 2000).

Chapter Ten: The Decision to Drop the Atomic Bomb

1. Ludwig Wittgenstein, "A Lecture on Ethics," in James C. Klagge and Alfred Nordmann, eds., *Philosophical Occasions, 1912–1951* (Hackett, 1993), 37–44.
2. In framing my arguments and moral judgments in this chapter, I have drawn heavily on the following sophisticated and richly detailed accounts: Frank, *Downfall;* Tsuyoshi Hasegawa, *Racing the Enemy: Stalin, Truman, and the Surrender of Japan* (Belknap, 2005); Michael J. Hogan, ed., *Hiroshima in History and Memory* (Cambridge University Press, 1996); and Rhodes, *The Making of the Atomic Bomb*. The most comprehensive and up-to-date bibliography on the debates surrounding this subject is provided in Frank, *Downfall*. For a judicious overview of the debates, see J. Samuel Walker, "The Decision to Use the Bomb: A Historiographical Debate," in Hogan, ed., *Hiroshima in History and Memory*, 11–37.
3. The lower estimates come from Frank, *Downfall*, Chapters 1 and 10; the higher

estimate of 900,000 comes from Kennedy, *The American People in World War II*, 422.

4. Excerpts taken from Rhodes, *The Making of the Atomic Bomb*, 474.

5. Excerpts taken from ibid., 713–33.

6. See the discussion in John Dower, "The Bombed," in Hogan, ed., *Hiroshima in History and Memory*, Chapter 5.

7. Henry Stimson, quoted in Rhodes, *The Making of the Atomic Bomb*, 642.

8. Henry Wallace, quoted in Barton Bernstein, "Understanding the Atomic Bomb and the Japanese Surrender," in Hogan, ed., *Hiroshima in History and Memory*, 73.

9. Barton Bernstein, "Understanding the Atomic Bomb and the Japanese Surrender," in Hogan, ed., *Hiroshima in History and Memory*, 73.

10. Robert S. McNamara, in Errol Morris, *The Fog of War* (documentary film), Columbia Tristar DVD, 2004.

11. Nikita Khrushchev to Leo Szilard (November 4, 1962), in Leo Szilard, Helen S. Hawkins, G. Allen Greb, and Gertrud Weiss Szilard, eds., *Toward a Livable World: Leo Szilard and the Crusade for Nuclear Arms Control* (MIT Press, 1987), 305.

12. See Hasegawa, *Racing the Enemy*, 166–67; and Frank, *Downfall*, Chapters 14–15. See also Weinberg, *A World at Arms*, 888.

13. Frank, *Downfall*, 29.

14. See ibid., Chapter 11.

15. Ibid., Chapters 11, 14.

16. Ibid., 234.

17. Kantaro Suzuki, quoted in ibid., 234.

18. See, for example, William J. Coughlin, "The Great *Mokusatsu* Mistake: Was This the Deadliest Error of Our Time?" *Harper's* 206:1234 (1953), 31–40.

19. See Frank, *Downfall*, Chapter 14.

20. Hasegawa, *Racing the Enemy*, Chapter 3.

21. Rhodes, *The Making of the Atomic Bomb*, 693–96.

22. Frank, *Downfall*, Chapter 18; and Hasegawa, *Racing the Enemy*, 195–213.

23. In the surrender rescript of August 15, Hirohito made explicit reference to the atomic bomb but not to the Soviet attack; in the rescript of August 17, directed to Japan's military officers, he mentioned the Soviet attack but not the atomic bomb. Hasegawa, 297–98.

24. Michihiko Hachiya, quoted in Frank, *Downfall*, 321.

25. Sadao Asada, "The Shock of the Atomic Bomb and Japan's Decision to Surrender: A Reconsideration," *Pacific Historical Review* 64:4 (November 1998).

26. Frank, *Downfall*, 215.

27. Dower, *War Without Mercy*, 53–54.

28. See the detailed discussion of the internal State Department debates on this issue in Hasegawa, *Racing the Enemy*, 80–82, 116–20.

29. In his radio address of February 12, 1943, explaining the policy of unconditional surrender, Roosevelt explicitly linked the doctrine to this long-term aim of reordering the Axis nations in the aftermath of war. He harked back to the prin-

ciples laid out by the United States and Britain in the Atlantic Charter of 1941, in which the two nations had set forth their vision of a postwar world:

> In our uncompromising policy we mean no harm to the common people of the Axis nations. But we do mean to impose punishment and retribution in full upon their guilty, barbaric leaders. . . . In the years of the American and French revolutions the fundamental principle guiding our democracies was established. The cornerstone of our whole democratic edifice was the principle that from the people and the people alone flows the authority of government. It is one of our war aims, as expressed in the Atlantic Charter, that the conquered populations of today be again the masters of their destiny. There must be no doubt anywhere that it is the unalterable purpose of the [Allies] to restore to conquered peoples their sacred rights.

Full text available on http://www.ibiblio.org/hyperwar/Dip/casablanca-cnf.html.

30. Hasegawa, *Racing the Enemy*, 291.
31. Daikichi Irokawa, *The Age of Hirohito* (Free Press, 1995), quoted in Frank, *Downfall*, 351.
32. Frank, *Downfall*, Chapter 13.
33. Rhodes, *The Making of the Atomic Bomb*, 628–51.
34. Robert Oppenheimer, quoted in ibid., 647.
35. James Byrnes, quoted in ibid.
36. Frank, *Downfall*, 303.
37. Barton Bernstein, "Understanding the Atomic Bomb and the Japanese Surrender," in Hogan, ed., *Hiroshima in History and Memory*. See also Barton Bernstein, "The Atomic Bombings Reconsidered," *Foreign Affairs* 74:1 (January–February 1995).
38. On Szilard's quest for peace, see Bess, *Realism, Utopia, and the Mushroom Cloud;* Szilard, Hawkins, Greb, and Szilard, eds., *Toward a Livable World;* William Lanouette with Bela Silard, *Genius in the Shadows: A Biography of Leo Szilard* (Macmillan, 1992); and Spencer R. Weart and Gertrud Weiss Szilard, eds., *Leo Szilard: His Version of the Facts* (MIT Press, 1978).
39. Leslie Groves, quoted in Frank, *Downfall*, 257.
40. Kantaro Suzuki, quoted in Frank, *Downfall*, 235.
41. Not surprisingly, since this counterfactual scenario requires quite a few speculative assumptions, historians differ in their appraisals of how long it would have taken for the Japanese to surrender after a Soviet attack (but in the absence of atomic bombing of cities). Sadao Asada believes that in such a situation, "there was a possibility that Japan would not have surrendered before November 1." Barton Bernstein and Tsuyoshi Hasegawa, by contrast, believe that under these circumstances the Japanese surrender would probably have come "before November 1." See Hasegawa, *Racing the Enemy*, 294–96.
42. Frank, *Downfall*, 312–13.
43. Ibid., 277–80, 325.

44. Gordon, *A Modern History of Japan*, 211.

45. Frank, *Downfall*, 163.

46. In order to err on the side of a conservative estimate, I am not including in this figure of 850,000 one other significant factor in the equation. By September 15, General LeMay's bombers would have completed the airborne destruction of Japan's railway system, thereby setting into motion the process of mass starvation throughout the Japanese home islands. There is no telling how many Japanese civilians would have died, under this scenario, during the fall of 1945—even after capitulation. Therefore, I am opting not to include this factor in the statistical estimate of the "Soviet shock" scenario, even though we can be sure that the number of lives lost because of this factor would have been extremely high. What this underscores, once again, is that the figure of 850,000 is a deliberately conservative estimate.

47. See, for example, Gar Alperovitz, Peter Dimok, and Sanho Tree, *The Decision to Use the Atomic Bomb* (Vintage, 1996); and Martin Sherwin, *A World Destroyed: The Atomic Bomb and the Grand Alliance* (Knopf, 1975).

48. See the overview of the debates in J. Samuel Walker, "The Decision to Use the Bomb: A Historiographical Debate," in Hogan, ed., *Hiroshima in History and Memory*, 11–37.

49. The most comprehensive and persuasive discussion of the topic is given in Frank, *Downfall*, Chapters 11–14. See also John Ray Skates, *The Invasion of Japan: Alternative to the Bomb* (University of South Carolina Press, 1994); and the detailed historiographical discussions in Hogan, ed., *Hiroshima in History and Memory*, particularly Chapters 1–4, 8; and in Alperovitz, Dimok, and Tree, *The Decision to Use the Atomic Bomb*.

50. Frank, *Downfall*, Chapters 11–14.

51. Ibid., 194–96.

52. Irokawa, *The Age of Hirohito*, quoted in ibid., 351.

53. Hasegawa, *Racing the Enemy*, 185–86, 198.

54. Frank, *Downfall*, 270.

55. Ensign Bernard O'Keefe, quoted in ibid., 283–84.

56. Frank, *Downfall*, Chapter 15.

57. See Alperovitz, Dimok, and Tree, *The Decision to Use the Atomic Bomb*; and Sherwin, *A World Destroyed*.

58. Henry Stimson, quoted in Gar Alperovitz, "Hiroshima: Historians Reassess," *Foreign Policy* 99 (Summer 1995), 29.

59. Lord Alanbrooke, quoted in ibid., 31.

60. Henry Stimson, quoted in ibid., 30–31.

61. For perceptive discussions of this evolving consensus among historians, see the chapters by J. Samuel Walker and Barton Bernstein in Hogan, ed., *Hiroshima in History and Memory*, Chapters 2 and 3.

62. On this remarkable initiative, known initially as the Acheson-Lilienthal Proposal and in a second phase as the Baruch Plan, see Lawrence S. Wittner, *One World or None: A History of the World Nuclear Disarmament Movement Through 1953* (Stanford University Press, 2005), Chapter 14.

63. Hasegawa, *Racing the Enemy,* 181–83.
64. Ibid., Chapters 3–5.
65. Ibid., 299.
66. Ibid., 297, 299.
67. See Elshtain, ed., *Just War Theory,* particularly Chapters 5 and 7; Howard, ed., *Restraints on War;* and Walzer, *Just and Unjust Wars.*
68. Elshtain, *Just War Theory,* Chapters 5 and 7.
69. Walzer, *Just and Unjust Wars.*
70. See Howard, ed., *Restraints on War.*
71. See the discussion in Rhodes, *The Making of the Atomic Bomb,* 605–10.
72. William Styron, *Sophie's Choice* (Random House, 1976), 480–84.
73. Excerpts taken from Rhodes, *The Making of the Atomic Bomb,* 717–18; 726.

Part Three: Long-Term Consequences of the War

1. Hiroo Onoda, *No Surrender: My Thirty-Year War,* trans. Charles Terry (Kodansha International, 1974), 160.
2. Ibid., 201.
3. Ibid., 14.
4. "Ex-Japanese Soldier Unhappy After Years in Philippine Jungle," *New York Times* (November 29, 1974), 46.

Chapter Eleven: Justice for the Unspeakable?

1. The episode is reported in Joseph E. Persico, *Nuremberg: Infamy on Trial* (Penguin, 1994), 8.
2. "Judgment of the International Military Tribunal for the Trial of German Major War Criminals," reproduced on the Web site of the Avalon Project at Yale Law School, at: http://www.yale.edu/lawweb/avalon/imt/proc/judcont.htm.
3. See the detailed discussion in Gary J. Bass, *Stay the Hand of Vengeance: The Politics of War Crimes Tribunals* (Princeton University Press, 2000), Chapter 5.
4. Anthony Eden, quoted in ibid., 13.
5. On the failure of the post-1919 efforts at international criminal justice, see James F. Willis, *Prologue to Nuremberg: The Politics and Diplomacy of Punishing War Criminals of the First World War* (Greenwood, 1982).
6. Hermann Göring, quoted in Lawrence Douglas, *The Memory of Judgment: Making Law and History in the Trials of the Holocaust* (Yale University Press, 2001), 11.
7. Ann Tusa and John Tusa, *The Nuremberg Trial* (Atheneum, 1984), 486.
8. See Igarashi, *Bodies of Memory,* Chapter 1; and Richard H. Minear, *Victor's Justice: The Tokyo War Crimes Trial* (Princeton University Press, 1971).
9. Stephen Large, "Far East War Crimes Trials," in Dear and Foot, eds., *The Oxford Companion to World War II,* 349.
10. Ibid., 350.
11. Dower, *Embracing Defeat,* 513.

12. See the excellent Web site on the Geneva Conventions at http://www.genevaconventions.org/.

13. Martens Clause, quoted in Jackson N. Maogoto, *War Crimes and Realpolitik: International Justice from World War I to the 21st Century* (Rienner, 2004), 25.

14. See the lucid discussion in Maogoto, *War Crimes and Realpolitik*, 107.

15. Richard Minear provides a particularly damning indictment of the conspiracy argument in his book *Victor's Justice*, Chapter 3. See also the discussion in Michael Biddiss, "Nuremberg Trials," in Dear and Foot, eds., *The Oxford Companion to World War II*, 825–27. For a dissenting view, arguing that the conspiracy count was valid and reasonable, see Whitney R. Harris, *Tyranny on Trial: The Trial of the Major German War Criminals at the End of World War II at Nuremberg, Germany, 1945–1946* (Southern Methodist University Press, 1999).

16. See Minear, *Victor's Justice*, Chapter 4; Large, "Far East War Crimes Trials," in Dear and Foot, eds., *The Oxford Companion to World War II*, 349–50; and Michael Biddiss, "Nuremberg Trials," in Dear and Foot, eds., *The Oxford Companion to World War II*, 825–27.

17. General Iola Nikitchenko, quoted in Harris, *Tyranny on Trial*, 17.

18. Large, "Far East War Crimes Trials," in Dear and Foot, eds., *The Oxford Companion to World War II*, 349.

19. Ibid.

20. Minear, *Victor's Justice*, Chapter 4.

21. Large, "Far East War Crimes Trials," in Dear and Foot, eds., *The Oxford Companion to World War II*, 349.

22. See Daniel Barenblatt, *A Plague upon Humanity: The Secret Genocide of Axis Japan's Germ Warfare Operation* (HarperCollins, 2004); and Sheldon H. Harris, *Factories of Death: Japanese Biological Warfare, 1932–45, and the American Cover-up* (Routledge, 1994).

23. Yoshio Shinozuka, quoted in Barenblatt, *A Plague upon Humanity*, 51.

24. Douglas MacArthur, radio message to State-War-Navy Coordinating Committee, May 6, 1947, quoted in Barenblatt, *A Plague upon Humanity*, 212. SWNCC was the high-level government body that oversaw United States occupation policy for Japan.

25. Harris, *Factories of Death*, 222.

26. For detailed descriptions of these (and other similar) organizations, see Deborah E. Lipstadt, *Denying the Holocaust: The Growing Assault on Truth and Memory* (Free Press, 1993); Richard J. Evans, *Lying About Hitler: History, Holocaust, and the David Irving Trial* (Basic Books, 2001); and Kenneth S. Stern, *Holocaust Denial* (American Jewish Committee, 1993).

27. For overviews (and systematic rebuttals) of the Holocaust deniers' positions, see Lipstadt, *Denying the Holocaust*; and Stern, *Holocaust Denial*.

28. For an overview of the documents assembled by the prosecution at Nuremberg, see Robert Storey, "Foreword," in Harris, *Tyranny on Trial*, xii–xiv. For direct online access to a great many of the documents themselves, see the excellent Web site maintained by the Avalon Project at Yale Law School: http://www.yale.edu/lawweb/avalon/imt/imt.htm. See also Donald Bloxham, *Genocide on Trial:*

War Crimes Trials and the Formation of Holocaust History and Memory (Oxford University Press, 2001).

29. See Kathleen Dalton, *Theodore Roosevelt: A Strenuous Life* (Knopf, 2002), 288.

30. See Maogoto, *War Crimes and Realpolitik,* 24–27.

31. An excellent recent survey is Frank Ninkovich, *The Wilsonian Century: U.S. Foreign Policy Since 1900* (University of Chicago Press, 2001); two broader surveys are Maogoto, *War Crimes and Realpolitik;* and Geoffrey Robertson, *Crimes Against Humanity: The Struggle for Global Justice* (New Press, 1999). See also Sterling Johnson, *Peace Without Justice: Hegemonic Instability or International Criminal Law?* (Ashgate, 2003).

32. See the detailed account of the history of the Convention Against Genocide in Power, *"A Problem from Hell,"* Chapters 3, 4, 7.

33. On this limbo period for international justice, see Maogoto, *War Crimes and Realpolitik,* Chapter 4.

34. Power, *"A Problem from Hell,"* 164.

35. For a detailed discussion of the Yugoslavian and Rwandan debacles, see Power, *"A Problem from Hell."*

36. See Maogoto, *War Crimes and Realpolitik,* Chapters 5 and 6.

37. On the ICC, see ibid., Chapter 7; Robertson, *Crimes Against Humanity,* Chapter 9; Johnson, *Peace Without Justice;* and Bruce Broomhall, *International Justice and the International Criminal Court: Between Sovereignty and the Rule of Law* (Oxford University Press, 2003).

38. For a discussion of the difficulties encountered in defining these crimes, see Maogoto, *War Crimes and Realpolitik,* Chapter 7; and Johnson, *Peace Without Justice,* Chapters 5 and 6.

39. For a listing of the nations that are parties to the court's statute, see the court's Web site at http://www.icc-cpi.int/statesparties.html.

40. See the ICC Web site at http://www.icc-cpi.int/ataglance/whatistheicc/history.html.

Chapter Twelve: Generations Under a Shadow

1. Wouk, *War and Remembrance,* 1289.

2. Helmut von Moltke, in Daniel J. Hughes, ed., *Moltke on the Art of War* (Presidio, 1993), 22.

3. Robert Oppenheimer, quoted in Rhodes, *The Making of the Atomic Bomb,* 758.

4. I draw heavily in this chapter on the ideas laid out in the insightful collection of lectures by the economist and peace researcher Kenneth Boulding, *Stable Peace* (University of Texas Press, 1978). See also Robert J. Art and Robert Jervis, eds., *International Politics: Enduring Concepts and Contemporary Issues* (Harper-Collins, 1996); Bess, *Realism, Utopia, and the Mushroom Cloud;* Richard Falk, *Reframing the International: Law, Culture, Politics* (Routledge, 2002); Johan Galtung, *Searching for Peace: The Road to Transcend* (Pluto, 2002); Stanley Hoffmann, *Duties Beyond Borders: On the Limits and Possibilities of Ethical International Relations* (Syracuse University Press, 1981); Robert S. McNamara,

Wilson's Ghost: Reducing the Risk of Conflict, Killing, and Catastrophe in the 21st Century (Public Affairs, 2003); Donald Puchala, *Theory and History in International Relations* (Routledge, 2003); James N. Rosenau and Ernst-Otto Czempiel, eds., *Governance Without Government: Order and Change in World Politics* (Cambridge University Press, 1992); and Jonathan Schell, *The Unconquerable World: Power, Nonviolence, and the Will of the People* (Metropolitan, 2003).

5. Interview by Michael Bess with Alain Beltran (Paris, January 1993).

6. T. S. Eliot, "The Waste Land," *Collected Poems* (Faber, 1963), 63.

7. On the evolving nature of the postwar Franco-German partnership, see Dominique Bocquet, Christian Deubner, and Quentin Peel, *The Future of the Franco-German Relationship: Three Views* (Royal Institute of International Affairs, 1997); Alistair Cole, *Franco-German Relations* (Longman, 2001); John E. Farquharson and Stephen C. Holt, *Europe from Below: An Assessment of Franco-German Popular Contacts* (Allen & Unwin, 1975); Robin F. Laird, ed., *Strangers and Friends: The Franco-German Security Relationship* (St. Martin's, 1989); Patrick McCarthy, ed., *France-Germany, 1983–1993: The Struggle to Cooperate* (St. Martin's, 1993); Patrick McCarthy, ed., *France-Germany in the Twenty-first Century* (Palgrave, 2001).

8. See the article "Fortieth Anniversary of the Elysée Treaty, January 22, 2003," on http://www.info-france-usa.org/news/statmnts/2003/elysee2.asp.

9. Farquharson and Holt, *Europe from Below*, 128.

10. Ibid., Chapter 8.

11. Most people are not aware that France and Germany, in the early 1950s, came close to fusing their armies into a single supranational military force. This radical innovation, known as the European Defense Community (EDC), had been proposed by the French as a way of allowing West Germany to rearm—while still exercising direct control from Paris over how the resurrected Wehrmacht would be employed. The idea was to model the EDC on the successful example of the six-nation European Coal and Steel Community: a multinational army governed by a consortium of representatives from France, Germany, Italy, Belgium, the Netherlands, and Luxembourg. The proposal met with strong approval from the United States, and was passed by five of the six member nations, some of which had to alter their constitutions to allow the transfer of military sovereignty to an external governing body. But in the end it was the French themselves who balked at their own idea: the Gaullists rejected it for straightforwardly nationalist reasons; the French communists voted against it because Stalin disliked the prospect of a potent West European army; and some French politicians still feared the Germans too much to entrust them with safeguarding French security. In 1954, by a vote of 309 against 250 in the French parliament, the EDC went down to defeat; memories of wartime were still too fresh for so radical a departure from traditional national sovereignty. The following year, without much fanfare, West Germany created its own national armed force, the Bundeswehr, and immediately subordinated it to the broader identity of NATO.

12. Cole, *Franco-German Relations*, 110, 115–16.

13. This is set forth as "Boulding's First Law" in his book *Stable Peace*.
14. This distinction between stable and unstable peace forms the foundation of Kenneth Boulding's argument in *Stable Peace*.
15. Boulding, *Stable Peace*. See also Kenneth Boulding, *Three Faces of Power* (Sage, 1990); and Larry D. Singell, ed., *Kenneth Boulding: Collected Papers*, vol. 6, *Toward the Twenty-first Century: Political Economy, Social Systems, and World Peace* (University Press of Colorado, 1985).
16. Hans Morgenthau, *Politics Among Nations* (McGraw-Hill, 1992).
17. See Roger B. Myerson, *Game Theory: Analysis of Conflict* (Harvard University Press, 1997).
18. Here, once again, the relevant literature is too immense to cite. A good starting point is Albert-Laszlo Barabasi, *Linked: How Everything Is Connected to Everything Else and What It Means for Business, Science, and Everyday Life* (Plume, 2002).
19. See Wittner, *One World or None*.
20. George C. Marshall, "Speech to the New York Herald Tribune Forum," October 29, 1945, in Larry Bland, ed., *The Papers of George Catlett Marshall*, vol. 5 (Johns Hopkins University Press, 2003), 337–38. Emphasis in original.
21. See the persuasive case made for this position by the historian E. P. Thompson in *The Heavy Dancers* (Merlin, 1985), 61–105.
22. See, for example, Jeffrey Sachs, *The End of Poverty: Economic Possibilities for Our Time* (Penguin, 2005); and Hoffmann, *Duties Beyond Borders*.
23. For a lucid discussion of this kind of reeducation, see Michael Nagler, *Is There No Other Way?: The Search for a Nonviolent Future* (Berkeley Hills, 2001).
24. Churchill, *Memoirs of the Second World War*, 1015–16.
25. George C. Marshall, "Nobel Lecture," reprinted on http://nobelprize.org/peace/laureates/1953/marshall-lecture.html.

Chapter Thirteen: The Politics of Memory

1. William Faulkner, *Requiem for a Nun* (Random House, 1950, 1951), 92.
2. See John E. Bodnar, *Remaking America: Public Memory, Commemoration, and Patriotism in the Twentieth Century* (Princeton University Press, 1992); John R. Gillis, ed., *Commemorations: The Politics of National Identity* (Princeton University Press, 1994); Warren Leon and Roy Rosenzweig, eds., *History Museums in the United States: A Critical Assessment* (University of Illinois Press, 1989); Edward T. Linenthal and Tom Engelhardt, eds., *History Wars: The Enola Gay and Other Battles for the American Past* (Holt, 1996); Gary Nash, Charlotte Crabtree, and Ross Dunn, *History on Trial: Culture Wars and the Teaching of the Past* (Vintage, 2000); Roy Rosenzweig and David Thelen, *The Presence of the Past: Popular Uses of History in American Life* (Columbia University Press, 2000).
3. See Linenthal and Engelhardt, eds., *History Wars*, Chapters 1 and 5.
4. Richard H. Kohn, "History at Risk," in Linenthal and Engelhardt, eds., *History Wars*, 164–66.

5. See the accounts by Edward Linenthal, John Dower, Paul Boyer, and Richard H. Kohn in Linenthal and Engelhardt, eds., *History Wars*.

6. Dower, *Embracing Defeat*, Chapter 16.

7. See the discussion in Igarashi, *Bodies of Memory*.

8. Buruma, *The Wages of Guilt*.

9. Ibid., 114.

10. Ibid., 129–34.

11. Ibid., 134.

12. Teresa Watanabe and Mary Williams Walsh, "Japan, Germany Forced to Face WWII's Ghosts," *Seattle Times* (August 13, 1995), A3.

13. Guo Aibing, "Azuma Supported in Appeal to UN," *China Daily* (North American edition) (April 29, 2000), 1.

14. Reported on the Web site of the Network of Concerned Historians, (NCH) #17 (Annual Report 2000): http://odur.let.rug.nl/~nch/action17.htm.

15. Watanabe and Walsh, "Japan, Germany Forced to Face WWII's Ghosts," A3.

16. The most penetrating comparative account is Buruma, *The Wages of Guilt*.

17. Watanabe and Walsh, "Japan, Germany Forced to Face WWII's Ghosts," A3.

18. Roderick Stackelberg, *Hitler's Germany: Origins, Interpretations, Legacies* (Routledge, 1999), Chapter 16.

19. Ernst Nolte, *Three Faces of Fascism*, trans. Leila Vennewitz (Holt, 1966), 399.

20. See the summary of Nolte's article and the reaction it generated in Stackelberg, *Hitler's Germany*, 257–59.

21. Ernst Nolte, quoted in ibid., 257–58.

22. See Peter Baldwin, ed., *Reworking the Past: Hitler, the Holocaust, and the Historians' Debate* (Beacon, 1990); Charles S. Maier, *The Unmasterable Past: History, Holocaust, and German National Identity* (Harvard University Press, 1988); and Stackelberg, *Hitler's Germany*, Chapter 16.

23. A sophisticated discussion of these issues is presented by Maier in *The Unmasterable Past*.

24. Benjamin Schwartz, "A Job for Rewrite: Stalin's War," *New York Times* (February 21, 2004), A17, A19; Glantz and House, *When Titans Clashed*; Murray and Millett, *A War to Be Won*.

25. For an overview of the response by one young communist intellectual (E. P. Thompson) to the events of 1956, see Bess, *Realism, Utopia, and the Mushroom Cloud*, 99–107.

26. Among the many excellent books that have been published on the Gorbachev era in the Soviet Union, my favorite remains David Remnick, *Lenin's Tomb: The Last Days of the Soviet Empire* (Random House, 1993).

27. Nina Andreyeva, quoted in ibid., 82.

28. Two fine recent works on the "memory wars" in France are Eric Conan and Henry Rousso, *Vichy: An Ever-Present Past*, trans. Nathan Bracher (University Press of New England, 1998); and Richard J. Golsan, *Vichy's Afterlife: History and Counterhistory in Postwar France* (University of Nebraska Press, 2000).

29. See Sarah Farmer, *Martyred Village: Commemorating the 1944 Massacre at Oradour-sur-Glane* (University of California Press, 1999).

30. Hallie, *Lest Innocent Blood Be Shed;* and Pierre Sauvage, *Weapons of the Spirit* (1986), VHS tape, 91 minutes.

31. Farmer, *Martyred Village.*

32. Marcel Ophuls, *Le Chagrin et la Pitié* [*The Sorrow and the Pity*] (1972), reissued on DVD by Image Entertainment, 2001.

33. Conan and Rousso, *Vichy,* Chapter 1.

34. Mitterrand held a post from 1942 to 1943 in the Vichy government's documentation service of the Légion Française des Combattants. In 1943 he left the government and secretly joined the anti-fascist Resistance. See Ronald Tiersky, *François Mitterrand* (Palgrave, 2000), Chapters 3 and 11.

35. Conan and Rousso, *Vichy,* 24.

36. Jacques Chirac, quoted in ibid., 39–41.

37. Quoted in Conan and Rousso, *Vichy,* 42.

38. The text of Chirac's speech is reproduced on http://www.chambon.org/lcsl_chirac_speech_en.htm.

39. Probert, *Bomber Harris,* Chapters 15–16.

40. Ibid., Chapters 17–21.

41. See Ian Buruma, "The Destruction of Germany," *New York Review of Books* (October 21, 2004), 8–12.

42. Keegan, *The Second World War,* 433.

43. Glenn Frankel, "The Raging WWII Battle; Controversial Statue Honors Briton 'Bomber' Harris," *Washington Post* (June 1, 1992), B1.

44. John Ezard, " 'Bomber' Harris Statue Unveiled to Jeers, Cheers, and Scuffles," *The Guardian* (June 1, 1992), 3.

45. Denis Bols, quoted in Frankel, "The Raging WWII Battle," B1.

46. Kenneth James, quoted in Frankel, "The Raging WWII Battle," B1.

47. For a lucid discussion of the epistemological basis of historical knowledge, see Joyce Appleby, Lynn Hunt, and Margaret Jacob, *Telling the Truth About History* (Norton, 1994), Chapter 7.

48. Leon and Rosenzweig, eds., *History Museums in the United States.* See also James E. Young, *The Texture of Memory: Holocaust Memorials and Meaning* (Yale University Press, 1993).

49. See the discussions of this aspect of the subject in Linenthal and Engelhardt, eds., *History Wars.*

50. National Air and Space Museum, Smithsonian Institution, "Exhibition Planning Document" (July 1993), reprinted on the Web site of the Air Force Association: http://www.afa.org/media/enolagay/07-93.asp.

51. Quoted in Edward T. Linenthal, "The Anatomy of a Controversy," in Linenthal and Engelhardt, eds., *History Wars,* 52.

Conclusion

1. *Newsweek* (November 26, 1984), 56.

2. See, for example, Trevor-Roper, *The Last Days of Hitler;* Jäckel, *Hitler's World*

View; Kershaw, *Hitler, 1889–1936: Hubris;* and Kershaw, *Hitler, 1936–1945: Nemesis.*

3. For accounts of the values espoused by the Resistance, see Claude Bourdet, *L'Aventure Incertaine: De la Résistance à la Restauration* (Stock, 1975); Italo Calvino, *The Path to the Spiders' Nests* (Ecco, 2000); Basil Davidson, *Scenes from the Anti-Nazi War* (Monthly Review Press, 1981); Charles Delzell, *Mussolini's Enemies: The Italian Antifascist Resistance* (Fertig, 1974); Milovan Djilas, *Wartime* (Harcourt Brace Jovanovich, 1980); Carlo Levi, *The Watch* (Steerforth, 1999; 1st English-language ed., 1951); Henri Noguères, *Histoire de la Résistance en France, de 1940 à 1945,* 5 vols. (Laffont, 1981); Ignazio Silone, *Bread and Wine* (Signet, 1988); E. P. Thompson, "The Liberation of Perugia," in Thompson, *The Heavy Dancers;* and E. P. Thompson, *There Is a Spirit in Europe: A Memoir of Frank Thompson* (Gollancz, 1947).

4. See in particular Bourdet, *L'Aventure Incertaine;* Davidson, *Scenes from the Anti-Nazi War;* Levi, *The Watch;* and Thompson, *There Is a Spirit in Europe.*

5. On the social and cultural impact of the war, see John Barber and Mark Harrison, *The Soviet Home Front, 1941–45: A Social and Economic History of the U.S.S.R. in World War II* (Longman, 1991); Earl R. Beck, *Under the Bombs: The German Home Front, 1942–45* (University Press of Kentucky, 1999); Dower, *Embracing Defeat;* Lewis Erenberg and Susan E. Hirsch, eds., *The War in American Culture: Society and Consciousness During World War II* (University of Chicago Press, 1996); Kennedy, *The American People in World War II;* Martel, ed., *The World War Two Reader;* Alan S. Milward, *War, Economy, and Society, 1939–1945* (University of California Press, 1979); Thomas A. Schwartz, *America's Germany: John J. McCloy and the Federal Republic of Germany* (Harvard University Press, 1991); Harold L. Smith, ed., *War and Social Change: British Society in the Second World War* (Manchester University Press, 1986); and Gordon Wright, "The Impact of Total War," in *The Ordeal of Total War, 1939–1945* (Waveland, 1997), Chapter 11.

6. Alex Shulman, quoted in Terkel, *"The Good War,"* 280.

BIBLIOGRAPHY

Since the literature on World War II is prodigious, I make no attempt here to offer a comprehensive bibliography, but restrict myself to listing only the works I directly consulted or cited in writing this book. The reader who seeks a general orientation regarding the scholarship and other writings on World War II would do well to start with the fine bibliographic essays presented by Gerhard Weinberg in *A World at Arms* (Cambridge University Press, 1994), 921–44; and by David M. Kennedy in *The American People in World War II* (Oxford University Press, 1999), 435–40. See also the Web site of the World War II Studies Association, which offers periodically updated bibliographies on the war: http://www.h-net.org/~war/wwtsa/. For a general guide to Web sites on the war, see J. Douglas Smith and Richard Jensen, *World War II on the Web* (Scholarly Resources, 2003).

Adamthwaite, Anthony. *The Lost Peace: International Relations in Europe, 1918–1939.* St. Martin's, 1981.

Alibek, Ken, and Stephen Handelman. *Biohazard.* Delta, 2000.

Alperovitz, Gar, Peter Dimok, and Sanho Tree. *The Decision to Use the Atomic Bomb.* Vintage, 1996.

Ambrose, Stephen. *Citizen Soldiers: The U.S. Army from the Normandy Beaches to the Bulge to the Surrender of Germany.* Simon & Schuster, 1998.

———. *D-Day, June 6, 1944: The Climactic Battle of World War II.* Simon & Schuster, 1994.

Appleby, Joyce, Lynn Hunt, and Margaret Jacob. *Telling the Truth About History.* Norton, 1994.

Art, Robert J., and Robert Jervis, eds. *International Politics: Enduring Concepts and Contemporary Issues.* HarperCollins, 1996.

Asada, Sadao. "The Shock of the Atomic Bomb and Japan's Decision to Surrender: A Reconsideration." *Pacific Historical Review* 64:4 (November 1998).

Axell, Albert, and Hideaki Kase. *Kamikaze: Japan's Suicide Gods.* Longman, 2002.

Baldwin, Peter, ed. *Reworking the Past: Hitler, the Holocaust, and the Historians' Debate.* Beacon, 1990.

Barabasi, Albert-Laszlo. *Linked: How Everything Is Connected to Everything Else and What It Means for Business, Science, and Everyday Life.* Plume, 2002.

Barber, John, and Mark Harrison. *The Soviet Home Front, 1941–45: A Social and Economic History of the U.S.S.R. in World War II.* Longman, 1991.

Barenblatt, Daniel. *A Plague upon Humanity: The Secret Genocide of Axis Japan's Germ Warfare Operation.* HarperCollins, 2004.

Barnett, Victoria J. *Bystanders: Conscience and Complicity During the Holocaust.* Greenwood, 1999.

———. *For the Soul of the People: Protestant Protest Against Hitler.* Oxford University Press, 1992.

Bass, Gary J. *Stay the Hand of Vengeance: The Politics of War Crimes Tribunals.* Princeton University Press, 2000.

Battin, M. Pabst. *Ethical Issues in Suicide.* Prentice-Hall, 1995.

Bauman, Zygmunt. *Modernity and the Holocaust.* Cornell University Press, 1989.

Beck, Earl R. *Under the Bombs: The German Home Front, 1942–45.* University Press of Kentucky, 1999.

Beevor, Antony, *The Fall of Berlin 1945.* Penguin, 2003.

———. *Stalingrad: The Fateful Siege, 1942–1943.* Penguin, 1999.

Benson, John, and Takao Matsumura. *Japan, 1868–1945: From Isolation to Occupation.* Pearson, 2001.

Bernstein, Barton. "The Atomic Bombings Reconsidered." *Foreign Affairs* 74:1 (January–February 1995).

Bess, Michael. *The Light-Green Society: Ecology and Technological Modernity in France, 1960–2000.* University of Chicago Press, 2003.

———. *Realism, Utopia, and the Mushroom Cloud: Four Activist Intellectuals and Their Strategies for Peace. Louise Weiss (France), Leo Szilard (USA), E. P. Thompson (England), Danilo Dolci (Italy).* University of Chicago Press, 1993.

Bird, Kai, and Martin Sherwin. *American Prometheus: The Triumph and Tragedy of J. Robert Oppenheimer.* Knopf, 2005.

Bloch, Marc. *Strange Defeat.* Norton, 1999.

Bloxham, Donald. *Genocide on Trial: War Crimes Trials and the Formation of Holocaust History and Memory.* Oxford University Press, 2001.

Bocquet, Dominique, Christian Deubner, and Quentin Peel. *The Future of the Franco-German Relationship: Three Views.* Royal Institute of International Affairs, 1997.

Bodnar, John E. *Remaking America: Public Memory, Commemoration, and Patriotism in the Twentieth Century.* Princeton University Press, 1992.

Bolle, Pierre, et al., eds. *Le Plateau Vivarais-Lignon: Accueil et Résistance, 1939–1944.* Société d'Histoire de la Montagne, 1992.

Boulding, Kenneth. *Stable Peace.* University of Texas Press, 1978.

———. *Three Faces of Power.* Sage, 1990.

Bourdet, Claude. *L'Aventure Incertaine: De la Résistance à la Restauration.* Stock, 1975.

Boyne, Walter. *The Influence of Air Power upon History.* Pelican, 2003.

Brokaw, Tom. *The Greatest Generation.* Random House, 1998.

Broomhall, Bruce. *International Justice and the International Criminal Court: Between Sovereignty and the Rule of Law.* Oxford University Press, 2003.

Browning, Christopher. *Ordinary Men: Reserve Police Battalion 101 and the Final Solution in Poland.* HarperCollins, 1992.

Budiansky, Stephen. *Battle of Wits: The Complete Story of Codebreaking in World War II.* Free Press, 2002.

Buell, Thomas B. *The Quiet Warrior: A Biography of Admiral Raymond A. Spruance.* Little, Brown, 1974.

Buruma, Ian. *The Wages of Guilt: Memories of War in Germany and Japan.* Meridian, 1994.

Byrnes, James F. *All in One Lifetime.* Harper & Row, 1954.

Calvino, Italo. *The Path to the Spiders' Nests.* Ecco, 2000.

Carr, Edward Hallett. *The Twenty Years' Crisis, 1919–1939: An Introduction to the Study of International Relations.* Palgrave, 2001.

———. *What Is History?* Vintage, 1967.

Chang, Iris. *The Rape of Nanking.* Penguin, 1997.

Churchill, Winston S. *Memoirs of the Second World War,* one-volume abridged edition. Houghton Mifflin, 1959.

———. *The Second World War,* vol. 3, *The Grand Alliance.* Cassell, 1950.

Clark, Alan. *Barbarossa: The Russian-German Conflict, 1941–1945.* Harper & Row, 1985.

Clendinnen, Inga. *Reading the Holocaust.* Cambridge University Press, 1999.

Coffey, Thomas M. *Iron Eagle: The Turbulent Life of General Curtis LeMay.* Random House, 1986.

Cole, Alistair. *Franco-German Relations.* Longman, 2001.

Conan, Eric, and Henry Rousso. *Vichy: An Ever-Present Past.* Trans. Nathan Bracher. University Press of New England, 1998.

Cook, Haruko Taya, and Theodore F. Cook. *Japan at War: An Oral History.* New Press, 1992.

Crane, Conrad C. *Bombs, Cities, and Civilians: American Airpower Strategy in World War II.* University of Kansas Press, 1993.

Daqing, Yang. "A Sino-Japanese Controversy: The Nanjing Massacre As History." *Sino-Japanese Studies* 3 (November 1990), 14–35.

Davidson, Basil. *Scenes from the Anti-Nazi War.* Monthly Review Press, 1981.

Davis, Peter. *Hearts and Minds.* Criterion Collection, 1974; DVD reissue, 2002.

Dear, I. C. B., and M. R. D. Foot, eds. *The Oxford Companion to World War II.* Oxford University Press, 1995.

Delzell, Charles. *Mussolini's Enemies: The Italian Antifascist Resistance.* Fertig, 1974.

Deutscher, Isaac. *Stalin: A Political Biography.* Oxford University Press, 1967.

Dickers, Scott, ed. *Our Dumb Century.* Three Rivers, 1999.

Djilas, Milovan. *Wartime.* Harcourt Brace Jovanovich, 1980.

Douglas, Lawrence. *The Memory of Judgment: Making Law and History in the Trials of the Holocaust.* Yale University Press, 2001.

Dower, John W. *Embracing Defeat: Japan in the Wake of World War II.* Norton/New Press, 1999.

———. *War Without Mercy: Race and Power in the Pacific War.* Pantheon, 1986.

Elshtain, Jean Bethke, ed. *Just War Theory.* New York University Press, 1992.

Erenberg, Lewis, and Susan E. Hirsch, eds. *The War in American Culture: Society and Consciousness During World War II.* University of Chicago Press, 1996.

Eubank, Keith. *World War II: Roots and Causes,* 2nd ed. Heath, 1992.

Evans, Richard J. *In Defense of History.* Norton, 2000.

———. *Lying About Hitler: History, Holocaust, and the David Irving Trial.* Basic Books, 2001.

Falk, Richard. *Reframing the International: Law, Culture, Politics.* Routledge, 2002.

Farmer, Sarah. *Martyred Village: Commemorating the 1944 Massacre at Oradour-sur-Glane.* University of California Press, 1999.

Farquharson, John E., and Stephen C. Holt. *Europe from Below: An Assessment of Franco-German Popular Contacts.* Allen & Unwin, 1975.

Feis, Herbert. *Churchill, Roosevelt, and Stalin: The War They Waged and the Peace They Sought.* Princeton University Press, 1957.

Fischer, Fritz. *Germany's Aims in the First World War.* Norton, 1968.

Fitzpatrick, Sheila. *Everyday Stalinism: Ordinary Life in Extraordinary Times, Soviet Russia in the 1930s.* Oxford University Press, 2000.

Flower, Desmond, and James Reeves, eds. *The War, 1939–1945: A Documentary History.* Da Capo, 1997.

Frank, Richard B. *Downfall: The End of the Imperial Japanese Empire.* Penguin, 1999.

Fuchida, Mitsuo, and Masatake Okumiya. *Midway: The Battle That Doomed Japan.* Ballantine, 1955.

Gaddis, John Lewis. *The Landscape of History: How Historians Map the Past.* Oxford University Press, 2002.

Galbraith, John Kenneth. *The Anatomy of Power.* Houghton Mifflin, 1985.

Galtung, Johan. *Searching for Peace: The Road to Transcend.* Pluto, 2002.

Geertz, Clifford. *The Interpretation of Cultures.* Basic Books, 1977.

Gillis, John R., ed. *Commemorations: The Politics of National Identity.* Princeton University Press, 1994.

Glantz, David M., and Jonathan M. House. *When Titans Clashed: How the Red Army Stopped Hitler.* University Press of Kansas, 1995.

Goldhagen, Daniel. *Hitler's Willing Executioners: Ordinary Germans and the Holocaust.* Vintage, 1997.

———. *A Moral Reckoning: The Role of the Catholic Church in the Holocaust and Its Unfulfilled Duty of Repair.* Knopf, 2002.

Golsan, Richard J. *Vichy's Afterlife: History and Counterhistory in Postwar France.* University of Nebraska Press, 2000.

Gordon, Andrew. *A Modern History of Japan.* Oxford University Press, 2003.

Gray, J. Glenn. *The Warriors: Reflections on Men in Battle.* Harper & Row, 1970.

Grodzins, Morton. *Americans Betrayed.* University of Chicago Press, 1949.

Gutman, Israel, ed. *Encyclopedia of the Holocaust.* Macmillan, 1990.

Haas, Peter. *Morality After Auschwitz: The Radical Challenge of the Nazi Ethic.* Fortress, 1988.

Hallie, Philip. *Lest Innocent Blood Be Shed: The Story of the Village of Le Chambon and How Goodness Happened There.* Harper & Row, 1979.

Harris, Sheldon H. *Factories of Death: Japanese Biological Warfare, 1932–45, and the American Cover-up.* Routledge, 1994.

Harris, Whitney R. *Tyranny on Trial: The Trial of the Major German War Criminals at the End of World War II at Nuremberg, Germany, 1945–1946.* Southern Methodist University Press, 1999.

Hasegawa, Tsuyoshi. *Racing the Enemy: Stalin, Truman, and the Surrender of Japan.* Belknap, 2005.

Hastings, Max. *Armageddon: The Battle for Germany, 1944–1945.* Knopf, 2005.

Hawkins, Mike. *Social Darwinism in European and American Thought, 1860–1945: Nature As Model and Nature As Threat.* Cambridge University Press, 1997.

Hecht, Gabrielle. *The Radiance of France: Nuclear Power and National Identity After World War II.* MIT Press, 1998.

Henderson, Sir Nevile. *Failure of a Mission: Berlin, 1937–1939.* Putnam, 1940.

Herzer, Ivo, ed. *The Italian Refuge: Rescue of Jews During the Holocaust.* Catholic University of America Press, 1989.

Hilberg, Raul. *Perpetrators, Victims, Bystanders: The Jewish Catastrophe, 1933–1945.* HarperCollins, 1992.

Hoffmann, Stanley. *Duties Beyond Borders: On the Limits and Possibilities of Ethical International Relations.* Syracuse University Press, 1981.

Hogan, Michael J. *The Marshall Plan: America, Britain and the Reconstruction of Western Europe, 1947–1952.* Cambridge University Press, 1989.

Hogan, Michael J., ed. *Hiroshima in History and Memory.* Cambridge University Press, 1996.

Hough, Richard, and Denis Richards. *The Battle of Britain.* Norton, 1989.

Howard, Michael, ed. *Restraints on War: Studies in the Limitation of Armed Conflict.* Oxford University Press, 1979.

Hoyt, Edwin P. *How They Won the War in the Pacific: Nimitz and His Admirals.* Lyons, 2000.

Hughes, Daniel J., ed. *Moltke on the Art of War.* Presidio, 1993.

Igarashi, Yoshikuni. *Bodies of Memory: Narratives of War in Postwar Japanese Culture, 1945–1970.* Princeton University Press, 2000.

Iggers, Georg. *Historiography in the Twentieth Century: From Scientific Objectivity to the Postmodern Challenge.* Wesleyan University Press, 1997.

Inoguchi, Rikihei, Tadashi Nakajima, and Roger Pineau. *The Divine Wind: Japan's Kamikaze Force in World War II.* Greenwood, 1959.

Iriye, Akira. *The Origins of the Second World War in Asia and the Pacific.* Longman, 1987.

Irokawa, Daikichi. *The Age of Hirohito.* Free Press, 1995.

Irons, Peter. *Justice at War: The Story of the Japanese Internment Cases.* University of California Press, 1983.

Jäckel, Eberhard. *Hitler's World View.* Harvard University Press, 1981.

Johnson, Sterling. *Peace Without Justice: Hegemonic Instability or International Criminal Law?* Ashgate, 2003.

Jonas, Hans. *The Imperative of Responsibility: In Search of an Ethics for the Technological Age.* Trans. Hans Jonas and David Herr. University of Chicago Press, 1984.

Joy, Bill. "Why the Future Doesn't Need Us." *Wired* 8.04 (April 2000). Available online at http://www.wired.com/wired/archive/8.04/joy.html.

Keegan, John. *The Face of Battle.* Penguin, 1995.

———. *The Second World War.* Penguin, 1989.

Kennedy, David M. *The American People in World War II.* Oxford University Press, 1999.

Kershaw, Ian. *Hitler, 1889–1936: Hubris.* Norton, 1999.

———. *Hitler, 1936–1945: Nemesis.* Norton, 2001.

———. *The Nazi Dictatorship: Problems and Perspectives of Interpretation*, 4th ed. Arnold, 2000.

Kershaw, Ian, and Moshe Lewin, eds. *Stalinism and Nazism: Dictatorships in Compari-son*. Cambridge University Press, 1997.

Koestler, Arthur. *Darkness at Noon*. Bantam, 1984.

Kolakowski, Leszek. *Main Currents of Marxism*. Oxford University Press, 1981.

Lafore, Laurence. *The End of Glory: An Interpretation of the Origins of World War II*. Waveland, 1970.

Laird, Robin F., ed. *Strangers and Friends: The Franco-German Security Relationship*. St. Martin's, 1989.

Lanouette, William, with Bela Silard. *Genius in the Shadows: A Biography of Leo Szilard*. Macmillan, 1992.

Lederberg, Joshua, ed. *Biological Weapons: Limiting the Threat*. MIT Press, 1999.

Leon, Warren, and Roy Rosenzweig, eds. *History Museums in the United States: A Critical Assessment*. University of Illinois Press, 1989.

Levi, Carlo. *The Watch*. Steerforth, 1999; 1st English-language ed., 1951.

Levi, Primo. *Survival in Auschwitz*. Trans. Stuart Woolf. Summit, 1986.

Levine, Alan J. *The Strategic Bombing of Germany, 1940–1945*. Praeger, 1992.

Lichtheim, George. *Marxism: A Historical and Critical Study*. Routledge, 1964.

Lightman, Alan, Daniel Sarewitz, and Christina Desser, eds. *Living with the Genie: Essays on Technology and the Quest for Human Mastery*. Island, 2003.

Lindqvist, Sven. *A History of Bombing*. New Press, 2001.

Linenthal, Edward T., and Tom Engelhardt, eds. *History Wars: The Enola Gay and Other Battles for the American Past*. Holt, 1996.

Lipstadt, Deborah E. *Denying the Holocaust: The Growing Assault on Truth and Memory*. Free Press, 1993.

Litwack, Leon, et al. *The United States: Becoming a World Power*, 5th ed. Prentice-Hall, 1982.

Lord, Walter. *Midway: Incredible Victory*. Harper & Row, 1967.

Lukacs, John. *Five Days in London: May 1940*. Yale University Press, 2001.

Lukes, Steven. *Power: A Radical View*, 2nd ed. Palgrave, 2004.

Lukes, Steven, ed. *Power*. New York University Press, 1986.

MacIntyre, Alasdair. *After Virtue: A Study in Moral Theory*. University of Notre Dame Press, 1984.

Maier, Charles S. *The Unmasterable Past: History, Holocaust, and German National Identity*. Harvard University Press, 1988.

Malia, Martin. *The Soviet Tragedy: A History of Socialism in Russia, 1917–1991*. Free Press, 1995.

Manchester, William. *Goodbye, Darkness: A Memoir of the Pacific War*. Back Bay, 2002.

———. *The Last Lion: Winston Spencer Churchill: Alone, 1932–1940*. Little, Brown, 1988.

Mangold, Tom, and Jeff Goldberg. *Plague Wars: The Terrifying Reality of Biological War-fare*. St. Martin's, 2001.

Maogoto, Jackson N. *War Crimes and Realpolitik: International Justice from World War I to the 21st Century*. Rienner, 2004.

Marrus, Michael. *The Holocaust in History*. University Press of New England, 1987.

Marshall, George C. *Biennial Reports of the Chief of Staff of the United States Army to the Secretary of War: 1 July 1939–30 June 1945.* Center of Military History, U.S. Army, 1996.

———. "Speech to the New York Herald Tribune Forum," October 29, 1945. In Larry Bland, ed. *The Papers of George Catlett Marshall,* vol. 5. Johns Hopkins University Press, 2003, 337–38.

Martel, Gordon, ed. *The World War Two Reader.* Routledge, 2004.

McCarthy, Patrick, ed. *France-Germany, 1983–1993: The Struggle to Cooperate.* St. Martin's, 1993.

———, ed. *France-Germany in the Twenty-first Century.* Palgrave, 2001.

McCullough, David. *Truman.* Simon & Schuster, 1992.

McNamara, Robert S. *Wilson's Ghost: Reducing the Risk of Conflict, Killing, and Catastrophe in the 21st Century.* Public Affairs, 2003.

Meltzer, Milton. *Rescue: The Story of How Gentiles Saved Jews in the Holocaust.* Harper & Row, 1988.

Michalczyk, John J., ed. *Resisters, Rescuers, and Refugees: Historical and Ethical Issues.* Sheed & Ward, 1997.

Milgram, Stanley. *Obedience to Authority: An Experimental View.* Harper & Row, 1974.

Milward, Alan S. *War, Economy, and Society, 1939–1945.* University of California Press, 1979.

Minear, Richard H. *Victor's Justice: The Tokyo War Crimes Trial.* Princeton University Press, 1971.

Mitsuru, Yoshida. *Requiem for Battleship Yamato.* Trans. Richard Minear. University of Washington Press, 1985.

Montefiore, Simon Sebag. *Stalin: The Court of the Red Czar.* Knopf, 2004.

Morgenthau, Hans. *Politics Among Nations.* McGraw-Hill, 1992.

Morison, Samuel Eliot. *History of United States Naval Operations in World War II.* 15 vols. Book Sales, 2001.

Morris, Errol. *The Fog of War.* Columbia Tristar DVD, 2004.

Murray, Williamson, and Allan R. Millett. *A War to Be Won: Fighting the Second World War.* Harvard University Press, 2000.

Myerson, Roger B. *Game Theory: Analysis of Conflict.* Harvard University Press, 1997.

Nagler, Michael. *Is There No Other Way?: The Search for a Nonviolent Future.* Berkeley Hills, 2001.

Nash, Gary B., Charlotte Crabtree, and Ross E. Dunn. *History on Trial: Culture Wars and the Teaching of the Past.* Vintage, 2000.

Neillands, Robin. *The Bomber War: Arthur Harris and the Allied Bomber Offensive, 1939–1945.* John Murray, 2001.

Ninkovich, Frank. *The Wilsonian Century: U.S. Foreign Policy Since 1900.* University of Chicago Press, 2001.

Noguères, Henri. *Histoire de la Résistance en France, de 1940 à 1945.* 5 vols. Laffont, 1981.

Nolte, Ernst. *Three Faces of Fascism.* Trans. Leila Vennewitz. Holt, 1966.

Novick, Peter. *That Noble Dream: The "Objectivity Question" and the American Historical Profession.* Cambridge University Press, 1988.

Onoda, Hiroo. *No Surrender: My Thirty-Year War.* Trans. Charles Terry. Kodansha International, 1974.

Oppenheimer, Robert. "Speech Before the Association of Los Alamos Scientists" (November 1945). In Alice K. Smith and Charles Weiner, eds. *Robert Oppenheimer: Letters and Recollections*. Harvard University Press, 1980.

Overy, Richard. *The Road to War*. Penguin, 2000.

———. *Why the Allies Won*. Norton, 1995.

Parker, R. A. C. *The Second World War: A Short History*. Oxford University Press, 1989.

Paxton, Robert O. *Europe in the Twentieth Century*. Harcourt Brace Jovanovich, 1975.

———. *Vichy France: Old Guard and New Order*. Columbia University Press, 2001.

Persico, Joseph E. *Nuremberg: Infamy on Trial*. Penguin, 1994.

Polenberg, Richard. *War and Society: The United States, 1941–1945*. Lippincott, 1972.

Power, Samantha. *"A Problem from Hell": America and the Age of Genocide*. Perennial, 2003.

Prange, Gordon. *At Dawn We Slept*. Penguin, 1982.

———. *Miracle at Midway*. Penguin, 1982.

Probert, Henry. *Bomber Harris: His Life and Times—The Biography of Marshal of the Royal Air Force Sir Arthur Harris, the Wartime Chief of Bomber Command*. Greenhill, 2003.

Puchala, Donald. *Theory and History in International Relations*. Routledge, 2003.

Remnick, David. *Lenin's Tomb: The Last Days of the Soviet Empire*. Random House, 1993.

Rhodes, Richard. *The Making of the Atomic Bomb*. Simon & Schuster, 1986.

Rittner, Carol, and Sondra Myers, eds. *The Courage to Care: Rescuers of Jews During the Holocaust*. New York University Press, 1986.

Robertson, Geoffrey. *Crimes Against Humanity: The Struggle for Global Justice*. New Press, 1999.

Rosenau, James N., and Ernst-Otto Czempiel, eds. *Governance Without Government: Order and Change in World Politics*. Cambridge University Press, 1992.

Rosenzweig, Roy, and David Thelen. *The Presence of the Past: Popular Uses of History in American Life*. Columbia University Press, 2000.

Ross, Stewart H. *Strategic Bombing by the United States in World War II: The Myths and the Facts*. McFarland, 2003.

Sachs, Jeffrey. *The End of Poverty: Economic Possibilities for Our Time*. Penguin, 2005.

Said, Edward W. *Orientalism*. Vintage, 1979.

Sauvage, Pierre. *Weapons of the Spirit*. VHS tape, 91 minutes. Friends of Le Chambon, 1987.

Schaffer, Ronald. *Wings of Judgment: American Bombing in World War II*. Oxford University Press, 1985.

Schain, Martin A., ed. *The Marshall Plan: Fifty Years After*. Palgrave, 2001.

Schell, Jonathan. *The Unconquerable World: Power, Nonviolence, and the Will of the People*. Metropolitan, 2003.

Schwartz, Thomas A. *America's Germany: John J. McCloy and the Federal Republic of Germany*. Harvard University Press, 1991.

Selden, Kyoko, and Mark Selden. *The Atomic Bomb: Voices from Hiroshima and Nagasaki*. East Gate, 1989.

Sherry, Michael S. *The Rise of American Air Power: The Creation of Armageddon*. Yale University Press, 1989.

Sherwin, Martin. *A World Destroyed: The Atomic Bomb and the Grand Alliance.* Knopf, 1975.

Silone, Ignazio. *Bread and Wine.* Signet, 1988.

Singell, Larry D., ed. *Kenneth Boulding: Collected Papers,* vol. 6, *Toward the Twenty-first Century: Political Economy, Social Systems, and World Peace.* University Press of Colorado, 1985.

Skates, John Ray. *The Invasion of Japan: Alternative to the Bomb.* University of South Carolina Press, 1994.

Sledge, E. B. *With the Old Breed at Peleliu and Okinawa.* Oxford University Press, 1990.

Smith, Douglas, and Richard Jensen. *World War II on the Web.* Scholarly Resources, 2003.

Smith, Harold L., ed. *War and Social Change: British Society in the Second World War.* Manchester University Press, 1986.

Smith, Helmut Walser. *The Butcher's Tale: Murder and Anti-Semitism in a German Town.* Norton, 2002.

Smith, Merritt Roe, and Leo Marx, eds. *Does Technology Drive History? The Dilemma of Technological Determinism.* MIT Press, 2001.

Spector, Ronald. *Eagle Against the Sun: The American War with Japan.* Vintage, 1985.

Spiegelman, Art. *Maus: A Survivor's Tale.* 2 vols. Pantheon, 1973–1986.

Stackelberg, Roderick. *Hitler's Germany: Origins, Interpretations, Legacies.* Routledge, 1999.

Stanton, Fred, ed. *Fighting Racism in World War II.* Pathfinder, 1980.

Staub, Ervin. *The Roots of Evil: The Origins of Genocide and Other Group Violence.* Cambridge University Press, 1989.

Stern, Kenneth S. *Holocaust Denial.* American Jewish Committee, 1993.

Stoler, Mark A. *George C. Marshall: Soldier-Statesman of the American Century.* Twayne, 1989.

Styron, William. *Sophie's Choice.* Random House, 1976.

Szilard, Leo, Helen S. Hawkins, G. Allen Greb, Gertrud Weiss Szilard, eds. *Toward a Livable World: Leo Szilard and the Crusade for Nuclear Arms Control.* MIT Press, 1987.

Szilard, Leo. "Reminiscences." In Gertrud Weiss Szilard and Katherine Winsor, eds. *Perspectives in American History.* Harvard University, Charles Warren Center for the Study of American History, 1968.

Tanaka, Yuki. *Hidden Horrors: Japanese War Crimes in World War II.* Westview, 1998.

Taylor, A. J. P. *The Origins of the Second World War.* Simon & Schuster; rpt., 1996.

Teller, Edward. *Memoirs.* Perseus, 2001.

Terkel, Studs. *The "Good War": An Oral History of World War Two.* Ballantine, 1984.

Thomas, Gordon. *Voyage of the Damned.* Fawcett, 1976.

Thompson, E. P. *The Heavy Dancers.* Merlin, 1985.

———. *There Is a Spirit in Europe: A Memoir of Frank Thompson.* Gollancz, 1947.

Thucydides. *History of the Peloponnesian War.* Trans. Rex Warner. Penguin, 1972.

Tiersky, Ronald. *François Mitterrand.* Palgrave, 2000.

Trevor-Roper, Hugh. *The Last Days of Hitler.* Pan, 1952.

Tusa, Ann, and John Tusa. *The Nuremberg Trial.* Atheneum, 1984.

Walzer, Michael. *Just and Unjust Wars: A Moral Argument with Historical Illustrations.* Diane, 1977.

Watt, Donald Cameron. *How War Came: The Immediate Origins of the Second World War, 1938–1939*. Pantheon, 1989.

Weart, Spencer R., and Gertrud Weiss Szilard, eds. *Leo Szilard: His Version of the Facts*. MIT Press, 1978.

Weinberg, Gerhard. *The Foreign Policy of Hitler's Germany*. 2 vols. Prometheus, 1994.

———. *A World at Arms: A Global History of World War II*. Cambridge University Press, 1994.

Whitehead, Kenneth D. "The Pope Pius XII Controversy." *The Political Science Reviewer* 31 (2002).

Willis, James F. *Prologue to Nuremberg: The Politics and Diplomacy of Punishing War Criminals of the First World War*. Greenwood, 1982.

Willmott, H. P. *The War with Japan: The Period of Balance, May 1942–October 1943*. Scholarly Resources, 2002.

Wilson, Joe W., Jr., et al. *The 761st "Black Panther" Tank Battalion in World War II*. McFarland, 1999.

Wineburg, Sam. *Historical Thinking and Other Unnatural Acts*. Temple University Press, 2001.

Wittgenstein, Ludwig. "A Lecture on Ethics." In James C. Klagge and Alfred Nordmann, eds. *Philosophical Occasions, 1912–1951*. Hackett, 1993, 37–44.

Wittner, Lawrence S. *One World or None: A History of the World Nuclear Disarmament Movement Through 1953*. Stanford University Press, 1993.

Wohlstetter, Roberta. *Pearl Harbor: Warning and Decision*. Stanford University Press, 1962.

Wouk, Herman. *War and Remembrance*. Little, Brown, 1985.

———. *The Winds of War*. Little, Brown, 1985.

Wright, Gordon. *The Ordeal of Total War, 1939–1945*. Waveland, 1997.

Wynn, Neil. *The Afro-American and the Second World War*. Elek, 1976.

Yahil, Leni. *The Rescue of Danish Jewry: Test of a Democracy*. Jewish Publication Society, 1969.

Young, James E. *The Texture of Memory: Holocaust Memorials and Meaning*. Yale University Press, 1993.

Zich, Arthur, et al. *The Rising Sun*. Time-Life Books, 1977.

Zuccotti, Susan. *The Italians and the Holocaust*. Basic Books, 1987.

———. *Under His Very Windows: The Vatican and the Holocaust in Italy*. Yale University Press, 2002.

INDEX

PERMISSIONS ACKNOWLEDGMENTS

Grateful acknowledgment is made for permission to reprint the following copyrighted material.

Donadio & Olson, Inc.: Excerpts from *The Good War* by Studs Terkel, copyright © 1984 Studs Terkel (Pantheon Books, a division of Random House, Inc., New York, 1984). Reprinted by permission of Donadio & Olson, Inc.

HarperCollins Publishers: Excerpt from Chapter 7 and from Chapter 5 from *Obedience to Authority: An Experimental View* by Stanley Milgram, copyright © 1974 by Stanley Milgram. Excerpt from Chapter 3 from *A Plague upon Humanity* by Daniel Barenblatt, copyright © 2003 by Daniel Barenblatt. Reprinted by permission of Harper-Collins Publishers.

Little, Brown and Co., Inc.: Excerpt from *War and Remembrance* by Herman Wouk, copyright © 1978 by Herman Wouk. Reprinted by permission of Little, Brown and Co., Inc.

Naval Institute Press: Excerpt from *The Divine Wind: Japan's Kamikaze Force in World War II* by Rikihei Inoguchi, Tadashi Nakajima, and Roger Pineau, copyright © 1959 by Rikihei Inoguchi, Tadashi Nakajima, and Roger Pineau (Greenwood Press, 1959). Reprinted by permission of Naval Institute Press.

Oxford University Press: Excerpt from *Freedom From Fear, Part 2: The American People in World War 2* by David M. Kennedy, copyright © 1999 by David M. Kennedy. Reprinted by permission of Oxford University Press, Inc.

Simon & Schuster Adult Publishing Group: Excerpts from *The Making of the Atomic Bomb* by Richard Rhodes, copyright © 1986 by Richard Rhodes. Reprinted by permission of Simon & Schuster Adult Publishing Group.

Viking Penguin and Key Porter Books Ltd.: Excerpt from *The Second World War* by John Keegan, copyright © 1989 by John Keegan. Rights in Canada administered by Key Porter Books Ltd., Toronto. Reprinted by permission of Viking Penguin, a division of Penguin Group (USA) Inc., and Key Porter Books Ltd.

ILLUSTRATION CREDITS